National Mapping Agency
www.osi.ie

Compiled and published by Ordnance Survey Ireland,
Phoenix Park, Dublin 8, Ireland.

Arna thiomsú agus arna fhoilsiú ag Suirbhéireacht Ordanáis Éireann,
Páirc an Fhionnuisce, Baile Átha Cliath 8, Éire.

SPECIAL THANKS TO FÁILTE IRELAND, DUBLIN CITY COUNCIL,
DÚN - LAOGHAIRE RATHDOWN COUNTY COUNCIL,
FINGAL COUNTY COUNCIL AND SOUTH DUBLIN COUNTY COUNCIL.

Map data compiled from the OSi Database and validated to March 2012.

10th Edition Published 2013
9th Edition Published 2010   8th Edition Published 2009   7th Edition Published 2007
6th Edition Published 2005   5th Edition Published 2004   4th Edition Published 2002
3rd Edition Published 1999   2nd Edition Published 1997   1st Edition Published 1995

Route Planner	
M50 Map	II
Tourist Information	III-IV
Dublin Public Transport Frequent Services	V-VI
Dublin City Council Information	VII-VIII
Dublin City and District Maps	1-68
City Centre Maps	69-76
Town Maps	77-92

77	Ashbourne	86	Dunshaughlin
79	Balbriggan	87	Kilcock
81	Blessington	88	Lusk
82	Clane	89	Rush
83	Delgany/Greystones	91	Ratoath
85	Donabate	92	Skerries

Garda Road Safety Information	93-94
Embassies	95
List of Hospitals	96
Industrial Estates and Business Parks	97-98
Street Index	99

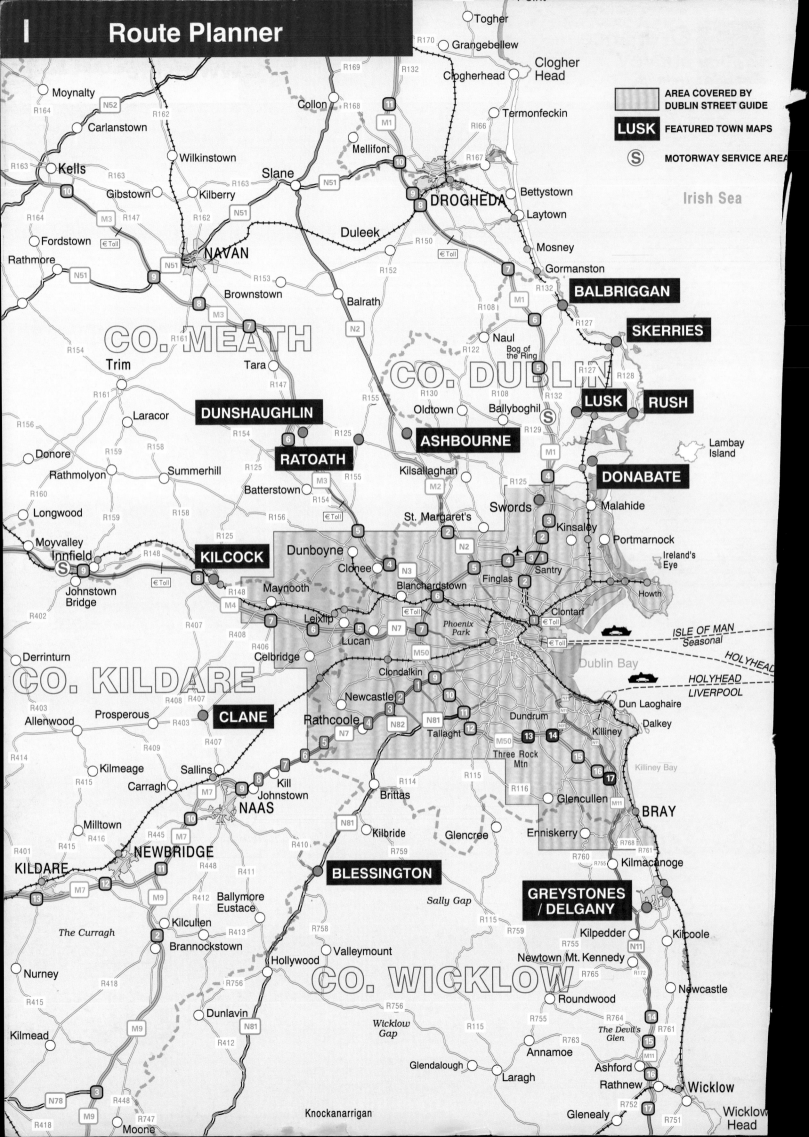

AREA COVERED BY DUBLIN STREET GUIDE

LUSK FEATURED TOWN MAPS

S MOTORWAY SERVICE AREA

Irish Sea

CO. MEATH

CO. DUBLIN

CO. KILDARE

CO. WICKLOW

BALBRIGGAN

SKERRIES

LUSK

RUSH

DONABATE

DUNSHAUGHLIN

RATOATH

ASHBOURNE

KILCOCK

CLANE

NEWBRIDGE

KILDARE

BLESSINGTON

GREYSTONES / DELGANY

Moynalty
Carlanstown
Kells
Gibstown
Wilkinstown
Slane
Kilberry
Fordstown
Rathmore
NAVAN
Trim
Tara
Brownstown
Balrath
Duleek
Mellifont
Termonfeckin
Togher
Grangebellew
Clogherhead
Clogher Head
DROGHEDA
Bettystown
Laytown
Mosney
Gormanston
Naul
Bog of the Ring
Oldtown
Ballyboghil
Kilsallaghan
St. Margaret's
Swords
Kinsaley
Malahide
Portmarnock
Lambay Island
Ireland's Eye
Howth
Clontarf
Finglas
Santry
Blanchardstown
Phoenix Park
Dublin Bay
ISLE OF MAN Seasonal
HOLYHEAD
HOLYHEAD LIVERPOOL
Dun Laoghaire
Dalkey
Killiney
Killiney Bay
BRAY
Kilmacanoge
Laracor
Donore
Rathmolyon
Summerhill
Batterstown
Longwood
Moyvalley
Innfield
Johnstown Bridge
Dunboyne
Clonee
Maynooth
Leixlip
Lucan
Celbridge
Clondalkin
Newcastle
Rathcoole
Brittas
Tallaght
Dundrum
Three Rock Mtn
Glencullen
Enniskerry
Kilbride
Glencree
Killiney
Derrinturn
Prosperous
Allenwood
Kilmeage
Sallins
Carragh
Kill
Johnstown
NAAS
Milltown
KILDARE
Ballymore Eustace
Kilcullen
Brannockstown
Nurney
Dunlavin
Kilmead
Moone
Kilpedder
Newtown Mt. Kennedy
Newcastle
Roundwood
The Devil's Glen
Annamoe
Ashford
Rathnew
Wicklow
Gleanely
Wicklow Head
Sally Gap
Valleymount
Hollywood
Wicklow Gap
Glendalough
Laragh
Knockanarrigan
The Curragh

Bray to Ballymount

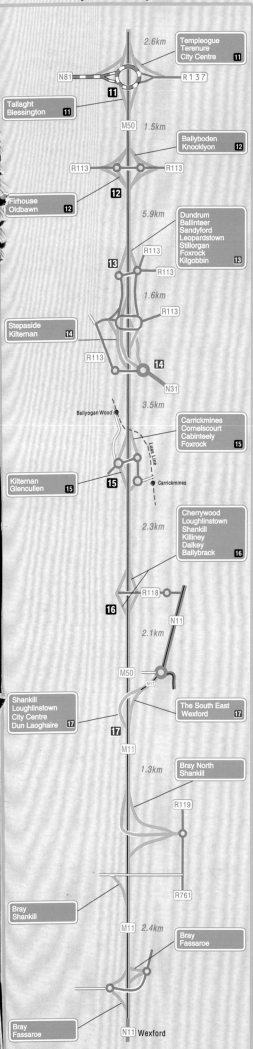

Ballymount to East Wall

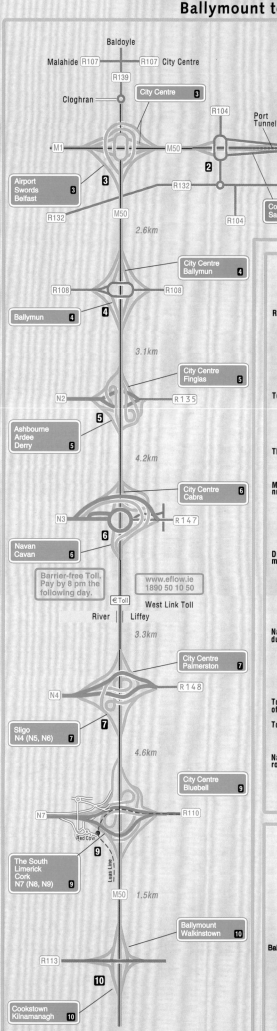

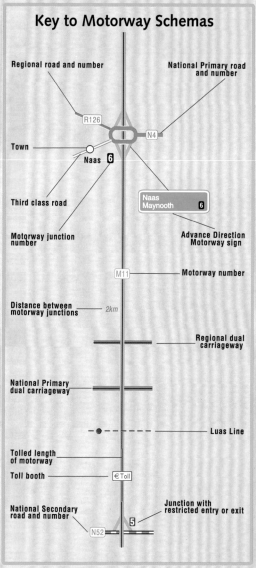

Key to Motorway Schemas

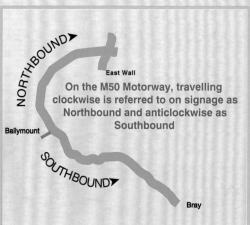

On the M50 Motorway, travelling clockwise is referred to on signage as Northbound and anticlockwise as Southbound

1. Take the weight off your feet...

2. Millennium wing of the National Gallery

Dublins Top 10

1. HOP ON A CITY TOUR...

Exploring a city is a beautiful thing. Sitting on a bus for two hours... not so much. That's why the Hop-on/Hop-off tours offered by Dublin Bus and City Sightseeing are such a brainwave. Stopping at multiple attractions around the city (think Dublin Zoo, Trinity College, the Guinness Storehouse), customers are free to hop on and off at their leisure. That means exploring your own interests, at your own pace, in your own sweet way. But there's more. Quality guides are on hand to offer entertainment and insight, multilingual audio commentary is available, kids go free on certain special offers, and tickets last for 48 hours, meaning you can pick up where you left off the following day. Genius.

2. ENJOY THE FREEDOM OF THE CITY...

Their contents are priceless, but entry to Dublin's top museums and galleries is free. Just think about the possibilities. That means you could skip from bog bodies at The National Museum of Archaeology to canvases by Caravaggio and Jack B Yeats at the National Gallery. You could check out four centuries of furnishings at The National Museum of Decorative Arts and History, before visiting Francis Bacon's reconstructed studio at Dublin City Gallery The Hugh Lane. Seven thousand items were meticulously transplanted here from Reece Mews in London, including books, brushes and, erm, several pairs of corduroy trousers. "I feel at home here in this chaos," Bacon once quipped. It's a world of riches that won't cost you a cent.

3. VISIT DUBLIN'S ANIMAL KINGDOM...

Over a million visitors pass through the gates of Dublin Zoo every year, and there are just as many reasons to join them. Tucked away in Phoenix Park, the zoo is constantly welcoming new arrivals – baby gorillas, hippos, rhino and red pandas to name but a few. Adult attractions include Harry, a 40-stone silverback lording it over the Gorilla Rainforest (he's watching you). Habitats range from the sweeping African Plains to a free-flying aviary, a family farm and lots of playgrounds. Modern principles of conservation, education and animal care govern everything and, yes, that includes the humans. The keepers at Dublin Zoo are walking, talking encyclopaedias. Throw them a bone.

4. PLAY KING OF THE CASTLE...

You want castles and cathedrals? Dublin has you covered. Take Malahide Castle, home to an amazing banqueting hall, a mischievous ghost named Puck and one of the best playgrounds in the country. Take Dublin Castle, dating from 1204AD and still central to the affairs of the nation. A tour of the State Apartments and medieval undercroft is essential here, but don't miss the Chester Beatty Museum and its excellent Silk Road Café, with Middle Eastern, North African, Mediterranean and vegetarian dishes. Dublin is also unique in boasting two landmark cathedrals within a short walk of each other – St Patrick's, where author and satirist Jonathan Swift famously served as Dean, and Christ Church, a chandelier of a building containing the bones of Strongbow.

5. DRINK A DROP OF DUBLIN...

You can't visit Dublin without tasting Guinness. Or better still, go the whole hog at the home of the black stuff. The state-of-the-art Guinness Storehouse, located beside the famous brewery at St James' Gate, wraps several floors of exhibitions and advertising displays around a pint-shaped atrium. You can even learn how to pour the perfect pint (tip: leave it settle for 119.5 seconds) before drinking in 360-degree views of Dublin from the Gravity Bar. Afterwards, enjoy another drop of Dublin on a tour of the Old Jameson Distillery in Smithfield, where you can learn about the triple distilling process before taking a tutored sup of the nectar itself. Sláinte!

6. GO TO GAOL...

Dating from 1796, Kilmainham Gaol was famous as "a machine for grinding rogues honest". Or perhaps infamous is a better word... the building stands empty today, but its thick walls, grim graffiti and foreboding atmosphere still evoke a shiver. Watch out for the striking Victorian wing, where scenes from Michael Collins and The Name of the Father were filmed; an AV presentation and guided tour further tease out the jail's place in Irish political and penal history. Robert Emmet, Charles Stuart Parnell and Eamonn de Valera were all imprisoned at Kilmainham, and the leaders of the 1916 Rising were executed by firing squad in the stone-breakers' yard. Yikes.

7. BROWSE THE CITY OF WORDS...

Dublin is one of just five UN ESCO Cities of Literature. The words of Nobel laureates like Yeats, Shaw, Beckett and Heaney echo in its streets. Statues of writers stand in parks; their names have been given to bridges. Visitors can celebrate Joyce's Bloomsday, take a literary pub crawl and see the Book of Kells at Trinity College. Literary Dublin is even one of Patricia Shultz's 1,000 Places to See Before You Die. But don't let this tempt you into thinking it's all about dead guys. Contemporary writers like Joseph O'Connor, Anne Enright and Paul Murray continue to carry the flame, as indeed, do Dubliners themselves, every time they utter the immortal greeting: "What's the story?"

3. Rooooaaaar of the wild in Dublin Zoo

4. Dublin Castle at the heart of the capital

5. Triple distilling at Jameson's

6. Kilmainham Gaol has stories to tell

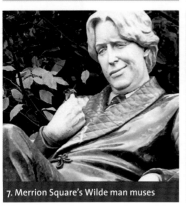
7. Merrion Square's Wilde man muses

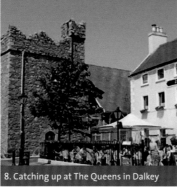
8. Catching up at The Queens in Dalkey

9. Knock, knock on Georgian doors

10. Long walks in Howth...

8. POP INTO A PUB...

There's not much to say ABOUT Dublin pubs that hasn't already been said IN Dublin pubs. These trusty little tabernacles are famous for their creamy pints, cosy snugs and quick-witted craic. Think of Mulligan's, Kehoe's, Toner's or McDaid's, all dripping with character, all dotted about the city like time machines. "In Dublin, you're never more than 20 paces from a pint," author JP Dunleavy once said. But yesterday's pints of plain are today deliciously diverse. Gastropubs do great grub; hotel bars are shaking up the cocktail scene; quality music, wine and coffee are mixing it up with flip-out fun in Temple Bar. Whatever your taste, there's a Dublin pub for you.

9. OPEN DUBLIN'S DOORS...

Paris has its beaux arts. Dublin has its Georgian streets and squares. Beaming out from beneath their fanlights, these brightly-painted doors are an iconic image of the city. But where did they come from? The answer lies between 1714 and 1830. In this period, four different Georges held the throne of England, Dublin entered an era of prosperity, and its medieval streetscape got one hell of a makeover. Grand buildings such as the Custom House, stately spaces such as Stephen's Green and sumptuous interiors like those at the Georgian House Museum are just some of the results on view today. Download a Georgian iWalk, and experience the "gorgeous eighteenth" for yourself.

10. CITY BY THE SEA...

With so much to do in the city centre, it's easy to forget that Dublin is a city by the sea. But a short ride on the Dart is all it takes to get out along its sparkling necklace of seaside villages and beaches. Within half an hour you could be bobbing along in a small boat on the way to Dalkey Island, eating Michelin starred food in Malahide, or walking the Victorian pier at Dun Laoghaire. Double that, and you might find yourself eating snap-fresh seafood in Howth, building sandcastles on Portmarnock's "Velvet Strand", or winding your way down wildflower-strewn cliff paths to White Rock beach in Killiney. Dublin Bay even has its own resident dolphins. How many capital cities can say that?

DUBLIN, COME JOIN THE 2013 PARTY!

The best part about any visit to Dublin is choosing what to do! And we have every kind of activity imaginable to keep you busy but Dublin doesn't stop there – we have a host of events that celebrate a myriad of unique aspects of Dublin. From traditional music, theatre, dance and fashion, to national celebrations, start planning your visit!

To plan your visit and events see **visitdublin.com/events**

Temple Bar Trad Fest	22nd – 27th January
Jameson Dublin International Film Festival	14th – 24th February
St. Patrick's Festival	14th – 18th March
Irish Fest	14th – 18th March
Dublin Bay Prawn Festival	24th – 28th April
International Dublin Gay Theatre Festival	6th – 19th May
Dublin Street Performance World Championship	12th – 14th July
Dublin Rock 'n' Roll Half Marathon	5th August
Dublin Horse Show	7th – 11th August
Dublin Fashion Festival	5th – 8th September
Festival Season	1st Sept – 31st October
Hard Working Class Heroes	3rd – 5th October
NYE Festival	31th Dec – 1st January

the gathering
IRELAND 2013
thegatheringireland.com

Dublin Public Transport Frequent Services

V

KEY

Bus services

▬▬▬	4	Harristown - Monkstown Avenue
▬▬▬	7	Mountjoy Square - Loughlinstown/Cherrywood
▬▬▬	9	Charlestown - Limeklin Avenue
▬▬▬	11	Wadelai Park - Sandyford Industrial Estate
▬▬▬	13	Harristown - Grange Castle
▬▬▬	14	Beaumont - Dundrum Luas Station
▬▬▬	15	Clongriffin - Ballycullen Road
▬▬▬	15a	Grand Canal Dock - Limeklin Avenue
▬▬▬	15b	Grand Canal Dock - Stocking Avenue
▬▬▬	16	Ballinteer (Brehonfield Road) - Dublin Airport
▬▬▬	17a	Blanchardstown - Howth Junction
▬▬▬	18	Palmerston - Sandymount
▬▬▬	25a	Lucan (Esker Church) - Merrion Square
▬▬▬	25b	Adamstown Station - Merrion Square
▬▬▬	27	Clare Hall - Jobstown
▬▬▬	29a	Lower Abbey Street - Baldoyle
▬▬▬	39a	UCD (Belfield) - Ongar
▬▬▬	40	Finglas Village - Liffey Valley (Shopping Centre)
▬▬▬	40d	Parnell Street - Tyrrelstown
▬▬▬	41	Lower Abbey Street - Swords Manor
▬▬▬	46a	Phoenix Park (Infirmary Road and Zoo) - Dun Laoghaire
▬▬▬	77a	Ringsend Road - Citywest Campus
▬▬▬	79a	Parkwest & Cherry Orchard - City Centre
▬▬▬	83	Harristown - Kimmage
▬▬▬	120	Parnell Street - Ashtown Station
▬▬▬	122	Ashington - Crumlin Hospital
▬▬▬	123	Walkinstown - Marino
▬▬▬	130	Lower Abbey Street - Castle Avenue (Clontarf)
▬▬▬	140	Finglas IKEA - Palmerston Park
▬▬▬	145	Heuston Station - Kilmacanogue
▬▬▬	150	Fleet Street - Rossmore
▬▬▬	151	Docklands - Foxborough
▬▬▬	747	Heuston Station - Dublin Airport
▬▬▬	A	Aircoach
▬▬▬	S	Swords Express
▬▬▬		Multiple bus routes

Rail services

▬▬▬	COMMUTER rail route
▬▬▬	DART rail route

Luas tram services

▬▬▬	Luas green line
▬▬▬	Luas red line

○	Principal stop
◆	Stop served by certain journeys only

Transfer Points
Locations where it is possible to change
to a different form of transport

🚆	Rail (DART, COMMUTER or Intercity)
🚌	Bus coach (regional or intercity)
P&R	Park & Ride (larger car parks)
✈	Airport
⚓	Ferry Port

Points of Interest

Public Park

Information correct from November 2012
(Map D17-10/2012)

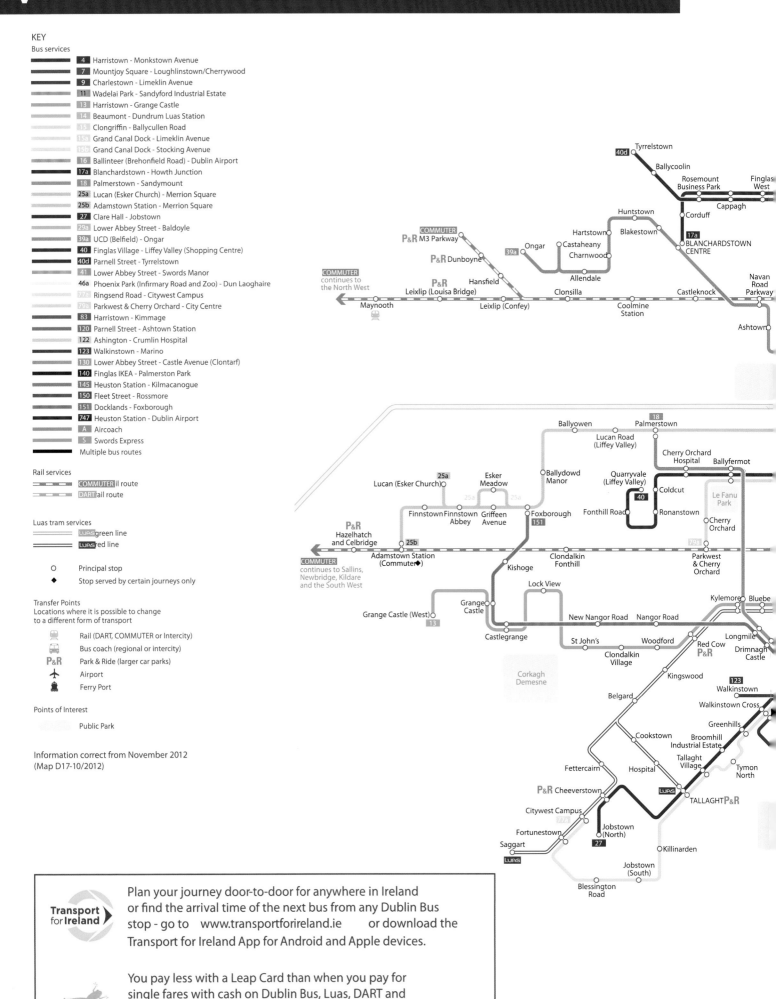

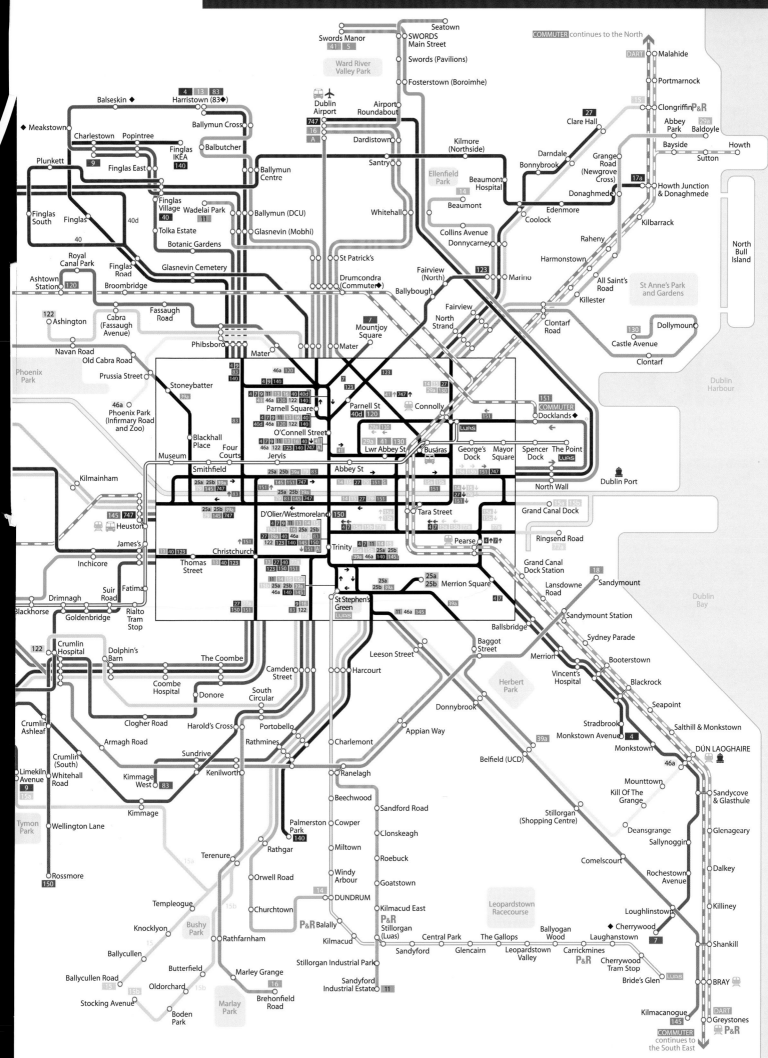

Cycling in Dublin

Dublin City Council has played a big role in the growth in popularity of cycling in Dublin. Council initiatives such as dublinbikes, which has seen over 4.5million journeys taken since its launch in 2009, awareness raising events like Dublin Bike Week and better cycling facilities have contributed to this growth. For information on cycling in Dublin, safety tips, maps of family-friendly cycling trails in Dublin city parks and much more see **www.dublincitycycling.ie**

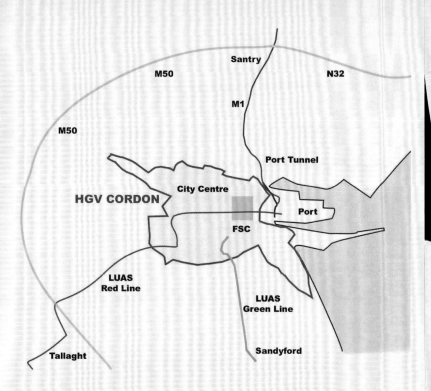

dublinbikes

Around 80,000 people have joined dublinbikes since its launch in September 2009. It's one of the world's most successful public bike rental schemes and as the first 30 minutes of any journey are free it's a great way to get around the city. dublinbikes has 550 bikes based at 44 stations in the city centre. You can join the scheme via **www.dublinbikes.ie** for an annual fee of €10. You can also join for three days for €2 at selected credit card-enabled stations.

dublinbikes is due to expand in 2012. Dublin City Council has prioritised the area around Dublin Docklands and Hueston Station in its incremental plans to expand dublinbikes.

Secure bike parking at Drury Street   75 B1

The ground floor of **Drury Street Car Park** features a free indoor, dedicated bike park area. An entire floor of car parking spaces was removed to provide space for bikes. The facility is designed for short-term use so this means anyone from commuters, to tourists, to shoppers can use it. It's conveniently located near shops, bars, restaurants and cafes, right in the heart of the city. The cycle parking area is under constant **CCTV** surveillance and is free to use to the public. It's open **Monday to Saturday between 7.30am and 1am and on Sunday between 11am and 7pm**.

Canal Way Cycle Route   pp 72, 75, 76

The Canal Way Cycle Route is proving very popular with cyclists and has increased the amenity value of the Grand Canal. The mainly off road cycle route is approximately 3.6km long and runs along the Grand Canal from Rathmines Road Lower/Portobello to Sheriff Street at Spencer Dock, Royal Canal. The new cycle route features a 3.5 metre wide 2-way cycle track along the northern bank of the Grand Canal and redesigned junctions at a number of locations featuring dedicated cyclist signals and so is ideal for families. It includes a 100 metre long boardwalk on the western approach to Leeson Street Bridge, to provide additional space for pedestrians and cyclists. The facility was officially opened on 22nd March, 2012, by the then Lord Mayor Andrew Montague, and Minister of State Alan Kelly T.D. It is the first phase of a cycle track building programme to cater for cyclists of all ages and capabilities.

Photo: Jason Clarke photography

5+ Axle HGV Ban

A 5+ HGV ban operates in certain area of Dublin City at certain time periods. A limited permit scheme is in operation for those that need to load/unload during the restricted time period.

When HGVs CANNOT enter the restricted zone: During the hours of 07.00-19.00, seven days a week, HGVs with 5+ axles are not allowed to enter the restricted zone during these times unless they have a **valid permit.**

When HGVs can enter the restricted zone: During the hours 19.00-07.00, seven days a week HGVs with 5+ axles are allowed to enter the restricted zone, even without a permit. HGVs with 4 axles or less are allowed to enter the restricted zone at any time, day or night. For more details see **www.dublincity.ie**

College Green Bus Corridor   71 D4

In May 2009 Dublin City councillors agreed to introduce the College Green Bus Corridor. This diverts private motor traffic away from College Green with only public transport being allowed to travel through the area between 7am and 10am and 4pm and 7pm, Monday to Friday.

The Bus Corridor reduces congestion in the area and improves conditions for perdestrians, cyclists and public transport. The scheme significantly reduces journey times for cross-city public transport and allows increased reliability and frequency. It's a natural progression in traffic management in Dublin city.

Park with Parking Tag

Parking Tag is Dublin City Council's cashless, mobile phone-based parking system which allows you to pay and top up by your mobile. Parking Tag is a Pay by Phone solution provided in the Dublin City Council area. Once registered, you simply text or call to pay for parking. All it takes is another quick SMS to extend parking for an additional period of time and no more rushing out to top-up the meter! You even get a reminder by SMS 10 minutes before your parking time expires. Registration is free on **www.parkingtag.ie** or T. 0818 300 161.

Photo: Jason Clarke photography

Walk Dublin – Dublin City Council's free app to get you around the city

Walk Dublin enables people to orientate themselves and obtain walking directions to all of the city's key cultural destinations. Discover what places of cultural significance are closest to you at any time, find out a little more about them and get walking! Walk Dublin is available on the App Store and is free to download.

Recycling in Dublin City

Dublin City Council operates a range of recycling facilities, these include Recycling Centre, WEE Collection, Bring Centres and over 100 Bottle Banks. For further information see **www.dublinwaste.ie**

Sports and Leisure Facilities

Dublin City Council operates 20 sports and leisure facilities. All offer excellent facilities and many contain pools, gyms. Gyms offer pay-as-you-go facilities. For information on opening times, locations, costs and facilities see **www.dublincity.ie**

IRISH SEA

Corballis Golf Links

18

Strand

COAST ROAD

The Lighthouse

Sports Ground

Castle Robbswall

ROBBSWALL WALK PATH

THE CRESCENT

The Anchorage

The Spinnaker

R106

THE CRESCENT

MONKS MEADOW

CONNEC LANE

ELBERY COURT

LIME TREE AVENUE

PADLETT GRO

WHEATFIELD ROAD

ASHLEY RISE

HEATHER GARDENS

WHEATFIELD GROVE

BRIAR WALK

BRACKEN DRIVE

Martello Tower

KELVIN CLOSE

WENDELL AVENUE

Alder Court

BLACKTHORN CLOSE

DEWBERRY PARK

HEATHER WALK

MARTELLO COURT

WENDELL AVE

STRAND ROAD

CARRICKHILL RISE

CARRICKHILL CLOSE

PORTMARNOCK

CARRICKHILL RISE

TILMARNOCK GROVE

CRESCENT

PARKVIEW

TILMARNOCK AVE

BURROW CT

The Quarry

PINE CT

CARRICKHILL HTS

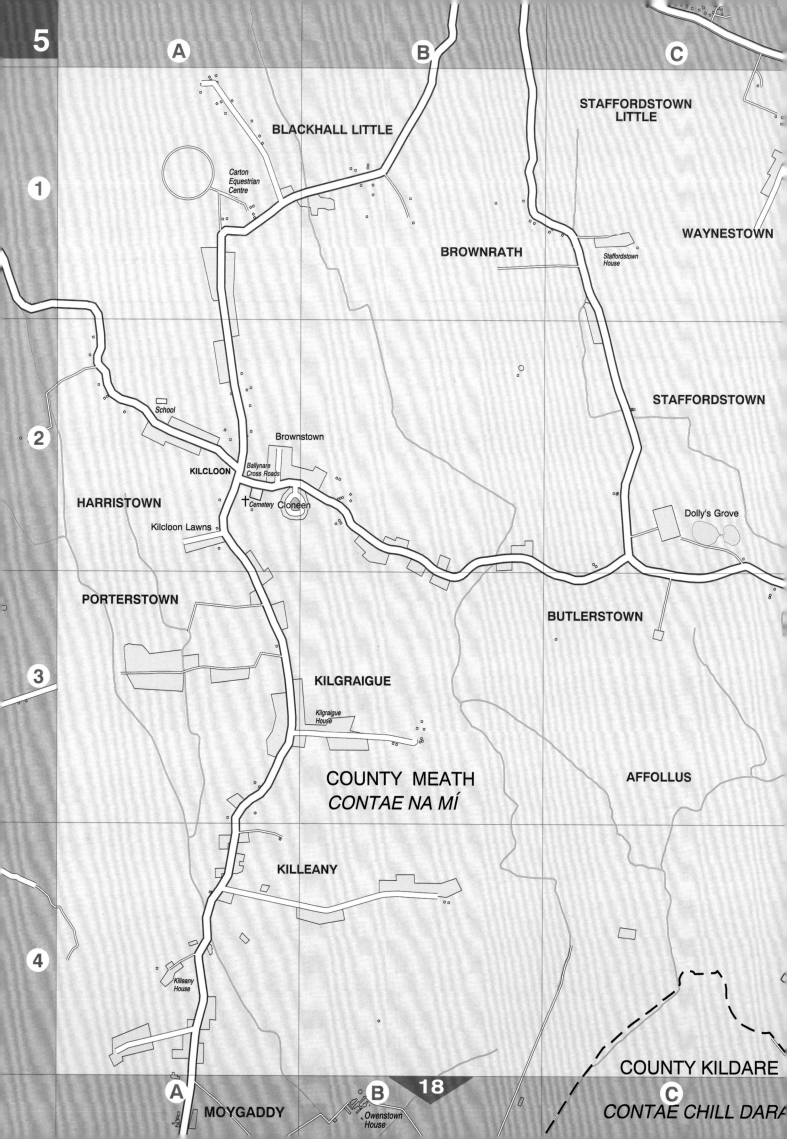

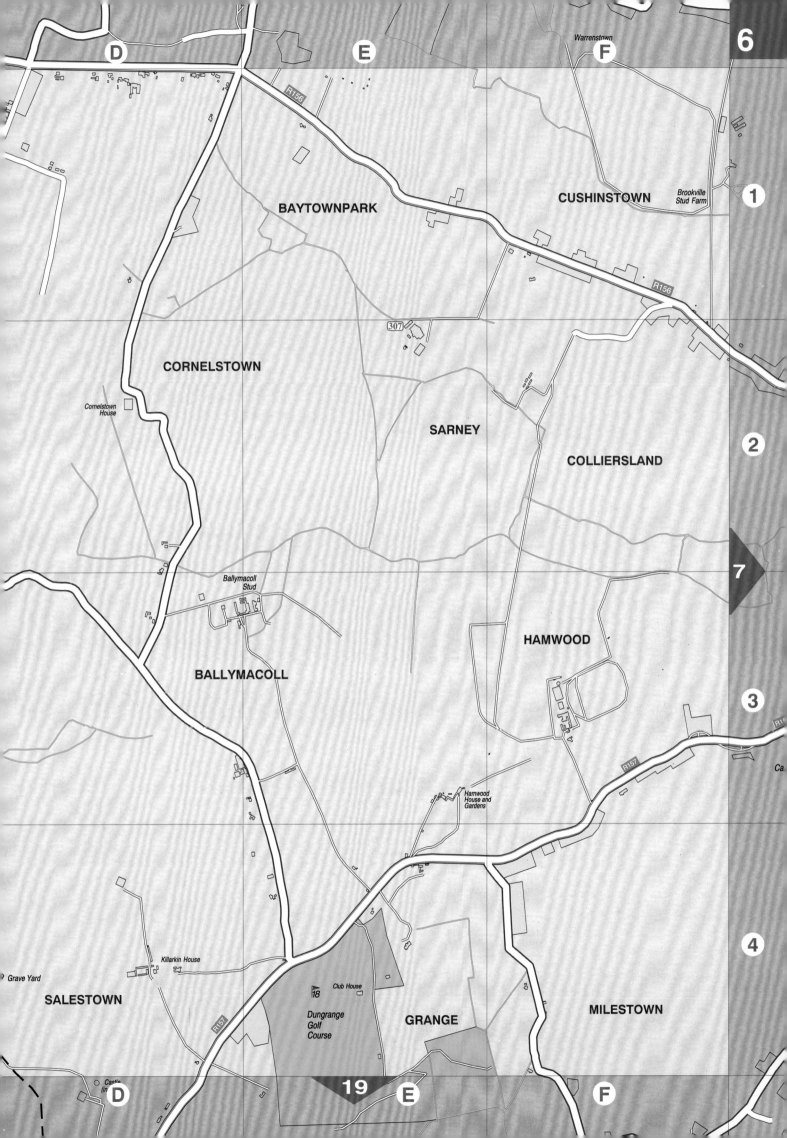

Warrenstown

R156

CUSHINSTOWN

Brookville
Stud Farm

1

BAYTOWNPARK

R156

307

CORNELSTOWN

Cornelstown
House

SARNEY

COLLIERSLAND

2

7

Ballymacoll
Stud

HAMWOOD

BALLYMACOLL

3

R1

R157

Hamwood
House and
Gardens

4

Killarkin House

Grave Yard

SALESTOWN

18
Club House

Dungrange
Golf
Course

GRANGE

MILESTOWN

R157

Castle
(in

CARRICKHILL RISE
CARRICKHILL CLOSE
PORTMARNOCK PARK
CARRICKHILL CRESCENT
STRAND
RISE
GROVE
WALK
The Quarry
PINE CT
CARRICKHILL DRIVE
CARRICKHILL HTS
BLACKBERRY
WOODLANDS
BEACH
BURROW CT
PORTMARNOCK AVE

296

1 Ardilaun

CARRICKHILL ROAD MIDDLE
CARRICKHILL ROAD
RISE
BLACKBERRY

R106

STRAND ROAD

Grave Yard

PORTMARNOCK

Carrick Court

The Dunes

Suncroft Avenue
Church Avenue

School
Pitch & Putt

Portmarnock Golf Links
⛳18

Velvet Strand

STRANDMILL AVENUE
PARK ROAD
STRANDMILL ROAD
GOLF LINKS ROAD

le Estuary Reserve

2

Murragh

ROAD

P

14

3

Mayne Bridge

COAST ROAD
R106

Portmarnock Golf Links

⛳18

Club House

APOLIN

4 BALDOYLE

Community Hall

COAST ROAD

School

WILLIE NOLAN ROAD
ADMIRAL
Admiral Court
Hosp
Georgian Hamlet
Sch
PARK
WELDONS LANE
MAIN STREET
COLLEGE STREET

GRANGE ROAD
Youth Club
Brookstone
Sch
Brookstone Lane
DUBLIN STREET
Nursing Home
Grave Yard
The Mall
STRAND ROAD

SEAGRANGE AVENUE
SEAGRANGE DRIVE
GRANGE PARK

Parkvale
TUSCANY
PARK
LAWN

A *Turnberry*
TURNBERRY SQUARE
WARRENHOUSE ROAD
WARREN
GREEN

IRISH

Portmarnock Point

Cush Point
Club House

Sutton

1

SEA

2

3

The Steer　◯ *Martello*
　　　　　　　Tower

**Ireland's
Eye**

Carrigeen Bay

Rowan Rocks

Thulla Rocks

Thulla

4

Lighthouse

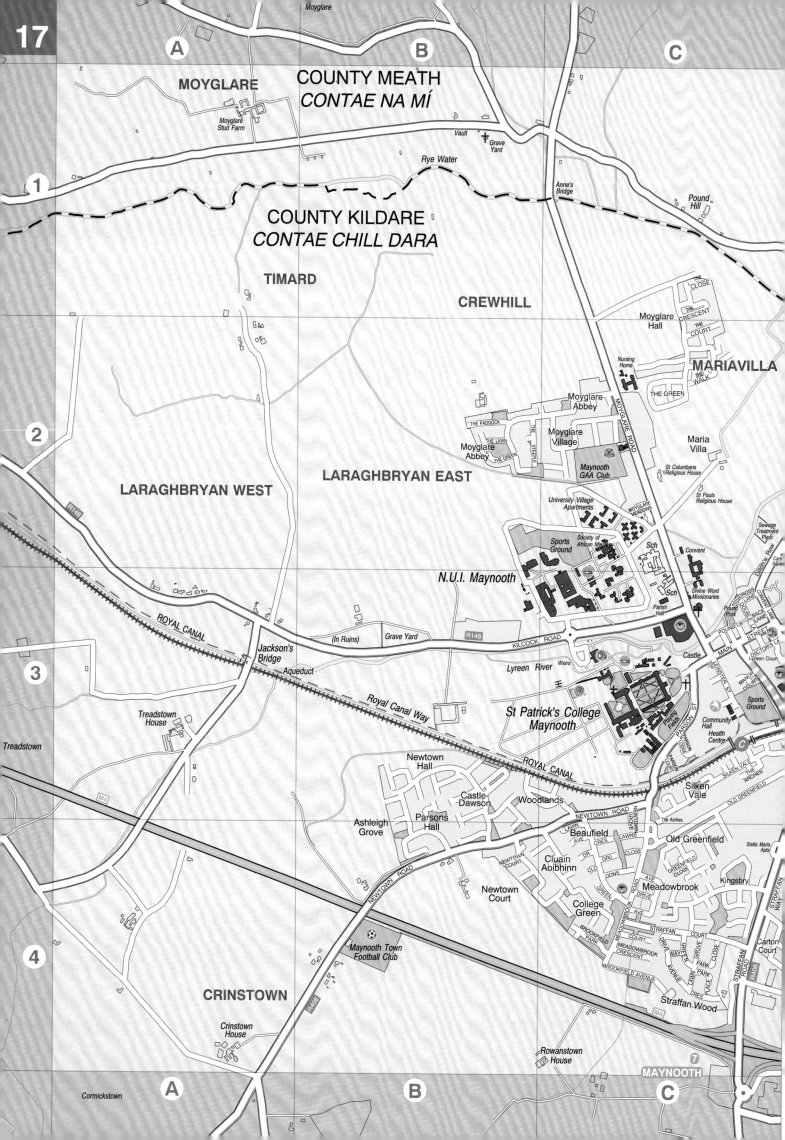

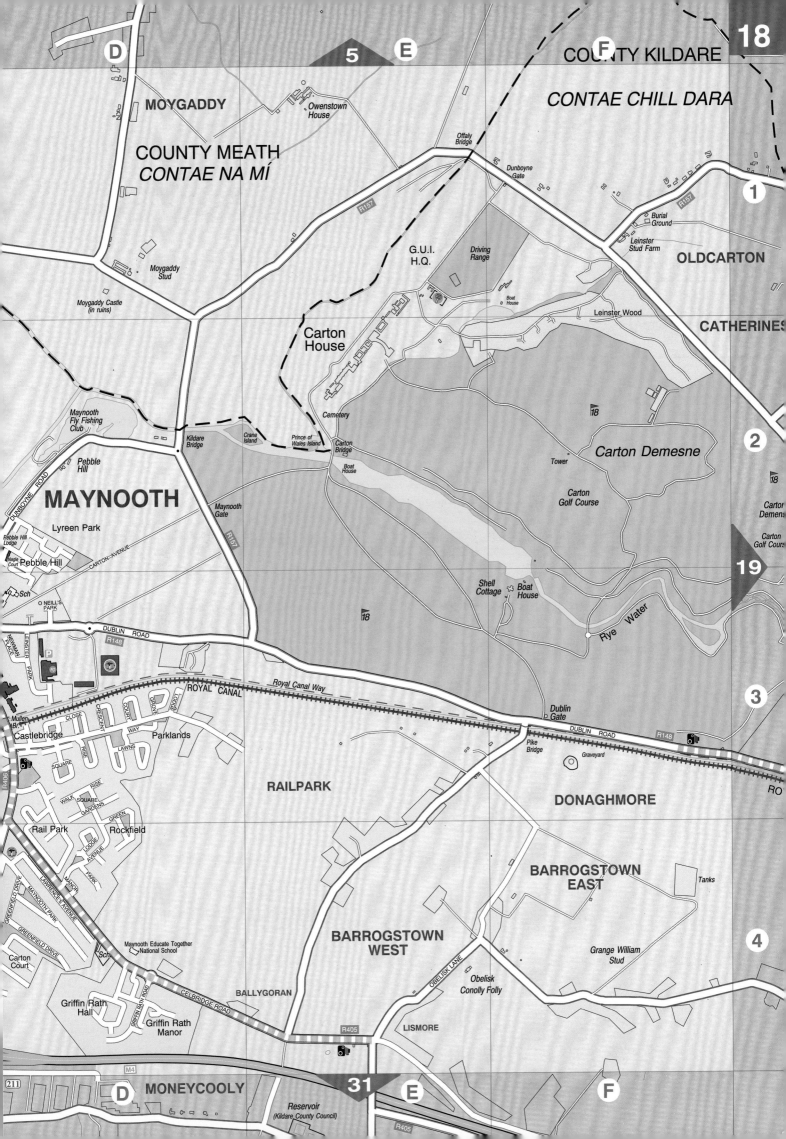

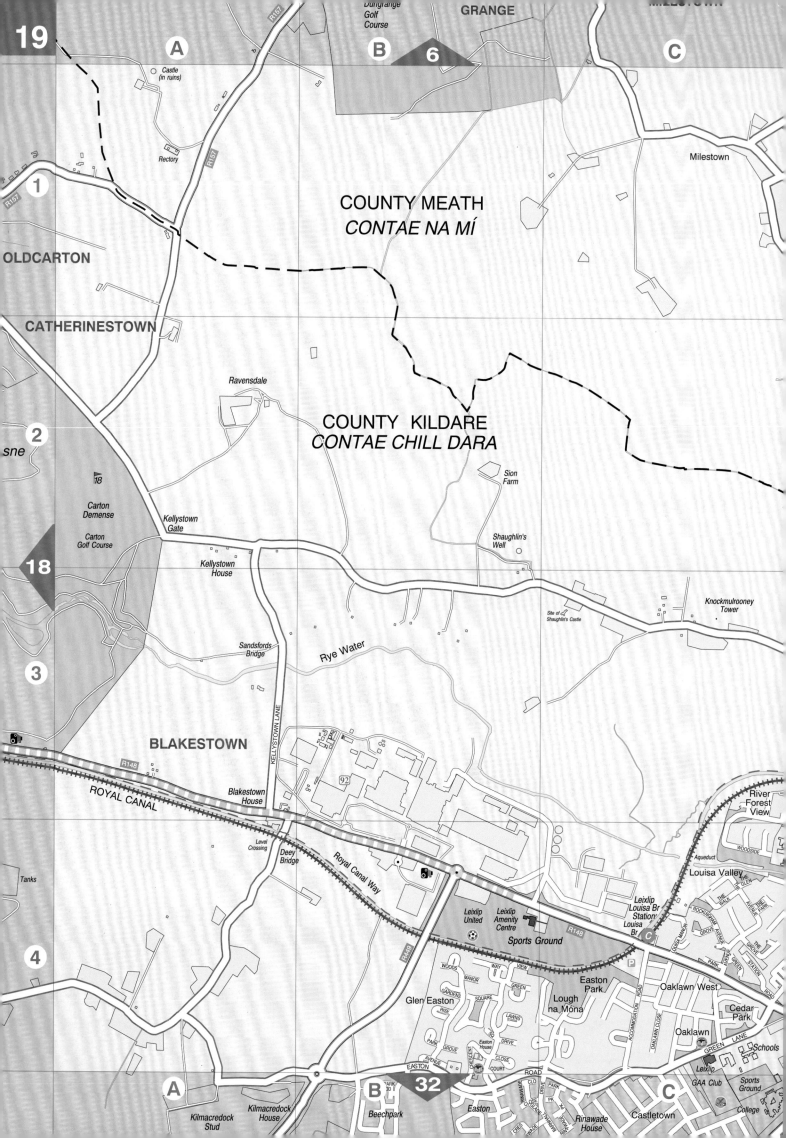

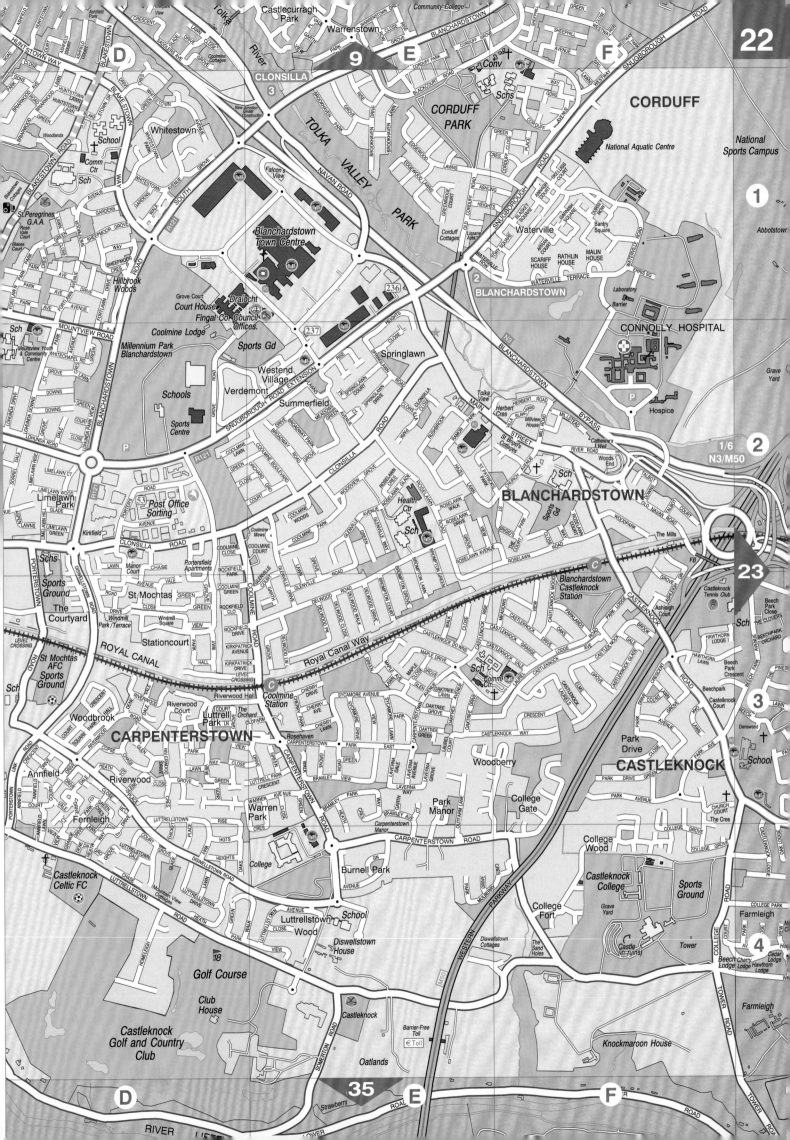

DUBLIN BAY

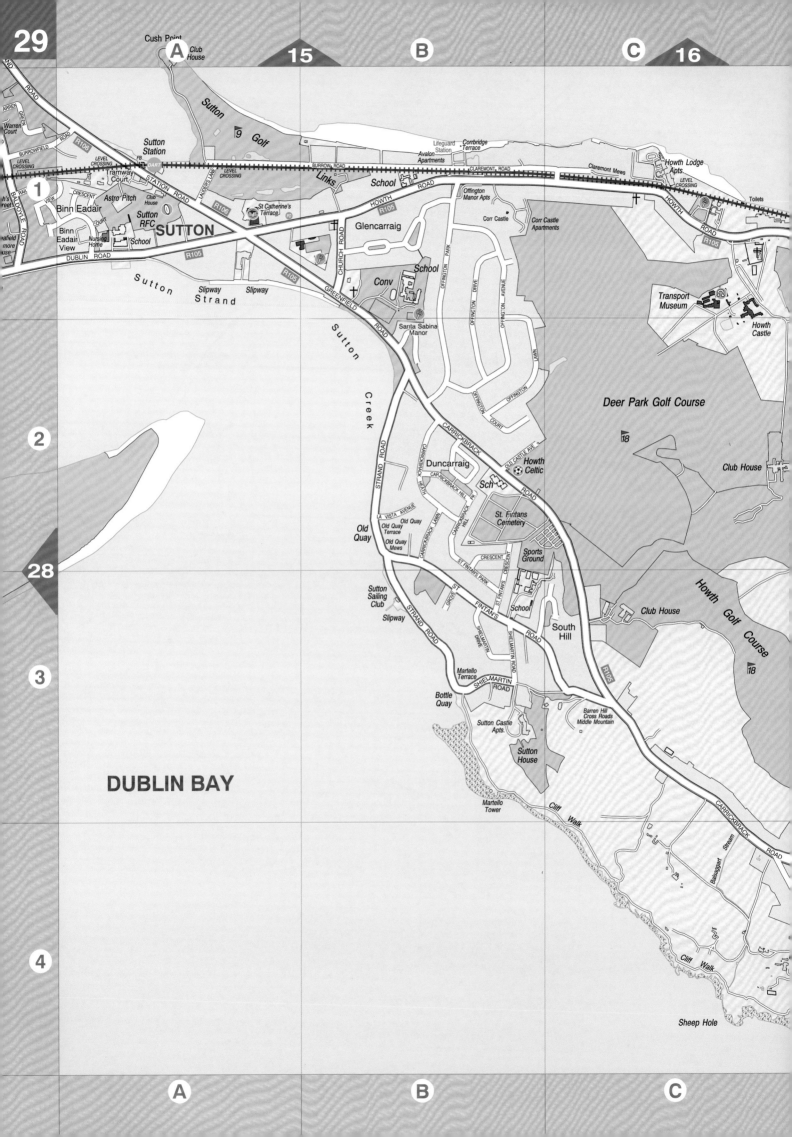

1

2

3

4

Lighthouse

Slipway

HOWTH HARBOUR

WEST PIER

Slipway

EAST PIER

Slipway

Slipway
Howth
Station
DART

P

Lifeboat
Station

Yacht
Club

Slipway

Toilets

HARBOUR
ROAD

CHURCH   ROAD

Tower

Asgard
Apts.

Balscadden Bay

Baths

STREET

Harbour
View

ABBEY   STREET

Evora Tce

Evora
Park

Evora
Crescent

ST LAWRENCE   ROAD

Health
Centre

GRACE O'MALLEY RD

St Lawrence's
Sports
Ground

School

BALSCADDEN   ROAD

Puck's Rocks

KILROCK   ROAD

NASHVILLE   PARK

P

Kilrock

Nose of Howth

HOWTH

NASHVILLE ROAD

R105

Sch

Crosstrees
Court

MAIN

STREET

ASGARD   LANE

ASGARD ROAD

COWBOOTER   LANE

ST PETERS
TERRACE

TUCKETTS

BALKILL   GROVE

BALKILL   PARK

Cannon Rock Estate

Cannon Rock

THORMANBY

Cannon
Rock
View

UPPER   CLIFF   ROAD

Gull
Cottage

**Cannon Rock
Cottage**

GRACE O'MALLEY DRIVE

BALKILL   PARK

BALGLASS   RD

BALKILL   ROAD

THORMANBY   LAWNS

DUNGRIFFAN
ROAD

GREYS   LANE

MARINERS
COVE

St Nessan's
Apartments

CASANA   VIEW

WOODCLIFF
HEIGHTS

Walk

Cliff

Casana Rock

Green Ivy

Reservoir

Beann Éadair
G.A.A. Club

Club
House

Woodside

Rockstown

*Thormanby
Woods*

THORMANBY   ROAD

*Thormanby
Lodge*

Deer

Park

Golf

Course

18

*Ben
of
Howth*

BALKILL   ROAD

WINDGATE

Loughoreen Hills
Green Hallows Quarries

*The Green
Hallows*

*Howth Hill
Lodge Nursing
Home*
Blakeney
House
(Mews)

KITESTOWN   RD

*The Gate
Lodge*

Piper's Gut

Fox Hole

Reservoir

Carrickbrack
Reservoir
(Disused)

WINDGATE   ROAD

NER RD

WINDGATE
RISE

BAILEY GREEN ROAD

**The
Summit**

Tower

Baily
Green

Reservoir

P

Highroom Bed

Lough Leven

P

OLD   CARRICKBRACK   ROAD

THORMANBY   ROAD

R105

CARRICKBRACK   ROAD

*Sisters of Charity
Stella Maris*

Gaskin's Leap

Whitewater Brook

Webb's Castle Rock

CEANCHOR ROAD

Cliff   Walk

*The Great
Baily*

Glenaveena

Helipad
*The Little
Baily*

*Hippy
Hole*

Doldrum Bay

Lion's Head

*The Needles or
Candlesticks*

Baily Lighthouse

Drumleck Point

D   E   F

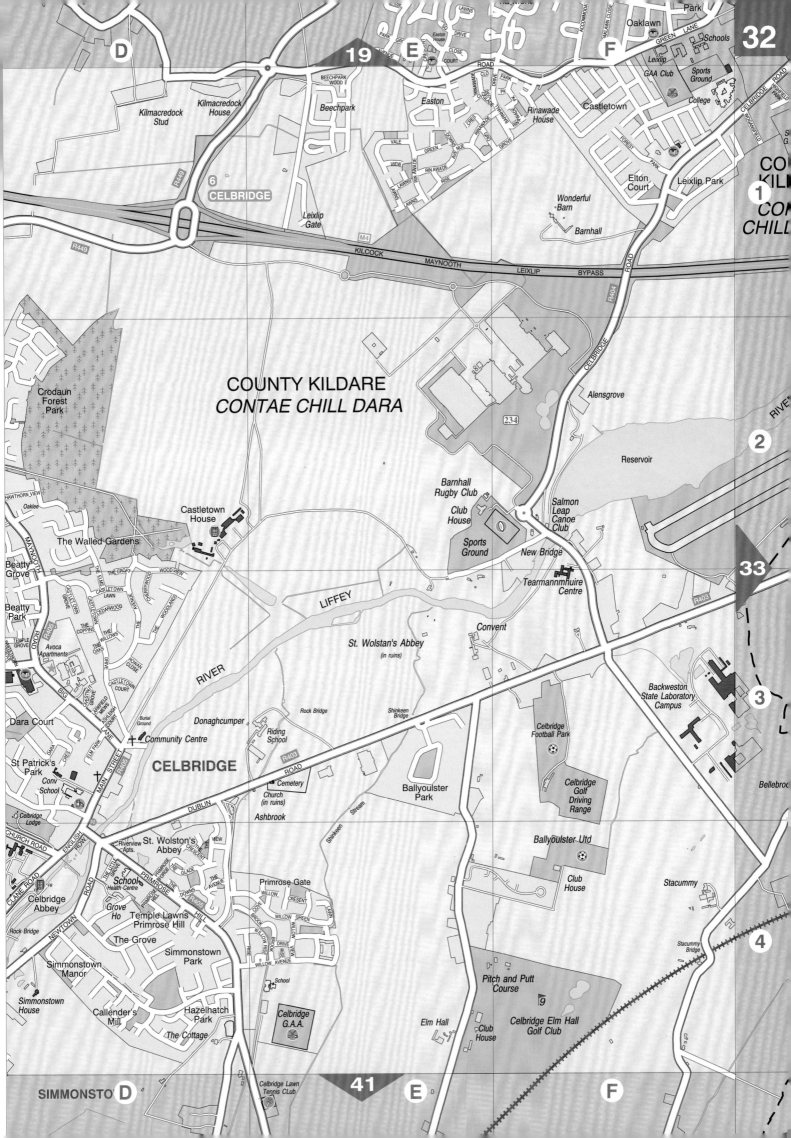

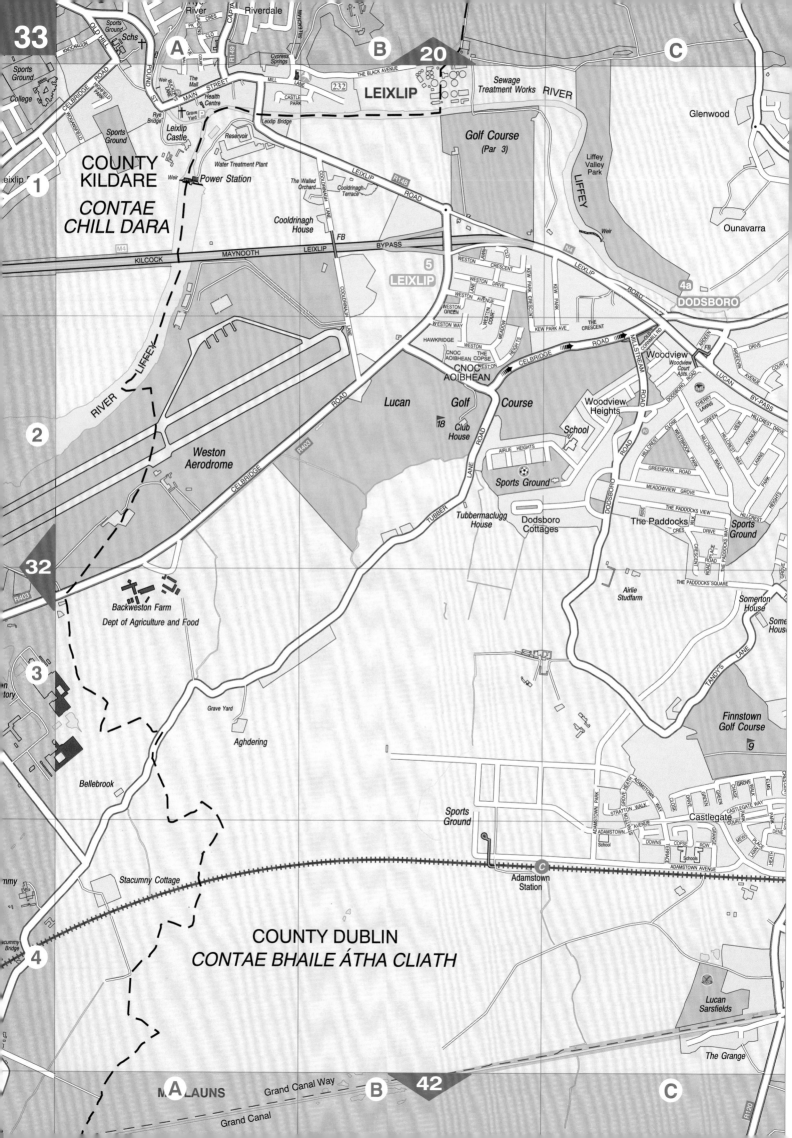

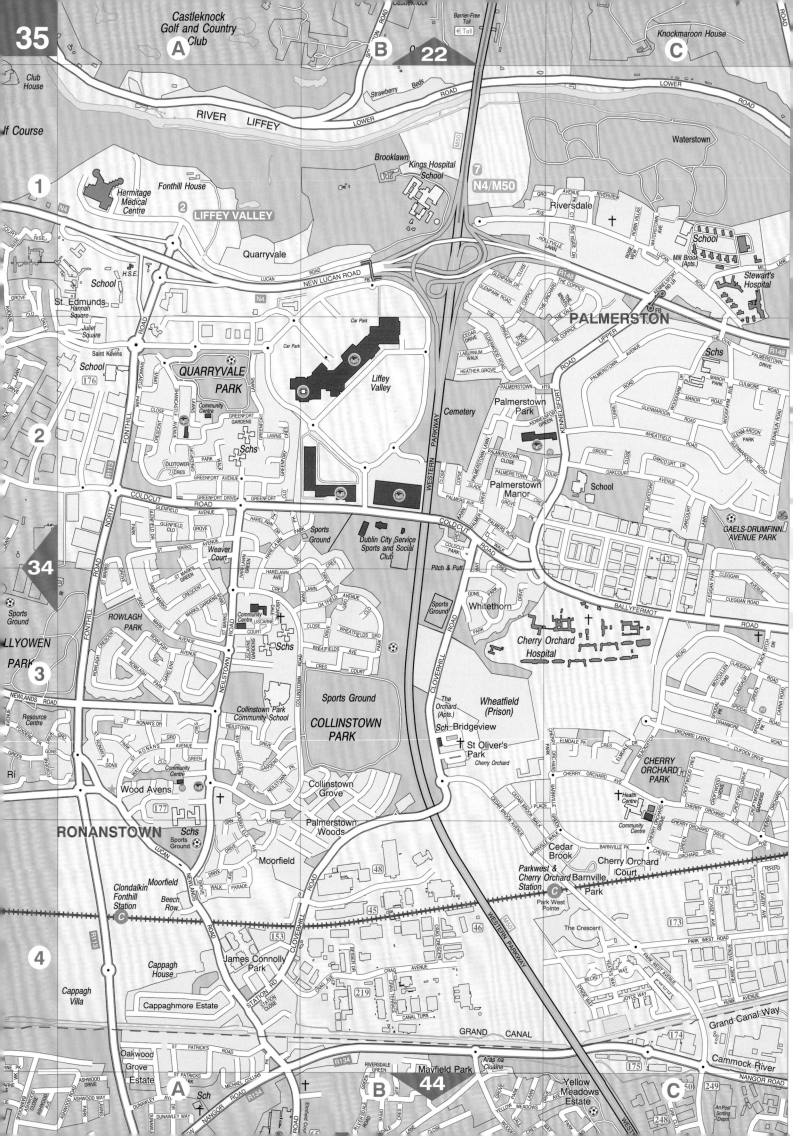

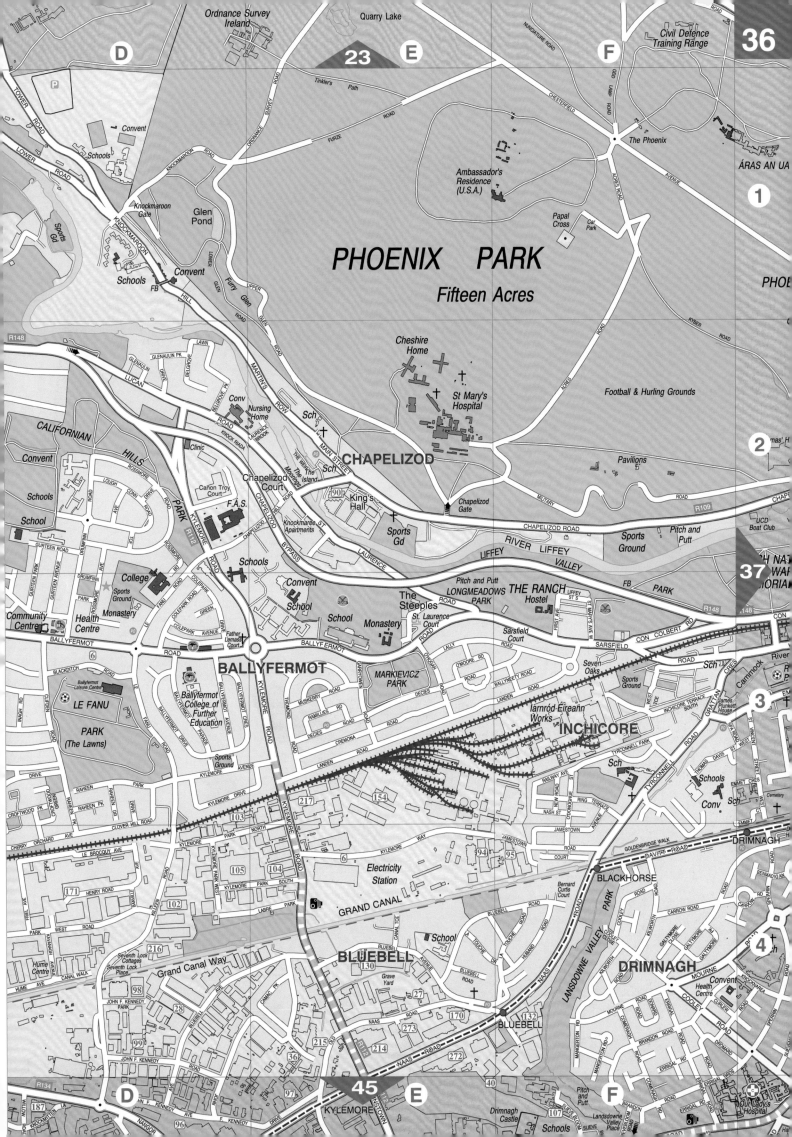

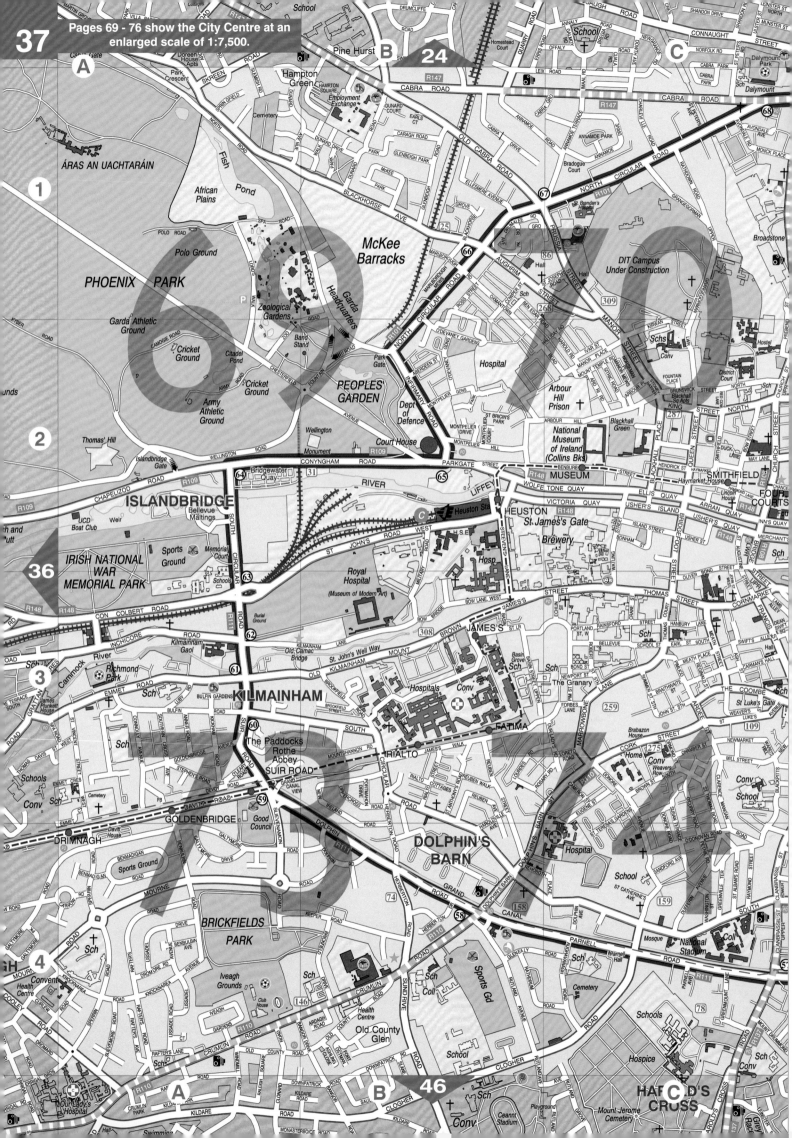

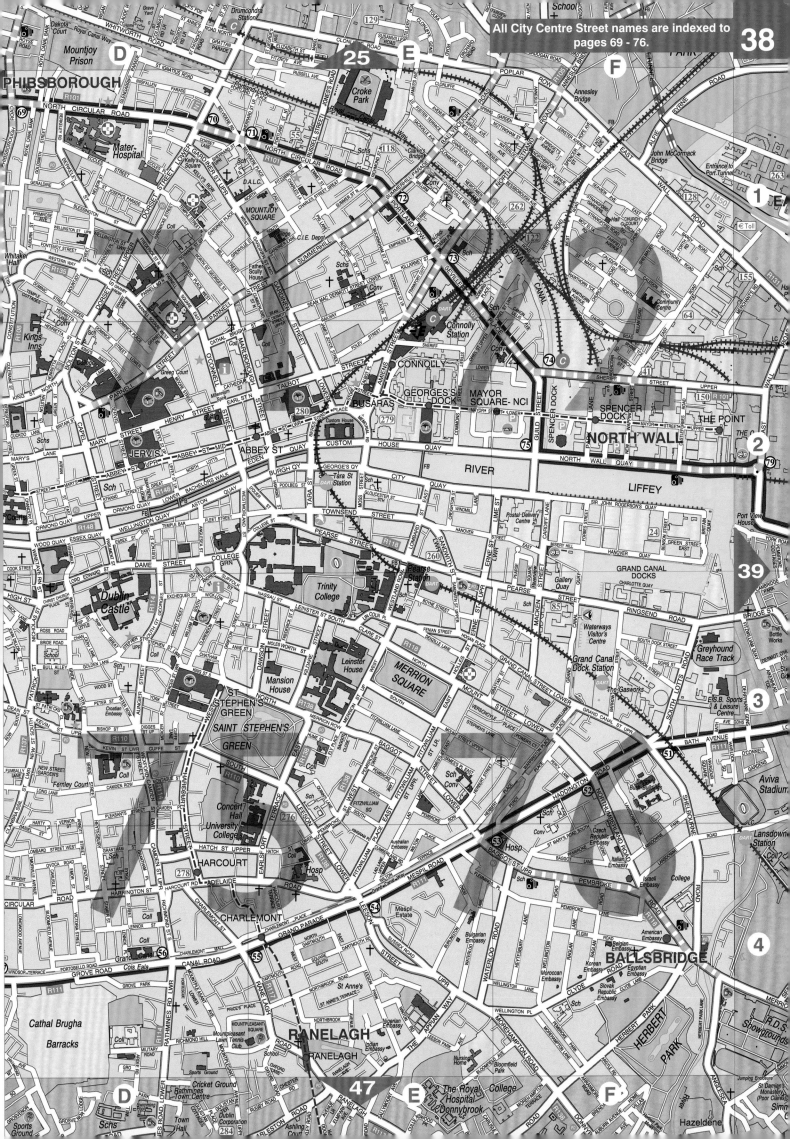

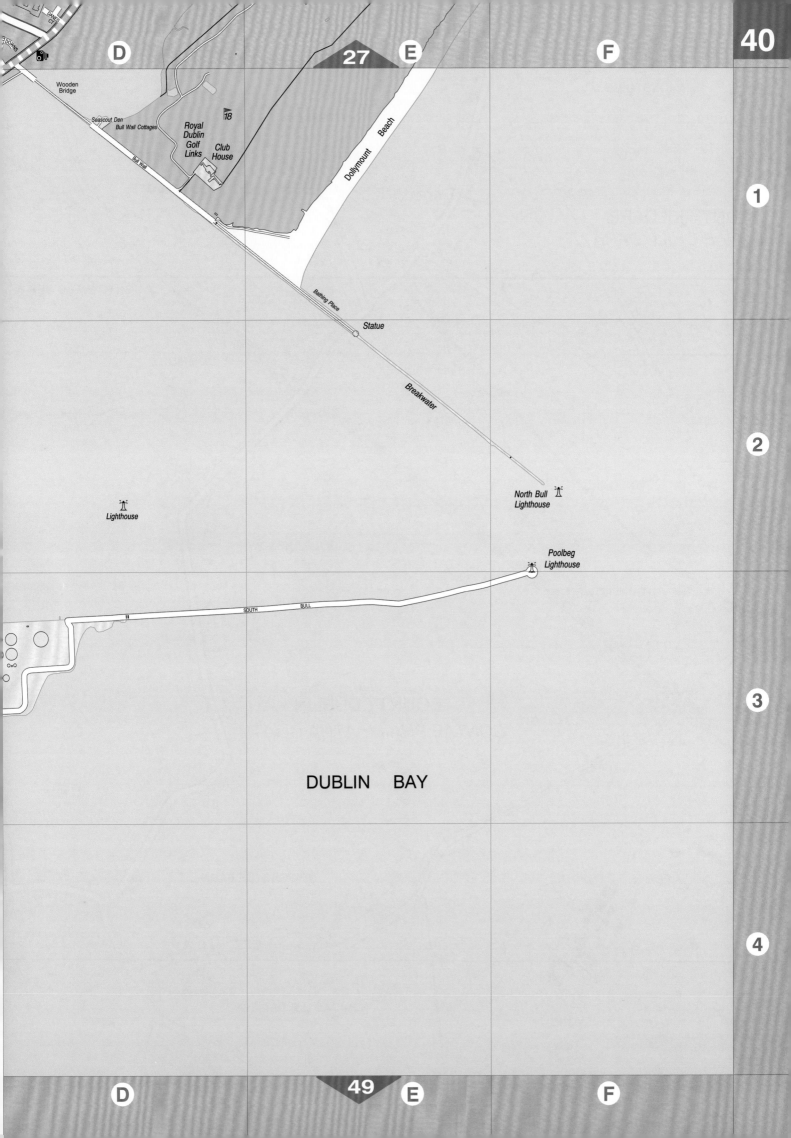

Wooden
Bridge

Seascout Den
Bull Wall Cottages

Royal
Dublin
Golf
Links

Club
House

⚑18

Bull Wall

Dollymount   Beach

Bathing Place

Statue

Breakwater

North Bull
Lighthouse

Poolbeg
Lighthouse

⊥̇
Lighthouse

SOUTH   BULL

DUBLIN   BAY

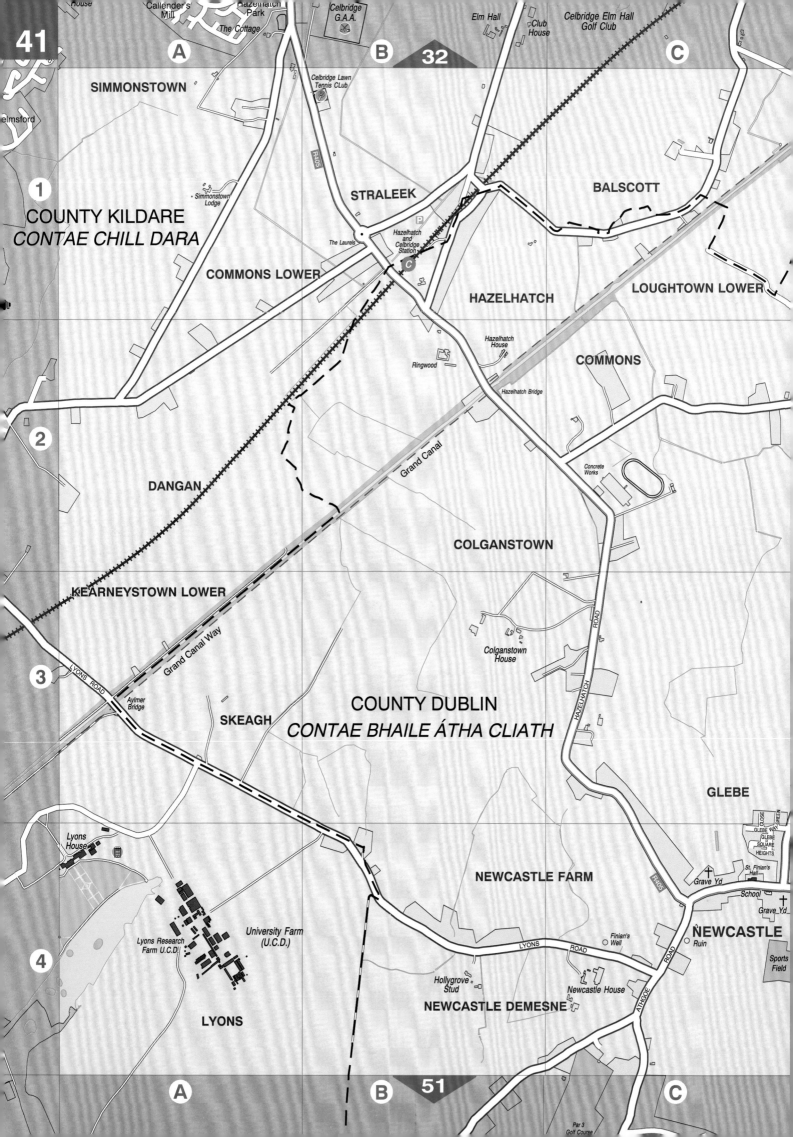

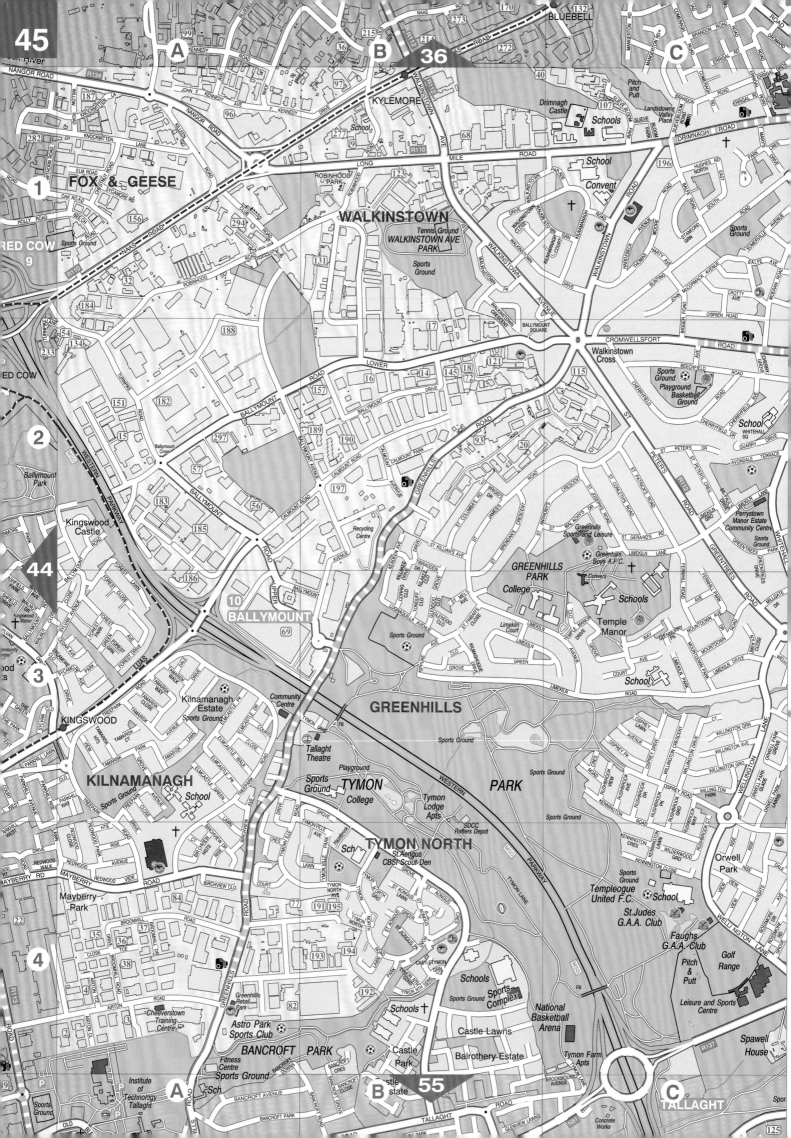

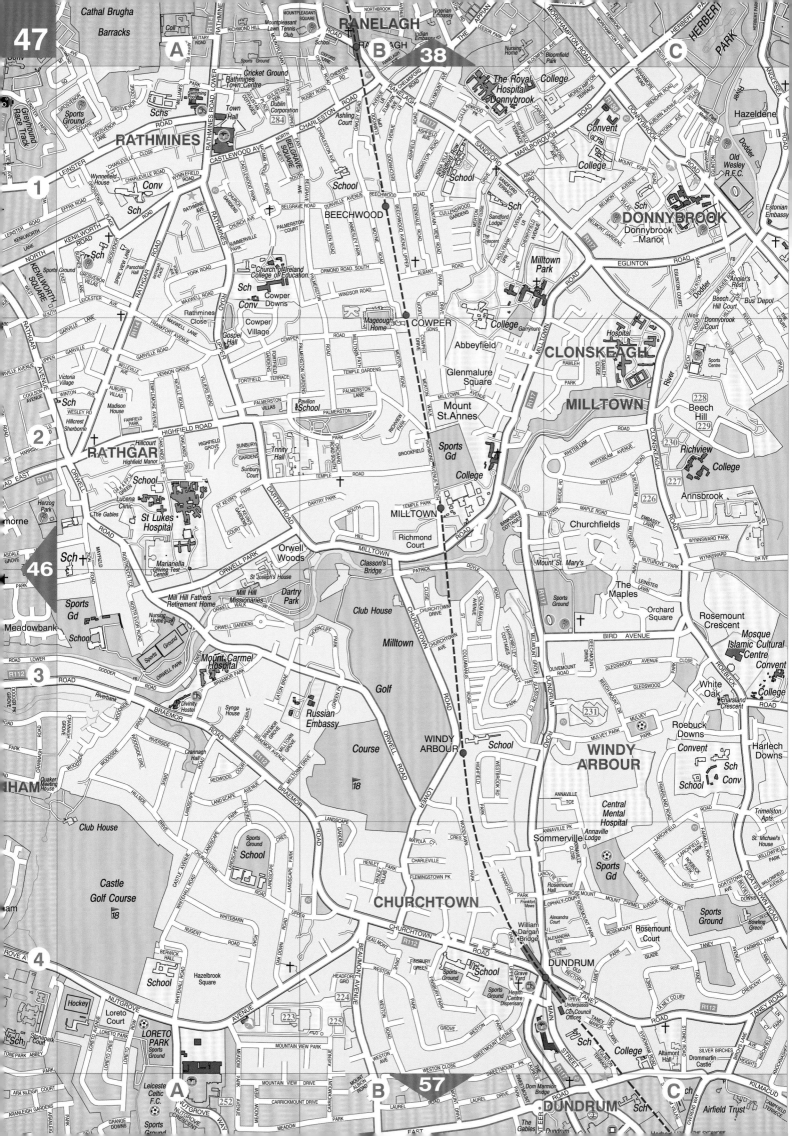

Lighthouse

Lighthouse

EAST PIER

Harbour

Car Ferry
Terminal

Yacht Club

i

Band Stand

CROFTON ROAD

HARBOUR ROAD

KELLY'S AVE

CROFTON AVE

GEORGE'S PLACE

Harbour
View

Harbour
Square

Dun-Laoghaire/Rathdown Town
Co. Council

Hall

Dún Laoghaire
Station

DART

Yacht Club

Yacht Club

Geographical Pointer

Toilets

QUEEN'S ROAD

GEORGE'S STREET LOWER

Hosp

Sch

MARINE RD

EBLINA AVE

R118

P

MORAN
PARK

Maritime
Museum

DÚN LAOGHAIRE

DOMINICK
ST

CROSS AVENUE

Sch

CONVENT ROAD

GEORGE'S STREET

HIGH TCE N

ADELAIDE STREET

MELLIFONT AVE

Baths

Health
Centre

TIVOLI TERRACE EAST

TIVOLI
TERRACE
SOUTH

PATRICK

MULGRAVE

NORTHUMBERLAND
AVENUE

CORRIG
AVENUE

GEORGE'S STREET UPPER

CLARINDA PARK WEST

CLARINDA
PARK N

PARK ROAD

P

WINDSOR TCE

P

PEOPLES
PARK

R119

Scotsman's Bay

MARINE PARADE

Forty Foot
Bathing Place

Harbour

Baths

SANDYCOVE POINT

Tower

SANDYCOVE AVE N

Youth
Club

Nursing
Home

E.H.B.
Nursing
Home

Children's
Home

CORRIG
ROAD

TIVOLI TERRACE
PARK

Clarinda
Manor

Sch

R118

GLENAGEARY RD LR

CLARINDA
PARK EAST

ROSSMEEN
GDNS

ROSSMEEN PARK

EDEN
PK

SUMMERHILL
PARK

Sandycove/
Glasthule
Station

DART
ROAD

GLASTHULE ROAD

EDEN RD UPR

EDEN
RD LR

Coll

Schs

BURDETT
AVENUE

SANDYCOVE

Gowran
Hall

SANDYCOVE AVE WEST

SANDYCOVE ROAD

SANDYCOVE AVE EAST

SANDYCOVE
LANE E

BREFFNI

R119

Bullock
Harbour

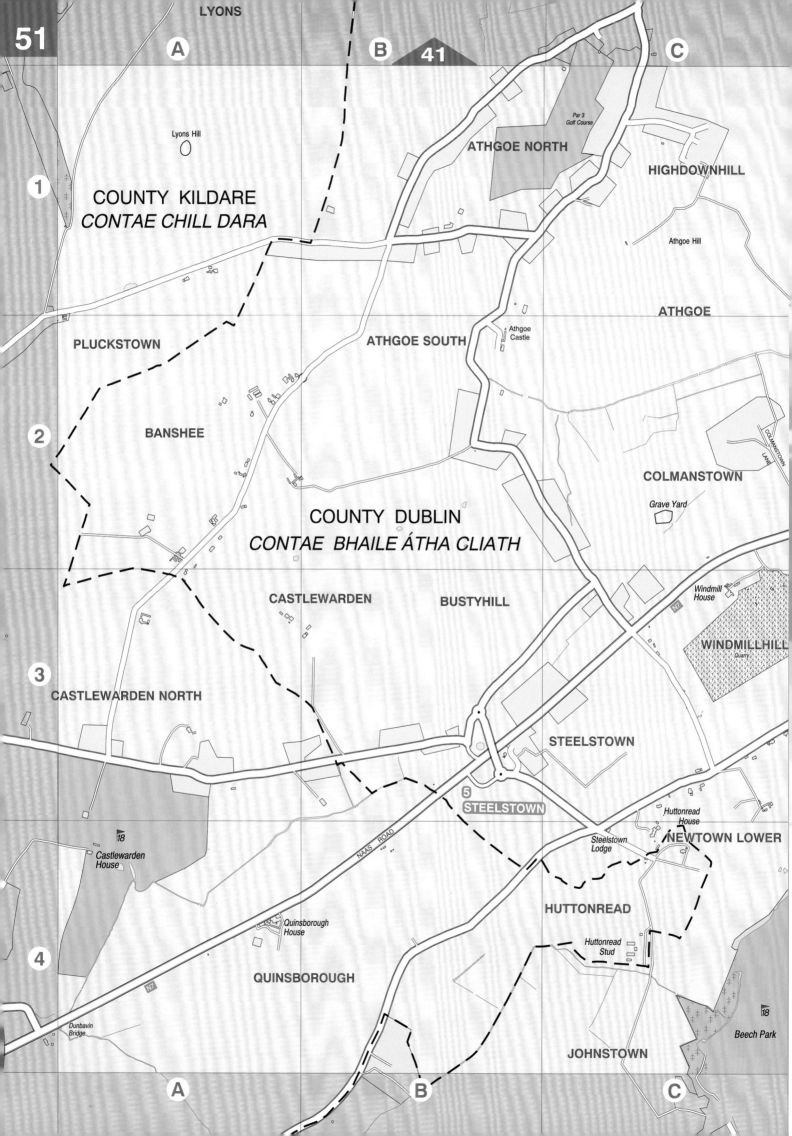

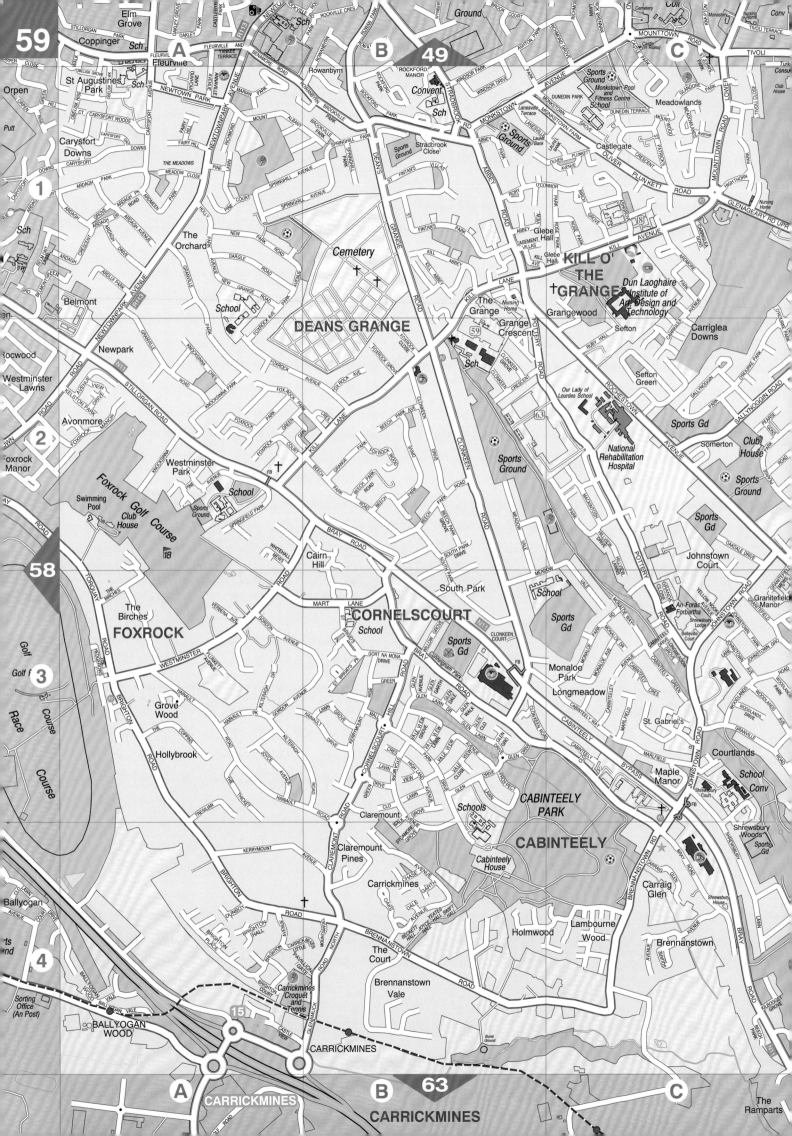

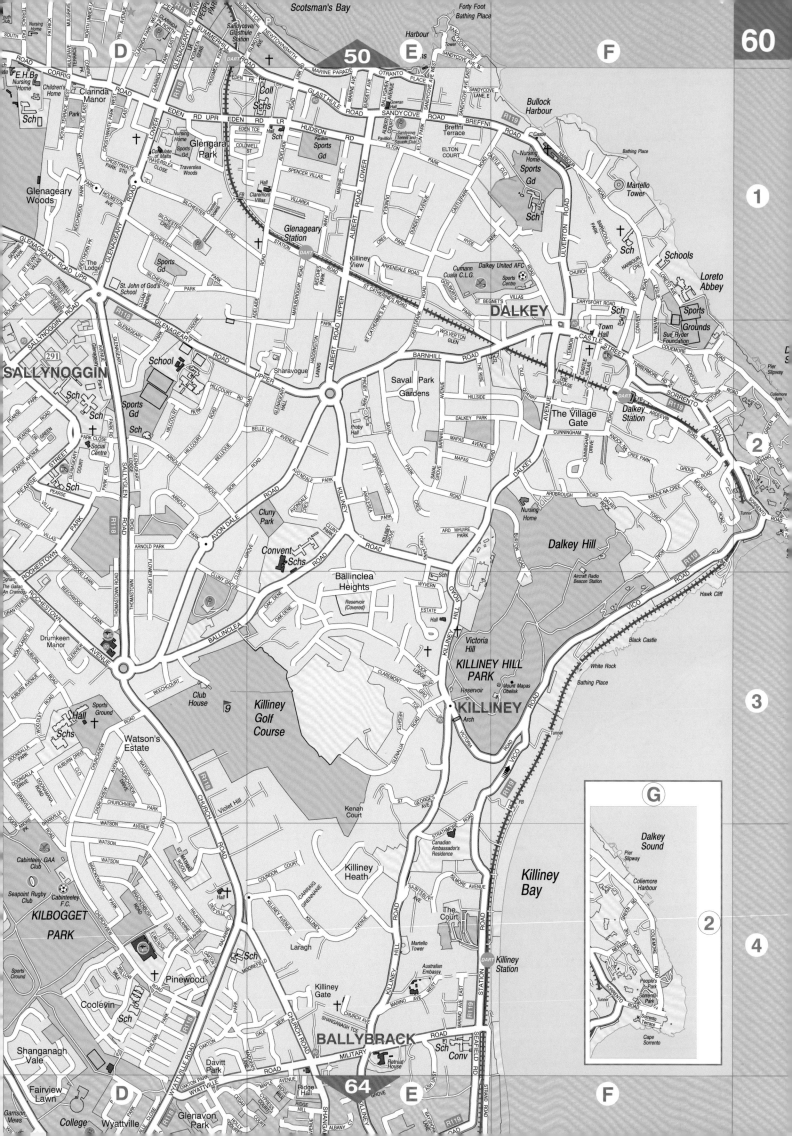

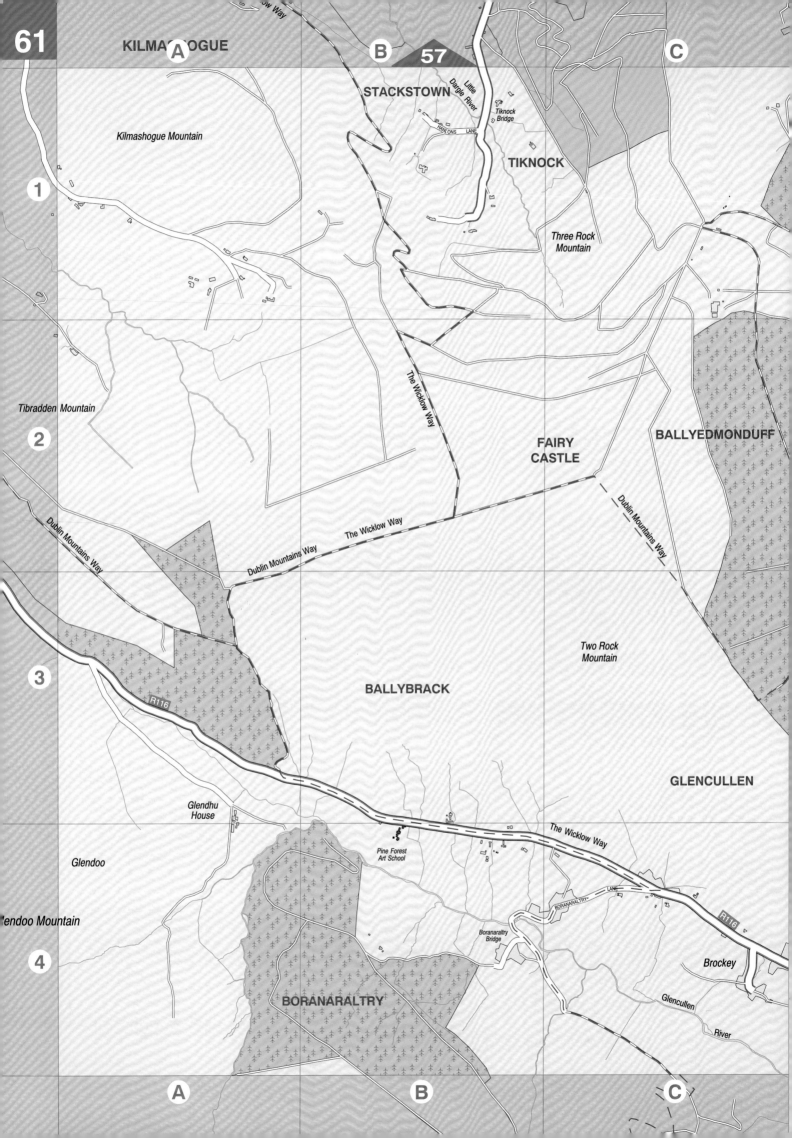

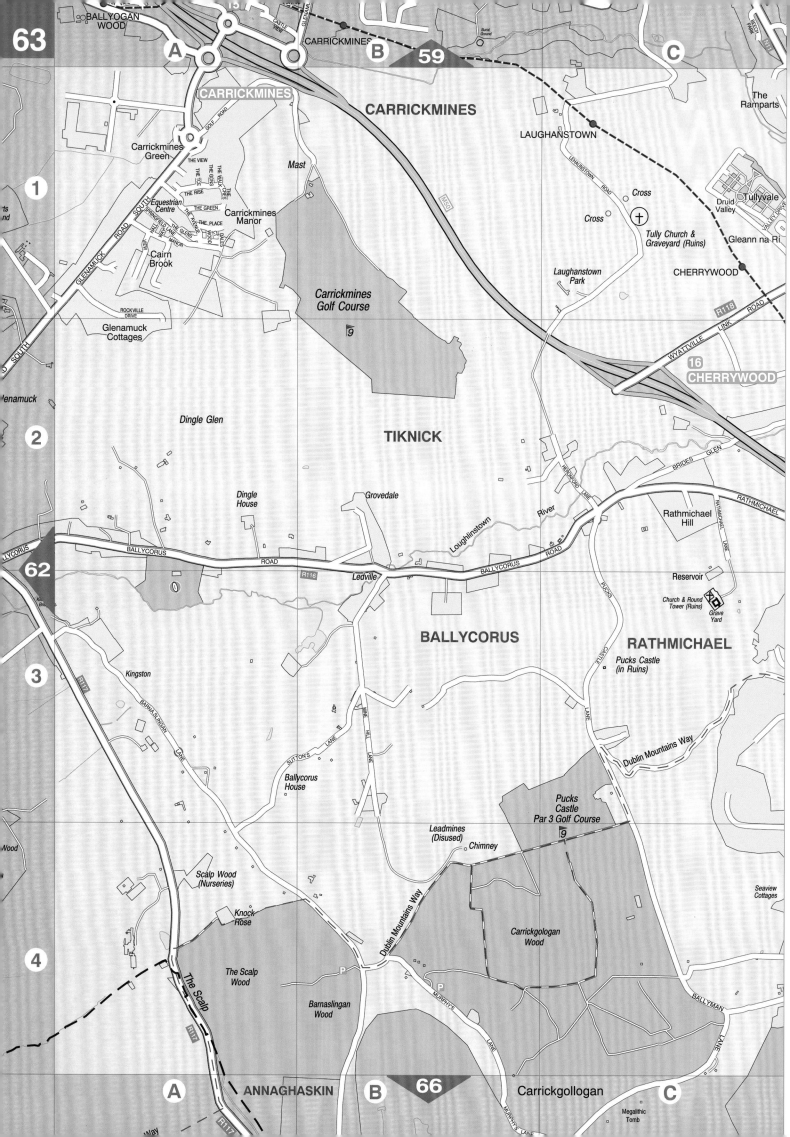

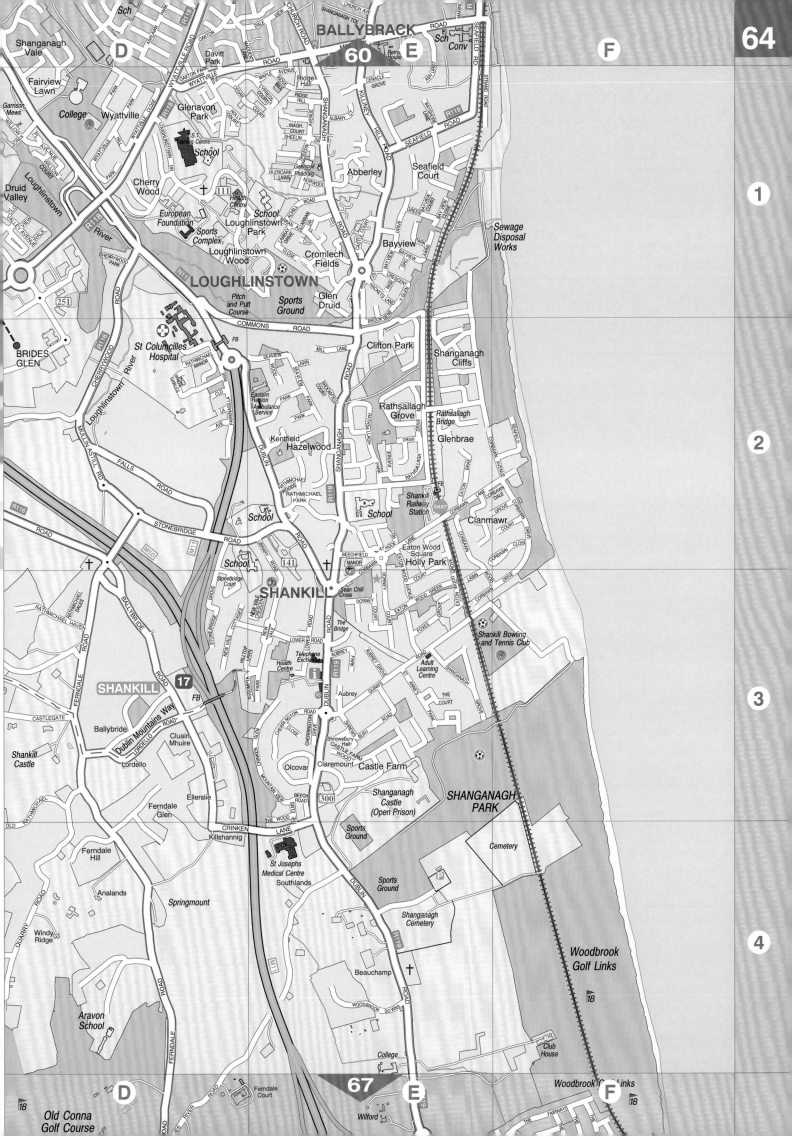

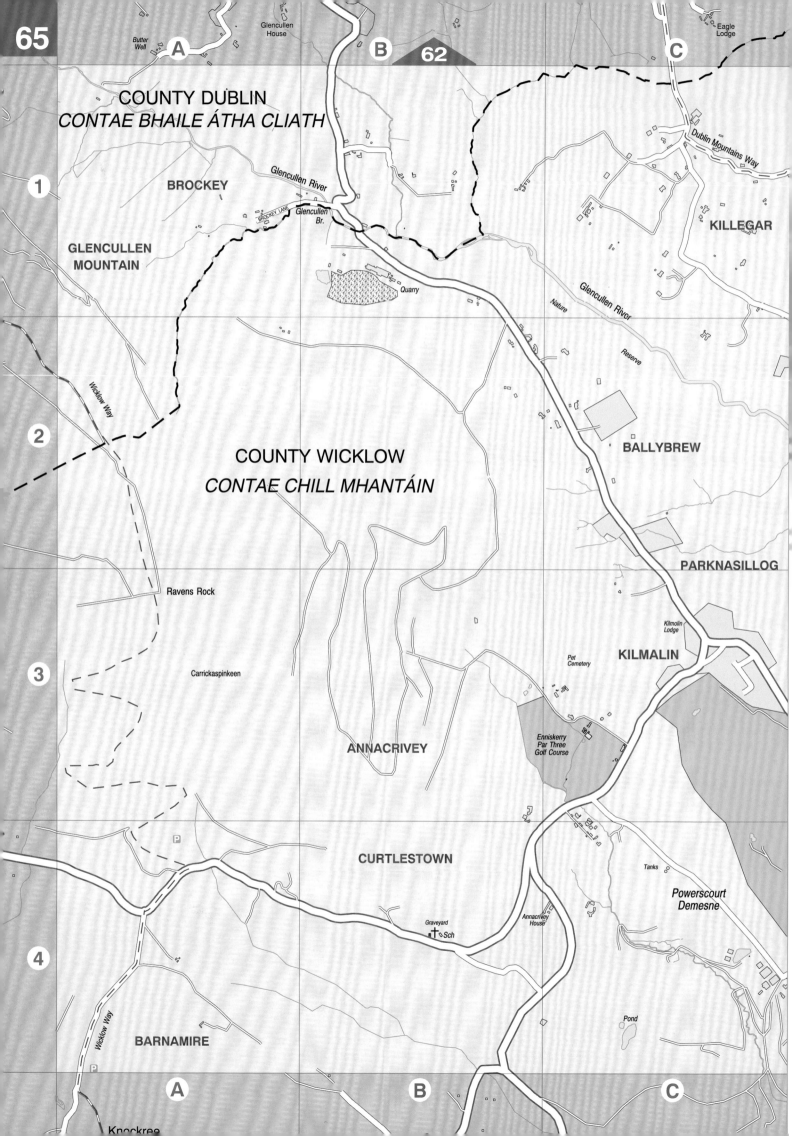

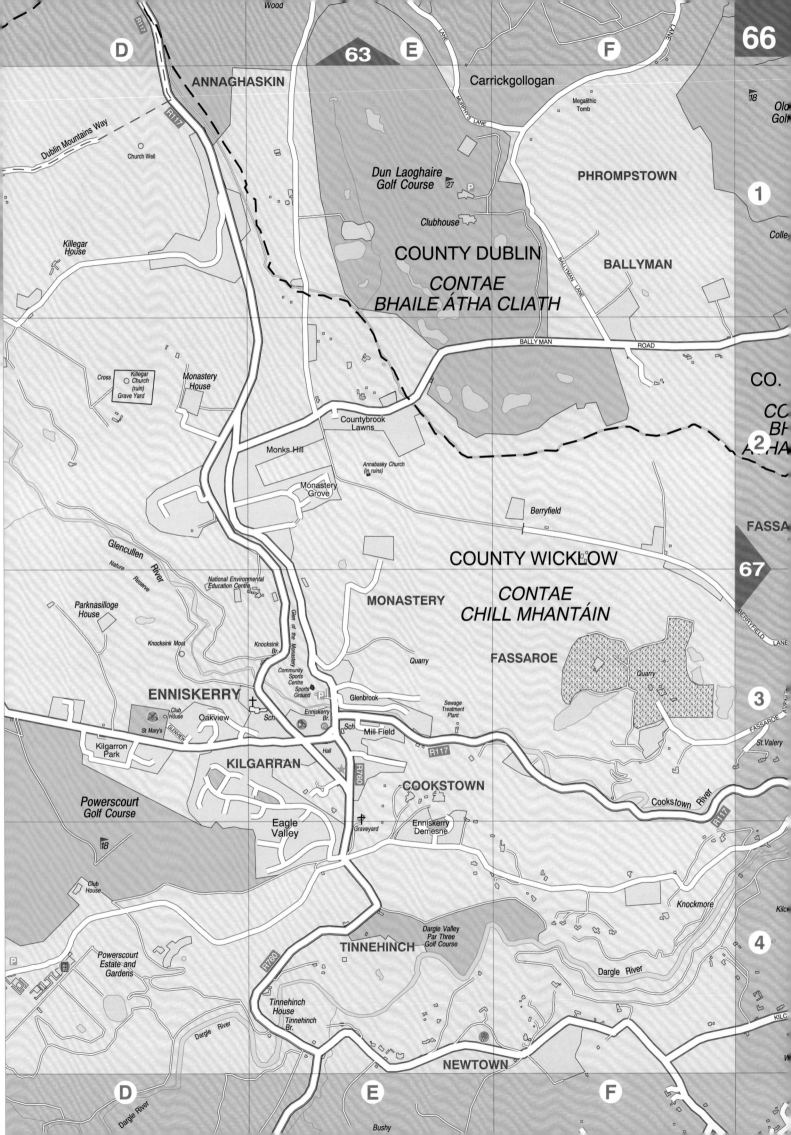

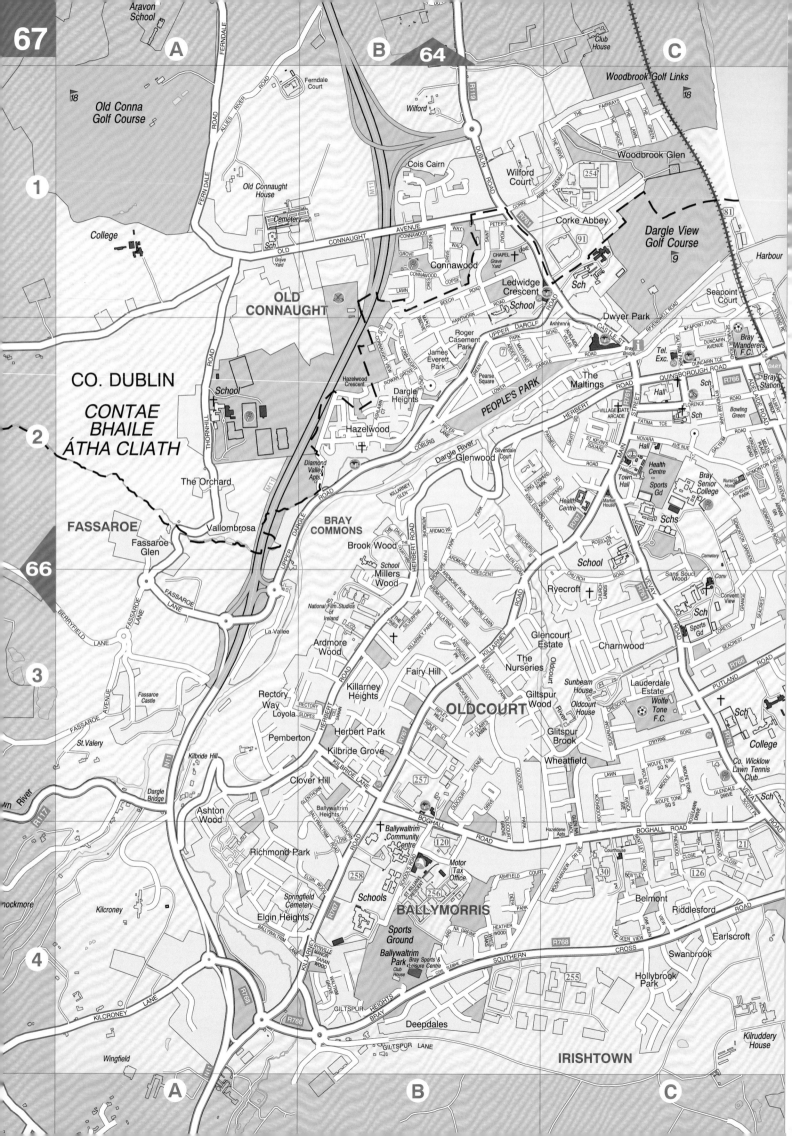

D E F

1

2

BRAY

National
Sea Life
Aquarium

IRISH   SEA

ALBERT AVE

SIDMONTON

South Esplanade

MEATH

Esplanade

STRAND   ROAD

ARATON CT

VICTORIA AVE

CONVENT AVENUE

Hall

R768

ROAD

SIDMONTON PK

STONHAM MEWS

WESTFIELD

NEWCOURT ROAD

Naylor's Cove

Fontenoy
Terrace

EDWARD ROAD

ROAD

RAHEEN PARK

PUTLAND

CUALA GROVE

CAMADERRY RD

NEWCOURT AVE

NEWCOURT AVE

RAHEEN PARK AVENUE

Raheenacluig Church
(in Ruins)

Golf Course

Eagle's
Nest

3

NEWCOURT ROAD

Briar
Wood

Bray
Head

Tunnel

NEWCOURT

R761

COUNTY WICKLOW

Bray Golf Club

18

CONTAE
CHILL MHANTÁIN

Tunnel

4

Tunnel

Tunnel
Tunnel

D E F

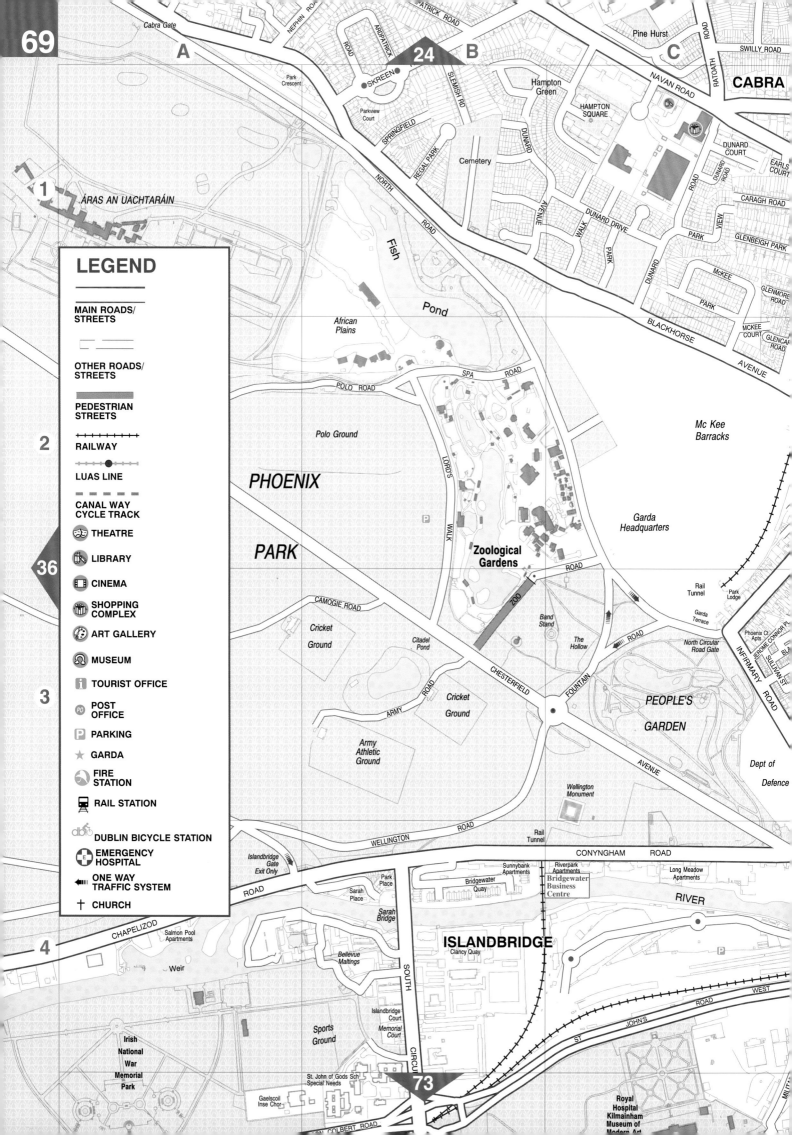

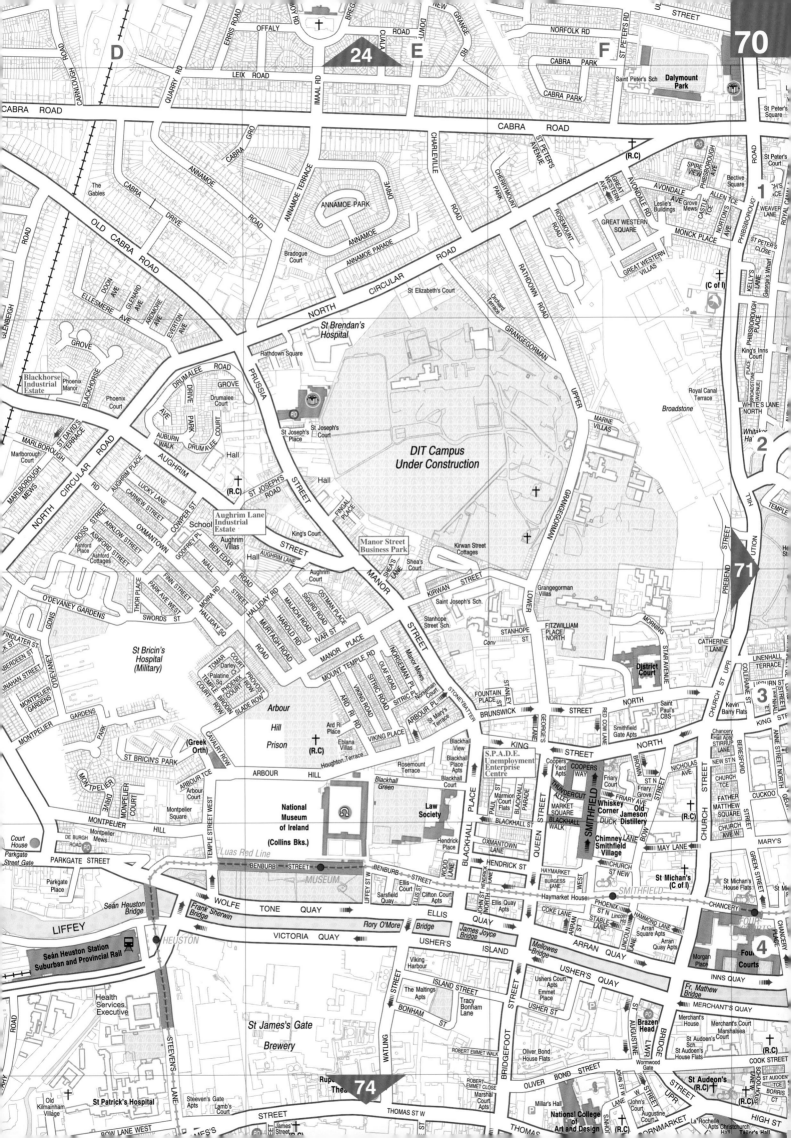

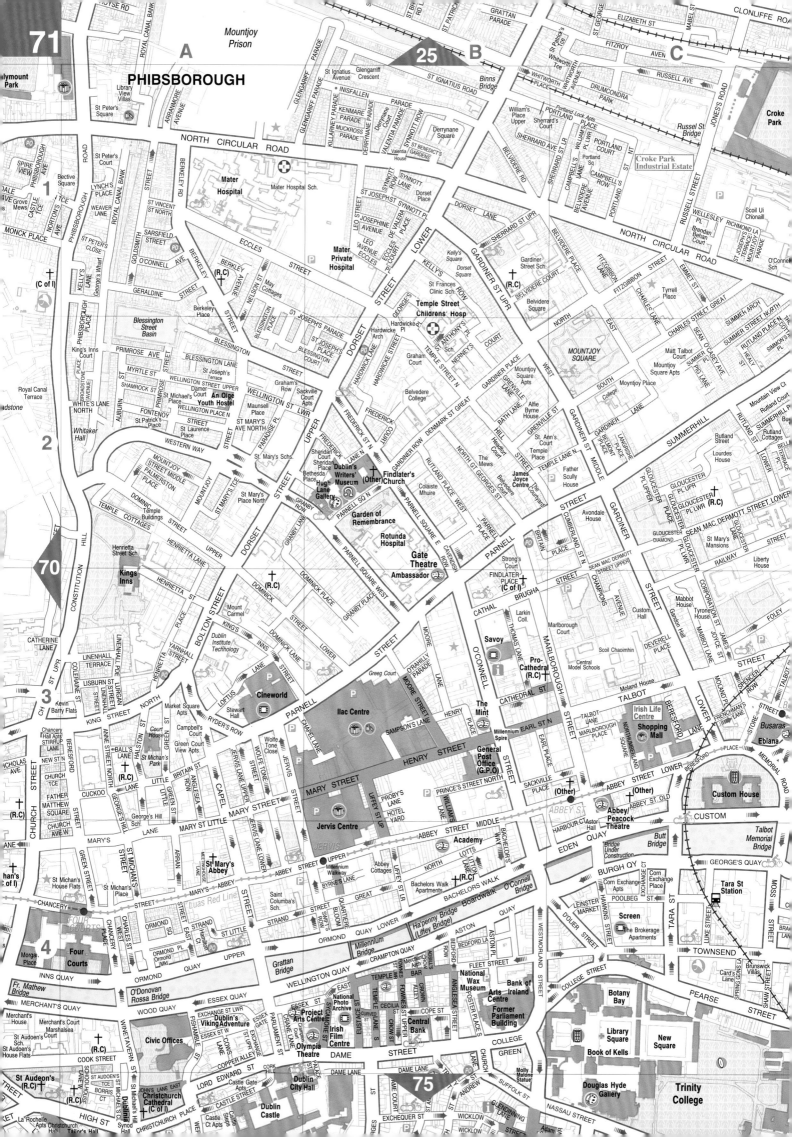

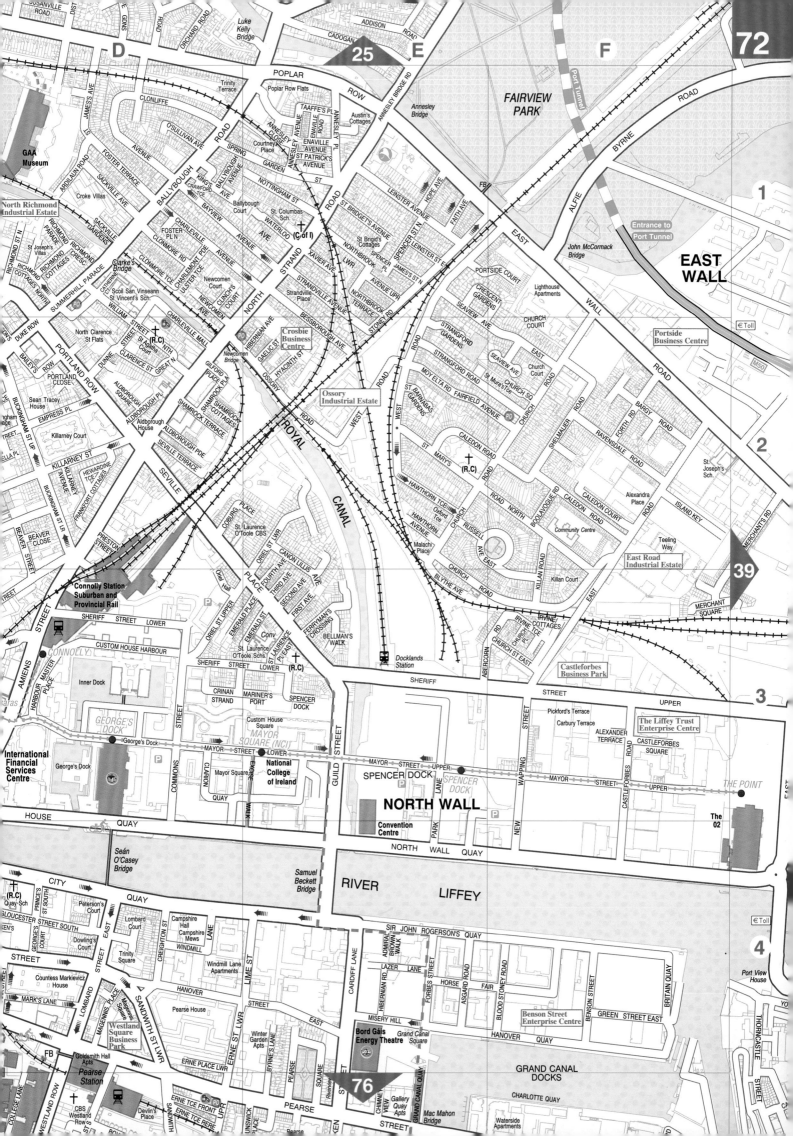

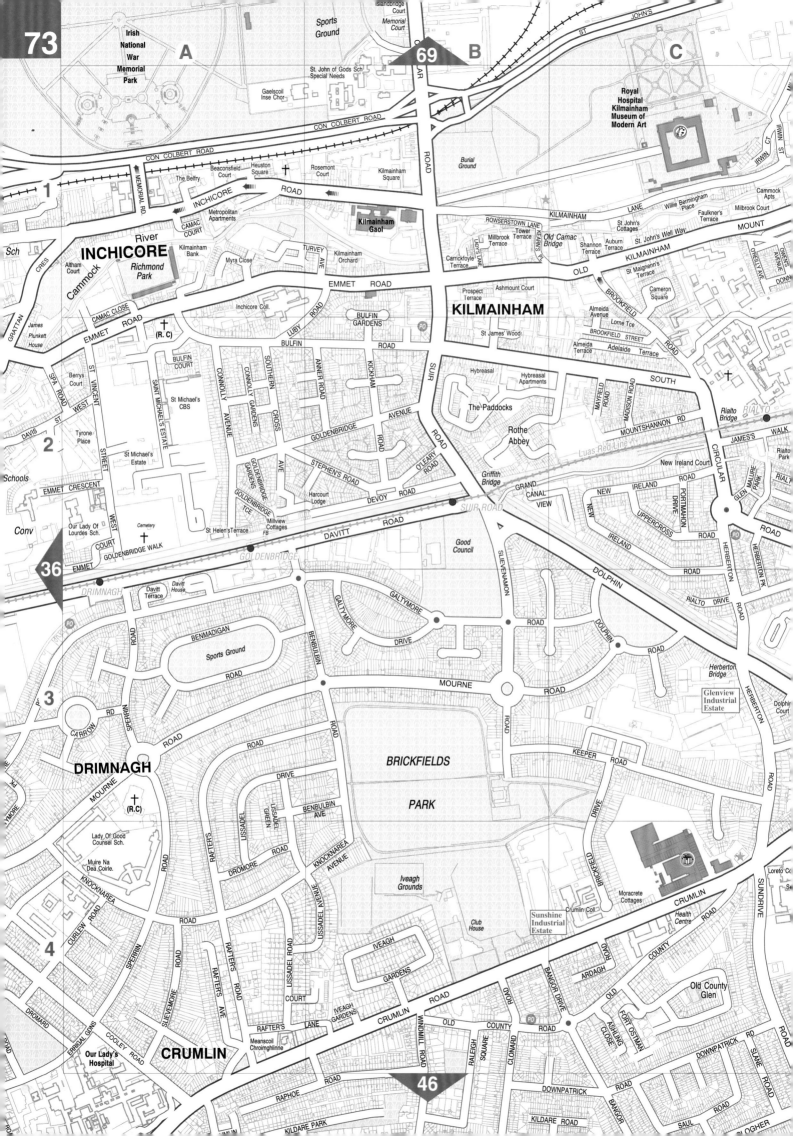

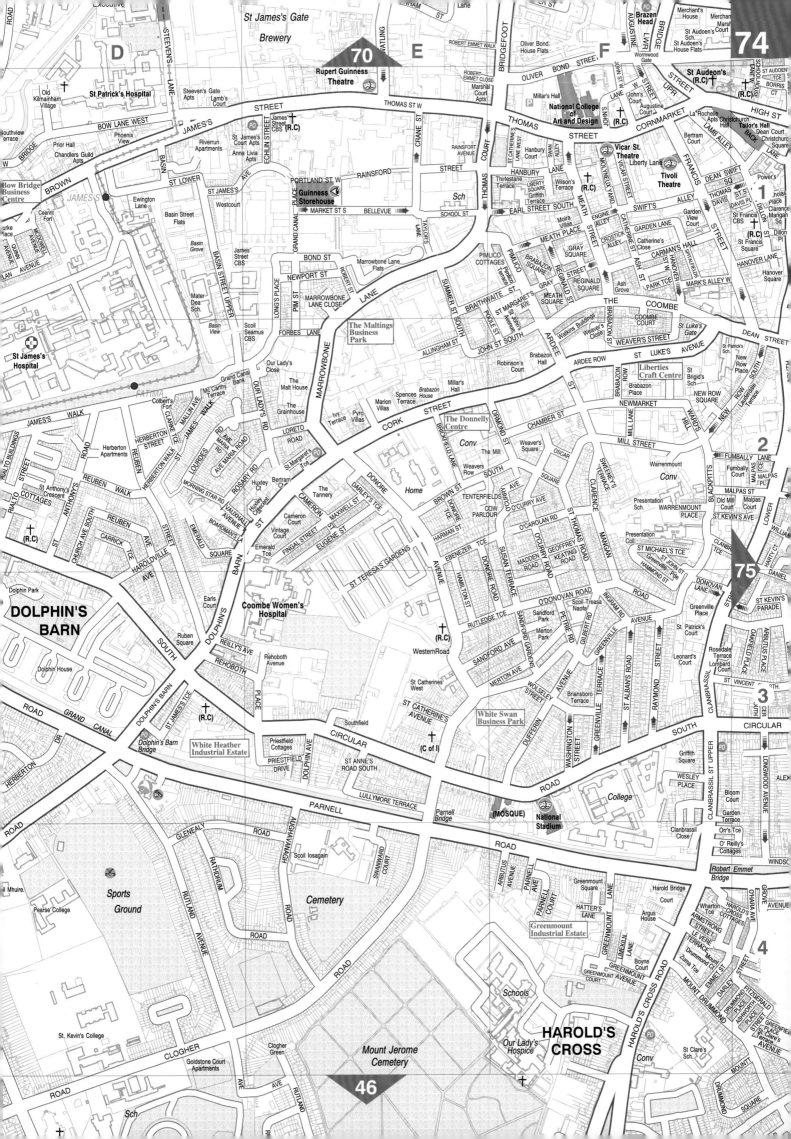

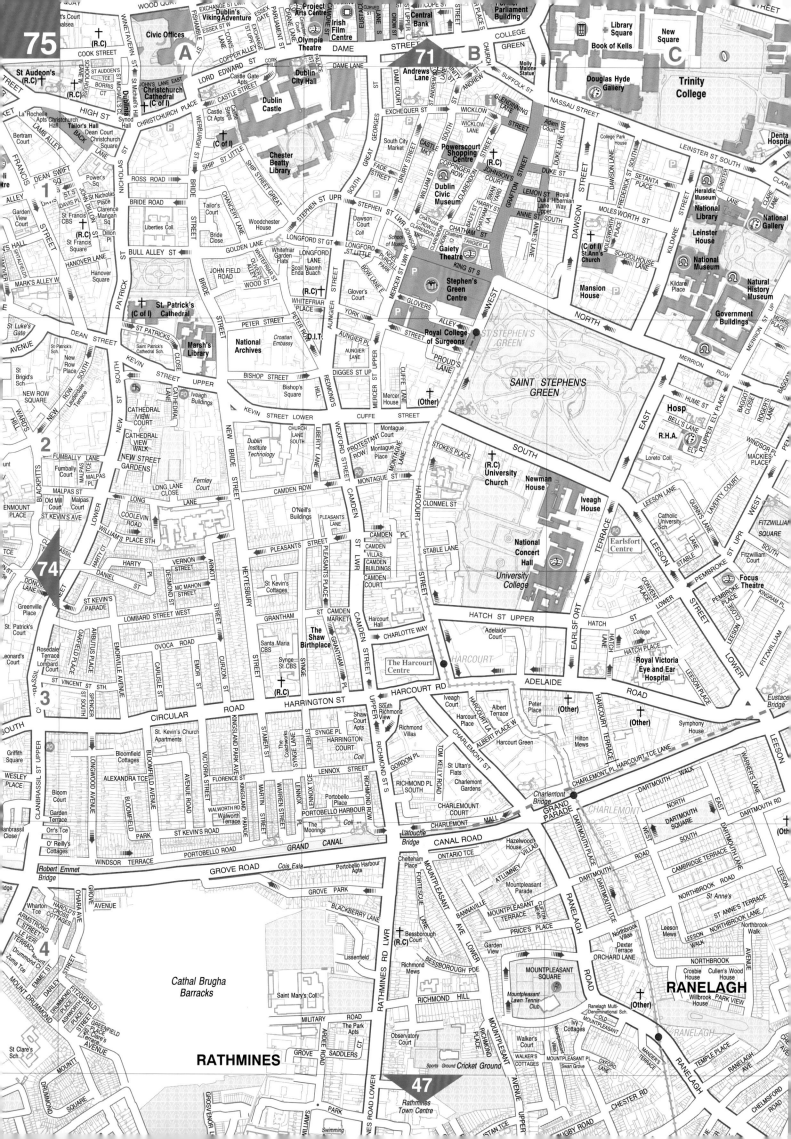

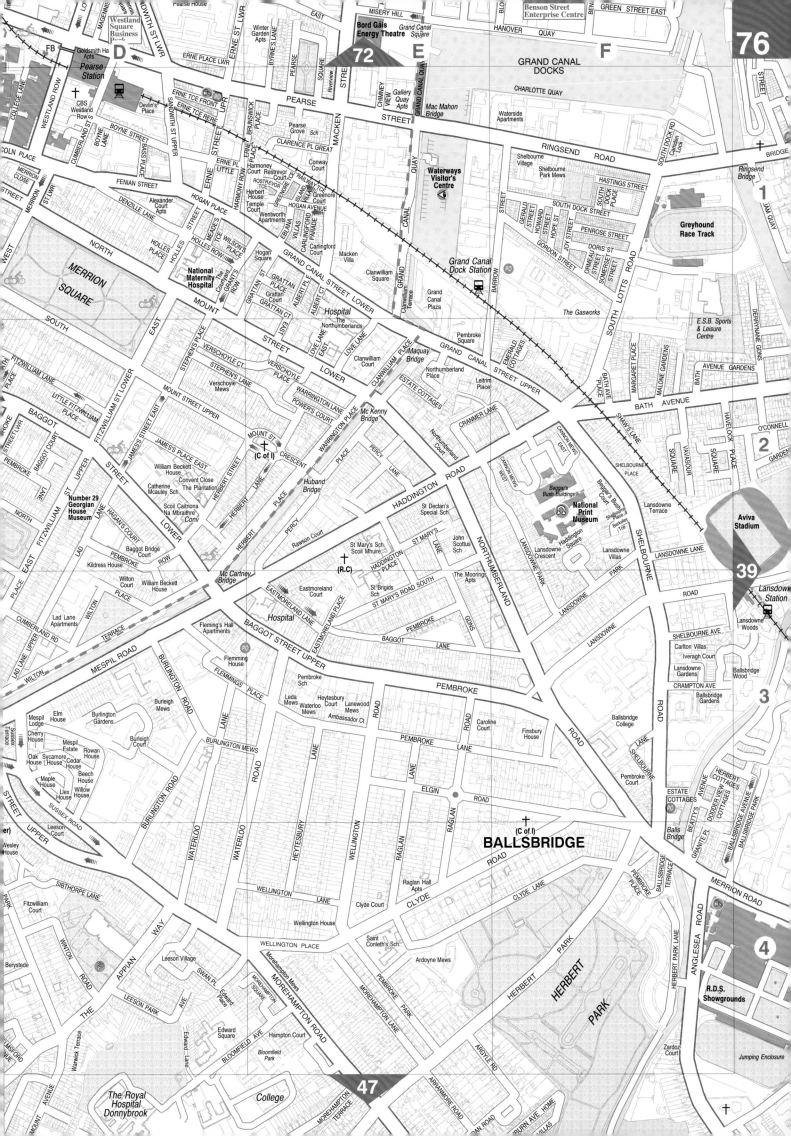

ASHBOURNE

LEGEND

M1	MOTORWAY
N9	NATIONAL PRIMARY ROAD
N81	NATIONAL SECONDARY ROAD
R683	REGIONAL ROAD
	MAIN ROADS/ STREETS
	OTHER ROADS STREETS
	NARROW STREET/ PRIVATE ROADS
	ROAD UNDER CONSTRUCTION
	PEDESTRIAN STREETS
	GREEN AREA
	WOODED AREA
	COMMERCIAL/ INDUSTRIAL
	HOSPITAL/ SCHOOL
	WATER
	HOSPITAL
	FIRE STATION
★	GARDA
P	PARKING
PO	POST OFFICE
†	CHURCH
■	MONUMENT/ STATUE
	LIGHTHOUSE
	ONE WAY STREETS
	MAINLINE RAIL STATION
	ART GALLERY
	SAMPLE LANDMARK BUILDING
	CINEMA
	GAELIC GROUND
	LIBRARY
	MUSEUM
	RUGBY GROUND
	TOURIST OFFICE
	SHOPPING COMPLEX
	SCHOOL/ COLLEGE
	SOCCER GROUND
	THEATRE
	VISITOR CENTRE
	GOLF COURSE
	CAMPING SITE
	CARAVAN SITE
	RAIL LINE

L C
(Level Crossing)

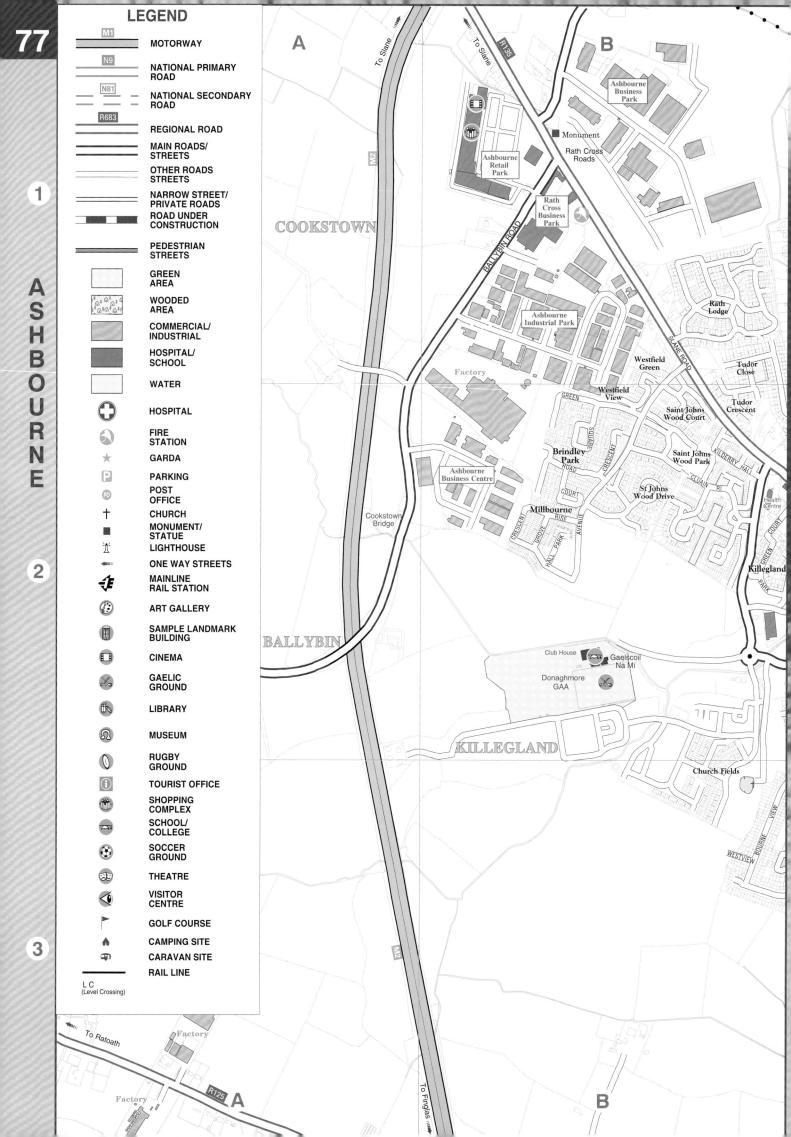

COOKSTOWN

BALLYBIN

KILLEGLAND

Ashbourne Business Park

Monument

Rath Cross Roads

Rath Cross Business Park

Rath Lodge

Ashbourne Retail Park

Ashbourne Industrial Park

Factory

Westfield Green

Westfield View

Saint Johns Wood Court

Tudor Close

Tudor Crescent

Brindley Park

Saint Johns Wood Park

Ashbourne Business Centre

Millbourne

St Johns Wood Drive

Health Centre

Killegland

Cookstown Bridge

Club House

Gaelscoil Na Mí

Donaghmore GAA

Church Fields

To Slane

To Slane

R135

To Ratoath

Factory

R125

To Finglas

Factory

ASHBOURNE

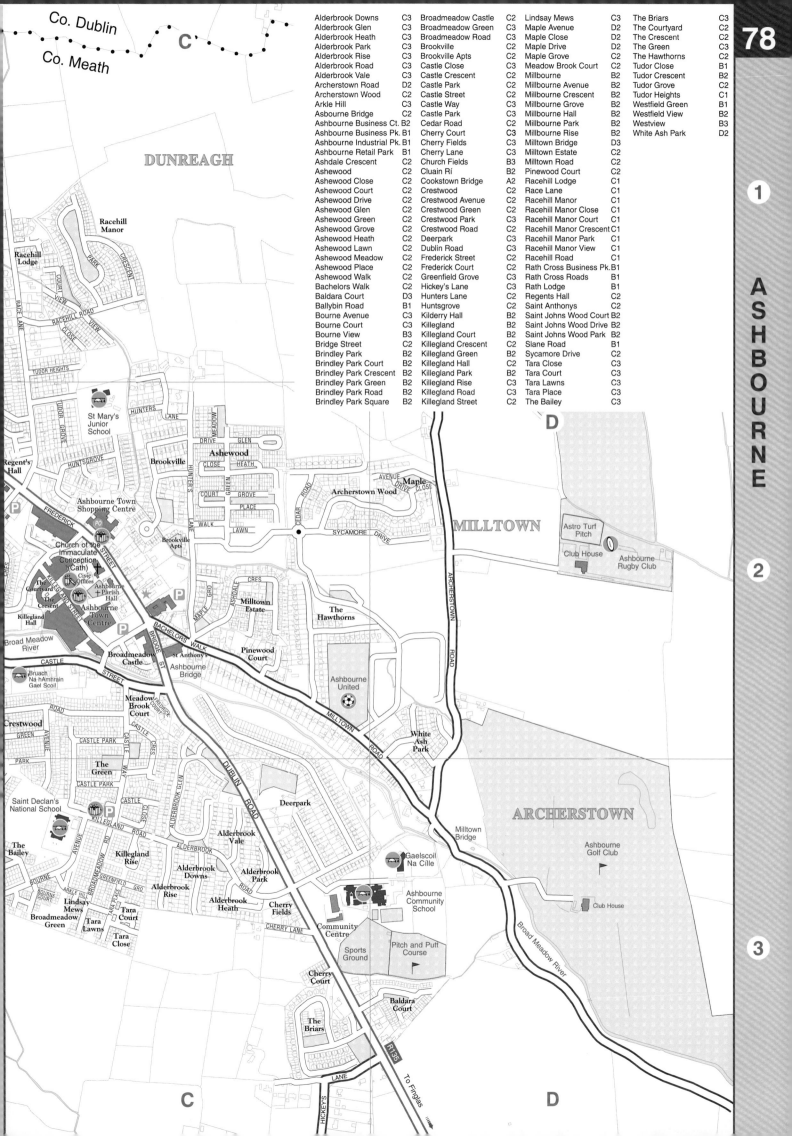

Alderbrook Downs	C3	Broadmeadow Castle	C2	Lindsay Mews	C3	The Briars	C3
Alderbrook Glen	C3	Broadmeadow Green	C3	Maple Avenue	D2	The Courtyard	C2
Alderbrook Heath	C3	Broadmeadow Road	C3	Maple Close	D2	The Crescent	C2
Alderbrook Park	C3	Brookville	C2	Maple Drive	D2	The Green	C3
Alderbrook Rise	C3	Brookville Apts	C2	Maple Grove	C2	The Hawthorns	C2
Alderbrook Road	C3	Castle Close	C3	Meadow Brook Court	C2	Tudor Close	B1
Alderbrook Vale	C3	Castle Crescent	C2	Millbourne	B2	Tudor Crescent	B2
Archerstown Road	D2	Castle Park	C2	Millbourne Avenue	B2	Tudor Grove	C2
Archerstown Wood	C2	Castle Street	C2	Millbourne Crescent	B2	Tudor Heights	C1
Arkle Hill	C3	Castle Way	C3	Millbourne Grove	B2	Westfield Green	B1
Asbourne Bridge	C2	Cedar Park	C3	Millbourne Hall	B2	Westfield View	B2
Ashbourne Business Ct.	B2	Cedar Road	C2	Millbourne Park	B2	Westview	B3
Ashbourne Business Pk.	B1	Cherry Court	C3	Millbourne Rise	B2	White Ash Park	D2
Ashbourne Industrial Pk.	B1	Cherry Fields	C3	Milltown Bridge	D3		
Ashbourne Retail Park	B1	Cherry Lane	C3	Milltown Estate	C2		
Ashdale Crescent	C2	Church Fields	B3	Milltown Road	C2		
Ashewood	C2	Cluain Rí	C2	Pinewood Court	C2		
Ashewood Close	C2	Cookstown Bridge	A2	Racehill Lodge	C1		
Ashewood Court	C2	Crestwood	C2	Race Lane	C1		
Ashewood Drive	C2	Crestwood Avenue	C2	Racehill Manor	C1		
Ashewood Glen	C2	Crestwood Green	C2	Racehill Manor Close	C1		
Ashewood Green	C2	Crestwood Park	C3	Racehill Manor Court	C1		
Ashewood Grove	C2	Crestwood Road	C2	Racehill Manor Crescent	C1		
Ashewood Heath	C2	Deerpark	C3	Racehill Manor Park	C1		
Ashewood Lawn	C2	Dublin Road	C3	Racehill Manor View	C1		
Ashewood Meadow	C2	Frederick Street	C2	Racehill Road	C1		
Ashewood Place	C2	Frederick Court	C2	Rath Cross Business Pk.	B1		
Ashewood Walk	C2	Greenfield Grove	C3	Rath Cross Roads	B1		
Bachelors Walk	C2	Hickey's Lane	C3	Rath Lodge	B1		
Baldara Court	D3	Hunters Lane	C2	Regents Hall	C2		
Ballybin Road	B1	Huntsgrove	C2	Saint Anthonys	C2		
Bourne Avenue	C3	Kilderry Hall	B2	Saint Johns Wood Court	B2		
Bourne Court	C3	Killegland	B2	Saint Johns Wood Drive	B2		
Bourne View	B3	Killegland Court	B2	Saint Johns Wood Park	B2		
Bridge Street	C2	Killegland Crescent	C2	Slane Road	B1		
Brindley Park	C3	Killegland Green	B2	Tara Close	C3		
Brindley Park Court	B2	Killegland Hall	C2	Tara Court	C3		
Brindley Park Crescent	B2	Killegland Park	B2	Tara Lawns	C3		
Brindley Park Green	B2	Killegland Rise	C3	Tara Place	C3		
Brindley Park Road	B2	Killegland Road	C3	The Bailey	C3		
Brindley Park Square	B2	Killegland Street	C2				

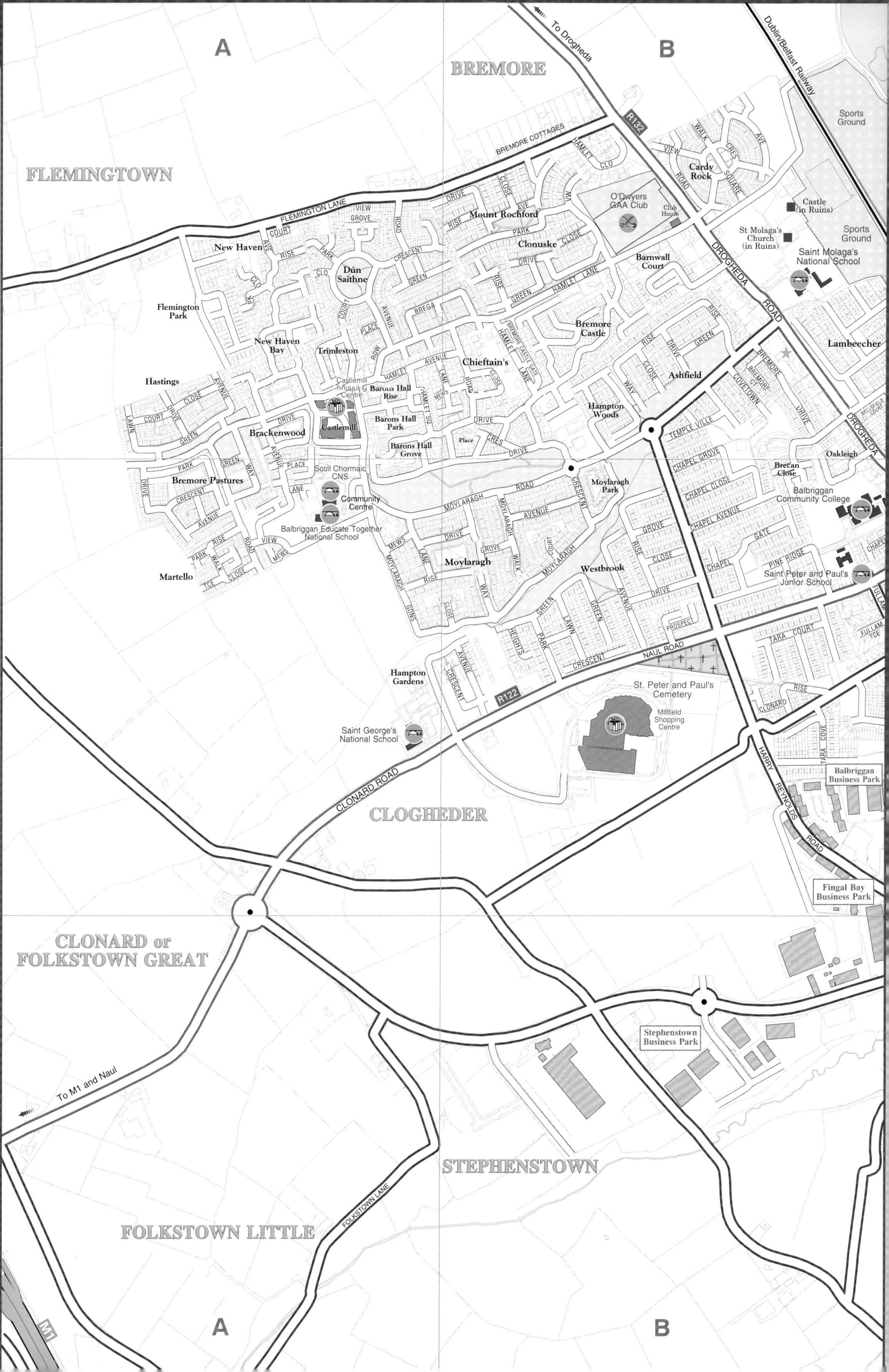

BALBRIGGAN

1

2

3

A

B

BREMORE

FLEMINGTOWN

To Drogheda

Dublin/Belfast Railway

R132

Sports Ground

BREMORE COTTAGES

Cardy Rock

Castle (in Ruins)

O'Dwyers GAA Club

Club House

St Molaga's Church (in Ruins)

Saint Molaga's National School

Sports Ground

Mount Rochford

Clonuske

New Haven

Barnwall Court

Dún Saithne

Lambeecher

Flemington Park

Bremore Castle

New Haven Bay

Trimleston

Chieftain's

Ashfield

Bremore Covetown

Hastings

Castlemill Shopping Centre

Barons Hall Rise

Hampton Woods

Tempe Vicke

Brecan Close

Oakleigh

Brackenwood

Castlemill

Barons Hall Park

Place

Moylaragh Park

Chapel Grove

Balbriggan Community College

Barons Hall Grove

Chapel Close

Bremore Pastures

Scoil Chormaic CNS

Chapel Avenue

Gate

Pine Ridge

Chapel

Saint Peter and Paul's Junior School

Community Centre

Moylaragh

Westbrook

Balbriggan Educate Together National School

Martello

Tara Court

Fullam Tce

Naul Road

Clonard

Prospect

Hampton Gardens

R122

St. Peter and Paul's Cemetery

Millfield Shopping Centre

Balbriggan Business Park

Saint George's National School

Harry Reynolds Road

Tara Cove

Fingal Bay Business Park

CLONARD ROAD

CLOGHEDER

CLONARD or FOLKSTOWN GREAT

Stephenstown Business Park

To M1 and Naul

STEPHENSTOWN

M1

FOLKSTOWN LITTLE

FOLKSTOWN LANE

DROGHEDA ROAD

FLEMINGTON LANE

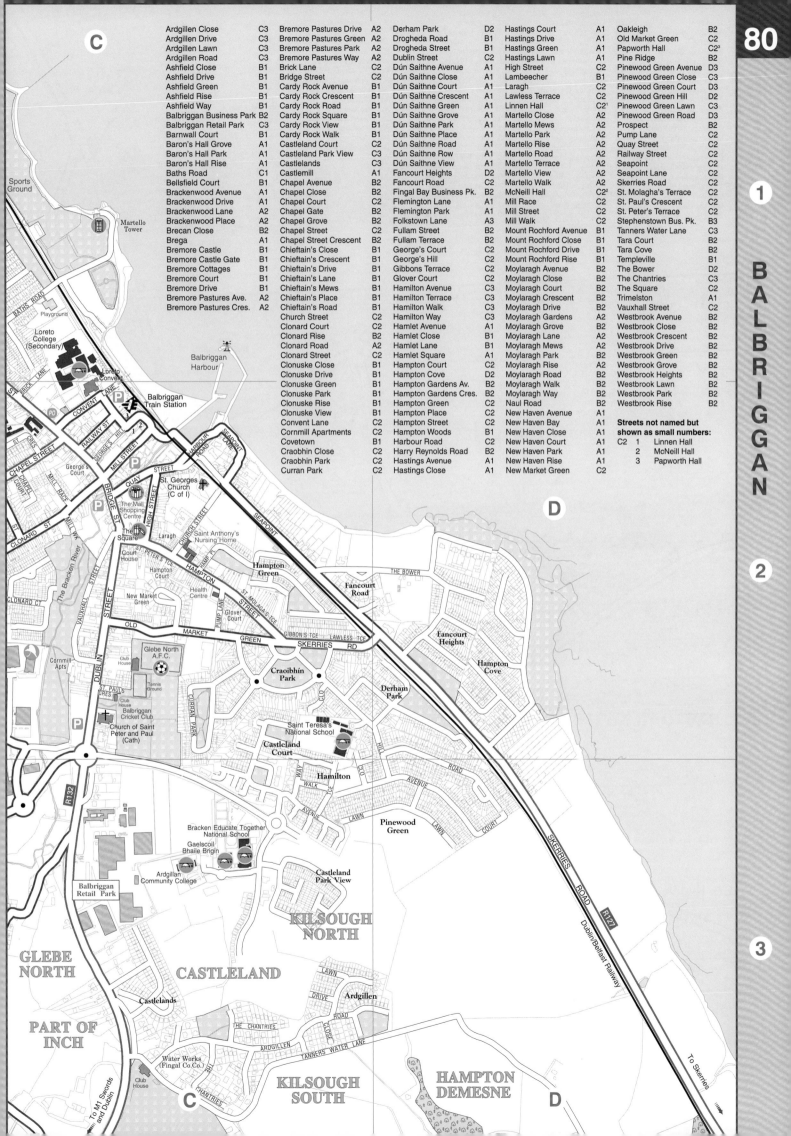

BALBRIGGAN

Street	Ref	Street	Ref	Street	Ref	Street	Ref	Street	Ref
Ardgillen Close	C3	Bremore Pastures Drive	A2	Derham Park	D2	Hastings Court	A1	Oakleigh	B2
Ardgillen Drive	C3	Bremore Pastures Green	A2	Drogheda Road	B1	Hastings Drive	A1	Old Market Green	C2
Ardgillen Lawn	C3	Bremore Pastures Park	A2	Drogheda Street	B1	Hastings Green	A1	Papworth Hall	C2³
Ardgillen Road	C3	Bremore Pastures Way	A2	Dublin Street	C2	Hastings Lawn	A1	Pine Ridge	B2
Ashfield Close	B1	Brick Lane	C2	Dún Saithne Avenue	A1	High Street	C2	Pinewood Green Avenue	D3
Ashfield Drive	B1	Bridge Street	C2	Dún Saithne Close	A1	Lambeecher	B1	Pinewood Green Close	C3
Ashfield Green	B1	Cardy Rock Avenue	B1	Dún Saithne Court	A1	Laragh	C2	Pinewood Green Court	D3
Ashfield Rise	B1	Cardy Rock Crescent	B1	Dún Saithne Crescent	A1	Lawless Terrace	A2	Pinewood Green Hill	D2
Ashfield Way	B1	Cardy Rock Road	B1	Dún Saithne Green	A1	Linnen Hall	C2¹	Pinewood Green Lawn	C3
Balbriggan Business Park	B2	Cardy Rock Square	B1	Dún Saithne Grove	A1	Martello Close	A2	Pinewood Green Road	D3
Balbriggan Retail Park	C3	Cardy Rock View	B1	Dún Saithne Park	A1	Martello Mews	A2	Prospect	B2
Barnwall Court	B1	Cardy Rock Walk	B1	Dún Saithne Place	A1	Martello Park	A2	Pump Lane	C2
Baron's Hall Grove	A1	Castleland Court	C2	Dún Saithne Road	A1	Martello Rise	A2	Quay Street	C2
Baron's Hall Park	A1	Castleland Park View	C3	Dún Saithne Row	A1	Martello Road	A2	Railway Street	C2
Baron's Hall Rise	A1	Castlelands	C3	Dún Saithne View	A1	Martello Terrace	A2	Seapoint	C2
Baths Road	C1	Castlemill	A1	Fancourt Heights	D2	Martello View	A2	Seapoint Lane	C2
Bellsfield Court	B1	Chapel Avenue	B2	Fancourt Road	C2	Martello Walk	A2	Skerries Road	C2
Brackenwood Avenue	A1	Chapel Close	B2	Fingal Bay Business Pk.	B2	McNeill Hall	C2²	St. Molagha's Terrace	C2
Brackenwood Drive	A1	Chapel Court	C2	Flemington Lane	A1	Mill Race	C2	St. Paul's Crescent	C2
Brackenwood Lane	A2	Chapel Gate	B2	Flemington Park	A1	Mill Street	C2	St. Peter's Terrace	C2
Brackenwood Place	A2	Chapel Grove	B2	Folkstown Lane	A3	Mill Walk	C2	Stephenstown Bus. Pk.	B3
Brecan Close	B2	Chapel Street	C2	Fullam Street	B2	Mount Rochford Avenue	B1	Tanners Water Lane	C3
Brega	A1	Chapel Street Crescent	C2	Fullam Terrace	B2	Mount Rochford Close	B1	Tara Court	B2
Bremore Castle	B1	Chieftain's Close	B1	George's Court	C2	Mount Rochford Drive	B1	Tara Cove	B2
Bremore Castle Gate	B1	Chieftain's Crescent	B1	George's Hill	C2	Mount Rochford Rise	B1	Templeville	B1
Bremore Cottages	B1	Chieftain's Drive	B1	Gibbons Terrace	C2	Moylaragh Avenue	B2	The Bower	D2
Bremore Court	B1	Chieftain's Lane	B1	Glover Court	C2	Moylaragh Close	B2	The Chantries	C3
Bremore Drive	B1	Chieftain's Mews	B1	Hamilton Avenue	C3	Moylaragh Court	B2	The Square	C2
Bremore Pastures Ave.	A2	Chieftain's Place	B1	Hamilton Terrace	C3	Moylaragh Crescent	B2	Trimelston	A1
Bremore Pastures Cres.	A2	Chieftain's Road	B1	Hamilton Walk	C3	Moylaragh Drive	B2	Vauxhall Street	C2
		Church Street	C2	Hamilton Way	C3	Moylaragh Gardens	A2	Westbrook Avenue	B2
		Clonard Court	C2	Hamlet Avenue	A1	Moylaragh Grove	B2	Westbrook Close	B2
		Clonard Rise	B2	Hamlet Close	B1	Moylaragh Lane	A2	Westbrook Crescent	B2
		Clonard Road	A2	Hamlet Lane	B1	Moylaragh Mews	A2	Westbrook Drive	B2
		Clonard Street	C2	Hamlet Square	A1	Moylaragh Park	A2	Westbrook Green	B2
		Clonuske Close	B1	Hampton Court	C2	Moylaragh Rise	A2	Westbrook Grove	B2
		Clonuske Drive	B1	Hampton Cove	D2	Moylaragh Road	B2	Westbrook Heights	B2
		Clonuske Green	B1	Hampton Gardens Av.	B2	Moylaragh Walk	B2	Westbrook Lawn	B2
		Clonuske Park	B1	Hampton Gardens Cres.	B2	Moylaragh Way	B2	Westbrook Park	B2
		Clonuske Rise	B1	Hampton Green	C2	Naul Road	B2	Westbrook Rise	B2
		Clonuske View	B1	Hampton Place	C2	New Haven Avenue	A1		
		Convent Lane	C2	Hampton Street	C2	New Haven Bay	A1		
		Cornmill Apartments	C2	Hampton Woods	B1	New Haven Close	A1		
		Covetown	B1	Harbour Road	C2	New Haven Court	A1		
		Craobhin Close	C2	Harry Reynolds Road	B2	New Haven Park	A1		
		Craobhin Park	C2	Hastings Avenue	A1	New Haven Rise	A1		
		Curran Park	C2	Hastings Close	A1	New Market Green	C2		

Streets not named but shown as small numbers:

C2 1 Linnen Hall
     2 McNeill Hall
     3 Papworth Hall

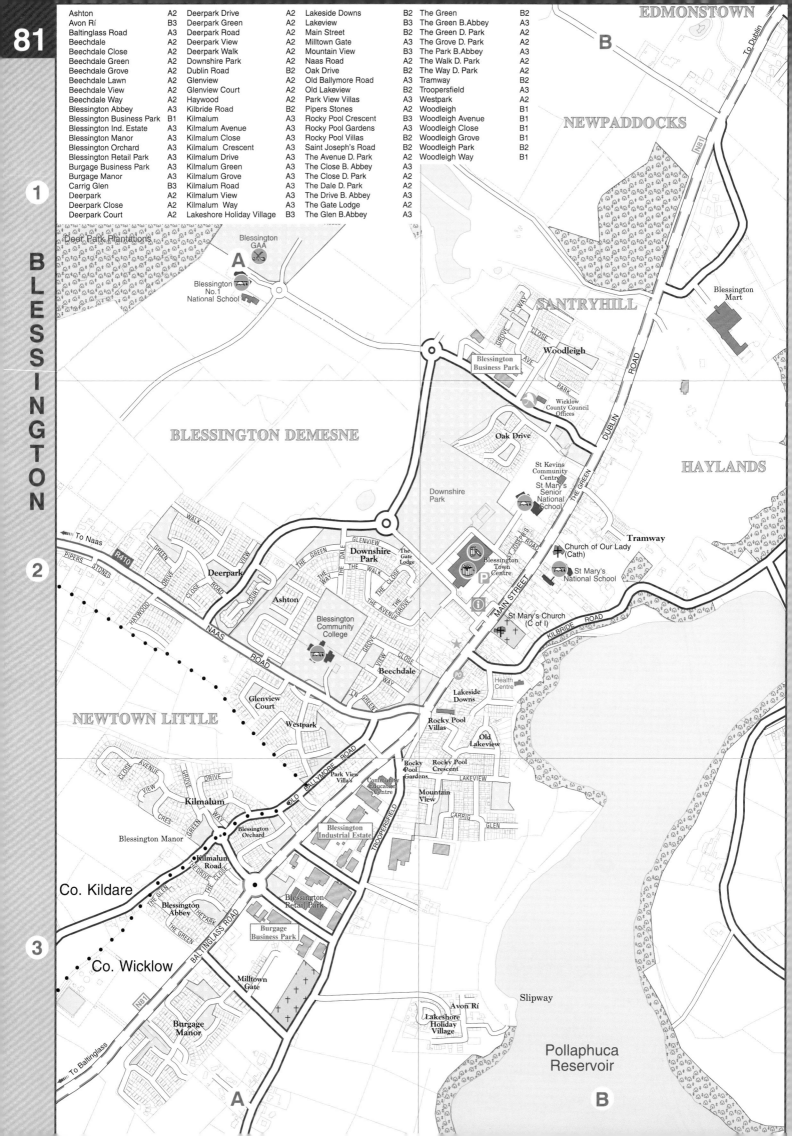

Ashton	A2	Deerpark Drive	A2	Lakeside Downs	B2	The Green	B2
Avon Rí	B3	Deerpark Green	A2	Lakeview	B3	The Green B.Abbey	A3
Baltinglass Road	A3	Deerpark Road	A2	Main Street	B2	The Green D. Park	A2
Beechdale	A2	Deerpark View	A2	Milltown Gate	A3	The Grove D. Park	A2
Beechdale Close	A2	Deerpark Walk	A2	Mountain View	B3	The Park B.Abbey	A3
Beechdale Green	A2	Downshire Park	A2	Naas Road	A2	The Walk D. Park	A2
Beechdale Grove	A2	Dublin Road	B2	Oak Drive	B2	The Way D. Park	A2
Beechdale Lawn	A2	Glenview	A2	Old Ballymore Road	A3	Tramway	B2
Beechdale View	A2	Glenview Court	A2	Old Lakeview	B2	Troopersfield	A3
Beechdale Way	A2	Haywood	A2	Park View Villas	A3	Westpark	A2
Blessington Abbey	A3	Kilbride Road	B2	Pipers Stones	A2	Woodleigh	B1
Blessington Business Park	B1	Kilmalum	A3	Rocky Pool Crescent	B3	Woodleigh Avenue	B1
Blessington Ind. Estate	A3	Kilmalum Avenue	A3	Rocky Pool Gardens	A3	Woodleigh Close	B1
Blessington Manor	A3	Kilmalum Close	A3	Rocky Pool Villas	A3	Woodleigh Grove	B1
Blessington Orchard	A3	Kilmalum Crescent	A3	Saint Joseph's Road	B2	Woodleigh Park	B2
Blessington Retail Park	A3	Kilmalum Drive	A3	The Avenue D. Park	A2	Woodleigh Way	B1
Burgage Business Park	A3	Kilmalum Green	A3	The Close B. Abbey	A3		
Burgage Manor	A3	Kilmalum Grove	A3	The Close D. Park	A2		
Carrig Glen	B3	Kilmalum Road	A3	The Dale D. Park	A2		
Deerpark	A2	Kilmalum View	A3	The Drive B. Abbey	A3		
Deerpark Close	A2	Kilmalum Way	A3	The Gate Lodge	A2		
Deerpark Court	A2	Lakeshore Holiday Village	B3	The Glen B.Abbey	A3		

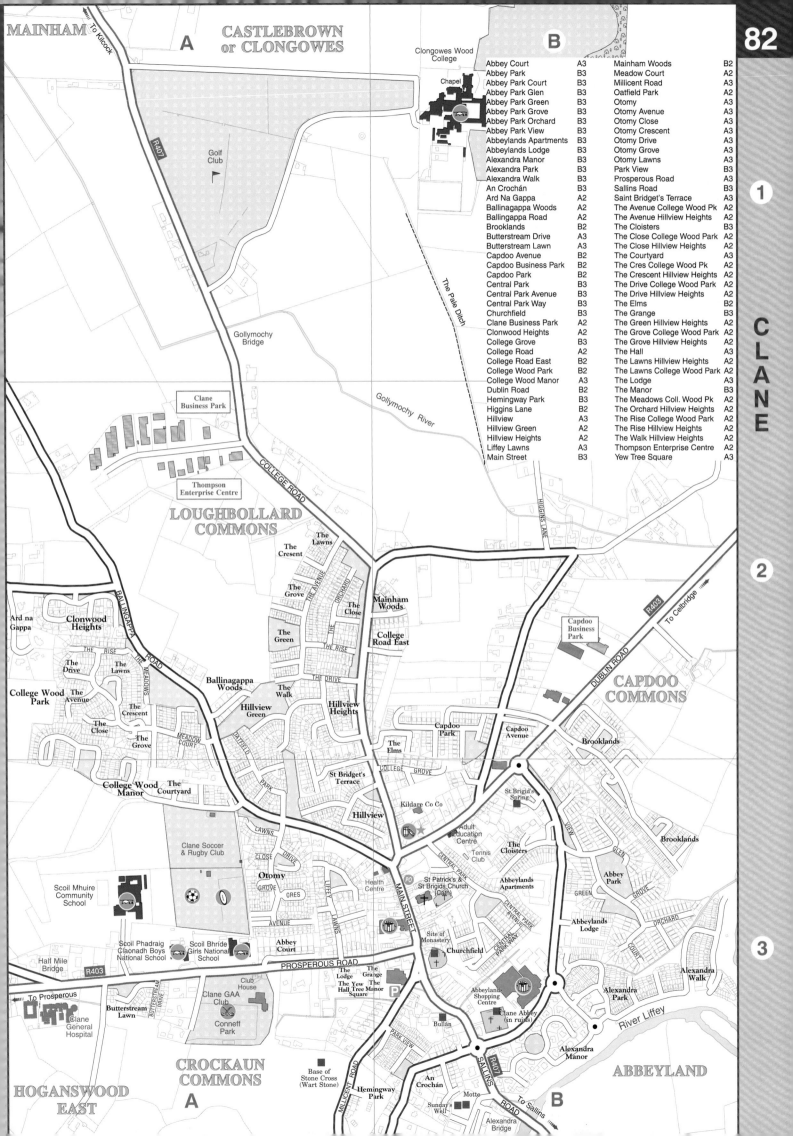

MAINHAM
To Kilcock

CASTLEBROWN
or CLONGOWES

Clongowes Wood College

Chapel

CLANE

Abbey Court	A3	Mainham Woods	B2
Abbey Park	B3	Meadow Court	A2
Abbey Park Court	B3	Millicent Road	A3
Abbey Park Glen	B3	Oatfield Park	A2
Abbey Park Green	B3	Otomy	A3
Abbey Park Grove	B3	Otomy Avenue	A3
Abbey Park Orchard	B3	Otomy Close	A3
Abbey Park View	B3	Otomy Crescent	A3
Abbeylands Apartments	B3	Otomy Drive	A3
Abbeylands Lodge	B3	Otomy Grove	A3
Alexandra Manor	B3	Otomy Lawns	A3
Alexandra Park	B3	Park View	B3
Alexandra Walk	B3	Prosperous Road	A3
An Crochán	B3	Sallins Road	B3
Ard Na Gappa	A2	Saint Bridget's Terrace	A3
Ballinagappa Woods	A2	The Avenue College Wood Pk	A2
Ballingappa Road	A2	The Avenue Hillview Heights	A2
Brooklands	B2	The Cloisters	B3
Butterstream Drive	A3	The Close College Wood Park	A2
Butterstream Lawn	A3	The Close Hillview Heights	A2
Capdoo Avenue	A3	The Courtyard	A3
Capdoo Business Park	B2	The Cres College Wood Pk	A2
Capdoo Park	B2	The Crescent Hillview Heights	A2
Central Park	B3	The Drive College Wood Park	A2
Central Park Avenue	B3	The Drive Hillview Heights	A2
Central Park Way	B3	The Elms	B2
Churchfield	B3	The Grange	B3
Clane Business Park	A2	The Green Hillview Heights	A2
Clonwood Heights	A2	The Grove College Wood Park	A2
College Grove	B3	The Grove Hillview Heights	A2
College Road	A2	The Hall	A3
College Road East	B2	The Lawns Hillview Heights	A2
College Wood Park	B2	The Lawns College Wood Park	A2
College Wood Manor	A3	The Lodge	A3
Dublin Road	B2	The Manor	B3
Hemingway Park	B3	The Meadows Coll. Wood Pk	A2
Higgins Lane	B2	The Orchard Hillview Heights	A2
Hillview	A3	The Rise College Wood Park	A2
Hillview Green	A2	The Rise Hillview Heights	A2
Hillview Heights	A2	The Walk Hillview Heights	A2
Liffey Lawns	A3	Thompson Enterprise Centre	A2
Main Street	B3	Yew Tree Square	A3

Golf Club

R407

Gollymochy Bridge

The Pale Ditch

Gollymochy River

Clane Business Park

Thompson Enterprise Centre

LOUGHBOLLARD COMMONS

COLLEGE ROAD

Higgins Lane

The Lawns

The Cresent

The Grove

THE AVENUE

THE ORCHARD

The Close

Mainham Woods

College Road East

BALLINGAPPA ROAD

Ard na Gappa

Clonwood Heights

THE RISE

The Drive

The Lawns

College Wood Park

The Avenue

THE MEADOWS

The Crescent

The Close

The Grove

MEADOW COURT

Ballinagappa Woods

The Green

THE RISE

THE DRIVE

The Walk

Hillview Green

Hillview Heights

OATFIELD PARK

College Wood Manor

The Courtyard

R403

To Celbridge

DUBLIN ROAD

Capdoo Business Park

CAPDOO COMMONS

Brooklands

Capdoo Park

Capdoo Avenue

The Elms

COLLEGE GROVE

St Bridget's Terrace

Hillview

Kildare Co Co

Adult Education Centre

Tennis Club

St Brigid's Spring

The Cloisters

Abbeylands Apartments

GLEN

Brooklands

VIEW

Abbey Park

GREEN

GROVE

ORCHARD

Clane Soccer & Rugby Club

LAWNS

CLOSE

DRIVE

GROVE

CRES

LIFFEY LAWNS

AVENUE

Otomy

Health Centre

PO

MAIN STREET

CENTRAL PARK

Central Park Avenue

St Patrick's & St Brigids Church (Cath)

Site of Monastery

Churchfield

CENTRAL PARK WAY

Abbeylands Lodge

Abbeylands Shopping Centre

COURT

Abbey Park

ORCHARD

Scoil Mhuire Community School

Scoil Phadraig Claonadh Boys National School

Scoil Bhríde Girls National School

Abbey Court

PROSPEROUS ROAD

The Lodge

The Grange

The Yew The Hall Tree Manor Square

P

Clane GAA Club

Club House

Conneff Park

Half Mile Bridge

R403

To Prosperous

Clane General Hospital

Butterstream Lawn

BUTTERSTREAM DRIVE

HOGANSWOOD EAST

CROCKAUN COMMONS

Base of Stone Cross (Wart Stone)

MILLICENT ROAD

Hemingway Park

An Crochán

PARK VIEW

Sunday's Well

Motte

Alexandra Bridge

SALLINS ROAD

To Sallins

Bullán

Clane Abbey (in ruins)

Alexandra Manor

Alexandra Park

Alexandra Walk

River Liffey

ABBEYLAND

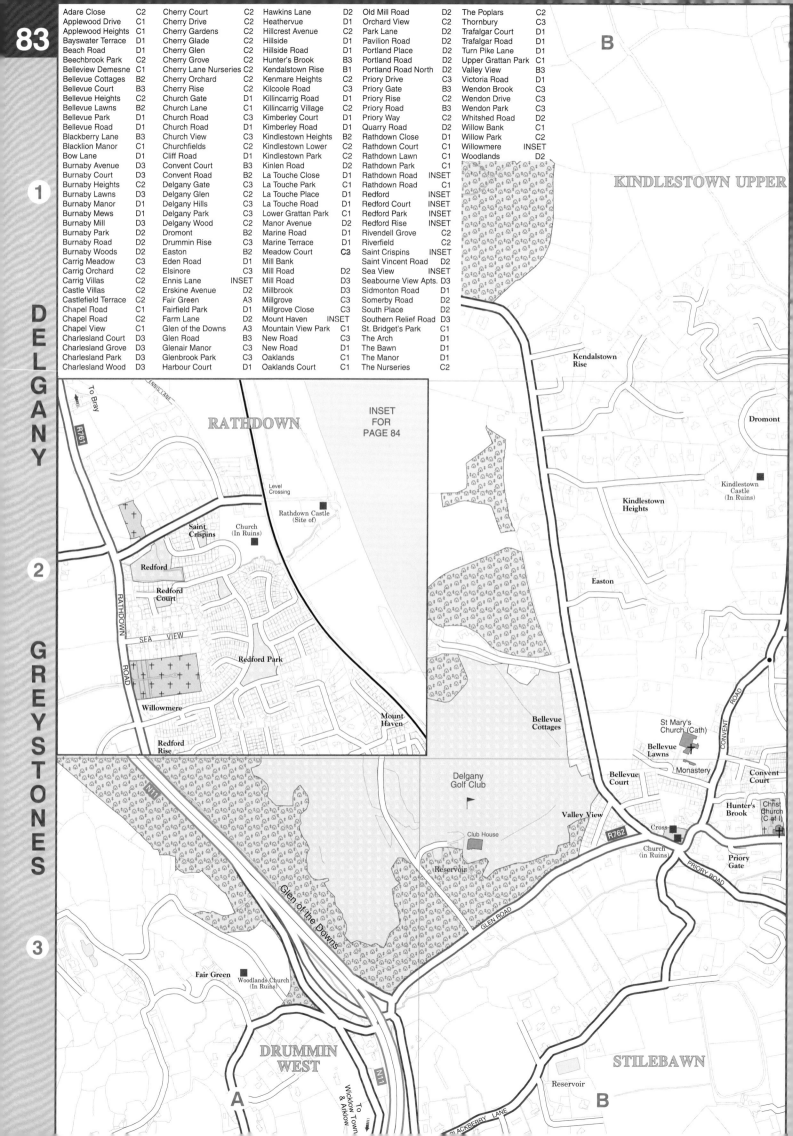

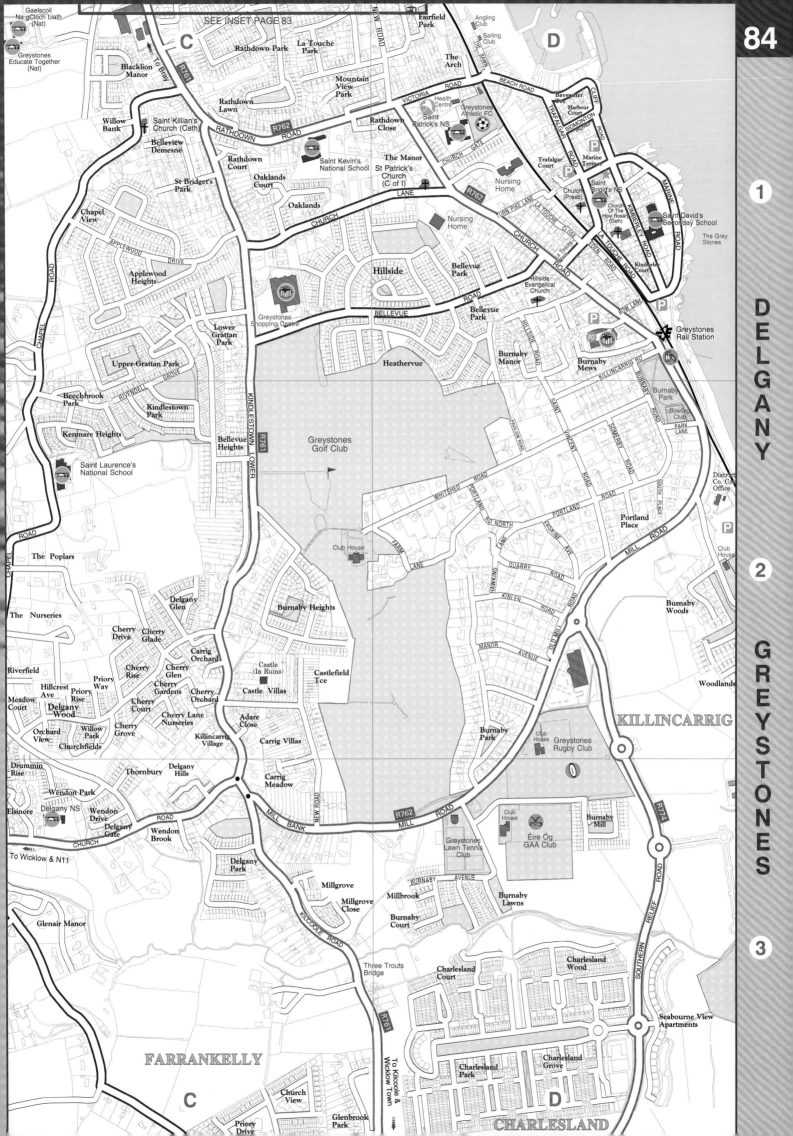

DONABATE

B

Rogerstown Estuary

Raheen Point

BEAVERSTOWN

RAHILLION

Windmill (in Ruins)

Club House

Dublin/Belfast Railway

Beaverstown Golf Club

Beaverbrook

Beaverstown Orchard

Orchard Close

Cois Inbhir

Carrs Mill

St. Patrick's Girls National School

Eden Grove

Benson Crés

Lambourne Park

St. Patrick's Boys National School

To Portraine

ROAD

Lambs Court

Somerton

The Priory

Barnewall

AVE

Educate Together National School

CRES

DRIVE

BALLISK COMMON

R126

PORTRANE

Beverton

WOOD

ORCHARD

GDNS

MEADOWS

GROVE

CLOSE

Donabate Community College

Donabate Community Centre

UPPER

WILLOWBROOK

BALLALEASE NORTH

Hazelwood

The Links

PORTRANE

ROAD

PARK

Beverton Court

Turvey

GREEN

WOODS

DRIVE

CRES

CLO

Keelings Court

STREET

Balalease Court

Baltra Hall

TURVEY

AVENUE

GROVE

TURVEY WALK

Ballisk Court

Fairways

DONABATE VILLAGE

BALLISK

Donabate Shopping Centre

St. Patrick's Church (Cath)

THE SPIRES

Sycamore Hill

St. Patricks (C of I)

The Square

Donabate Rail Station

FB

MAIN

St Patrick's Terrace

St Patrick's Park

BALLYMASTONE

NEWBRIDGE AVE

PO

ST MARY'S TERRACE

Prospect Hill

CHAPEL VIEW

Station Court

THE STRAND

HEARSE ROAD

R126

DONABATE

BALLALEASE SOUTH

NEW ROAD

To M1

CORBALLIS

Dublin/Belfast Railway

A

B

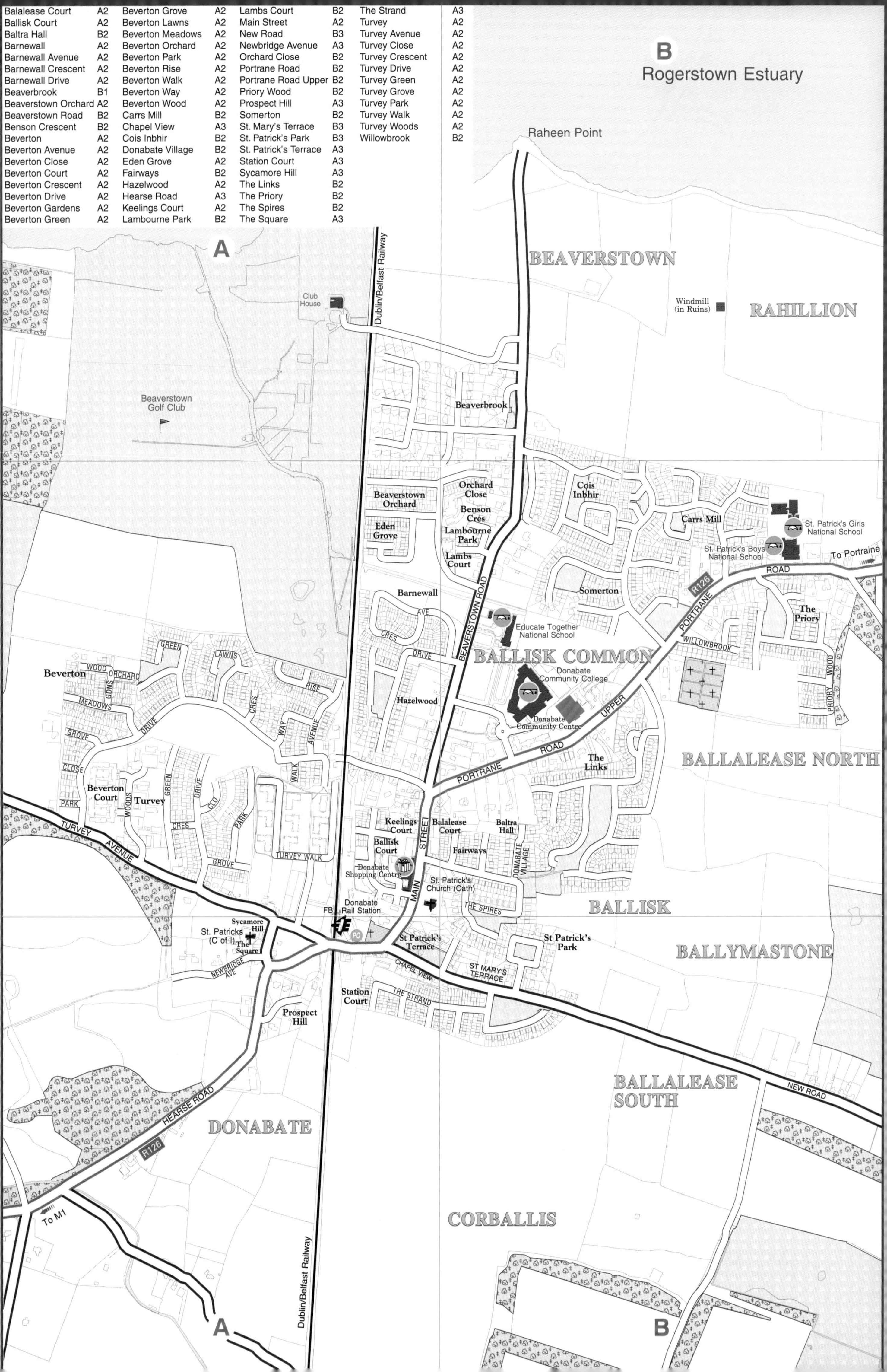

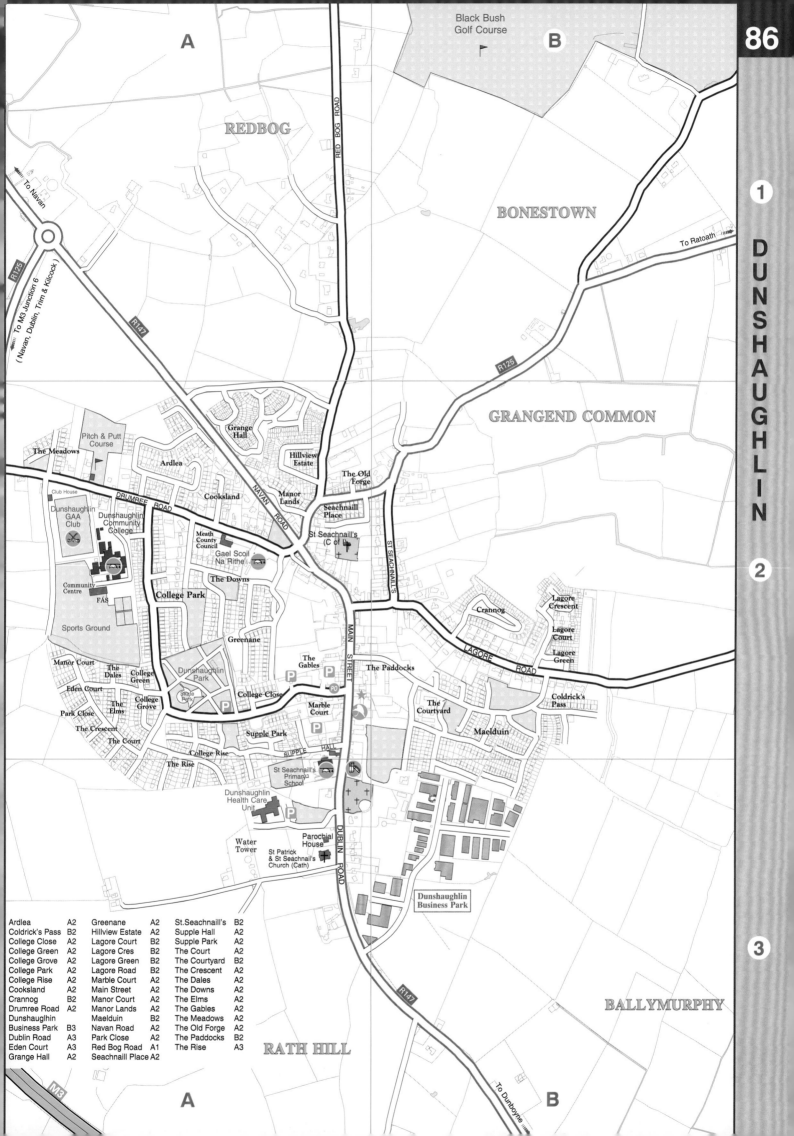

Black Bush
Golf Course

REDBOG

BONESTOWN

To Navan

To M3 Junction 6
(Navan, Dublin, Trim & Kilcock)

R125

R147

RED BOG ROAD

To Ratoath

GRANGEND COMMON

R125

The Meadows

Pitch & Putt
Course

Grange
Hall

Ardlea

Hillview
Estate

The Old
Forge

Club House

Cooksland

Manor
Lands

Seachnaill
Place

Dunshaughlin
GAA Club

DRUMREE ROAD

Dunshaughlin
Community
College

Meath
County
Council

St Seachnaill's
(C of I)

NAVAN ROAD

ST SEACHNAILL'S

Community
Centre

FÁS

Gael Scoil
Na Rithe

The Downs

College Park

Lagore
Crescent

Crannog

Lagore
Court

Sports Ground

Greenane

Lagore
Green

Manor Court

The
Dales

College
Green

Dunshaughlin
Park

The Gables

The Paddocks

MAIN STREET

LAGORE ROAD

Eden Court

The Elms

College
Grove

Skate
Park

College Close

Marble
Court

The Courtyard

Coldrick's
Pass

Park Close

The Crescent

Supple Park

PO

Maelduin

The Court

College Rise

SUPPLE HALL

The Rise

St Seachnaill's
Primary
School

Dunshaughlin
Health Care
Unit

DUBLIN ROAD

Water
Tower

Parochial
House

Dunshaughlin
Business Park

St Patrick
& St Seachnaill's
Church (Cath)

R147

RATH HILL

BALLYMURPHY

To Dunboyne

M3

A

B

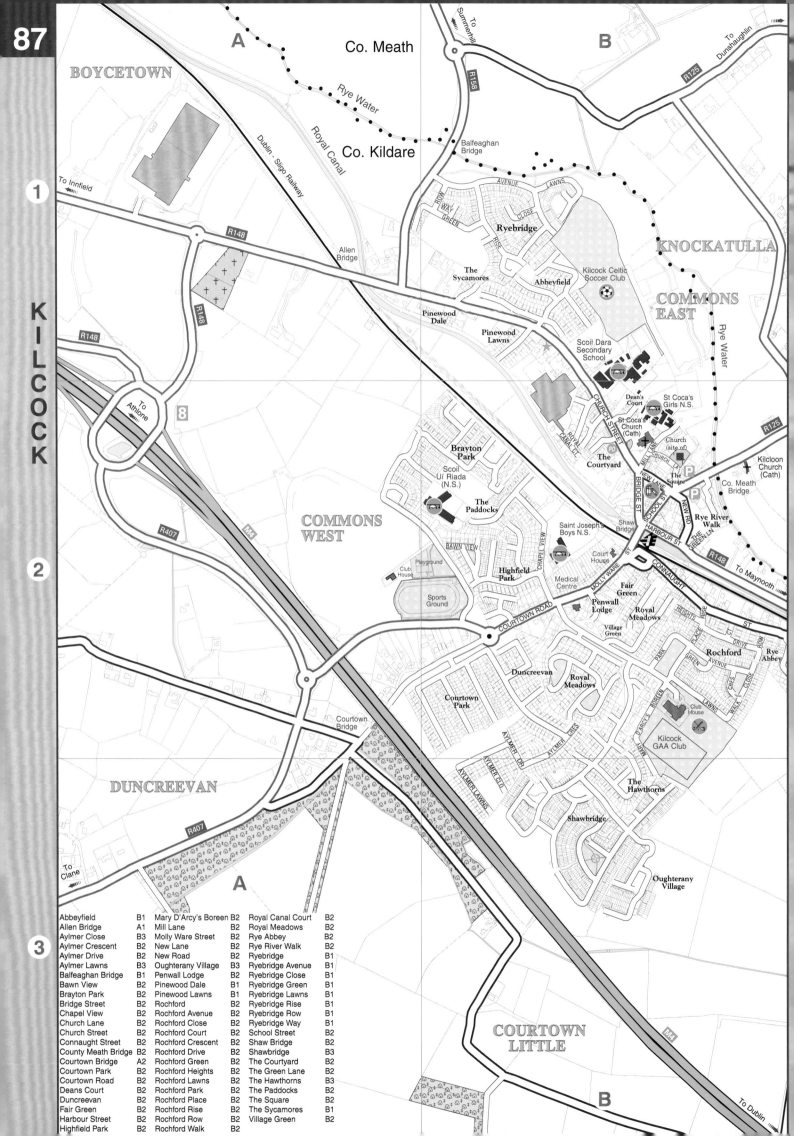

KILCOCK

BOYCETOWN

Co. Meath

Rye Water

Royal Canal

Co. Kildare

Dublin - Sligo Railway

To Innfield

R148

Allen Bridge

R148

R148

8

To Athlone

COMMONS WEST

R407

M4

DUNCREEVAN

R407

To Clane

Balfeaghan Bridge

AVENUE

LAWNS

CLOSE

ROW

WAY

GREEN

RISE

Ryebridge

The Sycamores

Abbeyfield

Pinewood Dale

Pinewood Lawns

Kilcock Celtic Soccer Club

Scoil Dara Secondary School

Dean's Court

St Coca's Girls N.S.

St Coca's Church (Cath)

Church (site of)

Kilcloon Church (Cath)

Co. Meath Bridge

KNOCKATULLA

COMMONS EAST

Rye Water

R125

R125

Brayton Park

Scoil Uí Riada (N.S.)

The Paddocks

BAWN VIEW

Playground

Club House

Sports Ground

CHURCH STREET

ROYAL CANAL CT.

The Courtyard

PO

The Square

NEW LANE

BRIDGE ST

SCHOOL ST

NEW RD

Rye River Walk

THE GREEN LN.

R148

To Maynooth

P

P

CHAPEL VIEW

Highfield Park

Saint Joseph's Boys N.S.

Court House

Medical Centre

Penwall Lodge

Fair Green

Village Green

Royal Meadows

MOLLY WARE ST

HARBOUR ST

Shaw Bridge

CONNAUGHT

HEIGHTS

RISE

ST

PLACE

GREEN

DRIVE

ROW

Rochford

Rye Abbey

COURTOWN ROAD

Duncreevan

Royal Meadows

Courtown Park

Club House

Kilcock GAA Club

AYLMER CRES

AYLMER DR.

AYLMER CLO.

AYLMER LAWNS

D'ARCY'S BOREEN

PARK

WALK

CRES

CLOSE

LAWNS

AVENUE

The Hawthorns

Shawbridge

Oughterany Village

Courtown Bridge

COURTOWN LITTLE

To Dublin

M4

A

B

1

2

3

A

B

Abbeyfield	B1	Mary D'Arcy's Boreen	B2	Royal Canal Court	B2
Allen Bridge	A1	Mill Lane	B2	Royal Meadows	B2
Aylmer Close	B3	Molly Ware Street	B2	Rye Abbey	B2
Aylmer Crescent	B2	New Lane	B2	Rye River Walk	B2
Aylmer Drive	B2	New Road	B2	Ryebridge	B1
Aylmer Lawns	B3	Oughterany Village	B3	Ryebridge Avenue	B1
Balfeaghan Bridge	B1	Penwall Lodge	B2	Ryebridge Close	B1
Bawn View	B2	Pinewood Dale	B1	Ryebridge Green	B1
Brayton Park	B2	Pinewood Lawns	B1	Ryebridge Lawns	B1
Bridge Street	B2	Rochford	B2	Ryebridge Rise	B1
Chapel View	B2	Rochford Avenue	B2	Ryebridge Row	B1
Church Lane	B2	Rochford Close	B2	Ryebridge Way	B1
Church Street	B2	Rochford Court	B2	School Street	B2
Connaught Street	B2	Rochford Crescent	B2	Shaw Bridge	B2
County Meath Bridge	B2	Rochford Drive	B2	Shawbridge	B3
Courtown Bridge	A2	Rochford Green	B2	The Courtyard	B2
Courtown Park	B2	Rochford Heights	B2	The Green Lane	B2
Courtown Road	B2	Rochford Lawns	B2	The Hawthorns	B3
Deans Court	B2	Rochford Place	B2	The Paddocks	B2
Duncreevan	B2	Rochford Rise	B2	The Square	B2
Fair Green	B2	Rochford Row	B2	The Sycamores	B1
Harbour Street	B2	Rochford Walk	B2	Village Green	B2
Highfield Park	B2				

Street	Grid
Abbeylands	B2
Ashgrove	A2
Baker's Close	B2
Balleally Lane	B3
Barrack Lane	B2
Belfry Place	B2
Blackraven Court	B2
Blacksmith's Road	B2
Bramble Lane	B2
Chapel Farm	A2
Chapel Farm Avenue	A2
Chapel Farm Close	A2
Chapel Farm Copse	A2
Chapel Farm Court	A3
Chapel Farm Cresent	A2
Chapel Farm Drive	A3
Chapel Farm Green	A2
Chapel Farm Grove	A2
Chapel Farm Lane	A2
Chapel Farm Lawn	A2
Chapel Farm Mews	A2
Chapel Farm Park	A2
Chapel Farm Place	A3
Chapel Farm Road	A2
Chapel Farm Row	A2
Chapel Farm Square	A3
Chapel Farm Terrace	A3
Chapel Farm Walk	A2
Chapel Farm Way	A2
Chapel Farm Wood	A2
Chapel Green	A2
Chapel Lane	A2
Chapel Road	A2
Church Road	B2
Cobbler's Walk	B2
Coleman	B2
Coleman Crescent	B2
Coleman Way	B2
Common's Lane	B1
Coopers Walk	B2
Danes Court	B2
Dublin Road	B2
Dun Emer	A2
Dun Emer Avenue	A2
Dun Emer Close	A2
Dun Emer Court	A2
Dun Emer Crescent	A2
Dun Emer Dale	A2
Dun Emer Drive	A2
Dun Emer Gardens	A2
Dun Emer Glade	A2
Dun Emer Green	A2
Dun Emer Grove	A2
Dun Emer Lawn	A2
Dun Emer Park	A2
Dun Emer Place	A2
Dun Emer Rise	A2
Dun Emer Road	A2
Dun Emer View	A2
Dun Emer Walk	A2
Dun Emer Way	A2
Forge Avenue	B3
Forge Lane	B2
Forge View	B3
Gleann Ribh	A2
Great Commons	B2
Hands Lane	A2
Hill Lane	B1
Huntsman's Road	B2
Huntsman's Way	A2
Joyce Road	B2
Kelly Park	A2
Kielys Lane	A3
Kilhedge Lane	A3
Little Commons	B2
Macullens Close	A2
Main Street	B2
Miller's Square	B2
Minister's Park	A2
Minister's Rise	A2
Minister's Road	A2
Netterville Place	B2
Norsemans Walk	B2
Orlynn Park	B2
Perrin Way	B2
Post Office Road	A2
Quickpennies Road	A1
Raheny Lane	B2
Rathmore Road	B3
Remount	B3
Saddlers Place	B2
Scholar's Walk	B2
Scribes Court	B2
Skerries Road	B1
Station Road	B2
Stonemason's	B2
Stonemason's Close	B2
Stonemason's Road	B2
Sweetman Walk	B2
Tanner's Way	B2
Thatcher's Way	B2
The Green	A2
The Square	B2
T. Avenue Orlynn Park	B2
The Close Orlynn Park	B2
The Drive Orlynn Park	B3
The Grove Orlynn Park	B2
The Park Orlynn Park	B3
Thornigne-Foullard Ln.	A2
Tower View	A2
Treen Hill	A2
Tyrell's Row	B2
Village Road	B2
Weaver's Crescent	B2
Wendy Walsh Close	B2
Whitethorn Walk	B2
Windward Way	B2

R
U
S
H

An Tearmann	B3	Golden Ridge Close	C2	Mill Bank Court	B2	St Catherines Park	C1
Barrack Lane	C2	Golden Ridge Crescent	C2	Mill Bank Walk	B2	St Catherines View	C1
Bawn Road	C2	Golden Ridge Drive	C2	North Beach	C2	St Catherines Way	C1
Bayview Villas	C2	Golden Ridge Green	C2	Old Barrack Road	D3	St. Joseph's Road	C3
Bollum Lane	C2	Golden Ridge Lodge	C2	Old Haystown	B2	St. Maur's Park	C2
Brook Lane	B2	Golden Ridge Mews	C2	Old Road	B2	Sundrive Road	B3
Brookfield Park	C2	Golden Ridge Square	C2	Old Road Court	B2	Sunlock Court	C2
Brookford	B2	Golden Ridge View	C2	Old Road Grove	B2	Sunset Court	C2
Brookford Park	B2	Golden Ridge Walk	C2	Palmer Avenue	C1	Tayleurs Point	D3
Brookside Gardens	B2	Golden Ridge Way	C2	Palmer Court	C1	The Cairn	C1
Carthy's Lane	A3	Golf Road	B3	Palmer Road	C1	The Forge	D2
Carrig Leathan	C2	Hand Park	D2	Park Road	C2	The Mall	C2
Ceol na Mara	C2	Hands Lane	C3	Quay Road	D2	The Millbank	B2
Channel Road	A3	Harbour Road	D2	Ravenswell	C1	Thorn Chase	C1
Chapel Green	B2	Haystown	B2	Rogerstown Court	B3	Thornleigh	C2
Clann Beag	B3	Haystown Close	C2	Rogerstown Park	B3	Thornleigh Court	C2
Clifflands	C1	Haystown Road	C2	Sandy Lane	C3	Tower Street	D2
Clifflands Court	C1	Healy's Lane	B3	Sandy Road	C2	Upper Main Street	C2
Clifflands Rise	C1	Hoskyn Bank	C3	Sea Brook	B2	Whitestown Road	A3
Coast Guard Road	INSET	Kenure Crescent	C2	Seafield Court	D2	Woodbury	C2
Cois Tra	C2	Kenure Lawns	C1	Skerries Road	C2	Wooddale Road	C1
Congress Gardens	C3	Kenure Park	C2	Six Cross Lane	C1	Woodland Court	C2
Convent Lane	C3	Kilbush Lane	C2	South Shore Cove	B3	Woodland Park	C2
Cooper's Lane	C2	Kilbush View	C2	South Shore Road	C3		
Coopersfield	C2	Knockabawn	D2	South Strand	C3		
Crescent Road	B3	Lady Cove	C1	Spout Road	A3		
Daly's Lane	B3	Lambay View	C1	St Catherines Avenue	C1		
Doctor's Lane	B2	Linkside	INSET	St Catherines Close	C1		
Echlin Court	C2	Linn Ban	B2	St Catherines Court	C1		
Eden Terrace	C2	Linn Beag	B2	St Catherines Crescent	C1		
Farran's Lane	C2	Linn Cuin	B2	St Catherines Drive	C1		
Finistere	D2	Linn Dubh	B2	St Catherines Estate	C1		
Golden Ridge	C2	Lower Main Street	C2	St Catherines Green	C1		
Golden Ridge Avenue	C2	Melbourne Gardens	C3	St Catherines Grove	C1		
Golden Ridge Court	C2	Mill Bank	B2	St Catherines Lawn	C1		

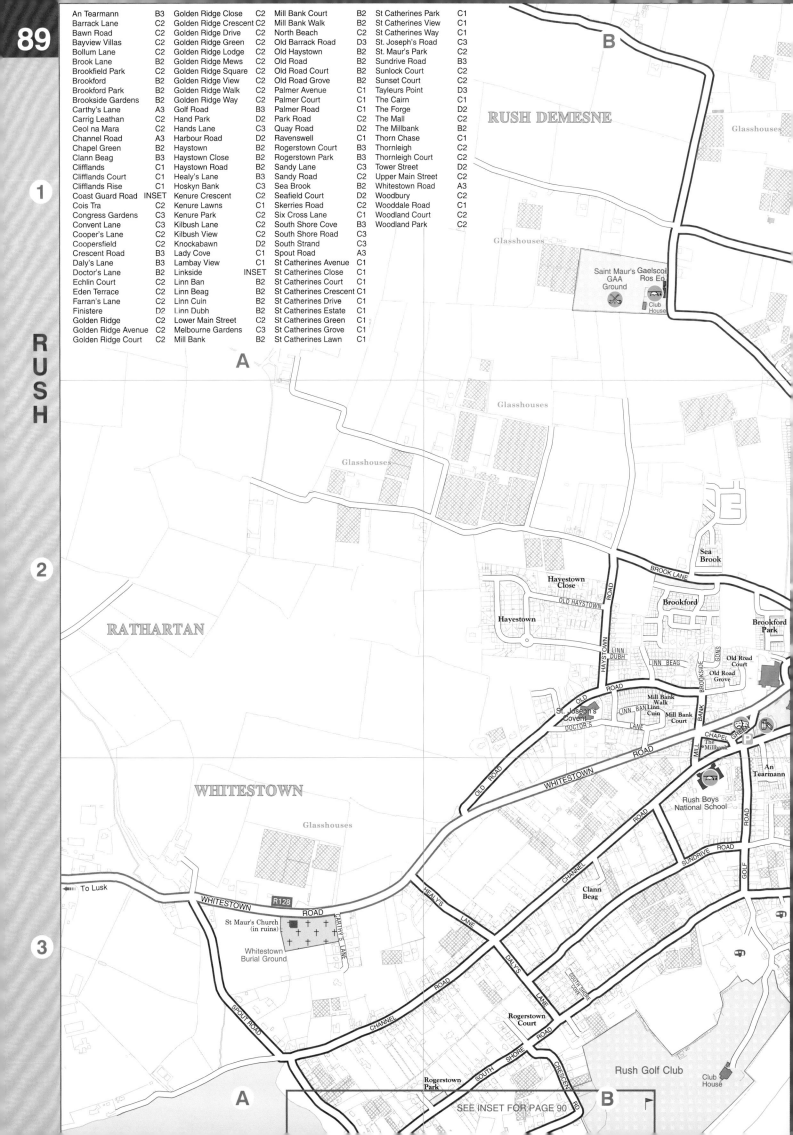

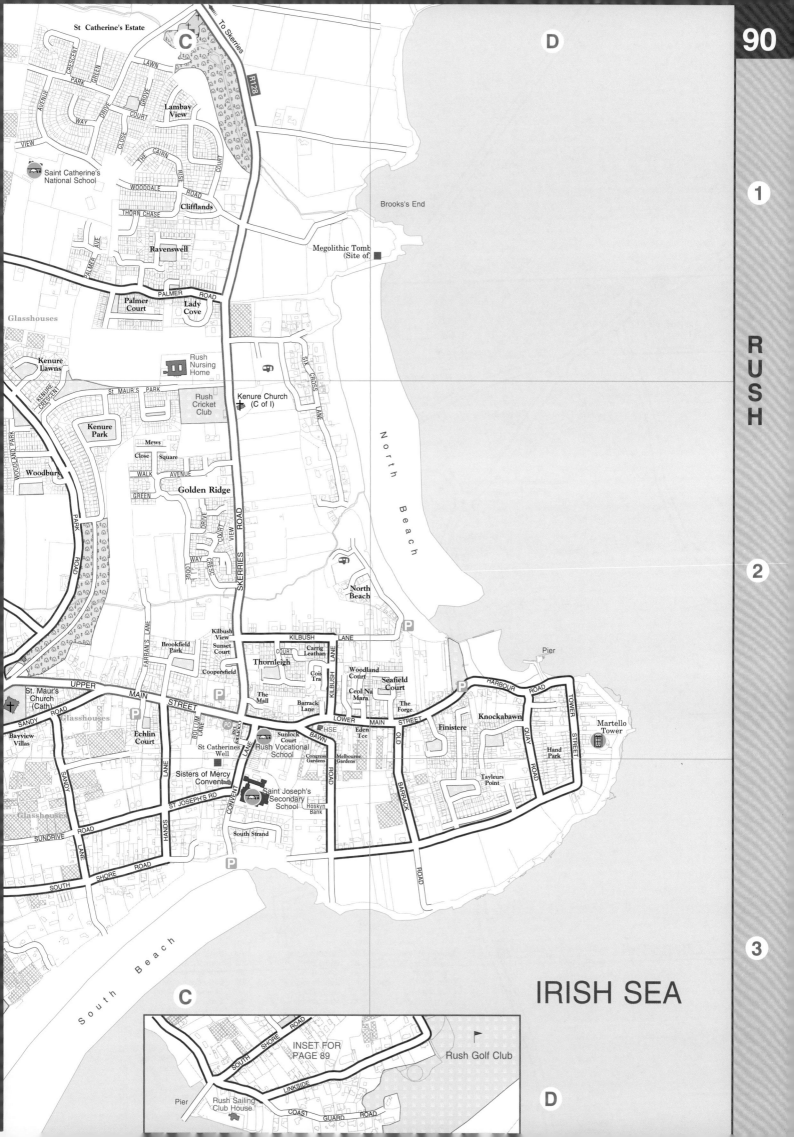

RUSH

IRISH SEA

St Catherine's Estate

To Skerries

R128

Lambay View

Saint Catherine's National School

Clifflands

Ravenswell

Glasshouses

Palmer Court

Lady Cove

PALMER ROAD

Rush Nursing Home

Kenure Lawns

ST. MAUR'S PARK

Rush Cricket Club

Kenure Church (C of I)

Brooks's End

Megolithic Tomb (Site of)

North Beach

Kenure Park

Mews

Close Square

Golden Ridge

Woodbury

SKERRIES ROAD

SIX CROSS LANE

North Beach

Kilbush View

Brookfield Park

Sunset Court

Thornleigh

Coopersfield

Carrig Leathan

KILBUSH LANE

Cois Tra

The Mall

Barrack Lane

Woodland Court

Ceol Na Mara

Seafield Court

The Forge

KILBUSH LANE

UPPER MAIN STREET

St. Maur's Church (Cath)

Glasshouses

Echlin Court

Bayview Villas

SANDY

BOLUM LANE

PO

St Catherines Well

Sunlock Court

Rush Vocational School

Congress Gardens

Melbourne Gardens

HSE

Eden Tce

LOWER MAIN STREET

OLD STREET

Finistere

Knockabawn

HARBOUR ROAD

Pier

QUAY ROAD

Hand Park

TOWER STREET

Martello Tower

Sisters of Mercy Convent

Saint Joseph's Secondary School

Hoskyn Bank

BARRACK ROAD

Tayleurs Point

SANDY ROAD

SUNDRIVE ROAD

Glasshouses

HANDS LANE

CONVENT LANE

ST JOSEPH'S RD

South Strand

SOUTH SHORE ROAD

P

South Beach

C

D

INSET FOR PAGE 89

SHORE ROAD

SOUTH

LINKSIDE

COAST GUARD ROAD

Pier

Rush Sailing Club House

Rush Golf Club

D

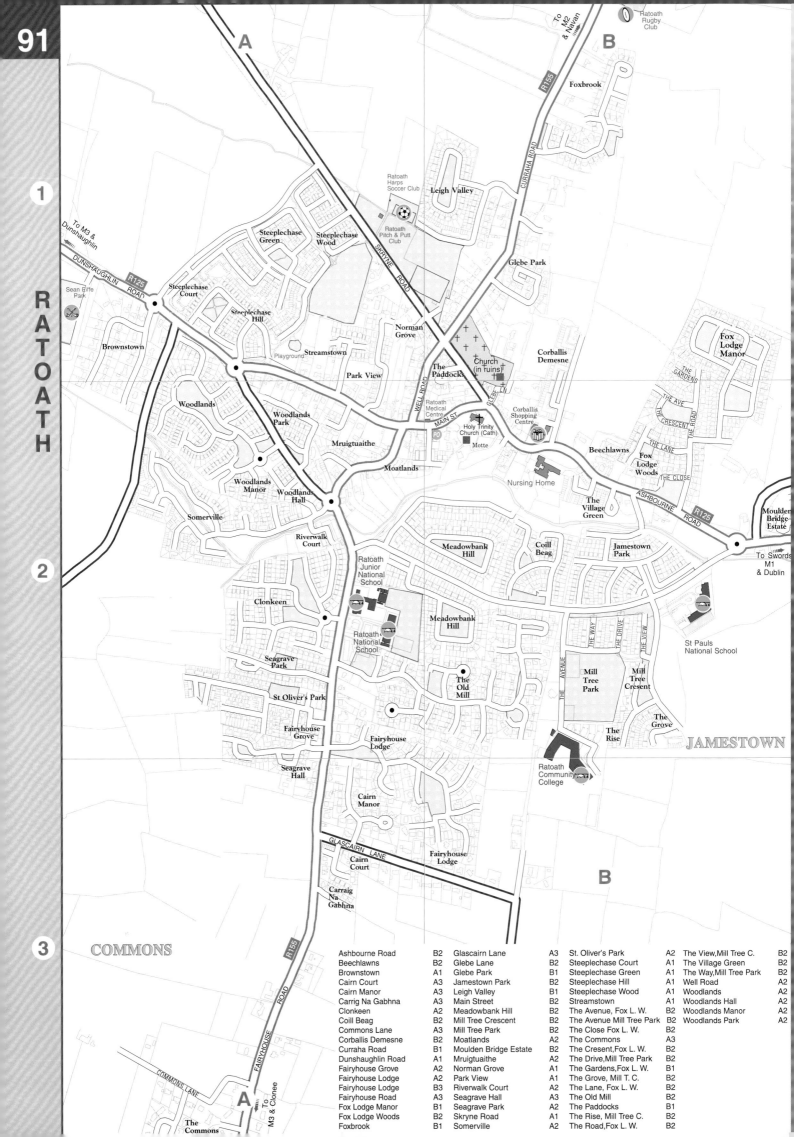

RATOATH

A   B

1

2

3

To M2
& Navan

Ratoath Rugby Club

R155

Foxbrook

CURRAHA ROAD

Leigh Valley

Ratoath Harps Soccer Club

Ratoath Pitch & Putt Club

Glebe Park

SKRYNE ROAD

Steeplechase Green

Steeplechase Wood

Steeplechase Court

To M3 & Dunshaughlin

DUNSHAUGHLIN ROAD

R125

Sean Eiffe Park

Steeplechase Hill

Norman Grove

Corballis Demesne

Brownstown

Playground

Streamstown

Park View

Church (in ruins)

The Paddocks

GLEBE LN

Corballis Shopping Centre

Woodlands

WELL ROAD

MAIN ST

Ratoath Medical Centre

Beechlawns

Fox Lodge Manor

THE GARDENS

THE AVE

THE CRESCENT

THE ROAD

Woodlands Park

Mruigtuaithe

PO

Holy Trinity Church (Cath)

Motte

Fox Lodge Woods

THE LANE

THE CLOSE

Moatlands

Nursing Home

The Village Green

ASHBOURNE ROAD

R125

Moulden Bridge Estate

Woodlands Manor

Woodlands Hall

Somerville

Riverwalk Court

Meadowbank Hill

Coill Beag

Jamestown Park

To Swords M1 & Dublin

Clonkeen

Ratoath Junior National School

Meadowbank Hill

THE WAY

THE DRIVE

THE VIEW

St Pauls National School

Seagrave Park

Ratoath National School

The Old Mill

THE AVENUE

Mill Tree Park

Mill Tree Cresent

St Oliver's Park

Fairyhouse Grove

Fairyhouse Lodge

The Rise

The Grove

JAMESTOWN

Seagrave Hall

Cairn Manor

Ratoath Community College

GLASCAIRN LANE

Cairn Court

Fairyhouse Lodge

B

R155

Carraig Na Gabhna

FAIRYHOUSE ROAD

COMMONS

COMMONS LANE

A

To M3 & Clonee

The Commons

Ashbourne Road	B2	Glascairn Lane	A3	St. Oliver's Park	A2	The View,Mill Tree C.	B2
Beechlawns	B2	Glebe Lane	B2	Steeplechase Court	A1	The Village Green	B2
Brownstown	A1	Glebe Park	B1	Steeplechase Green	A1	The Way,Mill Tree Park	B2
Cairn Court	A3	Jamestown Park	B2	Steeplechase Hill	A1	Well Road	A1
Cairn Manor	A3	Leigh Valley	B1	Steeplechase Wood	A1	Woodlands	A2
Carrig Na Gabhna	A3	Main Street	B2	Streamstown	A1	Woodlands Hall	A2
Clonkeen	A2	Meadowbank Hill	B2	The Avenue, Fox L. W.	B2	Woodlands Manor	A2
Coill Beag	B2	Mill Tree Crescent	B2	The Avenue Mill Tree Park	B2	Woodlands Park	A2
Commons Lane	A3	Mill Tree Park	B2	The Close Fox L. W.	B2		
Corballis Demesne	B2	Moatlands	A2	The Commons	A3		
Curraha Road	B1	Moulden Bridge Estate	B2	The Cresent,Fox L. W.	B2		
Dunshaughlin Road	A1	Mruigtuaithe	A2	The Drive,Mill Tree Park	B2		
Fairyhouse Grove	A2	Norman Grove	A1	The Gardens, Fox L. W.	B1		
Fairyhouse Lodge	A2	Park View	A1	The Grove, Mill T. C.	B2		
Fairyhouse Lodge	B3	Riverwalk Court	A2	The Lane, Fox L. W.	B2		
Fairyhouse Road	A3	Seagrave Hall	A3	The Old Mill	B2		
Fox Lodge Manor	B1	Seagrave Park	A2	The Paddocks	B1		
Fox Lodge Woods	B2	Skryne Road	A1	The Rise, Mill Tree C.	B2		
Foxbrook	B1	Somerville	A2	The Road,Fox L. W.	B2		

An Claddagh	A2	Kelly's Bay Heights	INSET	Rush Road	B3	The Drive, Skerries Rock	A2
Arcadia Court	B2	Kelly's Bay Inlet	INSET	Saint Patrick's Close	B3	The Green	A3
Ardgillan View	A2	Kelly's Bay Jetty	INSET	Sandy Banks	B2	The Grove, Skerries Rock	A2
Balbriggan Road	A2	Kelly's Bay Moorings	INSET	Seacrest	A2	The Haven	B2
Balbriggan Street	B2	Kelly's Bay Parade	INSET	Selskar Avenue	A2	The Heights, Skerries Rk.	A2
Barnageeragh Cove	INSET	Kelly's Bay Pier	INSET	Selskar Court	A2	The Hoar Rock	A2
Barnageeragh Road	INSET	Kelly's Bay Promenade	INSET	Selskar Rise	A2	The Kybe	B2
Beau-Piers Lane	B2	Kelly's Bay Rise	INSET	Selskar Road	A2	The Lawn, Skerries Rock	A2
Brookville Lane	B2	Kelly's Bay Rocks	INSET	Shalloch Hill Grove	A2	The Maltings	B3
Cabra Hill	B3	Kelly's Bay Shore	A2	Shenick Avenue	B3	The Park	A2
Callaghan's Lane	B2	Kelly's Bay Strand	INSET	Shenick Drive	B3	The Park, Skerries Rock	A2
Chapel Lane	B2	Kelly's Bay Tide	INSET	Shenick Grove	B3	The Quays	B2
Church Street	B2	Kelly's Bay Tower	INSET	Shenick Park	B3	The Rise, Skerries Rock	A2
Churchfield Close	B3	Kelly's Bay View	A1	Shenick Road	B3	The Rope Walk	B2
Churchfield Lawns	B3	Kelly's Bay Weir	INSET	Sherlock Park	B3	The Square	B2
College Court	B2	Little Strand Street	B2	Sherlock Terrace	B3	The Stableyard	B2
Convent Lane	B2	Manning's Opening	B2	Skerries Rock	A2	The Vale, Skerries Rock	A2
Derhams Lane	A2	Martine Court	B2	South Strand	B2	The View, Skerries Rock	A2
Downside Heights	B3	Marywell	B3	Station Road	A3	The Walk, Skerries Rock	A2
Downside Park	B3	McLoughlin's Lane	B2	Strand Street	B2	The Way, Skerries Rock	A2
Dublin Road	A3	Mill Lane	A3	Tennis Court Lane	B2	Thomas Hand Street	B2
Friar's Lane	B2	Miller's Lane	B3	The Avenue, Skerries Rock	A2	Townparks	A2
Foxgrove	A2	Millhill Park	B2	The Brambles	A2	Weldon's Lane	B3
Gavneys Gap	A2	Millview	B2	The Brock	A2	Windmill Close	B3
Golf Links Road	B3	Mooring Cove	A2	The Close, Skerries Rock	A2	Windmill Court	B3
Greenlawns	A3	Mourne Close	A2	The Court, Skerries Rock	A2	Windmill Drive	B3
Harbour Road	B2	Mourne Court	A2	The Crescent, Skerries RK.	A2	Windmill Lane	B3
Harrison's Cove	A2	Mourne Drive	A2	The Cross	B2	Windmill View	B3
Healy's Lane	B2	Mourne Grove	A2				
Heeney's Lane	B2	Mourne Park	A2				
Hillside Close	B3	Mourne View	A2				
Hillside Gardens	A3	New Street	B2				
Holmpatrick	B2	Newtownparks	A2				
Holmpatrick Terrace	B3	North Strand	A2				
Kelly's Bay Beach	INSET	Northcliffe Heights	A2				
Kelly's Bay Cliffs	INSET	Osprey	INSET				
Kelly's Bay Cove	INSET	Pump Lane	A2				
Kelly's Bay Drive	INSET	Quay Street	B2				
Kelly's Bay Harbour	INSET	Red Island	B1				

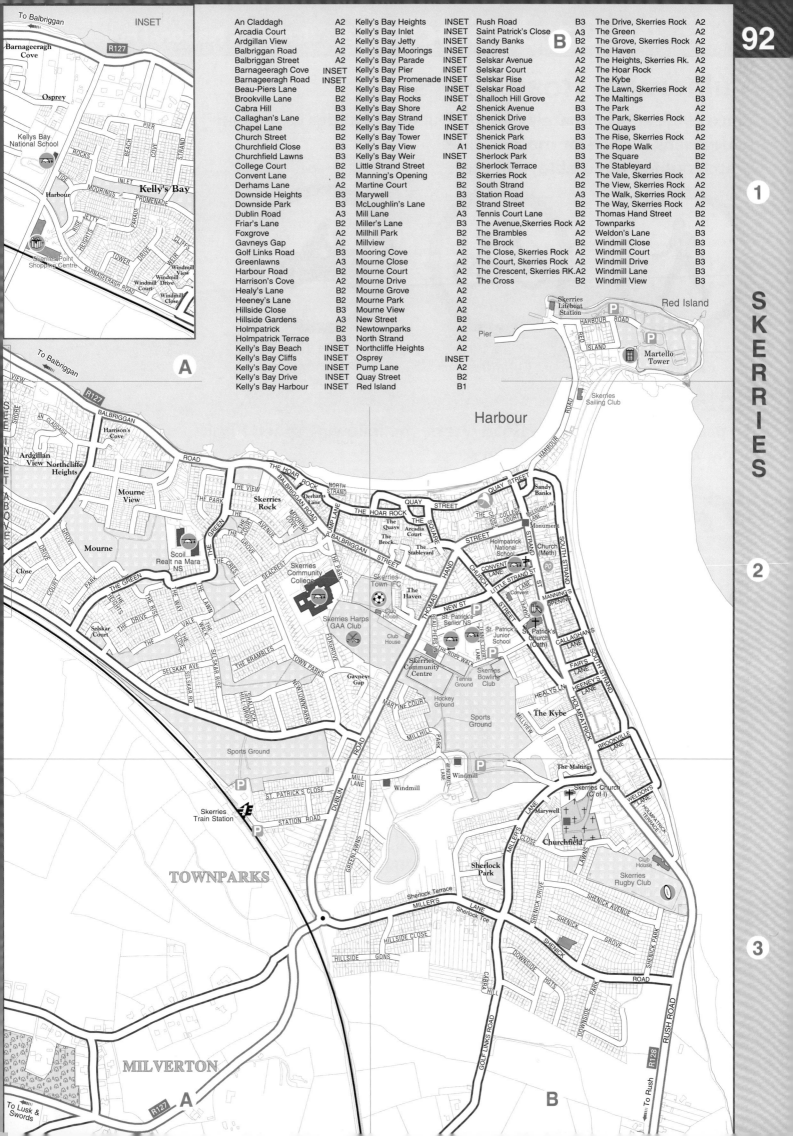

Vulnerable Road Users

Since 2007, approximately 60% of Dublin's fatalities have been pedestrians, cyclists or motorcyclists.
Watch out for vulnerable road users

| 4 in 10 Fatalities | 1 in 10 Fatalities | 1 in 10 Fatalities |

Speed Limits

To protect our Vulnerable Road Users, the following speed Limits apply within the Greater Dublin Area

High Concentration of Vulnerable Road Users — **General built up areas** — **Primary approach roads to the city**

Statistics show that:

- ◎ 85% of pedestrians would be killed if hit at 60kph
- ◎ 45% of pedestrians would be killed if hit at 50kph
- ◎ 5% of pedestrians would be killed if hit at 30kph

Know your Speed Limits, know YOUR Speed!

Garda personnel conduct speed checks across the road network using handheld and in-car equipment as well as mobile safety camera vans. Safety camera vans are also operated by a service provider on behalf of An Garda Síochána in speed enforcement zones. These zones may be found at www.garda.ie

Take heed - do not speed!

Crime Prevention Advice

It pays to be careful. To reduce your chances of becoming a victim of crime, consider the following -

» **Be aware of your surroundings**

» **Avoid travelling alone, where possible**

» **Avoid walking alone at night**

» **Keep cash on your person to the minimum required**

» **Keep wallets / purses out of sight**

» **Keep hand or shoulder bags close to the body and not dangling by the straps**

» **Where possible, take a mobile phone with you when out & about**

» **If travelling by public transport, sit as close as possible to the driver or exit**

» **If travelling by car, keep all doors locked**

» **Be alert when parking and getting out of your vehicle**

» **Be alert to pickpockets**

» **Ideally, do not leave property in cars or other vehicles**

» **Be especially careful with small electronic equipment e.g. Sat Navs, digital cameras, mobile phones, music players etc.**

» **Close all windows and lock all doors**

» **Do not leave property on view in your vehicle**

» **Do not leave cash, cheque books, credit/debit cards in your vehicle**

» **Do not leave personal/valuable documents in your vehicle e.g. utility bills, bank statements etc.**

» **Avoid parking in isolated places and, at night-time, park with care in a well-lit area**

» **Always secure bicycles to an immovable object**

Apostolic Nunciature
183 Navan Road
Dublin 7
Tel: 838 0577   24 D4

Argentine Embassy
15 Ailesbury Drive
Dublin 4
Tel: 269 1546   48 D1

Australian Embassy
7th Floor,
Fitzwilton House
Wilton Terrace, Dublin 2
Tel: 664 5300   38 E4

Austrian Embassy
15 Ailesbury Court Apts.
93 Ailesbury Road
Dublin 4
Tel: 269 4577   48 D1

Belgian Embassy
1 Elgin Road
Dublin 4
Tel: 6315284   48 D1

Embassy of the Federative Republic of Brazil
Block 8 Sixth Floor
Harcourt Centre,
Charlotte Way.
Dublin 2.
Tel: 475 6000   38 D4

British Embassy
29 Merrion Road
Dublin 4
Tel: 205 3700   48 D1

Bulgarian Embassy
22 Burlington Road
Dublin 4
Tel: 660 3293   38 E4

Canadian Embassy
7/8 Wilton Terrace.
Dublin 2
Tel: 234 4000   38 E4

Chilean Embassy
44 Wellington Road
Ballsbridge
Dublin 4
Tel: 667 5094   38 F4

Embassy of the People's Republic of China
40 Ailesbury Road
Ballsbridge, Dublin 4
Tel: 269 1707   48 D1

Embassy of the Republic of Croatia
Adelaide Chambers
Peter Street
Dublin 8
Tel: 476 7181   38 D3

Embassy of the Republic of Cuba
2 Adelaide Court,
Adelaide Road,
Dublin 2
Tel: 475 0899   38 D4

Embassy of Republic of Cyprus
71 Lower Leeson Street
Dublin 2
Tel: 676 3060   38 E3

Embassy of The Czech Republic
57 Northumberland Road
Dublin 4
Tel: 668 1135   38 F4

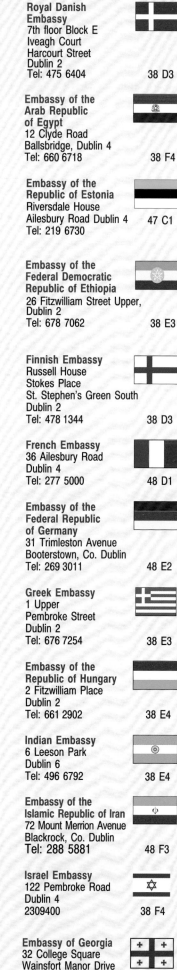

Royal Danish Embassy
7th floor Block E
Iveagh Court
Harcourt Street
Dublin 2
Tel: 475 6404   38 D3

Embassy of the Arab Republic of Egypt
12 Clyde Road
Ballsbridge, Dublin 4
Tel: 660 6718   38 F4

Embassy of the Republic of Estonia
Riversdale House
Ailesbury Road Dublin 4
Tel: 219 6730   47 C1

Embassy of the Federal Democratic Republic of Ethiopia
26 Fitzwilliam Street Upper,
Dublin 2
Tel: 678 7062   38 E3

Finnish Embassy
Russell House
Stokes Place
St. Stephen's Green South
Dublin 2
Tel: 478 1344   38 D3

French Embassy
36 Ailesbury Road
Dublin 4
Tel: 277 5000   48 D1

Embassy of the Federal Republic of Germany
31 Trimleston Avenue
Booterstown, Co. Dublin
Tel: 269 3011   48 E2

Greek Embassy
1 Upper
Pembroke Street
Dublin 2
Tel: 676 7254   38 E3

Embassy of the Republic of Hungary
2 Fitzwilliam Place
Dublin 2
Tel: 661 2902   38 E4

Indian Embassy
6 Leeson Park
Dublin 6
Tel: 496 6792   38 E4

Embassy of the Islamic Republic of Iran
72 Mount Merrion Avenue
Blackrock, Co. Dublin
Tel: 288 5881   48 F3

Israel Embassy
122 Pembroke Road
Dublin 4
2309400   38 F4

Embassy of Georgia
32 College Square
Wainsfort Manor Drive
Terenure Dublin 6W
Tel: 406 7956   46 D3

Italian Embassy
63/65 Northumberland Road
Ballsbridge,
Dublin 4
Tel: 660 1744   38 F4

Japanese Embassy
Nutley Building
Merrion Centre
Nutley Lane, Dublin 4
Tel: 202 8300   48 E1

Embassy of the Republic of Kenya
11 Elgin Road
Ballsbridge, Dublin 4
Tel: 613 6380   38 F4

Embassy of the Republic of Korea
15 Clyde Road
Ballsbridge, Dublin 4
Tel: 660 8800   38 F4

Embassy of the Republic of Latvia
92 St Stephen's Green
Dublin 2
Tel: 478 0161   38 E4

Embassy of Lesotho
2 Clanwilliam Square,
Grand Canal Quay,
Dublin 2.
Tel: 676 2233   38 F3[41]

Embassy of the Republic of Lithuania
47Ailsbury Road,
Ballsbridge, Dublin 4.
Tel: 203 5737   48 D1

Embassy of Malaysia
Level 3A-5A
Shelbourne House
Shelbourne Road
Ballsbridge Dublin 4.
Tel: 667 7280   38 F3

Maltese Embassy
15 Leeson Street Lower
Dublin 2
Tel: 6762340   38 E4

Mexican Embassy
19 Raglan Road
Dublin 4
Tel: 667 3105   38 F4

Embassy of the Kingdom of Morocco
39 Raglan Road
Dublin 4
Tel: 660 9449   38 F4

Netherlands Embassy
160 Merrion Road
Dublin 4
Tel: 269 3444   48 D1

Embassy of the Federal Republic of Nigeria
56 Leeson Park
Dublin 6
Tel: 660 4366   38 E4

Royal Norwegian Embassy
34 Molesworth Street,
Dublin 2
Tel: 662 1800   38 E3

Embassy of the Islamic Republic of Pakistan
1B Ailesbury Road
Ballsbridge Dublin 4
Tel: 261 3032   48 D1

Embassy of the Republic of The Philippines
4th Floor Hainault House
69-71 St. Stephens Green South
Dublin 2
Tel: 407 4040   72 F4

Embassy of the Republic of Poland
5 Ailesbury Road
Dublin 4
Tel: 283 0855   48 D1

Portuguese Embassy
15 Leeson Park
Dublin 6
Tel: 412 7040/5   38 E4

Embassy of Romania
26 Waterloo Road
Dublin 4
Tel: 668 1085   48 D1

Embassy of the Russian Federation
184/186 Orwell Road
Rathgar, Dublin 14
Tel: 492 2048   47 B3

Royal Embassy of Saudi Arabia
6/7 Fitzwilliam Square E
Dublin 2
Tel: 676 0704   76 D2

Embassy of the Slovak Republic
20 Clyde Road
Dublin 4
Tel: 660 0008 / 660 0012   38 F4

Embassy of the Republic of Slovenia
Morrison Chambers
2nd Floor,
32 Nassau Street Dublin 2
Tel: 670 5240   38 E3

Embassy of South Africa
Alexandra House,
Earlsfort Centre,
Earlsfort Terrace, Dublin 2
Tel: 661 5553   38 E3

Spanish Embassy
17A Merlyn Park
Dublin 4
Tel: 283 9900   48 E1

Swiss Embassy
6 Ailesbury Road
Ballsbridge
Dublin 4
Tel: 218 6382   48 D1

Embassy of the Republic of Turkey
11 Clyde Road
Ballsbridge, Dublin 4
Tel: 668 5240   38 F4

Embassy of Ukraine
16 Elgin Road,
Ballsbridge,
Dublin 4.
Tel: 668 8601   38 F4

Embassy of the United States of America
42 Elgin Road
Ballsbridge, Dublin 4
Tel: 630 6200   38 F4

**For further information contact:
Dept of Foreign Affairs,
80 St. Stephen's Green, Dublin 2.
Tel: 478 0822 / www.foreignaffairs.gov.ie**

HOSPITAL		ADDRESS		TEL No.	GRID
Tallaght Hosp. Adelaide & Meath (A&E) Hosp. & The National Childrens Hosp.		Tallaght	Dublin 24	01 414 2000	**54F1**
Beaumont Hosp. (A&E)	Beaumont Road	Beaumont	Dublin 9	01 809 3000	**26D1**
Cherry Orchard Hosp.		Ballyfermot	Dublin 10	01 620 6000	**35C3**
Cheeverstown House	Kilvare	Templeogue	Dublin 6W	01 499 3700	**46D4**
City of Dublin Skin & Cancer Hosp.		Hume Street	Dublin 2	01 676 6935	**38E3**
Connolly Hosp. (A&E)		Blanchardstown	Dublin 15	01 646 5000	**22F2**
Dublin Dental School & Hosp.		Lincoln Place	Dublin 2	01 612 7200	**38E3**
Cappagh National Orthopaedic Hosp.	Cappagh	Finglas	Dublin 11	01 814 0400	**23C1**
National Rehabilitation Hosp.		Dun Laoghaire	Co. Dublin	01 235 5000	**59C2**
Incorporated Orthopaedic Hosp. of Ireland	Castle Ave	Clontarf	Dublin 3	01 833 2521	**26E4**
Peamount Hosp.		Newcastle	Co. Dublin	01 601 0300	**42E2**
Royal Hosp. Donnybrook	off Morehampton Road	Dublin 4		01 406 6600	**47B1**
Royal Victoria Eye & Ear Hosp.		Adelaide Road	Dublin 2	01 664 4600	**38E4**
St.Bricins Military Hosp.		Infirmary Road	Dublin 7	01 677 6112	**37B2**
St.Columcilles Hosp. (A&E)		Loughlinstown	Co. Dublin	01 282 5800	**64D2**
St.James's Hosp. (A&E)		James's Street	Dublin 8	01 410 3000	**37B3**
St.Joseph's Hosp.		Clonsilla	Dublin 15	01 821 7177	**21B2**
St.Joseph's Hosp.	Springdale Road	Raheny	Dublin 15	01 877 4900	**27A2**
St.Luke's Hosp	Highfield Road	Rathgar	Dublin 6	01 406 5000	**47A2**
St.Mary's Hosp.		Phoenix Park	Dublin 20	01 625 0300	**36E2**
St.Michaels Hosp. (A&E)	Lr. Georges Street	DunLaoghaire	Co. Dublin	01 280 6901	**50D4**
St.Vincent's Hosp.(A&E)		Elm Park	Dublin 4	01 277 4000	**48E1**
Stewart's Hosp.		Palmerston	Dublin 20	01 626 4444	**35C1**
The Mater Hosp. (A&E)		Eccles Street	Dublin 7	01 803 2000	**38D1**

MATERNITY HOSPITALS

Coombe Women's Hosp		Dolphin's Barn	Dublin 8	01 408 5200	**37C4**
National Maternity Hosp.		Holles Street	Dublin 2	01 637 3100	**38E3**
Rotunda Hospital		Parnell Street	Dublin 1	01 873 0700	**38D1**

CHILDREN'S HOSPITALS

Temple Street Childrens University Hosp. (A&E)		Temple Street	Dublin 1	01 878 4200	**38D1**
National Childrens Hosp.		Tallaght	Dublin 24	01 414 2000	**54F1**
Our Lady's Hospital for Sick Children (A&E)		Crumlin	Dublin 12	01 409 6100	**46D1**

PSYCHIATRIC HOSPITALS

Central Mental Hospital		Dundrum	Dublin 14	01 298 9266	**47C3**
St.Brendan's Hospital		Rathdown Road	Dublin 7	01 869 3000	**37C1**
St.Edmundsbury Hospital	Old Lucan Road	Lucan	Co. Dublin	01 884 2400	**25B4**
St.Ita's Hospital	Portrane	Donabate	Co. Dublin	01 621 8200	**34E1**
St.John of God Hospital		Stillorgan	Co. Dublin	01 288 1781	**58F1**
St.Vincent's Hospital	Richmond Road	Fairview	Dublin 3	01 884 2400	**25B4**
St.Patrick's Hospital		James's Street	Dublin 8	01 249 3200	**37B3**

PRIVATE HOSPITALS

Beacon Hospital		Sandyford	Dublin 18	01 293 6600	**58D2**
Blackrock Clinic	Rock Road	Blackrock	Co. Dublin	01283 2222	**48F3**
Bon Secours Hospital Hospital		Glasnevin	Dublin 9	01 806 5300	**25A3**
Clane General Hospital	Prosperous Road	Clane	Co. Kildare	045 982 300	**82A3**
Hermitage Medical Clinic		Old Lucan Road	Dublin 20	01 645 9000	**35A1**
Mount Carmel Hospital	Braemor Park	Churchtown	Dublin 14	01 405 3400	**47A3**

Name	Pg	Grid /Ref	No.
Abbey Business Park	14	F4	112
Advance Business Park	12	F3	179
Aerodrome Business Park	52	F1	60
Airport Business Park	13	A1	213
Airport Industrial Campus	12	E4	01
Airside Business Park	02	D3	266
Airside Retail Park	01	C3	295
Airton Business Park	45	A4	2
Airton Business Park	45	A4	3
Airton Business Park	45	A4	4
Airton Coporate Park	45	A4	38
Airways Ind Est	12	F4	5
Allied Ind Est	36	E4	6
Alltech Technology Park	06	E2	307
Ardee Court	67	B2	007
Ashgrove Ind Est	59	C1	008
Aughrim Lane Ind Est	37	C1	268
Avonbeg Enterprise Centre	55	A1	085
Avonbeg Ind Est	45	B1	277
Avondale	49	A4	167
Baldonnel Business Park	43	A4	241
Baldoyle Ind Est	27	C1	10
Balfe Road Ind Est	45	C1	196
Balheary Industrial Park	02	D1	11
Ballyboggan Ind Est	24	D3	12
Ballycoolin Business Park	10	D4	13
Ballymount Business Centre	45	B2	14
Ballymount Court Business Centre	45	B2	72
Ballymount Cross Ind Est	45	A2	15
Ballymount Ind Est	45	B2	16
Ballymount Road Ind Est	45	B2	17
Ballymount Trading Centre	45	B2	18
Ballymun Ind Est	12	D4	19
Barbeque Poultry Business Park	64	E3	300
Base Enterprise Centre	09	A4	301
Beech Hill Office Campus	47	C2	228
Beechlawn Ind Complex	45	B2	20
Beechwood Close Ind Est	67	C4	21
Belfield Office Park	47	C2	229
Belgard Ind Est	44	F4	22
Bellevue Industrial Park	24	E3	86
Benson Street Enterprise Centre	38	F2	24
Blackhorse Ind Est	37	B1	25
Blackrock Business Park	49	A3	169
Blanchardstown Corporate Park	09	C3	165
Blanchardstown Industrial Park	09	C4	26
Bluebell Ind Est	36	D4	28
Bluebell Business Centre	36	E4	273
Bluebell Business Park	36	E4	27
Bow Bridge Business Centre	37	B3	308
Bracetown Business Park	07	C1	29
Bray Ind Est	67	C4	30
Bray Businese Park	67	C4	255
Bridges Ind Est	45	A1	32
Bridgewater Business Centre	37	B2	31
Brookfield Enterprise Centre	54	D1	247
Broombridge Ind Est	24	E3	33
Broomfield Business Park	03	B4	271
Broomhill Business Park	45	A4	84
Broomhill Business Park Close	45	A4	35
Broomhill Business Park Drive	45	A4	36
Broomhill Business Park Road	45	A4	37
Burton Hall Campus	58	E2	39
Butterly Business Park	26	D2	66
Calmount Business Park	45	B2	197
Carrigalea Ind Est	45	B1	40
Cashel Business Centre	46	E2	293
Castleforbes Business Park	38	F2	41
Cedar Industrial Park, Bray	67	B4	258
Celbridge Industrial Est	31	C3	238
Central Park Business Park	58	E2	253
Century Business Park	11	B4	206
Chapelizod Ind Est	36	E2	90
Charlestown Centre	11	A4	160
Cherry Orchard Ind Est	35	C2	42
Cherrywood Business Park	64	D1	251
Churchtown Business Park	47	B4	225
Cian Park Ind Est	25	B4	43

Name	Pg	Grid /Ref	No.
City Junction Business Park	13	C4	212
City Link Business Park	36	E4	215
City West Business Campus	53	B1	44
Clondalkin Business Centre	35	B4	46
Clondalkin Commercial Park	35	B4	45
Clondalkin Enterprise Centre	35	A3	177
Clonshaugh Business & Technology Park	13	A4	311
Clonshaugh Ind Est	13	A4	47
Clonskeagh House Office Park	47	C2	226
Clonskeagh Square Office Park	47	C2	227
Cloverhill Ind Est	35	B4	48
College Business and Technology Park	09	C4	200
Collinstown Ind Est	12	F3	50
Collinstown Ind Est (Intel)	19	B3	92
Collinstown Cross Ind Est	12	F2	49
Concord Ind Est Naas Road	36	E4	272
Cookstown Ind Est	44	F4	52
Cookstown Ind Est The Extension	44	E4	243
Cookstown Business Centre	44	F4	245
Cookstown Enterprise Park	44	F4	51
Cookstown Square	44	F4	244
Coolmine Ind Est	22	D2	53
The Courtyard Business Park	43	B2	269
Crag Avenue Ind Centre	35	B4	219
Cranford Centre, Stillorgan	48	D2	274
Croke Park Ind Est	38	E1	55
Crosbie Business Centre	38	F1	262
Crossbeg Ind Est	45	A2	56
Crosslands Business Park	45	A2	297
Crosslands Industrial Park	45	A2	57
Cruiserath Business Park	09	C3	199
Crumlin Business Park	46	E1	292
Damastown Ind Est	08	F3	58
Damastown Industrial Park	08	F3	302
Damastown Technology Park	08	E3	166
Dartmouth House Ind Centre	36	E3	217
Deansgrange Business Park	59	B2	59
Docklands Innovation Park	39	A1	155
Donnelly Centre	37	C3	275
Dublin Ind Est Glasnevin/Broombridge	24	E3	61
Dun Laoghaire Ind Est	59	B2	63
Dunboyne Ind Est	07	B2	62
Dundrum Business Park	47	C3	231
Earlscourt Ind Est	47	B4	224
Earlsfort Centre	38	E3	276
East Point Business Park	39	A1	263
East Road Ind Est	38	F1	64
Elmfield Ind Est	44	E1	65
Fashion City	45	A3	69
Feltrim Industrial Park	02	E3	67
Finches Industrial Park	45	B1	68
Finglas Business Centre	11	B4	140
Finglas Business Park	24	E3	023
Fonthill Retail Park	35	A2	176
Frank Fahey Centre	45	B1	9
Furry Park Ind Est	12	E3	181
Gaywood Ind Est	09	B3	70
Glasnevin Business Centre	24	D3	220
GlasnevinBusiness Park	24	D3	221
Glen Ind Est	24	E3	73
Glen Abbey Complex	44	F4	71
Glenageary Office Park	60	D2	291
Glenview Ind Est	37	B4	74
Glenville Ind Est	48	E3	75
Goldenbridge Ind Est	36	F3	315
Grange Castle Business Park	34	D4	218
Grange Castle International Business Park	43	B1	239
Grattan Business Park	13	A4	210
Great Keppel Business Centre	15	A1	296
Green Isle Business Park	44	D3	242
Greenhills Ind Est	45	A4	77
Greenhills Business Centre	45	B4	193
Greenhills Business Park	45	B4	192
Greenhills Centre	45	B4	191
Greenmount Ind Est	37	C4	078
Greenogue Business Park	42	E4	235
Grove Ind Est, Dubber Cross	11	B3	079
Grove Ind Est, Finglas	24	E1	080

Name	Pg	Grid /Ref	No.
Harbour Ind Est	67	C1	081
The Harcourt Centre	38	D4	278
Hewlett Packard Ind Park	32	F2	234
Hibernian Ind Est	45	A4	82
Hillcrest Ind Est	45	B2	93
Hills Ind Est	34	D1	83
Hollywood Business Park	09	C3	303
Horizon Logistics	11	B2	204
Howth Junction Business Park	27	B1	270
The Hub Logistics Park	7	C1	313
I.D.A.Tallaght Business Park	54	F2	89
Industrial Yarns Complex	67	C1	91
International Financial Services Centre (IFSC)	38	E2	279
Irish Life Centre	38	E2	280
J.F.K. Ave	45	A1	96
J.F.K. Drive	45	B1	97
J.F.K. Park	36	D4	98
J.F.K. Road	36	D4	99
Jamestown Business Park	11	A4	208
Jamestown Ind Centre	36	F4	95
Jamestown Ind Est	36	E4	94
Jamestown Little Ind Est	11	A4	298
KCR Ind Est	46	E2	100
Kilbarrack Ind Est	27	B1	101
Kilcarberry Industrial Park	43	A1	283
Kileen Industrial Park	36	D4	216
Killarney Road Business Park	67	B3	257
Killinardin Enterprise Park	54	F2	246
Kingswood Business Park	43	B3	312
Kinsealy Business Park	14	D1	281
Knockmitten Business Park	44	F1	282
Kore Development Park	36	E4	314
Kylemore Ind Est	36	D4	102
Kylemore Park North	36	D3	103
Kylemore Park South	36	E4	104
Kylemore Park West	36	D4	105
Landys Ind Est	56	D1	106
Lansdown Valley	45	C1	107
Leopardstown Office Park	58	E2	261
Leopardstown Retail Park	58	E2	108
Liberties Craft & Small Industries Centre	37	C3	109
The Liffey Trust Enterprise Centre	38	F2	150
Lilmar Ind Est	12	F4	110
Loughlinstown Ind Est	64	D1	111
Maltings Business Park	37	C3	259
Manor Street Business Park	37	C1	309
Maynooth Business Campus	17	C4	211
Merrywell Business Park	45	A2	188
Merrywell Ind Est	45	A2	182
Mill Lane Business Park	33	B1	232
Millbank Business Park	34	D1	87
Millenium Business Park	10	E3	202
Monarch Ind Est	44	F4	114
Montone Business Park	44	F1	248
Mount Pleasant Ind Est	47	A1	284
Mulcahy Keane Estate	45	C2	115
Mygan Park Industrial Park	11	B4	207
Naas Road Business Park	36	F4	132
Naas Road Ind Est	36	E4	170
Nangor Road Business Centre	35	C4	174
Newcastle Business Centre	42	E1	088
Newcourt Business Park	11	A2	205
Newlands Business Centre	44	E2	116
Newtown Ind Est	13	C4	117
North Park Business & Office Park	11	A4	209
North Richmond Ind Est	38	E1	118
North Ring Business Park	12	F3	180
Northern Cross Business Park	11	A4	285
Northwest Business Park	10	D3	201
Nutgrove Enterprise Park	57	A1	252
Nutgrove Office Park	47	A4	223
Oak Road Business Park	44	F1	250
Oakfield Ind Est	44	E1	119
Old Court Ind Est	67	B4	120
Old Sawmills Ind Est	45	B2	121
Ossory Ind Est	38	F1	122
Palmgrove Ind Est	25	B2	265
Park West Business Park	35	C4	173
Park West Enterprise Centre	35	C4	172

Name	Pg	Grid /Ref	No.
Park West Industrial Park	36	D4	171
Parkmore Ind Est	45	B1	123
Parkway Business Centre	45	A2	183
Phoenix Ind Est	23	B3	124
Pineview Ind Est	55	C1	125
Pinewood Close Ind Est	67	C4	126
Plato Business Park	09	A3	198
Poppintree Ind Est	11	B4	127
Port Tunnel Business Park	13	A4	310
Portside Business Centre	38	F1	128
Red Cow Business Park	45	A1	184
The Red Cow Interchange Est	44	F2	233
Richmond Road Ind Est	25	B4	129
Richview Park	47	C2	230
Riversdale Ind Est	36	E4	130
Riverview Business Centre	35	C4	175
Robinhood Business Park	45	A1	294
Robinhood Ind Est	45	B1	131
Rock Enterprise Centre	43	B3	240
Rosemount Business Park	10	D4	133
Royal Liver Retail Park	36	E4	214
S.P.A.D.E. Unemployment Enterprise Centre	37	C2	287
Sandyford Business Centre	58	E2	137
Sandyford Ind Est	58	E2	135
Sandyford Office Park	58	E2	136
Sandyford Park	58	E2	163
Santry Avenue Ind Est	12	E4	138
Santry Hall Ind Est	25	B1	139
Shankhill Business Centre	64	E2	141
Shanowen Ind Est	25	B1	142
Sitecast Ind Est	45	B4	194
Solas Retail Park	67	C1	254
South City Business Park	54	F2	306
South City Executive Park	46	E1	288
South County Business Park	58	F2	143
Southern Cross Business Park	67	B4	256
The Square Ind Complex	54	F1	289
St Joans Ind Est	45	A2	134
St John's Court Office Park	25	B1	264
St Margaret's Business Park	11	A4	286
St. Anthony's Business Park	45	A2	54
Stadium Ind Est	10	E4	203
Stillorgan Industrial Park	58	D2	144
Sunbury Ind Est	45	B2	145
Sunshine Ind Est	37	A4	146
Swanward Business Centre	45	A2	185
Swiftbrook Ind Est	53	A2	147
Swords Business Campus	02	D1	267
Swords Business Park	02	E1	148
Tallaght Enterprise Centre	55	A1	149
Taurus Business Park	45	B4	195
Terenure Business Park	46	F2	290
Terenure Enterprise Centre	46	F2	304
Tolka Industrial Park	24	D3	34
Tolka Valley Business Park	24	D3	222
Turnpike Ind Est see Ballymount Cross	45	A2	151
Unidare/Jamestown Business Park	24	E1	152
Weatherwell Ind Est	35	A4	153
West Pier Business Campus	48	C4	168
Westend Retail Park	22	E2	237
Western Business Park	44	F1	249
Western Ind Est	45	A1	156
Western Office Park	22	E1	236
Western Parkway Business Centre	45	B2	157
Western Parkway Business Park	45	B2	190
Westgate Business Park	45	A3	186
Westland Square Business Park	38	E2	260
Westlink Ind Est	36	E3	154
Westpoint Buisness Park	08	F4	164
Westway Centre	45	B2	189
White Heather Ind Est	37	B4	158
White Swan Business Park	37	C4	159
Whitestown Ind Est	54	F1	305
Willow Business Park	45	A1	187
Woodford Business Park	12	F3	178
Woodlawn Ind Est	12	F3	162

No.	Name	Pg	Grid/Ref
1	Airport Industrial Campus	12	E4
2	Airton Business Park	45	A4
3	Airton Business Park	45	A4
4	Airton Business Park	45	A4
5	Airways Ind Est	12	F4
6	Allied Ind Est	36	E4
7	Ardee Court	67	B2
8	Ashgrove Ind Est	59	C1
9	Frank Fahey Centre	45	B1
10	Baldoyle Ind Est	27	C1
11	Balheary Industrial Park	02	D1
12	Ballyboggan Ind Est	24	D3
13	Ballycoolin Business Park	10	D4
14	Ballymount Business Centre	45	B2
15	Ballymount Cross Ind Est	45	A2
16	Ballymount Ind Est	45	B2
17	Ballymount Road Ind Est	45	B2
18	Ballymount Trading Centre	45	B2
19	Ballymun Ind Est	12	D4
20	Beechlawn Ind Complex	45	B2
21	Beechwood Close Ind Est	67	C4
22	Belgard Ind Est	44	F4
23	Finglas Business Park	24	E3
24	Benson Street Enterprise Centre	38	F2
25	Blackhorse Ind Est	37	B1
26	Blanchardstown Ind Park	09	C4
27	Bluebell Business Park	36	E4
28	Bluebell Ind Est	36	D4
29	Bracetown Business Park	07	C1
30	Bray Ind Est	67	C4
31	Bridgewater Business Centre	37	B2
32	Bridges Ind Est	45	A1
33	Broombridge Ind Est	24	E3
34	Tolka Industrial Park	24	D3
35	Broomhill Business Park Close	45	A4
36	Broomhill Business Park Drive	45	A4
37	Broomhill Business Park Road	45	A4
38	Airton Coporate Park	45	A4
39	Burton Hall Campus	58	E2
40	Carrigalea Ind Est	45	B1
41	Castleforbes Business Park	38	F2
42	Cherry Orchard Ind Est	35	C2
43	Cian Park Ind Est	25	B4
44	City West Business Campus	53	B1
45	Clondalkin Commercial Park	35	B4
46	Clondalkin Business Centre	35	B4
47	Clonshaugh Ind Est	13	A4
48	Cloverhill Ind Est	35	B4
49	Collinstown Cross Ind Est	12	F2
50	Collinstown Ind Est	12	F3
51	Cookstown Enterprise Park	44	F4
52	Cookstown Ind Est	44	F4
53	Coolmine Ind Est	22	D2
54	St. Anthony's Business Park	45	A2
55	Croke Park Ind Est	38	E1
56	Crossbeg Ind Est	45	A2
57	Crosslands Industrial Park	45	A2
58	Damastown Ind Est	08	F3
59	Deansgrange Business Park	59	B2
60	Aerodrome Business Park	52	F1
61	Dublin Ind Est / Glasnevin/Broombridge	24	E3
62	Dunboyne Ind Est	07	B2
63	Dun Laoghaire Ind Est	59	B2
64	East Road Ind Est	38	F1
65	Elmfield Ind Est	44	E1
66	Butterly Business Park	26	D2
67	Feltrim Industrial Park	02	E3
68	Finches Industrial Park	45	B1
69	Fashion City	45	A3
70	Gaywood Ind Est	09	B3
71	Glen Abbey Complex	44	F4
72	Ballymount Court Business Centre	45	B2
73	Glen Ind Est	24	E3
74	Glenview Ind Est	37	B4
75	Glenville Ind Est	48	E3
77	Greenhills Ind Est	45	A4
78	Greenmount Ind Est	37	C4
79	Grove Ind Est Dubber Cross	11	B3
80	Grove Ind Est	24	E1
81	Harbour Ind Est	67	C1
82	Hibernian Ind Est	45	A4
83	Hills Ind Est	34	D1
84	Broomhill Business Park	45	A4
85	Avonbeg Enterprise Centre	55	A1
86	Bellevue Industrial Park	24	E3
87	Millbank Business Park	34	D1
88	Newcastle Business Centre	42	E1
89	I.D.A.Tallaght Business Park	54	F2
90	Chapelizod Ind Est	36	E2
91	Industrial Yarns Complex	67	C1
92	Collinstown Ind Est (Intel)	19	B3
93	Hillcrest Ind Est	45	B2
94	Jamestown Ind Est	36	E4
95	Jamestown Ind Centre	36	F4
96	J.F.K. Ave	45	A1
97	J.F.K. Drive	45	B1
98	J.F.K. Park	36	D4
99	J.F.K. Road	36	D4
100	KCR Ind Est	46	E2
101	Kilbarrack Ind Est	27	B1
102	Kylemore Ind Est	36	D4
103	Kylemore Park North	36	D3
104	Kylemore Park South	36	E4
105	Kylemore Park West	36	D4
106	Landys Ind Est	56	D1
107	Lansdown Valley	45	C1
108	Leopardstown Retail Park	58	E2
109	Liberties Craft & Small Industries Centre	37	C3
110	Lilmar Ind Est	12	F4
111	Loughlinstown Ind Est	64	D1
112	Abbey Business Park	14	F4
114	Monarch Ind Est	44	F4
115	Mulcahy Keane Estate	45	C2
116	Newlands Business Centre	44	E2
117	Newtown Ind Est	13	C4
118	North Richmond Ind Est	38	E1
119	Oakfield Ind Est	44	E1
120	Old Court Ind Est	67	B4
121	Old Sawmills Ind Est	45	B2
122	Ossory Ind Est	38	F1
123	Parkmore Ind Est	45	B1
124	Phoenix Ind Est	23	B3
125	Pineview Ind Est	55	C1
126	Pinewood Close Ind Est	67	C4
127	Poppintree Ind Est	11	B4
128	Portside Business Centre	38	F1
129	Richmond Road Ind Est	25	B4
130	Riversdale Ind Est	36	E4
131	Robinhood Ind Est	45	B1
132	Naas Road Business Park	36	F4
133	Rosemount Business Park	10	D4
134	St Joans Ind Est	45	A2
135	Sandyford Ind Est	58	E2
136	Sandyford Office Park	58	E2
137	Sandyford Business Centre	58	E2
138	Santry Avenue Ind Est	12	E4
139	Santry Hall Ind Est	25	B1
140	Finglas Business Centre	11	B4
141	Shankhill Business Centre	64	E2
142	Shanowen Ind Est	25	B1
143	South County Business Park	58	F2
144	Stillorgan Industrial Park	58	D2
145	Sunbury Ind Est	45	B2
146	Sunshine Ind Est	37	A4
147	Swiftbrook Ind Est	53	A2
148	Swords Business Park	02	E1
149	Tallaght Enterprise Centre	55	A1
150	The Liffey Trust Enterprise Centre	38	F2
151	Turnpike Ind Est see Ballymount Cross	45	A2
152	Unidare/Jamestown Business Park	24	E1
153	Weatherwell Ind Est	35	A4
154	Westlink Ind Est	36	E3
155	Docklands Innovation Park	39	A1
156	Western Ind Est	45	A1
157	Western Parkway Business Centre	45	B2
158	White Heather Ind Est	37	B4
159	White Swan Business Park	37	C4
160	Charlestown Centre	11	A4
162	Woodlawn Ind Est	12	F3
163	Sandyford Park	58	E2
164	Westpoint Buisness Park	08	F4
165	Blanchardstown Corporate Park	09	C3
166	Damastown Technology Park	08	E3
167	Avondale	49	A4
168	West Pier Business Campus	48	C4
169	Blackrock Business Park	49	A3
170	Naas Road Ind Est	36	E4
171	Park West Industrial Park	36	D4
172	Park West Enterprise Centre	35	C4
173	Park West Business Park	35	C4
174	Nangor Road Business Centre	35	C4
175	Riverview Business Centre	35	C4
176	Fonthill Retail Park	35	A2
177	Clondalkin Enterprise Centre	35	A3
178	Woodford Business Park	12	F3
179	Advance Business Park	12	F3
180	North Ring Business Park	12	F3
181	Furry Park Ind Est	12	E3
182	Merrywell Ind Est	45	A2
183	Parkway Business Centre	45	A2
184	Red Cow Business Park	45	A1
185	Swanward Business Centre	45	A2
186	Westgate Business Park	45	A3
187	Willow Business Park	45	A1
188	Merrywell Business Park	45	A2
189	Westway Centre	45	B2
190	Western Parkway Business Park	45	B2
191	Greenhills Centre	45	B4
192	Greenhills Business Park	45	B4
193	Greenhills Business Centre	45	B4
194	Sitecast Ind Est	45	B4
195	Taurus Business Park	45	B4
196	Balfe Road Industrial Est	45	C1
197	Calmount Business Park	45	B2
198	Plato Business Park	09	A3
199	Cruiserath Business Park	09	C3
200	College Business and Technology Park	09	C4
201	Northwest Business Park	10	D3
202	Millenium Business Park	10	E3
203	Stadium Ind Est	10	E4
204	Horizon Logistics	11	B2
205	Newcourt Business Park	11	A2
206	Century Business Park	11	B4
207	Mygan Park Industrial Park	11	B4
208	Jamestown Business Park	11	A4
209	North Park Business & Office Park	11	A4
210	Finglas Business Park	09	C3
211	Maynooth Business Campus	17	C4
212	City Junction Business Park	13	C4
213	Airport Business Park	13	A1
214	Royal Liver Retail Park	36	E4
215	City Link Business Park	36	E4
216	Kileen Industrial Park	36	D4
217	Dartmouth House Ind Centre	36	E3
218	Grange Castle Business Park	34	D4
219	Crag Avenue Industrial Centre	35	B4
220	Glasnevin Business Centre	24	D3
221	GlasnevinBusiness Park	24	D3
222	Tolka Valley Business Park	24	D3
223	Nutgrove Office Park	47	A4
224	Earlscourt Ind Est	47	B4
225	Churchtown Business Park	47	B4
226	Clonskeagh House Office Park	47	C2
227	Clonskeagh Square Office Park	47	C2
228	Beech Hill Office Campus	47	C2
229	Belfield Office Park	47	C2
230	Richview Park	47	C2
231	Dundrum Business Park	47	C3
232	Mill Lane Business Park	33	B1
233	The Red Cow Interchange Est	44	F2
234	Hewlett Packard Ind Park	32	F2
235	Greenogue Business Park	42	E4
236	Western Office Park	22	E1
237	Westend Retail Park	22	E2
238	Celbridge Industrial Est	31	C3
239	Grange Castle International Business Park	43	B1
240	Rock Enterprise Centre	43	B3
241	Baldonnel Business Park	43	A4
242	Green Isle Business Park	44	D3
243	Cookstown Ind Est The Extension	44	E4
244	Cookstown Square	44	F4
245	Cookstown Business Centre	44	F4
246	Killinardin Enterprise Park	54	F2
247	Brookfield Enterprise Centre	54	D1
248	Montone Business Park	44	F1
249	Western Business Park	44	F1
250	Oak Road Business Park	44	F1
251	Cherrywood Business Park	64	D1
252	Nutgrove Enterprise Park	57	A1
253	Central Park Business Park	58	E2
254	Solas Retail Park	67	C1
255	Bray Business Park	67	C4
256	Southern Cross Business Park	67	B4
257	Killarney Road Business Park	67	B3
258	Cedar Industrial Park	67	B4
259	Maltings Business Park	37	C3
260	Westland Square Business Park	38	E2
261	Leopardstown Office Park	58	E2
262	Crosbie Business Centre	38	F1
263	East Point Business Park	39	A1
264	St John's Court Office Park	25	B1
265	Palmgrove Ind Est	25	B2
266	Airside Business Park	02	D3
267	Swords Business Campus	02	D1
268	Aughrim Lane Ind Est	37	C1
269	The Courtyard Business Park	43	B2
270	Howth Junction Business Park	27	B1
271	Broomfield Business Park	03	B4
272	Concord Ind Est Naas Road	36	E4
273	Bluebell Business Centre	36	E4
274	Cranford Centre	48	D2
275	The Donnelly Centre	37	C3
276	Earlsfort Centre	38	E3
277	Avonbeg Ind Est	45	B1
278	The Harcourt Centre	38	D4
279	International Financial Services Centre (IFSC)	38	E2
280	Irish Life Centre	38	E2
281	Kinsealy Business Park	14	D1
282	Knockmitten Business Park	44	F1
283	Kilcarberry Industrial Park	43	A1
284	Mount Pleasant Ind Est	47	A1
285	Northern Cross Business Park	11	A4
286	St Margaret's Business Park	11	A4
287	S.P.A.D.E. Unemployment Enterprise Centre	37	C2
288	South City Executive Park	46	E1
289	The Square Ind Complex	54	F1
290	Terenure Business Park	46	F2
291	Glenageary Office Park	60	D2
292	Crumlin Business Park	46	E1
293	Cashel Business Centre	46	E2
294	Robinhood Business Park	45	A1
295	Airside Retail Park	01	C3
296	Great Keppel Business Centre	15	A1
297	Crosslands Business Park	45	A2
298	Jamestown Little Ind Est	11	A4
300	Barbeque Poultry Business Park	64	E3
301	Base Enterprise Centre	09	A4
302	Damastown Industrial Park	08	F3
303	Hollywood Business Park	09	C4
304	Terenure Enterprise Centre	46	F2
305	Whitestown Ind Est	54	F1
306	South City Business Park	54	F2
307	Alltech Technology Park	06	E2
308	Bow Bridge Business Centre	37	B3
309	Manor Street Business Park	37	C1
310	Port Tunnel Business Park	13	A4
311	Clonshaugh Business & Technology Park	13	A4
312	Kingswood Business Park	43	B3
313	The Hub Logistics Park	7	C1
314	Kore Development Park	36	E4
315	Goldenbridge Ind Est	36	F3

Due to limitations imposed by scale it has not been possible to include all street names on the map pages. Entries in the index prefixed by * are not shown on the map but are given a grid square reference and a bracketed indication as to its nearest location.

ABBREVIATIONS USED IN THIS INDEX

Apartments	Apts
Avenue	Ave
Crescent	Cres
Saint	St.

STREET NAME	PAGE / GRID REFERENCE	STREET NAME	PAGE / GRID REFERENCE	STREET NAME	PAGE / GRID REFERENCE	STREET NAME	PAGE / GRID REFERENCE
A		Acorn Drive	57 B1	Albert Ave	68 D2	Allendale Lawn	21 B1
		Acorn Road	57 B1	Albert College Ave	25 A2	Allendale Place	21 B1
1 Branch Road South	39 A2	Acres Road (Phoenix Park)	36 F2	Albert College Court	25 A2	Allendale Rise	21 B1
2 Branch Road North	39 B2	*Adair (off Sandymount Ave)	39 A4	Albert College Cres	25 A2	Allendale Square	21 B2
2 Branch Road North Extension	39 B1	*Adair Lane (off Aston Place)	71 B4	Albert College Drive	25 A2	Allendale Terrace	21 B1
2 Branch Road South	39 A2	*Adair Terrace		Albert College Grove	25 A2	Allendale View	21 B1
3 Branch Road South	39 A2	(on Saint Joseph's Parade)	71 A1	Albert College Lawn	25 A2	Allendale Walk	21 B1
4 Branch Road South	39 B2	Adam Court (off Grafton Street)	75 B1	Albert College Park	25 A2	Allenton Ave	55 A3
*A.W. Pugin House		Adams Town Court	34 D2	Albert Court		*Allenton Cres (off Allenton Road)	55 A2
(off Stonepark Court)	46 F4	Adamstown Ave	33 C4	(Grand Canal Street Lower)	76 E1	Allenton Drive	55 A3
Abberley	64 E1	Adamstown Park	33 C3	Albert Court (Sandycove Road)	60 E1	Allenton Gardens	55 A3
*Abberley Square Apts		Adamstown Road	34 D2	*Albert Park (off Hudson Road)	60 E1	Allenton Green	55 A3
(off Belgard Road)	54 F1	Adare Ave	26 E1	Albert Place East	76 E1	Allenton Lawns	55 A2
Abbey Cottages	71 B4	Adare Drive	26 E1	Albert Place West	75 B3	Allenton Park	55 A2
Abbey Court (Killester)	26 E3	Adare Green	26 E1	Albert Road Lower	60 E1	*Allenton Road (on Oldcourt Road)	55 B3
Abbey Court (Celbridge)	31 C4	Adare Park	26 E1	Albert Road Upper	60 E2	Allenton Way	55 A3
*Abbey Court		Adare Road	26 E1	*Albert Terrace (Charlemont Street)	75 B3	Allies River Road	67 A1
(off Abbey Road Monkstown)	59 B1	Addison Ave	24 F3	*Albert Terrace (off Crofton Road)	50 D4	Allingham Street	74 E2
Abbey Drive	24 D4	Addison Drive	24 F3	Albert Walk	67 C2	*Alma Court (off Alma Road)	49 B4
Abbey Green	31 C4	*Addison Hall (off Addison Lane)	24 F3	Aldborough House	72 D2	*Alma Park	
Abbey House	8 D3	*Addison Lane	24 F3	Aldborough Parade	72 D2	(off Carrickbrennan Road)	49 C4
Abbey Lane	31 C4	Addison Park	24 F3	Aldborough Place	72 D2	*Alma Place	
Abbey Park (Killester)	26 E3	*Addison Place (off Botanic Ave)	25 A3	Aldborough Square		(off Carrickbrennan Road)	49 C4
Abbey Park (Baldoyle)	27 C1	Addison Road	25 C4	(off Aldborough Place)	72 D2	Alma Road	49 B4
Abbey Park (Kill O'The Grange)	59 B1	Adelaide Court	75 B3	Aldemere	21 B2	*Alma Terrace	
Abbey Park (Celbridge)	31 C4	Adelaide Mews	48 E1	Alden Drive	27 C1	(off Mountplesant Ave Upper)	47 A1
Abbey Road	59 B1	Adelaide Road (Leeson Street)	75 B3	Alden Park	27 C1	Almeida Ave	73 C1
Abbey Street (Howth)	30 D1	Adelaide Road (Dún Laoghaire)	60 E1	Alden Road	27 C1	Almeida Terrace	73 C2
Abbey Street Lower	71 C3	Adelaide Road (Bray)	67 C2	Alder Court	4 D4	Alone Walk	26 E2
Abbey Street Middle	71 B4	*Adelaide Square (Peter Street)	75 A1	Alder Lodge	23 A4	Alpine Heights	44 D1
Abbey Street Old	71 C3	Adelaide Street	50 D4	Alderpark Court	54 F1	Alpine Rise	44 E4
Abbey Street Upper	71 B4	Adelaide Terrace		Alderwood Ave	54 E1	Altadore	60 D2
*Abbey Terrace (on Abbey Street)	30 D1	(off Brookfield Road)	73 C2	Alderwood Close	54 E1	Altamont Hall	47 C4
*Abbey Vale (Botanic Ave)	25 B4	*Adelaide Terrace		Alderwood Court	54 E1	Altham Court	73 A1
Abbey View	59 B1	(off Adelaide Road Dún Laoghaire)	60 E1	Alderwood Drive	54 F1	*Altham Court (Grattan Cres)	36 F3
Abbeydale	34 F3	*Adelaide Villas		Alderwood Green	54 E1	*Alverno (off Castle Ave)	39 B1
Abbeydale Close	34 F3	(off Adelaide Road Dún Laoghaire)	60 E1	Alderwood Grove	54 F1	Ambassador Court	
Abbeydale Cres	34 F3	Adelaide Villas (Bray)	67 C2	Alderwood Lawn	54 E1	(off Herbert Road)	76 E3
Abbeydale Gardens	34 F3	Admiral Brown Walk	72 E4	Alderwood Park	54 F1	Amber Vale	44 E4
Abbeydale Park	34 F3	Admiral Court		Alderwood Rise	54 E1	Amberwood	9 A4
Abbeydale Rise	34 F3	(off Willie Nolan Road)	15 A4	Alderwood Way	54 F1	*Amiens Square Apts	
Abbeydale Walk	34 F3	Admiral Park	15 A4	Aldrin Walk	26 E1	(Amiens Street)	72 D3
Abbeyfarm	31 C4	Adrian Ave	46 F1	*Alen Hall		Amiens Street	72 D3
Abbeyfield (Killester)	26 E3	*Aengus Hall		(off Belgard Square West)	54 F1	An Crannog	60 D3
Abbeyfield (Clonskeagh)	47 B2	(off Belgard Square West)	54 F1	Alensgrove	32 F2	Analands	64 D4
Abbeyfield Lawns	26 E3	Affollus	5 C3	Alexander Court Apts	76 D1	*Anastasia Lane	
Abbeylea Ave	1 C1	Aghards Road	31 C2	Alexander Terrace (North Wall)	72 F3	(off Sorrento Road)	60 F2
Abbeylea Close	1 C1	Aideen Ave	46 E2	*Alexander Terrace (Novara Ave)	67 C2	Anglers Rest	47 C1
Abbeylea Drive	1 C1	Aideen Drive	46 E2	Alexandra Court	47 C4	Anglesea Ave	49 A3
Abbeylea Green	1 C1	Aideen Place	46 E2	Alexandra Place	72 F2	*Anglesea House	
Abbeyvale Ave	1 B1	Aikenhead Terrace	39 A3	Alexandra Quay		(off Serpentine Ave)	39 A4
Abbeyvale Close	1 B1	Aiken's Village	58 D3	(Alexandra Basin)	39 A2	*Anglesea Lane (off Corrig Ave)	50 D4
Abbeyvale Court	1 B1	*Ailesbury (off Shanowen Road)	25 B1	*Alexandra Quay		Anglesea Park	60 E2
Abbeyvale Cres	1 B1	*Ailesbury Close		(off York Road, Ringsend)	39 A2	Anglesea Road	76 F4
Abbeyvale Drive	1 B2	(off Ailesbury Road)	48 D1	Alexandra Road	39 A2	Anglesea Row	71 A3
Abbeyvale Green	1 B2	Ailesbury Drive	48 D1	Alexandra Road Extension	39 C2	Anglesea Street	71 B4
Abbeyvale Grove	1 B1	Ailesbury Gardens	48 E1	*Alexandra Terrace (Portobello)	75 A3	Anley Court	34 E1
Abbeyvale Lawn	1 B1	Ailesbury Grove (Donnybrook)	48 D1	Alexandra Terrace (Terenure)	46 F2	Ann Devlin Ave	46 E4
Abbeyvale Place	1 B1	Ailesbury Grove (Dundrum)	57 B1	Alexandra Terrace (Dundrum)	47 C4	Ann Devlin Drive	46 E4
Abbeyvale Rise	1 B1	Ailesbury Lane		*Alexandra Villas		Ann Devlin Park	56 E1
Abbeyvale View	1 B2	(off Ailesbury Road)	48 D1	(off Dundrum Road)	47 C4	Ann Devlin Road	46 E4
Abbeyvale Way	1 B2	Ailesbury Lawn	57 B1	*Alexandra Walk Apts		Anna Livia Apts	74 E1
Abbeywood	34 F3	Ailesbury Mews	48 E1	(Wood Street)	75 A1	Anna Villa	47 B1
Abbeywood Ave	34 F3	Ailesbury Park	48 E1	Alfie Byrne House	71 B2	*Annabeg (off Wyattville Road)	60 D4
Abbeywood Close	34 F3	Ailesbury Road	48 D1	Alfie Byrne Road	72 F1	Annacrivey	65 B3
Abbeywood Court	34 E3	Ailesbury Wood	48 D1	All Hallows Green	25 B3	*Annadale	
Abbeywood Cres	34 F3	Airfield Court	48 D2	*All Hallows Lane		(off Churchtown Road Upper)	47 B4
Abbeywood Park	34 F3	*Airfield Drive		(off All Hallows Square)	25 B3	*Annadale Ave	
Abbeywood Way	34 F3	(off Churchtown Road)	47 B4	All Hallows Square	25 B3	(off Philipsburgh Ave)	25 C4
Abbots Hill	3 C3	Airfield Park	48 D2	All Saint's Close	27 A3	Annadale Cres	25 C3
Abbotstown Ave	23 C2	Airfield Road	46 F2	All Saints Drive	27 A3	Annadale Drive	25 C3
Abbotstown Drive	23 C1	Airlie Heights	33 B2	All Saints Park	27 A3	Annagh Court	22 F1
Abbotstown Road	24 D2	Airpark Ave	56 E2	All Saints Road	26 F3	Annaghaskin	66 D1
Abby Well	14 D1	Airpark Close	56 E2	Allen Park Drive	58 E1	Annaly Close	21 B1
Abercorn Road	72 E3	Airpark Court	56 E2	Allen Park Road	58 E1	Annaly Court	21 B1
*Abercorn Square		Airpark House	56 E2	Allen Terrace (off Avondale Ave)	70 F1	Annaly Drive	21 B1
(off Inchicore Terrace South)	36 F3	Airpark Rise	56 E2	Allendale Close	21 B2	Annaly Grove	21 B1
*Abercorn Terrace		Airside	2 D3	Allendale Copse	21 B1	Annaly Road	24 F4
(off Inchicore Terrace South)	36 F3	Airton Close	45 A4	Allendale Court	21 B1	Annaly Terrace	21 B1
Aberdeen Street	70 D3	Airton Road	45 A4	Allendale Drive	21 B1	Annamoe Drive	70 E1
Abington	2 F3	*Airton Terrace		Allendale Elms	21 B1	Annamoe Parade	70 E1
Accommodation Road	19 C4	(off Greenhills Road)	45 A4	Allendale Glen	21 B1	Annamoe Park	70 E1
Achill Road (Drumcondra)	25 B3	Albany Ave	49 B4	Allendale Green	21 B1	Annamoe Road	70 D1
Achill Road (Loughlinstown)	64 E1	Albany Court	64 E1	Allendale Grove	21 B1	Annamoe Terrace	70 E1
		Albany Road	47 B1	Allendale Heath	21 B1	Annaville Ave	59 A1

STREET NAME	PAGE / GRID REFERENCE		STREET NAME	PAGE / GRID REFERENCE		STREET NAME	PAGE / GRID REFERENCE		STREET NAME	PAGE / GRID REFERENCE
Annaville Close	47	C4	Ardagh Park Road	59	A1	Arranmore Ave	71	A1	Ashleigh Court (Celbridge)	32	D3
*Annaville Grove			Ardagh Road	73	C4	Arranmore Road	47	C1	Ashleigh Green	22	F3
(off Annaville Park)	47	C3	Ardara Ave	14	D4	Artane	26	E2	Ashleigh Grove (Maynooth)	17	B4
Annaville Lodge	47	C4	Ardbeg Cres	26	E2	*Artane Cottages Lower			Ashleigh Grove (Blanchardstown)	22	F3
Annaville Park	47	C4	Ardbeg Drive	26	E2	(off Malahide Road)	26	E2	Ashleigh Lawn	3	B3
*Annaville Residence Apts			Ardbeg Park	26	E2	*Artane Cottages Upper			Ashley Ave	2	D2
(off Annaville Terrace)	47	C3	Ardbeg Road	26	E2	(off Malahide Road)	26	E2	Ashley Drive	2	D2
Annaville Terrace	47	C3	*Ardbrugh Close			*Arthur Griffith Court			Ashley Grove	2	D2
Anne Street North	71	A3	(off Ardbrough Road)	60	F2	(off Esker Road at			*Ashley Heights		
Anne Street South	75	B1	Ardbrugh Road	60	F2	Arthur Griffith Park)	34	D2	(East of Dargle Heights)	67	B2
Anner Road	73	B2	*Ardbrugh Villas			Arthur Griffith Park	34	D3	Ashley Rise	4	D4
Anne's Bridge	17	C1	(off Ardbrough Road)	60	F2	*Arundel (off Monkstown Valley)	49	B4	Ashling Close	73	C4
Anne's Lane	75	B1	Ardcian Park	1	C1	Asdill's Row (off Temple Bar)	71	B4	Ashling Court	47	B1
Annesley Ave	72	E1	Ardcollum Ave	26	E2	Asgard Apts	30	D1	Ashling Heights	22	E1
Annesley Bridge (Tolka River)	72	E1	*Ardee Court (Ardee Row)	74	F2	Asgard Park	30	D2	Ashmount	9	A4
Annesley Bridge Road	72	E1	Ardee Grove	75	B4	Asgard Road (Grand Canal Dock)	72	E4	Ashmount Court	73	B1
Annesley Close	72	E1	Ardee Road	75	B4	Asgard Road (Howth)	30	D2	Ashton Ave (Swords)	1	Inset
*Annesley Mews			Ardee Row	74	F2	Ash Grove (Meath Street)	74	F1	Ashton Ave (Knocklyon)	56	D1
(off Annesley Park)	47	B1	Ardee Street (The Coombe)	74	F2	Ash Park Ave	34	E3	Ashton Close (Swords)	1	Inset
Annesley Park	47	B1	Ardee Street (Bray)	67	B2	Ash Park Court	34	E3	Ashton Close (Knocklyon)	56	D1
Annesley Place	72	E1	Ardeen	33	C2	Ash Park Grove	34	E2	Ashton Court	1	Inset
Annfield	22	D3	Ardeevin Ave	33	C2	Ash Park Heath	34	E2	Ashton Drive	1	Inset
Annfield Court	22	D3	Ardeevin Court	33	C2	Ash Street	74	F1	Ashton Green	1	Inset
Annfield Cres	22	D3	Ardeevin Drive	33	C2	Ashberry	34	D3	Ashton Grove (Swords)	1	Inset
Annfield Drive	22	D3	Ardeevin Road	60	F2	Ashbrook (Ashtown)	23	C3	Ashton Grove (Knocklyon)	56	D1
Annfield Lawn	22	D4	*Ardeevin Terrace			Ashbrook (Clontarf)	26	D4	Ashton Lawn	56	D1
Annsbrook	47	C2	(off Ardeevin Road)	60	F2	Ashbrook (Bray)	67	C2	Ashton Lawns	1	Inset
Annville Drive	58	E1	*Ardenza Park (off Seapoint Ave)	49	B3	Ashbrook (Celbridge)	32	E3	Ashton Park	49	B4
Apollo Way	26	D1	*Ardenza Terrace			*Ashbrook Terrace (Ranelagh)	47	B1	Ashton Rise	1	Inset
*Appian Close (on Leeson Park)	76	D4	(off Seapoint Ave)	49	B3	*Ashbrook Terrace			Ashton Wood	67	A3
Apples Road	58	D2	Ardglas Estate	57	C1	(off Sallymount Ave)	47	B1	Ashtown	23	C3
Applewood Ave East	1	Inset	Ardilaun	14	F1	*Ashbrook Villas (Ranelagh)	47	B1	Ashtown Court	23	C4
Applewood Ave West	1	Inset	Ardilaun Road	72	D1	Ashbury Park	67	C2	Ashtown Gate (Phoenix Park)	23	B4
Applewood Birch	1	Inset	*Ardilaun Square			Ashcroft	27	A2	Ashtown Gate Road (Phoenix Park)	23	B4
Applewood Court	1	Inset	(off Sackville Ave)	72	D1	*Ashcroft Court			Ashtown Grove	23	C4
Applewood Cres	1	Inset	Ardilea Downs	48	D4	(adjacent Blakestown Drive)	22	D1	Ashtown Lodge	23	C4
Applewood Drive (Swords)	1	Inset	Ardilea Wood	48	D4	*Ashcroft Grove			Ashtown Road	23	B3
Applewood Main Street	1	Inset	Ardlea Road	26	E2	(adjacent Blakestown Drive)	22	D1	Ashtowngate	23	C3
Applewood Mews	1	Inset	Ardlui Park	59	A1	Ashdale Ave	46	F2	*Ashurst (off Mount Merrion Ave)	48	E4
Applewood Place	1	Inset	Ardmeen Park	59	A1	Ashdale Close	2	E3	Ashurst (Ballybrack)	64	E1
Applewood Square	1	Inset	Ardmore Ave	70	D1	Ashdale Gardens	46	F2	Ashville Close	34	E1
Aranleigh Court	56	F1	Ardmore Close	26	D2	*Ashdale Park (off Ashdale Road)	46	F2	Ashwood Ave	43	C1
Aranleigh Dell	57	A1	Ardmore Cres (Artane)	26	D2	Ashdale Road (Swords)	2	E3	Ashwood Close	43	C1
Aranleigh Gardens	56	F1	Ardmore Cres (Bray)	67	B2	Ashdale Road (Terenure)	46	F2	Ashwood Drive	44	D1
Aranleigh Mount	56	F1	Ardmore Drive	26	D1	Ashe Court	2	E2	Ashwood Lawns	44	D1
Aranleigh Park	57	A1	Ardmore Grove	26	D1	Ashfield	46	D4	Ashwood Park	44	D1
Aranleigh Vale	56	F1	Ardmore Lawn	67	B3	Ashfield Ave (Clondalkin)	44	F3	Ashwood Road	44	D1
Arás na Cluaine	35	B4	Ardmore Park (Artane)	26	D2	Ashfield Ave (Ranelagh)	47	B1	Ashwood Way	44	D1
Aravon Court	68	D2	Ardmore Park			Ashfield Close (Clondalkin)	44	F3	Ashworth Place		
Arbour Court	70	D3	(Kill O'The Grange)	59	C1	Ashfield Court (Mulhuddart)	9	A4	(off Mount Drummond Ave)	75	A4
Arbour Hill	70	E3	Ardmore Park (Bray)	67	B2	Ashfield Court (Ballymorris)	67	B4	Aspen Drive	2	E3
Arbour Place	70	E3	Ardmore Wood	67	B3	Ashfield Drive (Clondalkin)	44	F3	Aspen Park (Kinsealy Court)	2	E3
Arbour Terrace	70	D3	Ardoyne Mews			Ashfield Gardens	9	A4	*Aspen Park (off Carriglea Ave)	59	C1
Arbutus Ave	74	F4	(off Claremont Road)	76	E4	Ashfield Green (Huntstown)	8	F4	Aspen Road	2	E3
*Arbutus Grove (off Beech Road)	67	B1	Ardpatrick Road	24	D4	Ashfield Grove	9	A4	Aspen Wood	21	C2
Arbutus Place	75	A3	*Ardtona Ave			Ashfield Lawn	8	F4	Aspin Ave	21	C2
Archers Wood	8	F4	(off Churchtown Road Lower)	47	B4	Ashfield Park (Huntstown)	9	A4	Aspin Lawns	22	D2
*Archway Court			Arena Road	58	E2	Ashfield Park (Clondalkin)	44	F3	Assumpta Park	64	E3
(off Mountjoy Street)	71	A2	Argus House	74	F4	Ashfield Park (Terenure)	46	F2	Aston Place	71	B4
Ard Cluain	8	D3	*Argyle House Apts			Ashfield Park (Booterstown)	48	E2	Aston Quay	71	B4
Ard Lorcain	58	F1	(off Claremont Road)	39	A4	Ashfield Road (Ranelagh)	47	B1	Astor Hall	71	C4
*Ard Lorcain Villas			Argyle Road	76	E4	Ashfield Way (Huntstown)	9	A4	Athgoe	51	C1
(off Ard Lorcain Stillorgan)	58	F1	*Argyle Square			Ashford Apts	24	F3	*Athgoe Drive		
Ard Mhacha	54	F2	(off Marlborough Road)	47	C1	Ashford Cottages	70	D2	(off Beechfield Manor)	64	E2
Ard Mhuire Park	60	E2	*Arkendale Court			Ashford Place	70	D2	Athgoe North	51	B1
Ard Mor Ave	53	C1	(off Arkendale Road)	60	E1	Ashford Street	70	D2	Athgoe Road (Newcastle)	41	C4
Ard Mor Close	53	C1	Arkendale Road	60	E1	Ashgrove (Baskin Lane)	13	C1	Athgoe Road (Shankill)	64	E2
Ard Mor Court	53	C1	*Arkendale Woods			Ashgrove (Celbridge)	31	C2	Athgoe South	51	B2
Ard Mor Cres	53	C1	(off Arkendale Road)	60	E1	Ashgrove (Tallaght)	54	E1	Atlumney Villas	75	B4
Ard Mor Dale	53	C1	Arkle Road	58	E2	Ashgrove (Kill O'The Grange)	59	C1	*Atmospheric Road		
Ard Mor Drive	53	C1	*Arkle Square (off Brewery Road)	58	F2	*Ashgrove Court			(off Castlepark Road)	60	E1
Ard Mor Green	53	C1	Arklow Street	70	D2	(off Sandyford Road)	57	C1	Aubrey	64	E3
Ard Mor Lawn	53	C1	Armagh Road	46	D1	*Ashgrove Terrace			Aubrey Grove	64	E3
Ard Mor Park	53	C1	Armstrong Street			(off Sandyford Road)	57	C1	Aubrey Park	64	E3
Ard Mor Walk	53	C1	(off Harold's Cross Road)	74	F4	Ashington Ave	24	D3	Auburn	26	D4
Ard na Glaise	48	F4	Armstrong Walk	26	E1	Ashington Close	24	D3	Auburn Ave (Castleknock)	23	A3
*Ard Na Gréine			Army Road	69	B3	Ashington Court	24	D3	Auburn Ave (Donnybrook)	47	C1
(off Orwell Road Rathgar)	47	A3	Arnold Grove	60	D2	Ashington Cres	23	C3	Auburn Ave (Cabinteely)	60	D3
Ard Na Gréine (Ballymorris)	67	B4	Arnold Park	60	D2	Ashington Dale	24	D3	Auburn Close (Castleknock)	23	A3
Ard na Mara	3	A3	Arnott Street	75	A2	Ashington Gardens	24	D3	Auburn Close (Cabinteely)	60	D3
Ard na Meala	12	D4	Arran Ave	64	E1	Ashington Green	24	D3	Auburn Drive (Castleknock)	23	A3
Ard Rí Place	70	E3	Arran Close	64	E1	Ashington Grove	24	D3	Auburn Drive (Cabinteely)	60	D3
Ard Rí Road	70	E3	Arran Court	22	F1	Ashington Heath	24	D3	Auburn Green	23	A3
Ardagh Ave	59	A1	Arran Drive	64	E1	Ashington Mews	24	D3	Auburn Grove	3	A3
*Ardagh Close			Arran Green	67	C2	Ashington North	24	D3	*Auburn House Apts		
(off Ardagh Park Road)	59	A1	Arran Quay	70	F4	Ashington Park	24	D3	(off Rathmines Road Upper)	47	A1
Ardagh Court	58	F1	Arran Quay Apts	70	F4	Ashington Rise	23	C3	*Auburn Park Apts		
Ardagh Cres	59	A1	*Arran Quay Terrace (Arran Quay)	70	F4	Ashlawn	57	C1	(off Navan Road / Auburn Ave)	23	A3
Ardagh Drive	59	A1	Arran Road	25	B3	Ashlawn Court	67	B2	*Auburn Road (off Victoria Ave)	47	C1
Ardagh Grove	59	A1	Arran Square Apts	70	F4	Ashlawn Park	60	D4	*Auburn Road		
Ardagh Park	59	A1	Arran Street East	71	A4	Ashleigh Court (Castleknock)	22	F3	(off Churchview Road)	60	D3
			Arran Street West	70	F4						

STREET NAME	PAGE / GRID REFERENCE

STREET NAME — PAGE / GRID REFERENCE

Auburn Road
(off Woodlands Road) — 60 D3
Auburn Street — 71 A2
Auburn Terrace (Old Kilmainham) — 73 C1
Auburn Villas (Rathgar) — 47 A2
*Auburn Villas
(Pearse Square, Bray) — 67 B2
Auburn Walk — 70 D2
Aughavannagh Road — 74 E4
Aughrim Court — 70 E3
Aughrim Lane — 70 E2
Aughrim Place — 70 D2
Aughrim Street — 70 D2
Aughrim Villas — 70 D2
Augustine Court
(Saint Margaret'sTce) — 74 F1
*Augustine Villas
(near Meath Place) — 67 C2
Aulden Grange — 12 F4
Aungier Lane — 75 B2
Aungier Place — 75 B2
Aungier Street — 75 B1
Austin's Cottages — 72 E1
*Avalon
(off Brighton Road Foxrock) — 59 A3
Avalon Apts — 29 B1
Ave Maria Road — 74 D2
Ave Road — 75 A3
*Avila Apts (off Carysfort Ave) — 59 A1
Avila Park — 23 C1
Avila Park Gardens — 23 C1
Avoca Apts — 32 D3
Avoca Ave (Stillorgan) — 48 F4
Avoca Ave (Dún Laoghaire) — 67 C3
Avoca Court — 48 F4
*Avoca Hall (off Avoca Park) — 49 A4
Avoca Park — 48 F4
Avoca Place — 49 A3
Avoca Road — 48 F4
Avoca Terrace — 48 F4
Avoca Wood — 48 F4
*Avonbeg Court
(off Avonbeg Drive) — 55 A1
Avonbeg Drive — 55 A1
Avonbeg Gardens — 55 B1
Avonbeg Park — 55 A1
Avonbeg Road — 55 B1
Avondale — 20 D4
*Avondale Apts (Lurgan Street) — 71 A3
Avondale Ave — 70 F1
Avondale Court (Blackrock) — 49 A4
*Avondale Court
(off Albert Road Lower) — 60 E1
*Avondale Court Apts
(Avondale Park) — 9 A3
Avondale Cres — 60 E2
Avondale House — 71 C2
Avondale Lawn — 49 A4
*Avondale Mews (off Kirkwood) — 39 A4
Avondale Park (Raheny) — 27 A2
*Avondale Park
(off Carysfort Ave Blackrock) — 49 A4
Avondale Park (Dalkey) — 60 E2
Avondale Park (Dún Laoghaire) — 67 B3
Avondale Park (Mulhuddart) — 9 A3
Avondale Road (Phibsborough) — 70 F1
Avondale Road (Dalkey) — 60 D2
Avondale Square — 7 B2
Avondale Terrace — 45 C2
Avonmore — 59 A2
*Avonmore Ave
(off Avonmore Road) — 55 B1
Avonmore Close — 55 B1
Avonmore Drive — 55 B1
*Avonmore Green
(off Avonmore Close) — 55 B1
Avonmore Grove — 55 B1
Avonmore Park — 55 B1
Avonmore Road — 55 B1
Aylesbury — 55 A2
Aylmer Ave — 42 D4
Aylmer Heath — 42 D4
Aylmer Road — 42 D4
Ayrefield Ave — 26 F1
Ayrefield Court — 26 F1
Ayrefield Drive — 26 F1
Ayrefield Grove — 26 F1
*Ayrefield Park (off Ayrefield Road) — 26 F1
Ayrefield Place — 26 F1
Ayrefield Road — 26 F1
Ayward Green — 24 D2

B

Bachelor's Walk — 71 B4
Bachelors Walk Apts — 71 B4
Bachelors Way — 71 B4
*Back Lane
(off Sandwith Street Upper) — 76 D1
Back Lane (High Street) — 75 A1
*Back Lane (Between College Street
and Main Street Baldoyle) — 15 A4
Back Lane (Maynooth) — 17 C3
Back Road — 3 B4
Baggot Bridge Court — 76 D2
Baggot Close — 75 C2
Baggot Court — 76 D2
Baggot Lane — 76 E3
*Baggot Rath House
(off Newbridge Ave) — 39 A3
Baggot Road — 23 C4
Baggot Street Lower — 76 D2
Baggot Street Upper — 76 E3
Baggot Terrace — 23 C4
Baggotrath Place — 76 D2
Bailey Green — 30 E3
Bailey Green Road — 30 E3
*Bailey View (off Harbour Road) — 60 F1
Bailey's Row — 72 D2
*Baker's Yard Apartment
(Portland Street North) — 71 C1
Balally Ave — 58 D1
Balally Close — 58 D1
Balally Drive — 58 D1
Balally Grove — 58 D2
Balally Hill — 58 D2
Balally Park — 58 D1
Balally Road — 57 C1
*Balally Terrace
(off Sandyford Road) — 58 D2
Balbutcher Drive — 11 C4
Balbutcher Lane — 11 C4
Balbutcher Lane Lower — 11 C4
Balbutcher Way — 11 C4
Balcurris Close — 12 D4
Balcurris Gardens — 12 D4
Balcurris Park East — 12 D4
Balcurris Park West — 12 D4
Balcurris Road — 12 D4
Baldoyle — 15 A4
Baldoyle Road — 28 D1
Balfe Ave — 45 C1
Balfe Road — 45 C1
Balfe Road East — 46 D1
Balfe Street — 75 B1
Balgaddy Road — 34 F3
Balglass Road — 30 D2
Balgriffin — 14 D3
Balgriffin Cottages — 14 D3
Balgriffin Park — 14 D3
Balgriffin Road — 14 D3
Balheary Road — 2 D1
Balkill Grove — 30 D2
Balkill Park — 30 D2
Balkill Road — 30 D2
Ballawley Court — 57 C2
Ballentree — 9 B2
Ballentree Ave — 9 B2
Ballentree Close — 9 B2
Ballentree Cres — 9 B2
Ballentree Drive — 9 B2
Ballentree Grove — 9 B3
Ballentree Lodge Apts — 9 B2
Ballentree Villa — 9 B3
*Ballinakelly Edge
(off Newcastle Boulevard) — 42 D4
*Ballinakelly Mews
(off Newcastle Boulevard) — 42 D4
*Ballinakelly Rise
(off Newcastle Boulevard) — 42 D4
Ballinakelly Village — 42 D4
Ballinclea Heights — 60 E3
Ballinclea Road — 60 D3
Ballinteer — 57 B2
Ballinteer Ave — 57 B2
Ballinteer Close — 57 B2
*Ballinteer Court
(off Ballinteer Ave) — 57 B2
Ballinteer Cres — 57 B2
Ballinteer Drive — 57 B2
Ballinteer Gardens — 57 C2
Ballinteer Grove — 57 B2
Ballinteer Park — 57 B2

Ballinteer Road (Dundrum) — 57 C1
Ballinteer Road (Delbrook Park) — 57 C2
Ballintrane Wood — 1 C2
Ballintyre Demesne — 57 B2
Ballintyre Downs — 57 B2
*Ballintyre Grove (Ballintyre) — 57 B2
Ballintyre Lane — 57 B2
Ballintyre Meadows — 57 B2
Ballintyre Square — 57 B2
Ballintyre Terrace — 57 B2
Ballintyre Walk — 57 B2
Ballintyre Woods — 57 B2
Ball's Lane — 71 A3
Ballsbridge (River Dodder) — 76 F4
*Ballsbridge Ave
(off Merrion Road) — 39 A4
*Ballsbridge Court — 76 F3
Ballsbridge Gardens
(off Merrion Road) — 76 F3
*Ballsbridge Park
(off Merrion Road) — 39 A4
Ballsbridge Terrace
(off Sandymount Ave) — 76 F4
Ballsbridge Wood — 76 F3
Ballybane — 43 A1
Ballybetagh — 62 F4
Ballybetagh Road — 62 E4
Ballyboden — 56 E1
Ballyboden Cres — 56 E1
Ballyboden Road — 56 E1
Ballyboden Way — 56 E1
Ballyboggan Road — 24 E3
Ballybough Ave — 72 D1
Ballybough Court — 72 D1
*Ballybough Lane (King's Ave) — 72 D1
Ballybough Road — 72 D1
Ballybrack (Village) — 60 E4
Ballybrack (Two Rock Mountain) — 61 B3
Ballybrew — 65 C2
Ballybride — 64 D3
Ballybride Road — 64 D3
Ballycoolin Road — 10 D4
Ballycorus — 63 B3
Ballycorus Road — 63 A2
Ballycullen Ave — 55 B2
*Ballycullen Cottages
(off Ballycullen Road) — 55 C2
Ballycullen Drive — 55 B2
Ballycullen Road — 55 C1
Ballydowd Grove — 34 E1
Ballydowd Manor — 34 E2
Ballyedmonduff
(Two Rock Mountain) — 61 C2
Ballyedmonduff (Stepaside) — 62 E1
Ballyedmonduff Road — 62 D1
Ballyfermot — 36 D3
Ballyfermot Ave — 36 D3
Ballyfermot Cres — 36 D3
Ballyfermot Drive — 36 D3
Ballyfermot Parade — 36 D3
Ballyfermot Road (Cherry Orchard) — 35 C3
Ballyfermot Road (Ballyfermot) — 36 E3
Ballygall Ave — 24 E1
Ballygall Cres — 24 E2
Ballygall Parade — 24 E2
Ballygall Place — 24 E2
Ballygall Road East — 24 F2
Ballygall Road West — 24 E1
Ballygihen Ave — 60 E1
*Ballygihen Villas
(off Sandycove Road) — 60 E1
Ballygoran — 18 E4
Ballygoran Court — 31 C2
Ballygoran View — 31 C2
Ballyhoy Ave — 27 A3
Ballymacartle — 13 C1
Ballymace Green — 46 E4
Ballymacoll — 6 D3
Ballymadrough Road — 2 F1
Ballymakealy Grove — 31 C4
Ballymakealy Lawns — 31 C4
Ballyman — 66 F1
Ballyman Lane (Carrickgollogan) — 63 C4
Ballyman Lane (Ballyman) — 66 F1
Ballyman Road — 66 F2
Ballymana — 54 E4
Ballymana Lane — 54 E4
*Ballymanagin Lane
(off Newlands Road) — 35 A4
*Ballymorris (off Killarney Road) — 67 B4
*Ballymoss Parade
(off Brewery Road) — 58 F2

Ballymoss Road — 58 E2
Ballymount Ave — 45 B2
*Ballymount Cottages
(off Ballymount Road Lower) — 45 B2
Ballymount Drive — 45 B2
Ballymount Road — 44 F3
Ballymount Road Lower — 45 B2
Ballymount Road Upper — 45 A2
Ballymount Square — 45 B2
Ballymun — 25 A1
Ballymun Road (M50 Junction 4) — 12 D4
Ballymun Road (Ballymun) — 25 A1
Ballymun Road (Glasnevin) — 25 A3
Ballynakelly Cottages — 42 D4
Ballynakelly Court — 42 D4
Ballynakelly Edge — 42 D4
Ballynakelly Green — 42 D4
Ballynakelly Mews — 42 D4
Ballynakelly Rise — 42 D4
Ballynakelly View — 42 D4
Ballynakelly Village — 42 D4
Ballyneety Road — 36 F3
*Ballynoe Court
(South of Kilbride Lane) — 67 B3
Ballyogan Ave — 58 F4
Ballyogan Close — 58 F4
Ballyogan Court — 58 F4
Ballyogan Cres — 58 F4
Ballyogan Drive — 58 F4
Ballyogan Estate — 58 F4
Ballyogan Green — 58 F4
Ballyogan Lawn — 58 F4
*Ballyogan Park
(off Ballyogan Drive) — 58 F4
Ballyogan Road — 58 F4
Ballyogen Vale — 59 A4
Ballyogen Wood — 59 A4
*Ballyolaf Manor (off Parkvale) — 57 C1
Ballyoulster Park — 32 E3
Ballyowen Ave — 34 F1
Ballyowen Court — 34 F1
Ballyowen Cres — 34 F1
Ballyowen Drive — 34 F1
Ballyowen Green — 34 F1
Ballyowen Grove — 34 F1
Ballyowen Hall — 34 F2
Ballyowen Lane — 34 F2
Ballyowen Lawn — 34 F1
Ballyowen Road — 34 F1
Ballyowen Square — 34 F2
Ballyowen View — 34 F1
Ballyowen Way — 34 F1
*Ballyroan Court
(off Knocklyon Drive) — 56 D1
Ballyroan Cres — 56 E1
Ballyroan Heights — 56 E1
Ballyroan Park — 56 D1
Ballyroan Road — 56 E1
Ballyshannon Ave — 25 C1
Ballyshannon Road — 26 D1
Ballystruan Lane — 12 D3
Ballytore Road — 46 F3
*Ballywaltrim Cottages
(Ballywaltrim Road) — 67 B4
Ballywaltrim Heights — 67 B3
Ballywaltrim Lane — 67 A4
Ballywaltrim Road — 67 B4
Ballywilliam Close — 67 B4
*Balnagowan (off Palmerston Park) — 47 B2
*Balrothery Cottages
(off Tallaght Road) — 55 C1
Balrothery Estate — 45 B4
Balscadden Road — 30 E1
Balscott — 41 C1
Bancroft Ave — 55 A1
Bancroft Close — 55 B1
*Bancroft Court
(off Bancroft Grove) — 55 B1
Bancroft Cres — 45 B4
Bancroft Downs — 45 A4
Bancroft Grove — 55 B1
Bancroft Park — 55 A1
Bancroft Road — 55 B1
Bangor Circle — 46 E1
Bangor Drive — 73 C4
Bangor Road — 46 E1
Bankside Cottages — 47 B2
Bann Road — 24 E3
Bannaville — 75 B4
Bannow Road — 24 E4
Banshee — 51 A2

STREET NAME	PAGE / GRID REFERENCE	STREET NAME	PAGE / GRID REFERENCE	STREET NAME	PAGE / GRID REFERENCE	STREET NAME	PAGE / GRID REFERENCE
Bantry Road	25 A3	*Bawnogue Cottages		*Beaumont House		Beechfield Heights	8 D4
Bantry Square	22 F1	(off Cherrywood Villas)	43 C1	(off Brighton Road)	46 F2	Beechfield Lawn	8 E4
Banville Ave	36 D4	Bawnogue Road	43 C1	Beaumont Road	25 C2	Beechfield Manor	64 E2
Barberstown Lane	1 A4	Bawnville Ave	55 A2	*Beaumont Wood		Beechfield Meadows	8 E4
Barclay Court	49 A3	Bawnville Close	55 A2	(off Ballyshannon Road)	25 C1	*Beechfield Mews	
Bargy Road	72 F2	Bawnville Drive	55 B2	*Beaupark Downs		(off Whitehall Road West)	46 D2
Barley Glen	54 F1	Bawnville Park	55 B2	(off Monkstown Valley)	49 B4	Beechfield Place	8 E4
Barnacoille Park	60 F1	Bawnville Road	55 A2	Beaupark Ave	14 E4	Beechfield Rise	8 E4
Barnamire	65 A4	Baymount Park	27 A4	Beaupark Close	14 E4	Beechfield Road (Clonee)	8 D4
Barnamore Cres	24 D3	Bayshore Lane	64 E1	Beaupark Cres	14 E4	Beechfield Road (Walkinstown)	45 C2
Barnamore Grove	24 D3	Bayside Boulevard North	27 C1	Beaupark Mews	14 E4	Beechfield View	8 E4
Barnamore Park	24 D3	Bayside Boulevard South	27 C1	Beaupark Place	14 E4	Beechfield Way	8 E4
Barnaslingan Lane	63 A3	*Bayside Cres (off Sarto Park)	27 C1	Beaupark Road	14 E4	Beechlawn	48 F3
Barneville Green	35 C3	Bayside Park	27 C1	Beaupark Row	14 E4	Beechlawn Ave (Coolock)	26 E1
Barneville Walk	35 C4	Bayside Square East	27 C1	Beaupark Square	14 E4	Beechlawn Ave (Ballinteer)	57 B1
Barnhall	32 F1	Bayside Square North	27 C1	Beaupark Street	14 E4	Beechlawn Close	26 E1
Barnhall Drive	32 F1	Bayside Square South	27 C1	Beaupark Terrace	14 E4	*Beechlawn Drive	
Barnhill Ave	60 E2	Bayside Square West	27 C1	Beauvale Park	26 D2	(Oscar Traynor Road)	26 E1
Barnhill Cross Road	34 D1	Bayside Walk	27 C1	Beaver Close	72 D2	Beechlawn Green	26 E1
*Barnhill Grove (off Barnhill Road)	60 F2	*Bayswater Terrace		Beaver Row	47 C1	Beechlawn Grove	26 E1
*Barnhill Lawn (off Barnhill Road)	60 E2	(off Breffni Road)	60 F1	Beaver Street	72 D2	*Beechlawn Manor	
*Barnhill Park		Baytownpark	6 E1	Beckett Hall	59 B4	(off Rathfarnham Road)	46 F2
(off Saval Park Gardens)	60 E2	Bayview (Loughlinstown)	64 E1	Beckett Way	35 C4	*Beechlawn Mews	
Barnhill Road	60 E2	*Bayview (near Bray Bridge)	67 C2	Bective Square	70 F1	(off Rathfarnham Road)	46 F2
*Barnhill Villas (on Barnhill Road)	60 F2	*Bayview (on Seapoint Road)	67 C2	*Bedford Court		Beechmount Drive (Windy Arbour)	47 C3
Barnville Park	35 C4	Bayview Ave	72 D1	(off Kimmage Road Lower)	46 E1	Beechpark	32 E1
Barnwell	21 A2	Bayview Close	64 E1	Bedford Lane (off Aston Quay)	71 B4	Beechpark Ave	26 E1
Barnwell Ave	21 A1	Bayview Court	64 E1	Bedford Row (off Aston Quay)	71 B4	Beechpark Close	23 A3
Barnwell Cres	21 A1	Bayview Cres	64 E1	Beech Drive	57 B1	Beechpark Court	26 E1
Barnwell Drive	24 F1	Bayview Drive	64 E1	Beech Grove (Lucan)	34 E2	Beechpark Orchard	23 A3
Barnwell Drive	21 A1	*Bayview Glade (Bayview)	64 E1	Beech Grove (Blackrock)	48 F2	Beechurst	67 B2
Barnwell Green	21 A1	Bayview Glen	64 E1	Beech Hill	47 C2	*Beechview	
Barnwell Lane	21 A1	Bayview Green	64 E1	Beech Hill Ave	47 C2	(off Edmondstown Road)	56 E2
Barnwell Lane	21 A1	Bayview Grove	64 E1	Beech Hill Court	47 C1	Beechwood	14 F1
Barnwell Road	21 A2	Bayview Lawn	64 E1	*Beech Hill Cres		Beechwood Ave Lower	47 B1
Barnwell Terrace	21 A1	Bayview Rise	64 E1	(off Beech Hill Drive)	47 C2	Beechwood Ave Upper	47 B1
Barnwell Way	21 A2	Beach Ave	39 A3	Beech Hill Drive	47 C2	Beechwood Close (Hartstown)	21 C1
*Baroma		Beach Drive	39 A3	Beech Hill Road	47 C2	Beechwood Close (Boghall Road)	67 C4
(off Kimmage Road Lower)	46 E2	Beach Park	15 A1	*Beech Hill Terrace		Beechwood Court	58 F1
Barrack Bridge	3 A2	Beach Road	39 A3	(off Beech Hill Drive)	47 C2	Beechwood Downs	21 C1
Barrack Court	52 F2	Beach View	27 C2	*Beech Hill Villas		*Beechwood Grove	
*Barrack Lane (off Irishtown Road)	39 A3	Beacon Court	58 D2	(off Beech Hill Drive)	47 C2	(off Beechwood Park)	60 D1
Barren Hill Cross Roads	29 C3	*Beacon Hill (off Nerano Road)	60 F2	Beech House (Sussex Road)	76 D3	*Beechwood House	
*Barrett Street		Beaconsfield Court	73 A1	Beech House (Swords)	1 Inset	(at Eaton Wood Square)	64 E2
(off York Road Dún Laoghaire)	49 C4	Bealing	9 B2	Beech Lawn	57 B1	Beechwood Lawn	60 D2
Barrogstown East	18 F4	Bealing Ave	9 B2	Beech Lodge	23 A4	Beechwood Lawns	52 F2
Barrogstown West	18 E4	Bealing Close	9 B3	Beech Park (Castleknock)	22 F3	*Beechwood Park	
*Barron Place (off Walsh Road)	25 A3	Bealing Cres	9 B2	Beech Park (Lucan)	34 E1	(off Dunville Ave Rathmines)	47 B1
Barrow Road	24 E3	Bealing Grove	9 B2	Beech Park (Cabinteely)	59 C4	Beechwood Park (Dún Laoghaire)	60 D1
Barrow Street	76 F1	Bealing Mews	9 B2	Beech Park Ave (Castleknock)	23 A3	Beechwood Road	47 B1
Barry Ave	24 D1	Bealing View	9 B2	Beech Park Ave (Deans Grange)	59 B2	Beggar's Bush Buildings	76 F2
Barry Close (off Barry Drive)	24 D1	Bealing Walk	9 B2	Beech Park Cres	23 A3	Beggars Bush Court	76 F2
Barry Drive	24 D1	Bealing Wood	9 B3	Beech Park Drive	59 B2	Belarmine	58 D4
Barry Green	24 D1	Bearna Park	58 D3	Beech Park Grove	59 B2	Belarmine Ave	58 D4
Barry Lane	21 A1	Beatty Grove	32 D2	Beech Park Lawn	23 A3	Belarmine Close	58 D4
Barry Park	24 D1	Beatty Park	32 D3	Beech Park Road	59 B2	Belarmine Court	58 D4
Barry Road	24 D1	Beatty's Ave		Beech Park Wood	32 E1	Belarmine Drive	58 D4
Barry's Park	2 D2	(off Sandymount Ave)	76 F3	Beech Road (Fox and Geese)	45 A1	Belarmine Grange	58 D4
Barryscourt Road	26 E1	Beauchamp	64 E4	Beech Road (Shankill)	64 E3	Belarmine Hall	58 D4
Barton Ave	56 F1	*Beaucourt (off Achill Road)	25 B3	Beech Road (Bray)	67 B1	Belarmine Heath	58 D4
*Barton Court		Beaufield	17 C4	Beech Row (Newlands Road)	35 A4	Belarmine Park	58 D4
(off Barton Road East)	57 A1	Beaufield Ave	17 C4	*Beech Row (off Nangor Road)	44 D1	Belarmine Place	58 D4
Barton Drive	56 F1	Beaufield Close	17 C4	*Beech Walk (off Brookwood)	56 E2	Belarmine Plaza	58 D4
Barton Road East	57 B1	Beaufield Cres	17 C4	Beechbrook Grove	14 D4	Belarmine Square	58 D4
Barton Road East Extension	57 A1	Beaufield Drive	17 C4	Beechcourt	60 D3	Belarmine Vale	58 D4
Barton Road Extension	57 A1	Beaufield Gardens	17 C4	Beechdale	7 B3	Belarmine Way	58 D4
Barton Road West	56 F1	Beaufield Green	17 C4	Beechdale Ave	55 B3	Belcamp Ave	13 B4
*Bartra Rock Apts		Beaufield Grove	17 C4	*Beechdale Close		Belcamp Cres	13 B4
(off Harbour Road)	60 F1	Beaufield Lawn	17 C4	(off Beechdale Ave)	55 B3	Belcamp Gardens	13 B4
Basin Grove	74 D1	Beaufield Manor	48 E4	Beechdale Court	55 B3	Belcamp Green	13 B4
Basin Lane Flats	74 D1	*Beaufield Mews		Beechdale Cres	55 B3	Belcamp Grove	13 B4
Basin Street Lower	74 D1	(off Beaufield Manor)	48 E4	Beechdale Lawn	55 B3	Belcamp Lane	13 C4
Basin Street Upper	74 D1	Beaufield Park	48 E4	*Beechdale Mews		Belcamp Park	13 A3
Basin View		*Beaufort (off Glasthule Road)	60 E1	(off Palmerston Road)	47 B1	Belclare Ave	11 C4
(off Basin Street Upper)	74 D2	*Beaufort Court		Beechdale Park	55 B3	Belclare Cres	11 C4
Baskin Cottages	13 C1	(off Beaufort Downs)	46 F4	Beechdale Place	55 C3	Belclare Drive	11 C4
Baskin Lane	13 B1	Beaufort Downs	46 F4	Beechdale Road	55 C3	Belclare Green	11 C4
Bass Place	76 D1	*Beaufort Villas		Beechdale Way	55 B3	Belclare Grove	11 C4
Bath Ave (Sandymount)	76 F2	(off Willbrook Road)	46 F4	Beeches		Belclare Lawns	11 C4
Bath Ave (Malahide)	3 C2	Beaumont	26 D1	(opposite Knockmaroon Gate)	36 D1	Belclare Park	11 C4
Bath Ave Gardens	76 F2	Beaumont Ave	47 B4	Beeches Park	60 E1	Belclare Terrace	11 C4
Bath Ave Place	76 F2	*Beaumont Close		Beeches Road	58 D1	Belclare View	11 C4
Bath Lane	71 B2	(off Beaumont Ave)	47 B4	Beechfield	8 D4	Belclare Way	11 C4
*Bath Place		Beaumont Cottages	34 D2	Beechfield Ave (Clonee)	8 D4	*Belfield Close (off Roebuck Road)	47 C3
(off Main Street Blackrock)	49 A3	*Beaumont Court		Beechfield Ave (Walkinstown)	45 C2	Belfield Court	48 D2
Bath Street	39 A3	(off Ballyshannon Road)	25 C1	Beechfield Close (Clonee)	8 D4	Belfield Downs	47 C4
Bawnlea Ave	54 D2	Beaumont Cres	26 D2	Beechfield Close (Walkinstown)	46 D2	Belfield Park Apts	48 E3
Bawnlea Close	54 D2	Beaumont Drive	47 B4	Beechfield Court	8 D4	Belfry Ave	53 C2
Bawnlea Cres	54 D2	Beaumont Gardens	48 F4	Beechfield Drive	8 D4	Belfry Close	53 C2
Bawnlea Drive	54 D2	Beaumont Grove	25 C2	Beechfield Green	8 D4	Belfry Court	53 C2
Bawnlea Green	54 D2	*Beaumont Hall (off The Park)	25 C2	*Beechfield Haven		Belfry Cres	53 C2
				(off Beechfield Manor)	64 E2		

STREET NAME	PAGE / GRID REFERENCE
Belfry Dale	53 C2
Belfry Downs	53 C2
Belfry Drive	53 C2
Belfry Gardens	53 C2
Belfry Green	53 C2
Belfry Grove	53 C2
Belfry Hall	53 C2
Belfry Lawn	53 C2
Belfry Lodge	53 C2
Belfry Manor	53 C2
Belfry Meadows	53 C2
Belfry Park	53 C2
Belfry Place	53 C2
Belfry Rise	53 C2
Belfry Road	53 C2
Belfry Square	53 C2
Belfry Terrace	53 C2
Belfry Walk	53 C2
Belfry Way	53 C2
*Belgard Close (off Garrynisk Road)	44 F3
Belgard Green	44 E4
Belgard Heights	44 F4
Belgard Road	44 E3
Belgard Square	54 F1
Belgard Square East	54 F1
Belgard Square North	54 F1
Belgard Square South	54 F1
Belgard Square West	54 F1
Belgrave Ave	47 B1
*Belgrave Court (off Mountpleasant Ave Upper)	47 A1
*Belgrave Mews (off Castlewood Ave)	47 A1
*Belgrave Place (off Belgrave Square West)	47 A1
*Belgrave Place (off Seapoint Ave Monkstown)	49 B4
Belgrave Road (Rathmines)	47 A1
Belgrave Road (Monkstown)	49 B4
Belgrave Square (Rathmines)	47 A1
Belgrave Square (Monkstown)	49 B4
Belgrave Square East (Rathmines)	47 A1
Belgrave Square East (Monkstown)	49 B4
Belgrave Square North (Rathmines)	47 A1
Belgrave Square North (Monkstown)	49 B4
Belgrave Square South (Rathmines)	47 A1
Belgrave Square South (Monkstown)	49 B4
Belgrave Square West (Rathmines)	47 A1
Belgrave Square West (Monkstown)	49 B4
*Belgrave Terrace (off Eaton Place Monkstown)	49 B4
*Belgrave Terrace (east side of text Meath)	68 D2
*Belgrave View (off Belgrave Ave)	47 B1
*Belgrave Villas (off Belgrave Ave Rathmines)	47 B1
*Belgrave Villas (east side of text Meath)	68 D2
Belgree	9 B2
Belgree Ave	9 B2
Belgree Close	9 B2
Belgree Court	9 B2
Belgree Drive	9 B2
Belgree Green	9 B2
Belgree Grove	9 B2
Belgree Heights	9 B2
Belgree Lawns	9 B2
Belgree Rise	9 B2
Belgree Walk	9 B2
Belgree Woods	9 B2
Belgrove Lawn	36 D2
Belgrove Park (Vernon Ave)	26 F4
Belgrove Park (Chapelizod)	36 D2
Belgrove Road	26 F4
*Bella Ave (off Bella Street)	72 D2
Bella Place (off Bella Street)	72 D2
Bella Street	71 C2
*Bella Vista Lodge (opposite Owendore Ave)	46 F4
Belleview Maltings	69 B4
Belleville	23 C4
Belleville Ave	47 A2
Belleville Court	59 C3
Bellevue	74 E1
Bellevue Ave (Merrion)	48 E2
Bellevue Ave (Dalkey)	60 E2
Bellevue Copse	48 E2
Bellevue Cottages (off Finglas Road Old)	24 F3
*Bellevue Court (off Dornden Park)	48 E2
Bellevue Park	48 E2
Bellevue Park Ave	48 E2
Bellevue Road	60 D2
Bellman's Walk	72 E3
Bell's Lane (off Merrion Row)	75 C2
Bell's Lane (Swords)	1 C2
Belmayne Ave	14 D3
Belmayne Park North	14 D3
Belmayne Park South	14 D4
Belmont (Stillorgan)	59 A1
Belmont (Irishtown)	67 C4
Belmont Ave	47 C1
*Belmont Court (off Belmont Ave)	47 C1
Belmont Gardens	47 C1
Belmont Green	58 F1
Belmont Grove	58 F1
Belmont Lawn	58 F1
Belmont Park (Raheny)	27 A2
*Belmont Park (off Donnybrook Road)	47 C1
Belmont Place (off Gardiner Street Middle)	71 C2
Belmont Square	27 A2
*Belmont Terrace (off Stillorgan Road)	58 F1
Belmont Villas	47 C1
*Belmount Court (off Philipsburgh Ave)	25 C4
Belton Park Ave	26 D3
Belton Park Gardens	26 D3
Belton Park Road	26 D3
Belton Park Villas	26 D3
*Belton Terrace (off Castle Street)	67 C2
Belvedere Court	71 B2
Belvidere Ave	71 C1
Belvidere Court	71 B1
Belvidere Place	71 C1
Belvidere Road	71 B1
Belvidere Square	71 B1
*Belville Apts (off ailesbury Road)	48 D1
Belvue	54 E1
Ben Edar Road	70 D2
*Ben Inagh Park (off Rock Road)	49 A3
Ben Of Howth	30 D3
*Benamore Court (off Newtownpark Ave)	49 A4
Benbulbin Ave	73 B3
Benbulbin Road	73 B3
Benburb Street	70 E4
Beneavin Court	24 F2
Beneavin Drive	24 F2
Beneavin Park	24 F1
Beneavin Road	24 F2
Bengal Terrace	24 F4
Benildus Ave	58 D1
Benmadigan Road	73 A3
Benson Street	72 F4
*Bentley Ave (off Bentley Road)	67 C4
Bentley Park	67 C4
Bentley Road	67 C4
*Bentley Villas (off George's Place)	49 C4
Berach Lodge	27 C2
Berehaven Place	27 B2
Beresford	25 B3
Beresford Ave	25 B3
Beresford Green	25 B3
Beresford Lane	71 C3
Beresford Lawn	25 B3
Beresford Place	71 C3
Beresford Street	71 A3
Berkeley Ave	71 A1
Berkeley Place	71 A1
Berkeley Road	71 A1
Berkeley Street	71 A1
Berkeley Terrace	76 F2
Bernard Curtis Court	36 F4
*Bernard Curtis House (off Bluebell Ave)	36 F4
Berryfield	34 D3
Berryfield Cres	24 D2
Berryfield Drive	24 D2
Berryfield Lane	67 A3
Berryfield Road	24 D2
Berrys Court	73 A2
Bertram Court	74 E2
Bertram Court	74 F1
Berwick Ave	1 B2
Berwick Court	1 B1
Berwick Cres	1 B1
Berwick Drive	1 B1
Berwick Grove	1 B1
Berwick Hall	47 A4
Berwick Lawn	1 B1
Berwick Place	1 B1
Berwick Rise	1 B2
Berwick View	1 B1
Berwick Walk	1 B2
Berwick Way	1 B1
Berystede	76 D4
Bessborough Ave	72 E1
Bessborough Court (Rathmines)	75 B4
*Bessborough Court (The Laurels)	46 F2
Bessborough Parade	75 B4
Besser Drive	35 B4
*Bethany House (off Gilford Road)	39 B4
Bethesda Place	71 B2
Bettyglen	27 B2
*Bettysford (off Monastery Road)	44 E1
Bettystown Ave	26 F3
Beverly Ave	56 D1
Beverly Court	26 F4
Beverly Cres	55 C2
Beverly Downs	55 C2
Beverly Drive	56 D2
Beverly Green	55 C2
Beverly Grove	56 D1
Beverly Heights	56 D2
Beverly Lawns	56 D2
Beverly Park	55 C1
Beverly Rise	55 C2
Bewley	34 E2
Bewley Ave	34 E2
Bewley Drive	34 E2
Bewley Grove	34 E2
Bewley Lawn	34 E2
Bianconi Ave	53 B1
Big Lane	32 D3
Bigger Road	45 C2
Bill Shelly Park	23 C2
Binn Eadair	29 A1
Binn Eadair Court	29 A1
Binn Eadair Cres	29 A1
Binn Eadair View	29 A1
Binns Bridge (Royal Canal)	71 B1
Birch Ave	58 D2
*Birch Dale (off Pine Ave Foxrock)	59 A2
*Birch Dale (off Carriglea Ave)	59 C1
Birch Grove	59 C1
Birchdale Close	2 E3
Birchdale Drive	2 E3
Birchdale Park	2 F3
Birchdale Road	2 E3
Birches Road	58 D1
Birchfield Ave	47 C4
Birchfield Court	47 C4
Birchfield Heights	47 C4
Birchfield Lawn	47 C4
Birchfield Park	47 C4
Birch's Lane	47 C4
Birchview Ave	45 A4
Birchview Close	45 A4
Birchview Court	45 A4
Birchview Drive	45 A4
Birchview Heights	45 A4
Birchview Lawn	45 A4
Birchview Rise	45 A4
Birchwood Close	44 E4
Birchwood Drive	54 E1
Birchwood Heights	54 E1
Bird Ave	47 C3
Biscayne	3 C3
Bishop Street	75 A2
Bishops Lane	62 F2
Bishop's Orchard	9 B2
Bishop's Orchard Boulevard	9 B2
Bishop's Orchard House Apts	9 B2
Bishop's Square	75 A2
*Bishopsmede Apts (Clanbrassil Terrace)	75 A2
Bissett's Loft Apts	3 B2
Bissett's Strand	3 B2
Black Street	69 C3
Blackberry Lane (Rathmines)	75 B4
Blackberry Lane (Portmarnock)	15 A1
Blackberry Rise	15 A1
*Blackburn Square (off Main Street Rathfarnham)	46 F4
Blackcourt Road	22 E1
Blackditch Drive	35 C3
Blackditch Road (Cherry Orchard)	35 C3
Blackditch Road (Le Fanu Park)	36 D3
Blackglen Court	58 D3
Blackglen Road	57 C3
Blackhall Court	70 E3
Blackhall Green	70 E3
Blackhall Little	5 B1
Blackhall Parade (Blackhall Street)	70 F3
Blackhall Place	70 E4
Blackhall Place Apts	70 E3
*Blackhall Square Apts (Brunswick Street North)	70 F3
Blackhall Street	70 F4
Blackhall View	70 E3
Blackhall Walk	70 F4
Blackheath Ave	26 F4
Blackheath Court	26 F4
Blackheath Drive	26 E4
Blackheath Gardens	26 E4
Blackheath Grove	26 E4
Blackheath Park	26 E4
Blackhorse Ave (North Circular Road)	69 C2
Blackhorse Ave (Ashtown)	23 C4
Blackhorse Grove	70 D2
Blackpitts	74 F2
Blackrock	49 A3
Blackthorn Ave	58 E2
Blackthorn Close (Portmarnock)	4 D4
*Blackthorn Close (off Spruce Ave Sandyford)	58 D2
*Blackthorn Court (off Moreen Ave)	58 D2
Blackthorn Drive	58 D2
*Blackthorn Green (off Moreen Ave)	58 D2
*Blackthorn Grove off Moreen Ave	58 D2
Blackthorn Hall	57 C3
Blackthorn Hill Ave	52 E2
Blackthorn Hill Close	52 E2
Blackthorn Hill Cres	52 E2
Blackthorn Hill Drive	52 E2
Blackthorn Hill View	52 E2
Blackthorn Road	58 D2
Blackwater Road	24 E3
Blackwood Close	21 A1
Blackwood Cres	21 A1
Blackwood Drive	21 A1
Blackwood Lane	3 C4
Blackwood Lawn	21 A1
Blackwood Mews	21 A1
Blackwood Park	21 A1
Blackwood Place	21 A1
Blackwoods	3 B4
Blakeney House (Swords)	2 E2
Blakeney House Mews (Howth)	30 E3
Blake's Court	22 D1
*Blakes Villas (on Grangegorman Lower)	70 F2
Blakestown Cottages	22 D1
Blakestown Drive	22 D1
Blakestown Road (Mulhuddart)	9 A4
Blakestown Road (Hartstown)	22 D1
Blakestown Way	22 D1
Blanchardstown	22 F2
Blanchardstown ByPass	22 F2
Blanchardstown Interchange	23 A2
Blanchardstown Road North	9 B4
Blanchardstown Road South	22 D2
Blarney Park	46 E1
Blasket Square	22 F1
Blessington Court	71 A2
Blessington Lane	71 A2
Blessington Place (off Saint Joseph's Parade)	71 A2
Blessington Road	53 C2
Blessington Street	71 A2
*Blind Quay Apts (Exchange Street Lower)	71 A4
Blizzard Apts	2 F3
Blood Stoney Road	72 F4
Bloom Court	74 F3
Bloomfield Ave (Morehampton Road)	76 D4
Bloomfield Ave (Portobello)	75 A3
Bloomfield Cottages	75 A3

STREET NAME	PAGE / GRID REFERENCE	STREET NAME	PAGE / GRID REFERENCE	STREET NAME	PAGE / GRID REFERENCE	STREET NAME	PAGE / GRID REFERENCE
*Bloomfield Lane (on Georges Street Lower)	50 D4	*Bow Bridge Court (on Kilmainham Lane)	73 C1	Brian Ave	25 C4	Broadford Road	57 B2
Bloomfield Park (Morehampton Road)	76 E4	*Bow Bridge House (Mount Brown)	74 D1	Brian Boru Ave	39 C1	Broadford Walk	57 B2
Bloomfield Park (Portobello)	75 A3	*Bow Bridge Place (Irwin Street)	74 D1	Brian Boru Street	39 C1	Broadmeadow	1 C1
Bluebell	36 E4	*Bow Bridge Place (off Military Road)	73 C1	Brian Road	25 C4	*Broadmeadow Mews (adjacent to railway, Strand Street Malahide)	3 B2
Bluebell Ave	36 E4	Bow Lane East	75 B1	Brian Terrace	25 C4	Broadstone	70 F2
Bluebell Road	36 E4	Bow Lane West	74 D1	Briansboro Terrace	74 F3	Broadstone Ave (off Royal Canal Bank)	71 A2
Blundelstown	42 E3	Bow Street	70 F4	Briar Walk	4 D4	*Broadstone Hall Apts (near Whitaker Hall)	71 A2
Blunden Drive	13 C4	Boyd House	14 F4	Briar Wood	68 D3	*Broadstone Place (off Royal Canal Bank)	71 A2
Blythe Ave	72 E3	Boyne Court	74 F4	*Briarfield Grove	27 B1	Broadway Drive	22 E2
Boardman's Lane (off Cork Street)	74 D2	Boyne Lane	76 D1	Briarfield Road	27 B2	Broadway Grove	22 E2
Boardwalk	71 B3	Boyne Road	24 E3	*Briarfield Villas (off Greendale Road)	27 B1	Broadway Park	22 E2
Boden Dale	56 F1	Boyne Street	76 D1	*Briarfield Villas (off Greendale Road)	27 B1	Broadway Road	22 E2
Boden Heath	56 E1	*Brabazon Buildings (Cork Street)	74 F2	*Briarly Court (off Churchtown Road)	47 B4	*Broc Hall (off Beech Hill Ave)	47 C1
Boden Heath Apts	56 E1	*Brabazon Cottages (near Adelaide Villas)	67 C2	*Briarsfield Walk (at Kilbarrack Station)	27 B1	Brockey (Glencullen)	61 C4
Boden Mill	56 E2	*Brabazon Court (off John Street South)	74 F2	Briarwood Ave	22 D1	Brockey (Glencullen Mountain)	65 A1
Boden Park	56 E1	Brabazon Hall	74 F2	Briarwood Close	9 A4	Brockey Lane	65 A1
Boden Wood	46 F4	Brabazon House	74 E2	Briarwood Gardens	22 D1	Brodin Row	70 D3
Boeing Road	12 F4	Brabazon Place	74 F2	Briarwood Green	22 D1	*Bromley Court (off Francis Street)	74 F1
Boghall Road (Killarney Road)	67 B4	Brabazon Row	74 F2	Briarwood Lawn	22 D1	Brompton Court	22 E3
Boghall Road (off Vevay Road)	67 C4	Brabazon Square	74 F1	Briarwood Park	22 D1	Brompton Green	22 E2
Bohammer	13 C2	Brabazon Street	74 F2	Briarwood Road	22 D1	Brompton Grove	22 E3
Boherboy	53 B2	Bracken Drive	4 D4	Brickfield	67 B3	Brompton Lawn	22 E2
Boherboy Road	53 B2	Bracken Hill	57 C3	Brickfield Drive	73 C4	Brook Court	49 B4
*Bohernabreena Cottages (off Bohernabreena Road)	55 A3	Bracken Road	58 D2	Brickfield Lane (The Coombe)	74 E2	*Brook House (off Richmond Road)	25 B4
Bohernabreena Road	55 A3	Brackenbush Park	60 D4	*Brickfield Lane (near Brickfield)	67 B3	Brook Wood	67 B2
*Bolbrook Ave (off Avonbeg Road)	55 B1	Brackenbush Road	60 D4	Bride Close	75 A1	Brookdale	55 A2
*Bolbrook Close (off Avonbeg Road)	55 B1	Bracken's Lane	71 C4	Bride Road	75 A1	Brookdale Ave	1 B3
*Bolbrook Drive (off Avonbeg Road)	55 B1	Brackenstown Ave	1 C2	Bride Street	75 A1	Brookdale Close	1 B2
Bolbrook Grove	55 B1	Brackenstown Road	1 C2	Brides Glen	63 C2	Brookdale Court	1 B3
Bolbrook Park	55 B1	Bradogue Court 70 E1	70 E1	Bride's Glen Ave	1 Inset	Brookdale Drive	1 B2
Bolbrook Villas	55 B1	Braeburn Terrace	1 Inset	Brides Glen Park	1 C1	Brookdale Green	1 B2
Bolton Green	1 A2	Braemor Ave	47 A3	Bride's Glen Park	1 Inset	Brookdale Grove	1 B2
*Bolton Square (Dominick Street Lower)	71 A3	Braemor Drive	47 A3	*Bridge Court	76 E2	Brookdale Lawns	1 B2
Bolton Street	71 A3	Braemor Grove	47 A3	*Bridge House Apts (off Lullymore Terrace)	74 E3	Brookdale Park	1 B2
Bond Drive	39 A1	Braemor Park	47 A3	Bridge Street (Swords)	2 D2	Brookdale Road	1 B2
Bond Road	39 A1	Braemor Road	47 A3	Bridge Street (Ringsend)	39 A3	Brookdale Walk	1 B2
Bond Street	74 E1	Braithwaite Street	74 E1	Bridge Street Lower	70 F4	Brookdale Way	1 B2
Bonham Street	70 E4	Bramblefield	8 F4	Bridge Street Upper	74 F1	Brookdene	64 E2
Boolavogue Road	72 F2	Bramblefield Court	8 F4	Bridgefoot Street	70 F4	Brookfield (Coolock)	26 F2
Boot Road	44 D2	Bramblefield Cres	8 F4	Bridgeview	35 B3	Brookfield (Lucan)	34 D3
Booterstown	48 E2	Bramblefield Drive	8 F4	*Bridgewater Hall (Clark's Bridge)	72 D1	Brookfield (Milltown)	47 B2
Booterstown Ave	48 F3	Bramblefield Park	8 F4	Bridgewater Quay	69 B4	*Brookfield (off Anglesea Road Donnybrook)	47 C1
*Booterstown Grove (off Booterstown Ave)	48 F2	Bramblefield View	8 F4	Bridon	62 F1	Brookfield (Blackrock)	48 F3
*Booterstown Hall (Rock Road)	48 F2	Bramblefield Walk	8 F4	*Brighton Ave (off Charlemont Road Clontarf)	26 D4	Brookfield Ave (Maynooth)	17 C4
Booterstown Park	48 F3	Bramley Ave	22 E3	Brighton Ave (Rathgar)	46 F2	Brookfield Ave (Blackrock)	49 A4
*Booterstown Woods (off South Hill Park)	48 E3	Bramley Court	22 E3	Brighton Ave (Monkstown)	49 B4	*Brookfield Ave (east side of Meath Road)	68 D3
Boranaraltry	61 B4	Bramley Cres	22 E3	Brighton Ave (Carrickmines)	59 A4	*Brookfield Court (at Rialto Bridge)	73 C2
Boranaraltry Bridge	61 B4	Bramley Garth	22 E3	*Brighton Cottages (off Brighton Road Foxrock)	59 A3	*Brookfield Court (off Ravensdale Park)	46 E2
Boranaraltry Lane	61 C4	Bramley Green	22 E3	Brighton Court	59 A4	*Brookfield Court (off Brookfield Place)	49 A4
Boroimhe Alder	1 C3	Bramley Grove	22 E3	Brighton Gardens	46 F2	*Brookfield Court (off Brookfield Road Tallaght)	54 D1
Boroimhe Ash	1 C3	Bramley Heath	22 E3	*Brighton Green (off Brighton Square)	46 F2	Brookfield Estate	46 E2
Boroimhe Aspen	1 C3	Bramley Park	22 E3	Brighton Hall	59 A4	*Brookfield Green (off Ravensdale Park)	46 E2
Boroimhe Beech	1 C3	Bramley Road	22 E3	*Brighton Lane (off Monkstown Road)	49 B4	*Brookfield Grove (off Brookfield Ave)	49 A4
Boroimhe Birches	1 C3	Bramley View	22 E3	*Brighton Lodge (off Brighton Road Foxrock)	59 A3	Brookfield Park	17 C4
Boroimhe Blackthorn	1 C3	Bramley Walk	22 E3	Brighton Place	59 A4	Brookfield Place	49 A4
Boroimhe Cedars	1 C3	Bramley Way	22 E3	Brighton Road (Terenure)	46 F2	Brookfield Road (Kilmainham)	73 C1
Boroimhe Cherry	1 C3	Brandon Road	36 F4	Brighton Road (Foxrock)	59 A3	Brookfield Road (Tallaght)	54 D1
Boroimhe Elms	1 C3	Bray	68 D1	Brighton Square	46 F2	Brookfield Street	73 C2
Boroimhe Hawthorns	1 C3	Bray Commons	67 B2	*Brighton Terrace (off Seapoint Ave Monkstown)	49 B4	Brookfield Terrace	49 A4
Boroimhe Hazel	1 C3	*Bray Head Terrace (Vevay Road, Putland Road)	67 C3	*Brighton Terrace (off Glasthule Road)	60 E1	Brookfield View	54 D1
Boroimhe Laurels	1 C3	Bray Road (Cornelscourt)	59 B2	Brighton Vale	49 B3	Brookhaven Drive	22 E1
Boroimhe Maples	1 C3	Bray Road (Shanganagh)	59 C4	Britain Place	71 B2	Brookhaven Grove	22 E1
Boroimhe Oaks	1 C3	Bray Southern Cross Road	67 B4	Britain Quay	72 F4	Brookhaven Lawn	22 E1
Boroimhe Pines	1 C3	Breakwater Road North	39 B2	Broadfield Ave	52 E2	Brookhaven Park	22 E1
Boroimhe Poplars	1 C3	Breakwater Road South	39 B2	Broadfield Close	52 E2	Brookhaven Rise	22 E1
Boroimhe Rowan	1 B3	Breffini Terrace	60 E1	Broadfield Court	52 E2	Brooklands	48 E1
Boroimhe Willows	1 C3	*Breffni Gardens (adjacent The Mall)	15 A4	Broadfield Drive	52 E2	Brooklawn (Clontarf)	26 D4
Borris Court (off High Street)	75 A1	Breffni Road	60 E1	Broadfield Heath	52 E2	Brooklawn (Lucan)	34 D3
Botanic Ave	25 A4	Bregia Road	24 F4	Broadfield Manor	52 E2	Brooklawn (Blackrock)	48 F3
*Botanic Court Apts (Prospect Way)	25 A4	Brehon Field Road	57 B2	Broadfield Meadows	52 E2	Brooklawn (Palmerston)	35 B1
Botanic Hall	24 F3	Brehon's Chair	57 A3	Broadfield Park	52 E2	*Brooklawn Ave (off Rockville Drive)	49 B4
*Botanic Mews (off Prospect Ave)	25 A4	Bremen Ave	39 A3	Broadfield View	52 E2	*Brooklawn Wood (off Stradbrook Road)	49 B4
*Botanic Park (off Botanic Ave)	25 A4	Bremen Grove	39 A3	Broadford Ave	57 B2	Brookmount Ave	55 C1
Botanic Road	25 A4	Bremen Road	39 A3	Broadford Close	57 B2	*Brookmount Court (off Butterfield Ave)	46 E4
*Botanic Square (off Botanic Ave)	25 A4	Brendan Behan Court	71 C1	Broadford Cres	57 B2	*Brookmount Lawns (off Tallaght Road)	55 C1
*Botanic Villas (off Botanic Road)	25 A4	Brendan Road	47 C1	Broadford Drive	57 B2	Brookpark	34 D3
Bóthair Katherine Tynan	44 E4	*Brennans Parade (between Sidmonton and Albert Ave)	68 D2	Broadford Hill	57 B2		
Bottle Works	39 A3	*Brennans Terrace (between Sidmonton and Albert Ave)	68 D2	Broadford Lawn	57 B2		
Boulevard Mount Eustace	9 B2	Brennanstown Ave	59 C4	Broadford Park	57 B2		
Boundary Road	39 A1	Brennanstown Road	59 B4	Broadford Rise	57 B2		
Bow Bridge (Camac River)	74 D1	Brennanstown Square	59 C4				
*Bow Bridge Court (Bow Bridge)	74 D1	Brennanstown Vale	59 B4				
		Brewery Road	58 F2				

STREET NAME	PAGE / GRID REFERENCE	STREET NAME	PAGE / GRID REFERENCE	STREET NAME	PAGE / GRID REFERENCE	STREET NAME	PAGE / GRID REFERENCE
Brookstone Lane	15 A4	Bunting Road	45 C1	Cabra Drive	70 D1	*Canal View	
Brookstone Road	15 A4	Burdett Ave	60 E1	Cabra Gate (Phoenix Park)	24 D4	(off Lullymore Terrace)	74 E3
Brookvale (off Lucan Road)	34 D1	Burg an Rí Glen	34 F3	Cabra Grove	70 D1	Canal Walk	36 D4
Brookvale Downs	46 F3	Burg an Rí Terrace	34 F3	Cabra Park	70 F1	*Cannon Mews	
Brookvale Road (Rathfarnham)	46 F3	Burgage	13 C3	*Cabra Park Mews (Cabra Park)	24 F4	(off Herbert Road)	39 A4
*Brookvale Road		*Burgage Cres (Burgage Street)	42 D4	Cabra Road	70 D1	Cannon Mews East	76 F2
(off Eglinton Road)	47 C1	*Burgage Green (Burgage Street)	42 D4	Caddell	14 F2	Cannon Mews West	76 F2
Brookview Ave	54 D1	*Burgage Green	56 E1	Cadogan Road	25 C4	*Cannon Place (off Herbert Road)	39 A4
Brookview Close	54 D1	Burgage Street	42 D4	Cairn Brook	63 A1	Cannon Rock Estate	30 E2
Brookview Court	54 D1	Burgess Lane	70 F4	Cairn Brook Hall	63 A1	Cannon Rock View	30 E2
Brookview Cres	54 D1	Burgh Quay	71 C4	Cairn Brook Manor	63 A1	Cannonbrook	34 D2
Brookview Drive	54 D1	Burke Place (off Mount Brown)	74 D1	Cairn Brook View	63 A1	Cannonbrook Ave	34 D2
Brookview Gardens	54 D1	Burleigh Court	76 D3	Cairn Brook Way	63 A1	Cannonbrook Court	34 D2
Brookview Green	54 D1	Burleigh Mews	76 D3	Cairn Court	12 D4	Cannonbrook Lawn	34 D2
Brookview Grove	54 D1	Burlington Gardens	76 D3	Cairn Hill	59 B2	Cannonbrook Park	34 D2
Brookview Lawns	54 D1	Burlington Mews	76 D3	Cairnfort	62 E1	*Canon Court (Bride Street)	75 A1
Brookview Park	54 D1	Burlington Road	76 D3	Cairnwood Ave	44 E4	Canon Lillis Ave	72 E2
Brookview Rise	54 D1	*Burmah Close (off Dalkey Ave)	60 F2	Cairnwood Court	44 E4	*Canon Mooney Gardens	
Brookview Terrace	54 D1	Burnell Park Ave	22 E4	Cairnwood Green	44 E4	(off Cambridge Road)	39 A3
*Brookview Walk		Burnell Park Green	22 E4	Caldbeck Way	44 E2	Canon Troy Court	36 D2
(Brookview Way)	53 C1	Burnell Square	14 D4	Calderwood Ave	25 C3	Capel Street	71 A3
Brookview Way	54 D1	Burnside	25 B1	*Calderwood Grove		Cappagh Ave	24 D1
Brookville	24 D1	Burren Court	11 C4	(off Calderwood Road)	25 C3	Cappagh Drive	24 D2
*Brookville Cres		*Burris Court (off High Street)	75 A1	Calderwood Road	25 C3	Cappagh Green	24 D1
(off Brookville Park)	26 E1	Burrow Court (Poppintree)	11 C4	Caledon Court	72 F2	Cappagh Road (Cappoge)	10 E4
Brookville Park (Coolock)	26 E1	Burrow Court (Portmarnock)	15 A1	Caledon Road	72 F2	Cappagh Road (Finglas)	24 D1
Brookville Park (Artane)	26 E2	Burrow Road (Sutton)	29 B1	Callaghan Bridge	21 C2	Cappaghmore Estate	35 A4
Brookville Park (Dean's Grange)	59 B1	Burrow Road (Stepaside)	58 D4	Callary Road	48 D3	Cappoge	10 F4
Brookwood	56 E2	Burrowfield Road	28 D1	Callender's Mill	32 D4	Cappoge Cottages	10 E4
*Brookwood Abbey		Burton Court	58 E2	Calmount Ave	45 B2	Captain's Ave	46 D1
(off Gracefield Road)	26 E2	Burton Hall Ave	58 E2	Calmount Park	45 B2	Captain's Drive	46 D2
Brookwood Ave	26 E2	Burton Hall Road	58 E2	Calmount Road	45 B2	Captain's Hill	20 D4
Brookwood Cres	26 F2	Burton Road	60 F2	Camac Close	73 A1	Captain's Road	46 D2
Brookwood Drive	26 E2	*Bushfield Ave		Camac Court	73 A1	Cara Park	13 B3
Brookwood Glen	26 F3	(off Marlborough Road)	47 B1	*Camac Cres Apts		*Caragh Court	
Brookwood Grove	26 E2	Bushfield Drive	44 D3	(off Turvey Ave)	73 A1	(off Philipsburgh Ave)	25 C4
Brookwood Hall	26 E3	Bushfield Green	44 D2	*Camac House (on Bow Bridge)	73 C1	Caragh Road	69 C1
Brookwood Heights	26 F2	Bushfield Grove	44 D3	Camac Park	36 E4	Carberry Road	25 C3
Brookwood Lawn	26 F2	Bushfield Lawns	44 D2	*Camac View Apts		*Carbury Place	
Brookwood Meadow	26 E2	*Bushfield Place		(on Kilmainham Lane)	73 C1	(off Newtown Ave Blackrock)	49 A3
Brookwood Park	26 E3	(off Bushfield Terrace)	47 B1	*Camac Way Apts		Carbury Terrace	72 F3
Brookwood Rise	26 F3	*Bushfield Square		(on Rowserstown Lane)	73 C1	Cardiff Castle Road	24 D2
Brookwood Road	26 E2	(off Philipsburgh Ave)	25 C4	Camaderry Road	68 D3	Cardiff Lane	72 E4
Broombridge Road	24 E4	Bushfield Terrace	47 B1	*Camberley Elms		Cardiffs Bridge	24 D3
Broomfield (Malahide)	3 B4	Bushy Park Gardens	46 F3	(off Churchtown Road Upper)	47 B4	Cardiffsbridge Ave	24 D2
Broomfield (Lucan)	21 B4	Bushy Park House	46 E3	*Camberley Oaks		Cardiffsbridge Grove	
Broomfield Court	64 E2	Bushy Park Road	46 F3	(off Churchtown Road Upper)	47 B4	(off Cappagh Road)	24 D1
Broomfield Mews	3 B4	Bustyhill	51 B3	*Cambridge Ave		Cardiffsbridge Road	24 D2
Broomhill Close	45 A4	*Butler's Place Apts (Benson Street)	72 F4	(off Pigeon House Road)	39 A3	Card's Lane (Pearse Street)	71 C4
Broomhill Drive	45 A4	Butlerstown	5 C3	*Cambridge Court		Carleton Road	25 C4
Broomhill Road	45 A4	Butt Bridge (River Liffey)	71 C4	(off Cambridge Park)	39 A3	Carlingford Court	76 E1
Broomhill Terrace		Buttercup Ave	13 C4	Cambridge Park	39 A3	Carlingford Parade	76 E1
(off Broomhill Road)	45 A4	Buttercup Close	13 C4	Cambridge Road (Ringsend)	39 A3	Carlingford Road	25 A4
Brown Street North	70 F3	Buttercup Drive	13 C4	Cambridge Road (Rathmines)	47 A1	Carlisle Ave	47 B1
Brown Street South	74 E2	Buttercup Green	13 C4	*Cambridge Square		*Carlisle Court	
Brownrath	5 B1	Buttercup Lawn	13 C4	(off Thorncastle Street)	39 A3	(off Terenure Road North)	46 F2
Brownsbarn	43 C4	Buttercup Mews	13 C4	*Cambridge Street		Carlisle Street	75 A3
Brownsbarn Court	43 C4	Buttercup Park	13 C4	(off Cambridge Park)	39 A3	*Carlisle Terrace	
Brownsbarn Garden	43 C4	Buttercup Square	13 C4	Cambridge Terrace (Ranelagh)	75 C4	(off North Circular Road)	70 F1
Brownsbarn Orchard	43 C4	Buttercup Terrace	13 C4	*Cambridge Terrace		Carlisle Terrace (Malahide)	3 B3
Brownsbarn Wood	43 C4	Butterfield Ave	46 E4	(off York Road Dún Laoghaire)	49 C4	*Carlisle Terrace (off Corrig Road)	60 D1
Brownstown (Kilcloon)	5 A2	Butterfield Close	46 E4	*Cambridge Villas		*Carlisle Terrace	
Brownstown (Peamount)	42 D1	Butterfield Court	46 F4	(off Castlewood Park)	47 A1	(on Seymour Road)	67 C2
*Bruce's Terrace		Butterfield Cres	46 F4	Camden Ave	23 C3	Carlton Court (Swords)	2 D2
(near Dargle Heights)	67 B2	Butterfield Drive	46 F4	Camden Buildings	75 B2	Carlton Court (Clontarf)	26 D4
*Brug Chroimlinn		Butterfield Grove	46 E4	Camden Court	75 B3	*Carlton Terrace (Novara Ave)	67 C2
(off Saint Agnes RoadCrumlin)	46 D1	*Butterfield Meadow		Camden Lock	76 F1	Carlton Villas	
Brunswick Place	76 E1	(off Butterfield Cres)	46 E4	Camden Market	75 B3	(off Sandymount Ave)	76 F3
Brunswick Street North	70 F3	Butterfield Orchard	46 E4	Camden Place	75 B2	*Carlton Villas (Novara Ave)	67 C2
Brunswick Villas (Pearse Street)	71 C4	Butterfield Park	46 E4	Camden Row	75 A2	Carmanhall Court	58 E2
*Brusna Cottages		*Byrne's Cottages (Francis Street)	74 E2	Camden Street Lower	75 B2	Carmanhall Road	58 E2
(off Main Street Blackrock)	49 A3	Byrnes Lane (Pearse Square West)	72 E4	Camden Street Upper	75 B3	*Carman's Court	
Buckingham Street Lower	72 D2	Byrne's Lane (Jervis Street)	71 B4	Camden Villas	75 B2	(off Carman's Hall)	74 F1
Buckingham Street Upper	72 D2	*Byrne's Terrace		Cameron Square	73 C1	Carman's Hall	74 F1
Buckingham Village	71 C2	(off Beech Hill Drive)	47 C2	Cameron Street	74 E2	Carna Road	35 C3
*Buckley Hall				Cammock Apts	73 C1	Carndonagh Drive	27 B1
(Buckingham Street Lower)	72 D2			Camogie Road (Phoenix Park)	69 B3	Carndonagh Lawn	27 B1
Buckleys Lane	33 A1	**C**		*Campbell Court		Carndonagh Park	27 B1
Bulfin Court	73 A2			(streets between Tuckett's Lane		Carndonagh Road	27 B1
Bulfin Gardens	73 B1	Cabinteely	59 C4	and Main Street)	30 D2	Carne Court	8 F4
*Bulfin House (off Bulfin Road)	73 B2	Cabinteely Ave	59 C3	Campbell's Court	71 A3	Carnegie Court	2 D1
Bulfin Road	73 A2	Cabinteely Bypass	59 C3	Campbell's Lane		Carnew Street	70 D2
Bull Alley Street	75 A1	Cabinteely Close	59 C3	(off Belvidere Ave)	71 C1	Carnlough Road	70 D1
*Bull Lane (Saint Kevin's Square)	67 C2	*Cabinteely Court		Campbell's Row		Carnlough Road	24 E4
Bull Wall	40 D1	(off Pottery Road)	59 C3	(off Portland Street North)	71 C1	Caroline Court	
Bull Wall Cottages	40 D1	Cabinteely Cres	59 C3	Campfield Terrace	57 C1	(off Sandymount Road)	76 E3
*Bullock Steps (off Harbour Road)	60 F1	Cabinteely Drive	59 C3	Campshire Hall	72 D4	*Caroline Row	
Bunbury Gate Ave	1 Inset	Cabinteely Green	59 C3	Campshire Mews	72 D4	(off Irishtown Road)	39 A3
Bunbury Gate Cres	1 Inset	*Cabinteely Park		Canal Road	75 B4	Carpenterstown	22 D3
Bunratty Ave	26 E1	(off Cabinteely Way)	59 C3	Canal Terrace	36 E4	Carpenterstown Ave	22 E3
Bunratty Drive	26 E1	Cabinteely Way	59 C3	Canal Turn	35 B4	Carpenterstown Manor	22 E3
Bunratty Road	26 E1	Cabra	69 C1			Carpenterstown Park East	22 E3

STREET NAME	PAGE / GRID REFERENCE	STREET NAME	PAGE / GRID REFERENCE	STREET NAME	PAGE / GRID REFERENCE	STREET NAME	PAGE / GRID REFERENCE
Carpenterstown Road	22 E4	Carton Demesne	18 F2	Castle Road (Lucan)	34 E2	Castlegrange Gardens	21 B1
Carraig Close	11 C4	Carton Square	17 C2	Castle Road (Saggart)	53 A2	Castlegrange Green (Swords)	2 D1
Carraig Glen	59 C4	Carwell Court	2 E2	Castle Rosse	14 F4	Castlegrange Green (Clonsilla)	21 B1
Carraig Grennane	60 E4	Carysfort Ave	49 A4	*Castle Side (off Castlefield Ave)	55 C1	Castlegrange Green (Clondalkin)	43 B1
Carraroe Ave	27 A1	Carysfort Downs	59 A1	Castle Steps (off Castle Street)	75 A1	Castlegrange Heights	2 D1
Carrick Court	14 F1	*Carysfort Drive		Castle Street (Cork Hill)	75 A1	Castlegrange Hill	2 D1
*Carrick Lawn		(off Carysfort Road)	60 F1	Castle Street (Dalkey)	60 F2	Castlegrange Lawn (Clonsilla)	21 B1
(off Kilmacud Road Upper)	58 D1	Carysfort Grove	59 A1	Castle Street (Bray)	67 C2	Castlegrange Lawn (Clondalkin)	43 C1
Carrick Terrace	74 D2	Carysfort Hall	49 A4	Castle Terrace (Phibsborough Ave)	70 F1	Castlegrange Park	21 B1
Carrickaspinkeen	65 A3	Carysfort Park	49 A4	Castle Terrace (Malahide)	3 B2	Castlegrange Road (Swords)	2 D1
Carrickbrack Heath	29 B2	Carysfort Road	60 F1	*Castle Terrace (off Ulverton Road)	60 F1	Castlegrange Road (Clondalkin)	43 C1
Carrickbrack Hill	29 B2	Carysfort Woods	59 A1	Castle View (Clondalkin)	44 E1	Castlegrange Row	21 B1
Carrickbrack Lawn	29 B2	Casana View	30 E2	*Castle View (off Dundrum Castle)	57 C1	Castlegrange Square (Clondalkin)	43 C1
Carrickbrack Park	29 B2	*Casement Close		Castle View (Carrickmines)	59 A4	Castlegrange Terrace	21 B1
Carrickbrack Road (Sutton)	29 B2	(beside school on Barry Road)	24 D1	*Castle View (off Oldcourt Road)	55 B3	Castlegrange Way	2 D1
Carrickbrack Road		Casement Drive	24 D1	*Castle View Apts		Castlekevin Road	26 D1
(The Summit Howth)	30 D4	Casement Green	24 D1	(opposite Fade Street)	75 B1	Castleknock	22 F3
Carrickbrennan Lawn	49 C4	Casement Grove	24 D1	Castle View Road	44 E1	Castleknock Ave	22 F3
Carrickbrennan Road	49 C4	Casement Park	24 D1	Castle Village	31 C2	Castleknock Brook	22 F3
Carrickfoyle Terrace	73 B1	Casement Road (Mellows Park)	24 D1	Castle Village Ave	31 C2	Castleknock Close	22 E3
Carrickhill Close	4 D4	Casement Road (Finglas South)	24 D2	Castle Village Close	31 C2	Castleknock Court	22 F3
Carrickhill Drive	15 A1	Casement Villas	59 B1	Castle Village Court	31 C2	Castleknock Cres	22 F3
Carrickhill Heights	15 A1	Cashel Ave	46 E2	Castle Village Cres	31 C2	Castleknock Dale	22 F3
Carrickhill Rise	4 D4	Cashel Road	46 D1	Castle Village Drive	31 C2	Castleknock Downs	22 E3
Carrickhill Road	15 A1	Casimir Ave	46 F1	Castle Village Green	31 C2	Castleknock Drive	22 F3
Carrickhill Road Middle	15 A1	*Casimir Court (off Casimir Ave)	46 F1	Castle Village Grove	31 C2	Castleknock Elms	22 F3
Carrickhill Road Upper	3 C4	Casimir Road	46 F1	Castle Village Lawns	31 C2	Castleknock Gate (Phoenix Park)	23 B4
Carrickhill Walk	4 D4	Casino Drive	3 B2	Castle Village Park	31 C2	Castleknock Glade	22 F3
Carrickmines	59 B4	Casino Park	26 D3	Castle Village Place	31 C2	Castleknock Grange	22 F3
Carrickmines Ave	59 B4	Casino Road	25 C4	Castle Village Rise	31 C2	Castleknock Green	23 A3
Carrickmines Chase	59 B4	*Cassian Court		Castle Village Walk	31 C2	Castleknock Grove	22 F3
Carrickmines Dale	59 B4	(at Lockkeeper's Walk)	24 D3	Castle Village Way	31 C2	Castleknock Laurels	22 F3
Carrickmines Garth	59 B4	Castaheany	8 E4	Castle Village Woods	31 C2	Castleknock Lodge	23 A4
Carrickmines Green	63 A1	Castilla Park	26 F4	Castle Villas (Dalkey)	60 F2	Castleknock Manor	23 A3
Carrickmines Little	59 A4	Castle Ave (Swords)	2 D2	*Castle Way Apts (Golden Lane)	75 A1	Castleknock Meadows	22 F3
Carrickmines Manor	63 A1	Castle Ave (Clontarf)	26 E4	Castlebridge	18 D3	Castleknock Oaks	22 F3
Carrickmines Oaks	59 B4	Castle Ave (Clondalkin)	44 E1	Castlebrook	57 C1	Castleknock Park	23 A3
Carrickmount Ave	57 B1	Castle Ave (Churchtown)	47 A4	Castlebyrne Park	49 A4	Castleknock Rise	22 E3
Carrickmount Drive	57 A1	Castle Close (Clondalkin)	44 E1	Castlecurragh Heath	9 A4	Castleknock Road	
Carrig Court	53 B1	Castle Close (Dalkey)	60 F1	Castlecurragh Park	9 B4	(Blanchardstown)	22 F3
Carrig Road	11 C4	Castle Court (Clontarf)	26 D4	Castlecurragh Vale	9 B4	Castleknock Road (Phoenix Park)	23 A4
Carrigallen Drive	24 E3	*Castle Court (off Cypress Lawn)	46 D4	Castledawson Ave	48 F3	Castleknock Vale	22 F3
Carrigallen Park	24 E3	*Castle Court		Castlefarm	1 C1	Castleknock View	22 F3
Carrigallen Road	24 E3	(off Main Street Rathfarnham)	46 F4	Castlefield Ave	55 C1	Castleknock Walk	22 E3
Carrigeen	52 D3	*Castle Court		Castlefield Court (Clonsilla)	21 C2	Castleknock Way	22 F3
Carriglea	55 B2	(off Whitehall Road Rathfarnham)	47 A4	Castlefield Court (Firhouse)	55 C1	Castleknock Wood	22 F3
Carriglea Ave (Tallaght)	55 B2	Castle Court (Booterstown)	48 F2	Castlefield Drive	55 C2	*Castlelands (off Hyde Road)	60 F1
Carriglea Ave		*Castle Court (off Dundrum Castle)	57 C1	Castlefield Green	55 C2	*Castlelands	
(Kill O'The Grange)	59 C2	Castle Court (Stepaside)	58 E4	Castlefield Grove	55 C2	Grove (off Hyde Road)	60 F1
Carriglea Court (Tallaght)	55 B2	Castle Court (Loughlinstown)	64 E1	Castlefield Lawn	55 C1	Castlelyons	42 D4
*Carriglea Court		Castle Court Apts (Dublin Castle)	75 A1	Castlefield Manor (Malahide)	3 B3	Castlemoyne	14 D3
(off Carriglea Gardens)	59 C1	*Castle Court Apts		Castlefield Manor (Firhouse)	55 C1	*Castlepark Court	
Carriglea Downs (Tallaght)	55 B2	(off Saint Margarets Ave Malahide)	3 B3	Castlefield Orchard	55 C1	(off Castlepark Road)	60 E2
Carriglea Downs		Castle Cove (Malahide)	3 A2	Castlefield Park (Clonsilla)	21 C2	Castlepark Road	60 E1
(Kill O'The Grange)	59 C2	*Castle Cove		Castlefield Park (Firhouse)	55 C2	Castlerosse Cres	14 F4
Carriglea Drive	55 B2	(off Castle Street Dalkey)	60 F2	Castlefield Way	55 C2	Castlerosse Drive	14 F4
Carriglea Gardens	59 C1	*Castle Cres (off Monastery Road)	44 E1	Castlefield Woods	21 C2	Castlerosse View	14 F4
Carriglea Grove	55 B2	Castle Dawson	17 B3	Castleforbes Road	72 F3	Castleside Drive	46 F3
Carriglea Rise	55 B2	Castle Down Croft	2 F2	Castleforbes Square	72 F3	Castletimon Ave	25 C1
Carriglea View	55 B2	Castle Down Grove	2 F2	Castlegate (Monkstown)	59 C1	Castletimon Drive	25 C1
Carriglea Walk	55 B2	Castle Down Road	2 F2	Castlegate (Shankill)	64 D3	Castletimon Gardens	25 C1
Carrigmore Ave	53 B2	Castle Drive (Swords)	2 D2	Castlegate Chase	33 C3	Castletimon Green	25 C1
Carrigmore Close (Saggart)	53 B2	Castle Drive (Clondalkin)	44 E1	Castlegate Close	33 C3	Castletimon Park	25 C1
Carrigmore Close (Oldbawn)	54 F3	Castle Drive (Ballyogan Road)	58 E4	Castlegate Copse	33 C4	Castletimon Road	25 C1
Carrigmore Court	53 C2	Castle Elms	26 E1	Castlegate Court	33 C4	Castletown	32 F1
Carrigmore Cres	53 C1	Castle Farm	64 E3	Castlegate Cres	33 C3	Castletown Court	32 D3
Carrigmore Dale	53 B2	Castle Farm Wood	64 E3	Castlegate Dene	33 C3	Castletown Drive	32 D3
Carrigmore Downs	53 B1	Castle Gate Apts	75 A1	Castlegate Downs	33 C4	Castletown Grove	32 D3
Carrigmore Drive	54 F2	Castle Grove (Swords)	2 D2	Castlegate Drive	33 C3	Castletown Lawn	32 D3
Carrigmore Elms	53 B2	Castle Grove (Clontarf)	26 E4	Castlegate Elms	33 C3	Castletymon Court	45 B4
Carrigmore Gardens	53 B1	Castle Grove (Clondalkin)	44 E1	Castlegate Grange	33 C4	Castletymon Gardens	45 B4
Carrigmore Glen	53 B1	Castle Heath	3 A3	Castlegate Green	33 C3	Castletymon Green	45 B4
Carrigmore Green	53 B3	Castle Lawn	58 E4	Castlegate Grove	33 C3	Castleview (Artane)	26 E2
Carrigmore Grove (Saggart)	53 B2	Castle Lawns (Malahide)	2 F2	Castlegate Heath	33 C4	Castleview (Clontarf)	26 E4
Carrigmore Grove (Oldbawn)	54 F3	Castle Lawns (Tallaght)	45 B4	Castlegate Lawn	33 C4	Castleview Court	1 Inset
Carrigmore Lawns	53 B1	Castle Market (off Drury Street)	75 B1	Castlegate Mews	33 C4	Castleview Ave	1 Inset
Carrigmore Manor	53 B2	*Castle Mews Apts		Castlegate Park	33 C3	Castleview Close	1 Inset
Carrigmore Meadows	53 B2	(Castle Street Dalkey)	60 F2	Castlegate Place	33 C3	Castleview Cres	1 Inset
Carrigmore Oak	53 B2	*Castle Oaks		Castlegate Row	33 C4	Castleview Drive	1 Inset
Carrigmore Park	54 F3	(adjacent to Lawson Spinney)	3 A3	Castlegate Square	34 D3	Castleview Estate	7 B3
Carrigmore Place	53 B2	Castle Park (Swords)	2 D2	Castlegate Terrace	33 C4	Castleview Green	1 Inset
Carrigmore Road	54 F2	Castle Park (Leixlip)	33 A1	Castlegate Walk	33 C3	Castleview Grove	1 Inset
Carrigmore Terrace	53 B2	Castle Park (Clondalkin)	44 E1	Castlegate Way	33 C3	Castleview Heights	1 Inset
Carrigmore View	54 F3	Castle Park (Tallaght)	45 B4	Castlegrange	21 B1	Castleview Lawns	1 Inset
Carrigmore Way	53 C2	Castle Park (Monkstown)	49 C4	Castlegrange Ave (Swords)	2 D1	Castleview Meadows	1 Inset
Carrigwood	55 C2	Castle Park Estate (Tallaght)	55 B1	Castlegrange Ave (Clonsilla)	21 B1	Castleview Park (Swords)	1 Inset
Carrington	12 E4	*Castle Place (on Breffni Road)	60 F1	Castlegrange Close (Swords)	2 D1	Castleview Park (Malahide)	3 A3
Carrow Road	73 A3	Castle Riada Ave	34 E2	Castlegrange Close (Clondalkin)	43 B1	Castleview Place	1 Inset
Carton Ave	18 D2	Castle Riada Cres	34 E2	Castlegrange Court (Clondalkin)	43 C1	Castleview Rise	1 Inset
Carton Bridge	18 E2	Castle Riada Drive	34 E3	Castlegrange Drive (Clonsilla)	21 B1	Castleview Row	1 Inset
Carton Court	17 C4	Castle Riada Grove	34 E2	Castlegrange Drive (Clondalkin)	43 B1	Castleview Walk	1 Inset
		Castle Road (Clontarf)	26 E4				

STREET NAME	PAGE / GRID REFERENCE
Castleview Way	1 Inset
Castlewarden	51 A3
Castlewarden North	51 A3
Castlewood	21 C1
Castlewood Ave	47 A1
*Castlewood Close (off Castlewood Ave)	47 A1
*Castlewood Court (off Oakley Road)	47 B1
Castlewood Park	47 A1
*Castlewood Place (off Church Gardens)	47 A1
*Castlewood Terrace (off Castlewood Ave)	47 A1
Cathal Brugha Street	71 B3
*Cathedral Court (New Street South)	75 A2
Cathedral Lane	75 A2
Cathedral Street	71 B3
Cathedral View Court	75 A2
Cathedral View Walk	75 A2
Catherine Court (off William Street North)	72 D1
Catherine Lane	70 F3
Catherine Street (Swift's Alley)	74 F1
Catherines Close	74 F1
Catherine's Well	22 F2
*Cats Ladder (off Torca Road)	60 F2
Causeway Road	27 B3
Cavalry Row	70 D3
Cavendish Row	71 B2
Caves Strand	3 A2
Ceanchor Road	30 D4
Ceannt Fort (off Mount Brown)	74 D1
Cecil Ave	26 D4
Cecilia Street (off Temple Bar)	71 B4
Cedar Ave	45 A3
Cedar Ave	1 B3
Cedar Brook	35 C4
Cedar Brook Ave	35 B3
Cedar Brook Place	35 B3
Cedar Brook Walk	35 B3
Cedar Close	1 B3
Cedar Court (Terenure)	46 F2
Cedar Court (Loughlinstown)	64 D1
Cedar Drive (Dunboyne)	7 B2
Cedar Drive (Palmerstown)	35 B2
*Cedar Grove (off Shelerin Road adjacent Lohonda Cres)	21 C2
Cedar Grove	1 B3
*Cedar Grove Apts (off Knocklyon Ave)	55 C1
*Cedar Hall (off Milltown Road)	47 C1
Cedar House	76 D3
Cedar House	1 Inset
Cedar Lawn	1 B3
Cedar Lodge	23 A4
Cedar Lodge Apts	56 E2
Cedar Park (Leixlip)	19 C4
Cedar Park (Donaghmede)	27 A1
Cedar Place	1 B3
Cedar Square (Swords)	1 B3
*Cedar Square (off Linden Grove)	48 F4
Cedar Walk	27 B2
Cedarhurst Green	23 B3
Cedarhurst Road	23 B3
Cedarmount Road	48 E4
Cedars (opposite Knockmaroon Gate)	36 D1
Cedarwood	32 D3
Cedarwood Ave	24 F1
Cedarwood Close	24 F1
Cedarwood Green	24 F1
Cedarwood Grove	24 F1
Cedarwood Park	24 F1
Cedarwood Rise	24 F1
Cedarwood Road	24 F1
Ceder Park	1 B3
Ceder View	1 B3
Celbridge	32 D3
Celbridge Abbey	31 C4
Celbridge Road (Maynooth)	18 D4
Celbridge Road (Leixlip)	32 F2
Celbridge Road (Lucan)	33 B2
*Celestine Ave (off Dermot O'Hurley Ave)	39 A3
Celtic Park Ave	25 C2
Celtic Park Road	25 C2
Cenecle Grove	64 E1
Chalet Gardens	34 E1
Chalfont Ave	3 B2

STREET NAME	PAGE / GRID REFERENCE
Chalfont Park	3 B2
Chalfont Place	3 B2
Chalfont Road	3 A2
*Chamber Court (off Chamber Street)	74 F2
Chamber Street	74 F2
*Chamberlain Court (off Richmond Ave)	25 C4
*Chamberlain Court (Richmond Ave)	25 B4
Chamley Gardens	2 F3
Chamley Park	2 F3
Champions Ave	71 C3
Chancel Mews	24 D4
*Chancery Court (Chancery Lane)	75 A1
Chancery Hall (John Street North)	70 E4
*Chancery Hall Apts (Ellis Quay / John Street North)	70 F4
Chancery Lane	75 A1
Chancery Place	71 A4
Chancery Street	71 A4
Chandlers Guild Apts	74 D1
Chandlers Mill	32 D4
Chanel Ave	26 E2
Chanel Grove	26 E1
Chanel Road	26 E2
*Chapel Ave (off Bath Street)	39 A3
*Chapel Cres	24 D3
Chapel Hill	34 D1
Chapel Lane (Parnell Street)	71 B3
Chapel Lane (Swords)	2 D2
Chapel Lane (Bray)	67 B1
*Chapel Manor (Knockmaroon Hill)	36 D1
Chapel Road (Kinsaley)	14 D1
Chapel View Apts	34 D1
Chapelizod	36 E2
Chapelizod Bypass	36 E2
Chapelizod Court	36 E2
Chapelizod Hill Road	36 E2
Chapelizod Road	69 A4
Chapellizod Gate (Phoenix Park)	36 E2
Chapelton	9 B1
*Chaplains Place (near Community Centre)	35 A3
*Chaplains Terrace (near Harelawn Green)	35 A3
Chaplegate	25 A4
Chaplewood Ave	9 C1
Chaplewood Cres	9 C1
Chaplewood View	9 C1
Charlemont	25 C3
*Charlemont Ave (off George's Place Dún Laoghaire)	50 D4
Charlemont Bridge (Grand Canal)	75 B3
Charlemont Court	75 B3
Charlemont Gardens	75 B3
Charlemont Mall	75 B4
Charlemont Parade	72 D1
Charlemont Place	75 C3
Charlemont Road	26 D4
Charlemont Street	75 B3
*Charlemont Terrace (off George's Place Dún Laoghaire)	50 D4
Charles Lane	71 C1
*Charles Sheils Houses	58 F2
Charles Street Great	71 C2
Charles Street West (off Ormond Quay Upper)	71 A4
Charleston Ave	47 B1
*Charleston Court Flats (off Charleston Road)	47 B1
Charleston Road	47 B1
Charlestown Ave	11 B4
Charlestown Court	11 B4
Charlestown Drive	11 B4
Charlestown Green	11 B4
Charlestown Mews	11 B4
Charlestown Park	11 B4
Charlestown Place	11 A4
Charlestown Way	11 B4
Charleville	47 B4
Charleville Ave	72 D1
Charleville Close	47 A1
Charleville Mall	72 D1
Charleville Road (Phibsborough)	70 E1
Charleville Road (Rathmines)	47 A1
Charleville Square	46 E4
*Charleville Terrace (on Charleville Road)	70 E1
Charlotte Quay	76 F1
*Charlotte Quay Apts	76 E1

STREET NAME	PAGE / GRID REFERENCE
*Charlotte Terrace (off Victoria Road Dalkey)	60 F2
Charlotte Way	75 B3
Charlton Lawn	48 D4
Charnwood (Clonsilla)	21 C2
Charnwood (Bray)	67 C3
Charnwood Ave	21 C2
Charnwood Court	21 C2
Charnwood Dale	21 C2
Charnwood Gardens	21 C2
Charnwood Green	21 C2
Charnwood Grove	21 C2
Charnwood Heath	21 C2
Charnwood Meadows	21 C2
Charnwood Park	21 C2
*Charter House (on Convent Lane)	17 C3
Chatham Court (on Chatham Street)	75 B1
Chatham Lane (off Chatham Street)	75 B1
Chatham Row	75 B1
Chatham Street	75 B1
*Chaworth Terrace (Hanbury Lane)	74 F1
Cheeverstown Road	54 D1
Chelmsford Ave	75 C4
*Chelmsford Lane (off Chelmsford Road)	47 B1
Chelmsford Road	47 B1
Chelsea Gardens	26 F4
Cheltenham Place	75 B4
Cherbury Court	48 F3
Cherbury Gardens	48 F3
*Cherbury Mews (off Cherbury Court)	48 F3
Cherbury Park Ave	34 D2
Cherbury Park Road	34 D2
Cherries Road	58 D2
Cherrington Close	64 E3
Cherrington Drive	64 E3
Cherrington Road	64 E3
Cherry Ave (Swords)	1 C3
Cherry Ave (Carpenterstown)	22 E3
Cherry Court (Terenure)	46 F2
*Cherry Court (off Loughlinstown Drive)	64 D1
Cherry Drive (Coolmine)	22 E3
Cherry Garth (Swords)	1 C2
Cherry Garth (Stillorgan)	48 E4
Cherry Grove (Swords)	1 B3
Cherry Grove (Crumlin)	45 C2
Cherry House	76 D3
Cherry Lawn	22 E3
Cherry Lawns	33 C2
Cherry Lodge	23 A4
Cherry Orchard Ave	35 C3
Cherry Orchard Ave	36 D4
Cherry Orchard Court	35 C4
Cherry Orchard Cres	35 C4
Cherry Orchard Drive	35 C4
Cherry Orchard Green	35 C4
Cherry Orchard Grove	35 C4
Cherry Orchard Parade	35 C4
*Cherry Orchard Way (off Cherry Orchard Drive)	35 C4
Cherry Park (Swords)	1 B3
Cherry Park (Carpenterstown)	22 E3
*Cherry Tree Drive (off Boghall Road)	67 C3
Cherry Wood	64 D1
Cherryfield Ave	45 C2
Cherryfield Ave Lower	47 B1
Cherryfield Ave Upper	47 B1
Cherryfield Close	21 C1
Cherryfield Court	21 B1
Cherryfield Drive	45 C2
Cherryfield Lawn	21 C1
Cherryfield Park	21 C1
Cherryfield Road	45 C2
Cherryfield View	21 B1
Cherryfield Walk	21 C1
Cherryfield Way	46 D4
*Cherrymount Cres (off Casino Park)	26 D3
*Cherrymount Grove (off Casino Park)	26 D3
Cherrymount Park	70 F1
Cherrywood	32 D3
Cherrywood Ave	44 D1
Cherrywood Cres	43 C1
Cherrywood Drive	43 C1
Cherrywood Grove	44 D1
Cherrywood Lawn	43 C2

STREET NAME	PAGE / GRID REFERENCE
Cherrywood Park (Clondalkin)	43 C2
Cherrywood Park (Loughlinstown)	64 D1
Cherrywood Road	64 D2
Cherrywood Villas (Cherrywood)	43 C1
*Cherrywood Villas (off Tower Road)	44 D1
Chester Downs	60 D1
Chester Road	47 B1
*Chester Square (off Albert Road Lower)	60 E1
Chesterfield Ave (Phoenix Park)	69 B3
Chesterfield Ave (Phoenix Park)	23 B4
Chesterfield Ave (Castleknock)	23 B4
Chesterfield Close	23 B4
Chesterfield Copse	23 B4
Chesterfield Grove	23 B4
Chesterfield Park	23 B3
Chesterfield View	23 B3
*Chestnut Court (off Collinswood)	25 C2
Chestnut Grove (Dunboyne)	7 B3
Chestnut Grove (Celbridge)	32 D3
Chestnut Grove (Clondalkin)	44 F3
Chestnut Grove (Ballinteer)	57 B2
Chestnut House (Swords)	1 Inset
*Chestnut Park (off Pine Ave Foxrock)	59 A2
Chestnut Road (Clondalkin)	45 A1
Chestnut Road (Mount Merrion)	48 E3
Chipping Row	21 A1
Chipping Terrace	21 A1
Christchurch Hall	74 F1
Christchurch Place	75 A1
Christchurch Square	75 A1
Church Ave (Portmarnock)	14 F2
Church Ave (Blanchardstown)	22 F2
*Church Ave (off Ballymun Road)	25 A3
Church Ave (Drumcondra)	25 B3
Church Ave (Irishtown)	39 A3
Church Ave (Rathmines)	47 A1
Church Ave (Killiney)	60 E4
Church Ave South (Dolphin's Barn)	74 D2
Church Ave West (Church Street)	70 F4
Church Court (East Wall)	72 F2
Church Court (Castleknock)	22 F3
Church Gardens	47 A1
Church Green	46 F1
Church Grove	55 A2
Church Lands	67 C3
Church Lane (College Green)	71 B4
Church Lane (Rathfarnham)	46 F3
*Church Lane (off Church Ave)	47 A1
Church Lane South	75 A2
Church Park	46 F1
Church Park Ave	46 F1
Church Park Court	46 F1
Church Park Drive	46 F1
Church Park Lawn	46 F1
Church Park Way	46 F1
Church Place (off Irvine Terrace)	72 F3
Church Road (East Wall)	72 E3
Church Road (Swords)	2 D2
Church Road (Malahide)	3 B3
Church Road (Mulhuddart)	9 A4
Church Road (Finglas)	24 D2
Church Road (Sutton)	29 B1
Church Road (Celbridge)	32 D4
Church Road (Rathcoole)	52 E2
Church Road (Killiney)	60 D3
Church Road (Ballybrack)	60 E4
Church Road (Dalkey)	60 F1
Church Road (Bray)	67 C3
Church Road (Saggart)	53 A2
*Church Row (off Irvine Terrace)	72 F3
Church Square 72 F2	72 F2
Church Street (Four Courts)	70 F4
Church Street (Finglas)	24 D2
Church Street (Howth)	30 D1
Church Street East	72 F3
Church Street New	70 F4
Church Street Upper	70 F3
Church Terrace (off Church Street)	70 F3
Church Terrace (Finglas)	24 E2
*Church Terrace (Main Street, Herbert Road)	67 C2
*Church View (adjacent Church Road)	24 D2
Church View (Drumcondra)	25 B3
Church View (Hollystown)	9 B1
*Church View (off Oak Way Clondalkin)	44 D2

STREET NAME	PAGE / GRID REFERENCE	
*Church Villas (off Brennanstown Road)	59	C4
Church Walk	24	D4
Churchfields (Clonskeagh)	47	C2
*Churchgate Ave (off Vernon Ave)	39	C1
*Churchill Mews (off Church Road)	60	F1
*Churchill Terrace (off Sandymount Ave)	39	A4
*Churchlands (off Sandyford Road)	58	D3
Churchtown	47	B4
Churchtown Ave	47	B3
Churchtown Close	47	B3
Churchtown Drive	47	B3
Churchtown Road	47	B4
Churchtown Road Lower	47	B3
Churchtown Road Upper	47	A4
Churchview Ave	60	D3
Churchview Drive	60	D3
Churchview Park	60	D3
Churchview Road	60	D3
Churchwell Ave	14	D3
Churchwell Close	14	D3
Churchwell Court	14	D3
Churchwell Drive	14	D3
Churchwell Mews	14	D3
Churchwell Place	14	D4
Churchwell Road	14	D4
Churchwell Square	14	D3
Cian Park	25	B4
Cianlea	1	B1
Cill Cais	54	F2
Cill Eanna	26	F2
*Cill Manntan Park (near Market House)	67	C2
Cill Sarain	67	B3
*City Gate Apts (near Brazen Head)	70	F4
City Quay	72	D4
Citywest Ave	53	C1
Citywest Interchange (Junction 3)	43	B4
Citywest Road	53	C1
*Claddagh Court	35	C3
Claddagh Green	35	C3
Claddagh Road	35	C3
*Claddagh Terrace (at Esplanade)	68	C2
Clanawley Road	26	E3
Clanboy Road	26	E3
Clanbrassil Close	74	F4
Clanbrassil Street Lower	74	F3
Clanbrassil Street Upper	74	F3
Clanbrassil Terrace	74	F2
Clancarthy Road	26	D3
Clancy Ave	24	E1
Clancy Quay	69	B4
Clancy Road	24	E1
Clandonagh Road	26	D3
Clane Road	31	B4
Clanfadda Wood	48	F3
Clanhugh Road	26	E3
Clanmahon Road	26	E3
Clanmaurice Road	26	D3
Clanmawr	64	E2
Clanmoyle Road	26	D3
Clanranald Road	26	D3
Clanree Road	26	D3
Clanwilliam Court	76	E2
Clanwilliam Place	76	E2
Clanwilliam Square	76	E1
Clanwilliam Terrace	76	E1
Clare Hall	14	D4
Clare Lane	75	C1
*Clare Park Villas (off Achill Road)	25	B3
Clare Road	25	B3
Clare Street	75	C1
*Claremont Ave (off Ballymun Road)	25	A3
Claremont Close	24	F4
Claremont Court (Finglas)	24	F4
*Claremont Court (off Shelbourne Road)	39	A4
*Claremont Court (off Claremont Road)	39	A4
Claremont Cres	24	F4
Claremont Drive	24	F2
Claremont Grove	60	E3
Claremont Lawn	24	F4
Claremont Mews	29	C1
Claremont Park	39	A4
Claremont Road (Sutton)	29	B1
Claremont Road (Sandymount)	39	A4

STREET NAME	PAGE / GRID REFERENCE	
Claremont Road (Carrickmines)	59	B4
Claremont Road (Killiney)	60	E3
*Claremont Terrace (off Main Street Dundrum)	47	C4
*Claremont Villas (off Adelaide Road)	60	E1
Claremont Villas (Glenageary)	60	E1
Claremount (Shankill)	64	E3
Claremount (Cornelscourt)	59	B3
Claremount Pines	59	B4
*Claremount Terrace (west side of text Meath)	68	D2
Clarence Mangan Road	74	F2
Clarence Mangan Square (off John Dillon Street)	75	A1
Clarence Place Great	76	E1
Clarence Street	49	C4
Clarence Street Great North	72	D2
Clarendon Market		
(off William Street South)	75	B1
Clarendon Row (off King Street South)	75	B1
Clarendon Street	75	B1
*Clareville Court (off Claremont Lawn)	24	F4
Clareville Grove	24	F4
Clareville Road	46	F1
Clarinda Manor	60	D1
Clarinda Park East (Dún Laoghaire)	50	D4
Clarinda Park North	50	D4
Clarinda Park West	50	D4
Clarion Quay	72	D3
Clarke Terrace	74	D2
Clarke's Bridge (Royal Canal)	72	D1
*Clarkeville Terrace (off Lucan Road Palmerston)	35	C1
Classon's Bridge	47	B2
Claude Road	25	A4
*Clayton Terrace (off Saint Laurence Road)	36	E2
Clearstream Court	24	E1
*Clearwater Apts (off Bath Ave Malahide)	3	C2
*Clearwater Court (at Lockkeeper's Walk)	24	D3
*Clearwater Cove (off Dunleary Road)	49	C4
Cleggan Ave	35	C3
Cleggan Park	35	C3
Cleggan Road	35	C3
Clifden Drive	35	C3
Clifden Road	36	D3
*Cliff Terrace (off Breffni Road)	60	E1
Clifford's Lane	2	E2
*Clifton Ave (off Monkstown Cres)	49	C4
Clifton Court Apts	70	E4
*Clifton Lane (off Monkstown Road)	49	C4
Clifton Mews	75	B4
Clifton Park	64	E2
*Clifton Terrace (off Seapoint Ave)	49	C4
Cliftonville Road	25	A4
Clinch's Court	72	D1
*Clipper Court (Liffey Street West)	70	E4
*Clipper Court Apts (off Liffey Street West)	70	E4
*Clipper View (Liffey Street West)	70	E4
*Clipper View Apts (off Liffey Street West)	70	E4
Clogher Green	74	E4
Clogher Road	74	D4
Cloghran	1	C4
Cloghran Roundabout	1	C4
Cloister Ave	49	A4
Cloister Close	48	F4
Cloister Court	24	D3
Cloister Gate	49	A4
Cloister Green	49	A4
Cloister Grove	49	A4
Cloister Park	49	A4
Cloister Square	49	A4
Cloister Way	49	A4
Clon Burgh	58	D3
*Clonallen (off Kimmage Road Lower)	46	E2
Clonard Ave	57	C2
Clonard Close	57	C2
*Clonard Court (off Poddle Close)	46	E2
Clonard Drive	57	C2
Clonard Grove	57	C2
Clonard Lawn	57	C2

STREET NAME	PAGE / GRID REFERENCE	
Clonard Park	57	C2
Clonard Road (Crumlin)	73	B4
Clonard Road (Sandyford)	57	C2
*Clonasleigh (off Beechfield Manor)	64	E2
Cloncourt Apts	8	D3
Clondalkin	44	D1
Clonee	8	D3
Clonee Bridge	8	D3
Clonee Bypass	8	D3
Cloneen	5	A2
Clonfert Road	46	E1
Clongriffin	14	E4
Clonkeen Court	59	B3
Clonkeen Cres	59	B2
Clonkeen Drive	59	B2
Clonkeen Grove	59	B2
*Clonkeen Lawn (off Clonkeen Road)	59	B3
Clonkeen Road	59	B2
Clonlara Ave	43	A4
*Clonlara Road (off Pine Road)	39	A3
Clonlara Road (Naas Road)	43	A4
Clonlea	57	C2
*Clonlea Wood (off Ballinteer Road)	57	C2
Clonliffe Ave	72	D1
Clonliffe Gardens	25	B4
Clonliffe Road	25	B4
*Clonliffe Square (off Distillery Road)	25	B4
*Clonmacnoise Grove (off Clonmacnoise Road)	46	E1
Clonmacnoise Road	46	E1
Clonmel Road	25	A2
Clonmel Street	75	B2
Clonmellon Grove	14	D4
*Clonmore Court (off Ballymun Road)	25	A3
Clonmore Road (Ballybough)	72	D1
Clonmore Road (Goatstown)	48	E4
Clonmore Terrace	72	D1
*Clonmore Villas (Clonmore Road)	72	D1
Clonrosse Court	26	F1
Clonrosse Drive	26	F1
Clonrosse Park	26	F1
Clonshaugh	13	B3
Clonshaugh Ave	13	A4
Clonshaugh Close	13	B4
*Clonshaugh Court (off Clonshaugh Cres)	13	B4
Clonshaugh Cres	13	A4
Clonshaugh Drive	13	B4
Clonshaugh Glen	13	B4
Clonshaugh Green	13	B4
Clonshaugh Grove	13	B4
Clonshaugh Heights	13	A4
Clonshaugh Lawns	13	B4
Clonshaugh Meadow	13	A4
Clonshaugh Park	13	B4
Clonshaugh Rise (off Clonshaugh Ave)	13	B4
Clonshaugh Road (Belcamp)	13	A3
Clonshaugh Road (Kilmore)	13	A4
Clonshaugh Walk	13	B4
Clonsilla	21	C2
Clonsilla Close	22	E2
Clonsilla Link Road	21	C2
Clonsilla Park	22	E2
Clonsilla Road	22	E2
Clonskeagh	47	C2
*Clonskeagh Drive (off Clonskeagh Road)	47	C2
Clonskeagh Road	47	C2
*Clonskeagh Square (off Clonskeagh Road)	47	C2
Clontarf	39	C1
Clontarf Park	39	C1
Clontarf Road (Fairview)	26	D4
Clontarf Road (Clontarf)	39	C1
*Clonturk Ave (off Drumcondra Road Upper)	25	B3
*Clonturk Court (off Church Ave)	25	B3
*Clonturk Gardens (off Clonturk Park)	25	B4
Clonturk Park	25	B4
Cloonlara Cres	24	E3
Cloonlara Drive	24	E2
Cloonlara Road	24	E3
Cloonlara Square	23	B3
Cloonmore Ave	54	D2
Cloonmore Close	54	E2

STREET NAME	PAGE / GRID REFERENCE	
Cloonmore Cres	54	D2
Cloonmore Drive	54	D2
Cloonmore Gardens	54	D2
Cloonmore Green	54	D2
Cloonmore Grove	54	D2
Cloonmore Lawn	54	D2
Cloonmore Park	54	D2
Cloonmore Road	54	D2
*Cloragh Mills (South of Springvale)	56	E2
*Cloragh Mills Apts (Edmonstown Park)	56	E2
Cloragh Road	56	E4
*Clounties Court (adjacent Chamley Park)	2	F3
Clover Hill	67	A3
Clover Hill Drive	36	D3
Clover Hill Road	36	D4
Cloverhill Road (Clondalkin)	35	A4
Cloverhill Road (Cherry Orchard)	35	B3
*Cloyne Road (off Blarney Park)	46	E1
Cluain Aoibhinn	17	C4
Cluain Mhuire (Glenageary)	60	D1
Cluain Mhuire (Shankill)	64	D3
*Cluain na Greine Court (at The Bridge)	64	E3
Cluain Rí	34	F2
Cluain Shee	58	D3
Club Road	45	A1
Clune Road	24	E1
Cluny Grove	60	D3
Cluny Park	60	E2
Clutterland	42	F1
Clyde Court (off Seafort Ave)	76	E4
*Clyde House (off Serpentine Ave)	39	A4
Clyde Lane	76	F4
Clyde Road	76	E4
Cnoc Aoibhean	33	B2
Coast Road (Malahide)	3	C2
Coast Road (Baldoyle)	15	A4
*Coates Lane (off main street and Pound Lane)	17	C3
Coburg	67	B2
Coburg Place	72	D2
*Coghill's Court (off Dame Street)	71	B4
Cois Cairn	67	B1
*Cois Coillte (off Loughlinstown Drive)	64	D1
Cois Eala	75	A4
Cois Na hAbhann	54	F2
Cois Sleibhe	67	B4
Coke Lane	70	F4
Coke Ovens Cottages	24	F4
Colbert's Fort (off Saint James Walk)	74	D2
Colbert's Fort (Tallaght)	44	F4
*Coldbeck Way (off Fonthill Road South)	46	E2
*Coldcut Cres (Coldcut Road)	35	B2
Coldcut Cres	35	B2
Coldcut Park	35	B2
Coldcut Road	35	B2
Coldwell Street	60	D1
Colepark Ave	36	D3
Colepark Drive	36	D3
Colepark Green	36	D3
Colepark Road	36	D3
Coleraine Street	71	A3
Colganstown	41	B2
Coliemore Apts.	60	G2
Coliemore Road	60	G2
*Coliemore Villas (off Coliemore Road)	60	F2
College Cres	46	D3
College Drive	46	E3
College Fort	22	F4
College Gate	22	F3
*College Gate Apts (Tara Street)	71	C4
College Green (Trinity College)	71	B4
College Green (Maynooth)	17	C4
College Grove (Castleknock)	22	F4
College Lane (Trinity College)	76	D1
College Lane (Rathcoole)	52	F1
*College Manor (off Millmount Ave)	25	B4
*College Mews (off Clonliffe Road)	25	B4
College Park (Castleknock)	23	A4
College Park (Kimmage)	46	E3
College Park Ave	57	C2
College Park Close	57	C2

STREET NAME	PAGE / GRID REFERENCE
*College Park Court (off College Park Ave)	57 C2
*College Park Drive (off College Park Ave)	57 C2
College Park Grove	57 C2
College Park House	75 C1
College Park Way	57 C2
College Road (Castleknock)	22 F4
College Road (Greenogue Industrial Estate)	42 E4
College Road (Whitechurch Road)	57 A3
College Square	46 D3
College Street (Trinity College)	71 C4
College Street (Baldoyle)	15 A4
College View (Drumcondra)	25 B3
*College View (off Main Street Tallaght)	55 A1
College Wood	22 F4
Collegeland	42 F4
*Collier's Ave (off Anna Villa)	47 B1
Colliersland	6 F2
*Collindale (off Beaumont Road)	25 C2
Collins Ave	25 C2
Collins Ave East	26 D3
Collins Ave Extension	25 A2
Collins Ave West	25 B2
Collins Bridge	20 F4
*Collins Close (off Collins Ave)	25 C3
*Collins Court (off Collins Ave)	25 C3
*Collins Court (off Temple Road)	49 A3
Collins Drive	24 E1
Collins Green	24 E1
Collins Park	26 D3
Collins Place	24 E1
*Collins Row (Glasaree Road)	24 E2
*Collinstown Cres (off Collinstown Road)	35 A3
Collinstown Cross	12 F2
Collinstown Grove	35 B3
Collinstown Road	35 A3
Collinswood	25 C2
Colmanstown	51 C2
Colmanstown Lane	51 C2
Colmcille Court	2 D2
Colthurst Close	34 F2
Colthurst Cres	34 F2
Colthurst Gardens	34 F2
Colthurst Green	34 F2
Colthurst Mews	34 F2
Colthurst Park	34 F2
Colthurst Rise	34 F2
Colthurst Road	34 F2
Colthurst Way	34 F2
Comeragh Road	36 F4
Comeran Court	74 E2
Commons (Hazelhatch)	41 C2
Commons (Rathcoole)	52 E1
Commons East	2 D3
Commons Little	42 D4
Commons Lower	41 A1
Commons Road (Saint John's Gate)	44 D2
Commons Road (Loughlinstown)	64 E2
Commons Street	72 D3
Compass Court	23 C3
*Compass Court Apts (at Lockkeeper's Walk)	24 D3
*Comyn Place (off Walsh Road)	25 A3
Con Colbert Road (Kilmainham)	73 A1
Con Colbert Road (Inchicore)	36 F3
Confey	20 D4
*Congress Gardens (off Hudson Road)	60 E1
Congress Hall	7 B3
Congress Park	7 B3
Connaught Parade (off Connaught Street)	24 F4
*Connaught Place (off Crofton Road)	50 D4
Connaught Street	24 F4
Connawood	67 B1
Connawood Copse	67 B1
Connawood Cres	67 B1
Connawood Drive	67 B1
Connawood Green	67 B1
Connawood Grove	67 B1
Connawood Lawn	67 B1
Connawood Walk	67 B1
Connawood Way	67 B1
Connolly Ave (Kilmainham)	73 A2
Connolly Ave (Malahide)	3 A4
Connolly Gardens	73 A2
Connolly's Folly	18 E4
Conor Clune Road	23 C4
Conquer Hill Ave	39 C1
Conquer Hill Road	39 C1
Constellation Road	12 F4
Constitution Hill	71 A3
Convent Ave (Marino)	25 B4
Convent Ave (Bray)	68 D2
Convent Close	76 D2
*Convent Court (off Coolnevaun Kilmacud)	58 E1
*Convent Hall Apts (off Milltown Ave)	47 B2
Convent Lane (Portmarnock)	4 D4
Convent Lane (Maynooth)	17 C3
Convent Lane (Willbrook)	46 F4
*Convent Lawns (off Kylemore Road)	36 E3
Convent Lodge	26 F2
Convent Place	75 C3
Convent Road (Clondalkin)	44 E2
Convent Road (Blackrock)	49 A4
Convent Road (Dún Laoghaire)	50 D4
Convent Road (Dalkey)	60 F2
Convent View (Oldcourt)	67 C3
*Convent View (Sidmonton Road Bray)	68 D2
Convent View Cottages (off Ratoath Road Cabra)	24 D4
Convent View Cottages (Saint John's Gate)	44 D2
*Convent View Cres (adjacent Convent View Cottages)	24 D4
Convent Way	24 D4
Conway Court	76 E1
Conyngham Road	69 C4
Cook Street	71 A4
Cooks Road	1 A4
Cookstown	66 E3
Cookstown Court	44 F4
Cookstown Road	44 E4
Cookstown Way	44 E4
*Coolamber Court (off Knocklyon Road)	56 D1
Coolamber Drive	52 F2
Coolamber Park	56 D1
Coolamber Road	52 F2
Coolatree Close	25 C2
Coolatree Park	25 C2
Coolatree Road	25 C2
Cooldrinagh Lane	33 B1
Cooldrinagh Terrace	33 B1
Cooldríona Court	2 D2
Cooleen Ave	25 C1
Coolevin (Ballybrack)	60 D1
Coolevin Road	75 A2
Cooley Close	36 F4
Cooley Road	73 A4
Coolgariff Road	25 C1
*Coolgraney (off Nutgrove Park)	47 C2
*Coolgraney Court (off Nutgrove Park)	47 C2
Coolgreena Close	25 C2
Coolgreena Road	25 C1
Coolkill	58 D3
Coolmine	52 F3
Coolmine Boulevard	22 E2
Coolmine Close	22 D2
Coolmine Cottages	9 A4
Coolmine Court	22 E2
Coolmine Green	22 D3
Coolmine Lawn	22 D2
Coolmine Mews	22 E2
Coolmine Park	22 E2
Coolmine Road (Carpenterstown)	22 E3
Coolmine Road (Saggart)	52 F2
Coolmine Woods	22 E2
Coolnevaun	58 E1
Coolock	26 E1
Coolock Drive	26 E1
Coolock Lane (Santry)	12 F4
Coolock Village	26 E1
*Coolock Village Close (off Coolock Village)	26 E1
Coolrua Drive	25 C1
Coolwater Lakes	53 B2
Coombe Court	74 F1
Coopers Way	70 F3
*Coopers Yard (Smithfield)	70 F3
Coopers Yard Apts	70 F3
Cope Bridge	20 D3
Cope Street	71 B4
Copeland Ave	26 D4
Copeland Grove	26 D4
Copper Alley (Eustace Street)	71 A4
*Copper Beech Grove (East of Hazelwood)	67 B2
Coppinger	49 A4
Coppinger Close	48 F4
Coppinger Glade	48 F4
Coppinger Row	75 B1
Coppinger Walk	49 A4
Coppinger Wood	48 F4
Corbally	53 C3
Corbally Ave	53 C2
Corbally Close	53 C2
Corbally Downs	53 C2
Corbally Drive	53 C2
Corbally Glade	53 C2
Corbally Green	53 C2
Corbally Heath	53 C2
Corbally Lawn	53 C2
Corbally Park	53 C2
Corbally Rise	53 C2
Corbally Square	53 C2
Corbally Vale	53 C2
Corbally Way	53 C2
Corbawn Ave	64 E2
Corbawn Close	64 F2
Corbawn Court	64 F2
Corbawn Dale	64 F2
Corbawn Drive	64 F2
*Corbawn Glade (near Corbawn Wood)	64 E2
Corbawn Grove	64 F2
Corbawn Lane	64 E2
Corbawn Lawn	64 E3
Corbawn Wood	64 E2
Corduff	22 F1
Corduff Ave	22 F1
Corduff Close	22 F1
Corduff Cottages	22 E1
Corduff Cres	22 F1
Corduff Gardens	22 F1
Corduff Green	22 F1
Corduff Grove	9 B4
Corduff Park	9 B4
Corduff Place	22 F1
Corduff Way	22 F1
Cork Hill (off Dame Street)	71 A4
Cork Street	74 E2
Corkagh View	44 D2
Corke Abbey	67 C1
Corke Abbey Ave	67 B1
Cormac Terrace	46 F2
Corn Exchange Apts	71 C4
Corn Exchange Place	71 C4
*Corn Mill (off Distillery Road)	25 B4
*Corn Mill (Blank Tony)	25 B4
*Corn Mill Apts. (Distillery Road)	25 B4
Cornelscourt	59 B3
Cornelscourt Hill Road	59 B3
Cornelstown	6 D2
Cornerpark	42 D3
Cornmarket	74 F1
Corporation Street	71 C3
Corr Castle	29 B1
Corr Castle Apts	29 B1
Corrbridge Terrace	29 B1
Corrib Road	46 E2
Corrig Ave	50 D4
Corrig Close	45 B3
*Corrig Court (off Corrig Road)	58 E2
Corrig Hall	57 C3
Corrig Park	50 D4
Corrig Road (Stillorgan)	58 E2
Corrig Road (Dún Laoghaire)	60 D1
Corrig Road (Dalkey)	60 F1
Corrybeg	46 D4
*Cosy Lodge (off William's Park)	47 A1
Coulson Ave	46 F2
Coultry Ave	25 B1
Coultry Close	25 A1
Coultry Court	12 D4
Coultry Cres	12 D4
Coultry Drive	12 D4
Coultry Gardens	12 D4
Coultry Green	12 D4
Coultry Grove	12 E4
Coultry Lawn	12 E4
Coultry Park	12 E4
Coultry Road	12 D4
Coultry Terrace	12 D4
Coultry Way	25 B1
Coundon Court	60 E4
Countess Markievicz House	72 D4
Countybrook Lawns	66 E2
*Court House Square (off Doctors Lane)	17 C3
Courthill	7 B2
Courthill Drive	7 B2
*Courthouse Square Apts (off Main Street Tallaght)	55 A1
Courtlands	59 C3
*Courtney House	76 D4
Courtney Place	72 E1
Courtview Apts	23 C3
Cow Parlour	74 E2
Cowbooter Lane	30 E2
Cowper Downs	47 A1
Cowper Drive	47 B2
Cowper Gardens	47 B2
*Cowper Mews (off Cowper Road)	47 A2
Cowper Road	47 B2
Cowper Street	70 D2
Cowper Village	47 A2
Cows Lane	71 A4
Crag Ave	35 B4
Crag Cres	35 B4
Crag Terrace	35 B4
Craigford Ave	26 E3
Craigford Drive	26 E3
Craigie Court	24 E2
*Craiglands (off Ardeevin Road)	60 F2
*Craigmore Gardens (off Temple Road)	49 A3
Crampton Ave (off Park Lane)	76 F3
Crampton Court (off Dame Street)	71 B4
Crampton Quay	71 B4
Crane Lane (off Dame Street)	71 A4
Crane Street	74 E1
*Crane Yard Apts (Crane Lane)	71 A4
Cranfield Place	39 A3
*Cranford Court (off Terenure Road West Kimmage)	46 E2
Cranford Court (Stillorgan Road)	48 D2
Cranmer Lane	76 E2
*Cranmer Place	76 E2
*Crannagh (off Milltown Road)	47 C2
*Crannagh Castle (off Crannagh Road)	46 F3
*Crannagh Court (off Crannagh Road)	46 F3
Crannagh Grove	47 A3
Crannagh Hall	47 A3
Crannagh Park	46 F3
Crannagh Road	46 F3
*Crannagh Way (off Crannagh Road)	47 A3
Crannogue Close	11 C4
Crannogue Road	11 C4
Crawford Ave	25 A4
Crawford Terrace (off Kings Ave)	72 D1
Creighton Street	72 D4
Cremona Road	36 E3
Cremore Ave	24 F3
Cremore Cres	24 F3
Cremore Drive	24 F3
*Cremore Heights	24 F2
Cremore Lawn	24 F3
Cremore Park	25 A3
Cremore Road	24 F3
Cremore Villas (off Cremore Cres)	24 F3
Cremorne (Terenure Road East)	46 F2
Cremorne (Knocklyon)	56 D1
Cres Gardens	72 E1
*Cres House (off Marino Cres)	26 D4
Cres Place	26 D4
Cres Villas	25 A4
Crestfield Ave	25 B2
Crestfield Close	25 B2
Crestfield Drive	25 B2
Crestfield Park	25 B2
Crestfield Road	25 B2
Creston	11 B3
Crewhill	17 B1
Crinan Strand	72 D3
Crinken Glen	64 E3
Crinken Lane	64 D4
Crinstown	17 A4
Croaghpatrick Road	24 D4
Crockshane	52 E3
Crodaun Court	31 C2
Crodaun Forest Park	32 D2

STREET NAME	PAGE	GRID
Crofton Ave	50	D4
*Crofton Mansions (off Crofton Road)	50	D4
Crofton Road	50	D4
*Crofton Terrace (off Crofton Road)	50	D4
Croftwood Cres	35	C3
Croftwood Drive	35	C3
Croftwood Gardens	35	C3
Croftwood Green	36	D3
Croftwood Grove	35	C3
Croftwood Park	36	D3
Croke Villas	72	D1
Cromcastle Ave	26	D1
*Cromcastle Close (off Cromcastle Green)	26	D1
*Cromcastle Court (off Kilmore Road)	26	D1
Cromcastle Drive	26	D1
Cromcastle Green	26	D1
Cromcastle Park	26	D1
Cromcastle Road	26	D1
Cromlech Close	62	F2
Cromlech Court	11	C4
Cromlech Fields	64	E1
Cromwellsfort Road	45	C2
Crooksling	53	B4
Crosbie House	75	C4
*Crosbie's Yard Apts (near Ossory Industrial Estate)	72	E2
Crosforge	53	A2
Cross Ave (Booterstown)	48	F3
Cross Ave (Dún Laoghaire)	50	D4
*Cross Guns Quay Apts (Prospect Road)	25	A4
Cross Lane	17	C3
Crosstrees Court	30	D2
Crosthwaite Park East	60	D1
Crosthwaite Park South	60	D1
Crosthwaite Park West	60	D1
*Crosthwaite Terrace (off Clarinda Park West)	50	D4
Crostick Alley (off Meath Street)	74	F1
Crotty Ave	45	C1
Crow Street (off Dame Street)	71	B4
Crown Alley (off Temple Bar)	71	B4
Croydon Gardens	25	C4
Croydon Green	25	C4
Croydon Park Ave	25	C4
*Croydon Terrace (off Griffith Ave)	25	C3
Cruagh Ave	62	E1
Cruagh Close	62	E1
Cruagh Court	62	E1
Cruagh Green	62	E1
Cruagh Lane	56	E4
Cruagh Rise	62	E1
Cruagh Road	56	E4
Cruagh Wood	62	E1
Cruise Park	9	A2
Cruise Park Ave	9	A2
Cruise Park Close	9	A2
Cruise Park Court	9	A2
Cruise Park Cres	9	A2
Cruise Park Drive	9	A2
Cruise Park Hall	9	A2
Cruise Park Rise	9	A2
Cruise Park Square	9	A2
Cruise Park Walk	9	A2
Cruiserath Road	9	C3
Crumlin	73	A4
*Crumlin Park (off Crumlin Road)	46	D1
Crumlin Road	73	C4
Cuala Grove	68	D3
Cuala Road (Cabra)	24	F4
Cuala Road (Bray)	68	D3
*Cuan na Mara (off Harbour Road, close to Post Office)	30	D1
Cuckoo Lane	71	A3
Cuffe Lane	75	B2
Cuffe Street	75	B2
Cuilenn Park	24	F1
Cul na Greine	54	F2
*Cullen's Cottages (off Annaville Ave)	49	A4
Cullen's Wood House	75	C4
*Cullenswood Court (off Cullenswood Park)	47	B1
Cullenswood Gardens	47	B1
Cullenswood Park	47	B1
*Cullenswood Road (off Charleston Road)	47	B1
*Culmore Park (off Culmore Road)	35	C2
Culmore Road	35	C2
*Cumberland Place North (on North Circular Road)	70	F1
Cumberland Road	76	D3
Cumberland Street	49	C4
Cumberland Street North	71	C2
Cumberland Street South	76	D1
Cunningham Drive	60	F2
Cunningham Park	59	B3
Cunningham Road	60	F2
Curlew Road	73	A4
*Curracloe Drive (off Kilfenora Drive)	27	A1
Curragh Hall	9	B3
Curragh Hall Ave	9	B3
Curragh Hall Close	9	B3
Curragh Hall Court	9	B3
Curragh Hall Cres	9	B3
Curragh Hall Drive	9	B3
Curragh Hall Gate	9	B3
Curragh Hall Green	9	B3
Curragh Hall Grove	9	B3
Curragh Hall House	9	B3
Curragh Hall Lane	9	B3
Curragh Hall Lodge	9	B3
Curragh Hall Road	9	B3
Curragh Hall View	9	B3
Curragh Hall Way	9	B3
Curragh Hall Wood	9	B3
Curtlestown	65	B4
Curved Street	71	B4
Curzon Street	75	A3
Cushinstown	6	F1
Cushlawn Ave	54	F2
Cushlawn Close	54	F3
Cushlawn Dale	54	F3
Cushlawn Drive	54	F2
Cushlawn Grove	54	F2
Cushlawn Park	54	F2
Cushlawn Walk	54	F3
Cushlawn Way	54	F3
Custom Hall	71	C3
Custom House Harbour	72	D3
Custom House Quay	71	C3
Custom House Square	72	E3
Cymric Road	39	A3
*Cypress Ave (off Brookwood)	56	E2
Cypress Court	64	E1
Cypress Drive	46	D3
Cypress Garth	46	D4
Cypress Grove North	46	D3
Cypress Grove Road	46	D3
Cypress Grove South	46	D4
Cypress House	28	D1
Cypress Lawn	46	D4
Cypress Park	46	D4
Cypress Road	48	E3
Cypress Springs	20	D4

D

STREET NAME	PAGE	GRID
*Daisy Market (off Arran Street)	71	A4
Dakota Ave	12	F4
Dakota Court	25	A4
Dal Riada	3	C4
Dalcassian Downs	24	F4
*Dale Close (off Dale Drive)	58	E1
Dale Drive	58	E1
Dale Road	58	E1
Dale View	60	E4
*Dale View Park (off Madden's Lane)	60	E4
Dalepark Road	55	A2
Daletree Ave	55	B2
Daletree Close	55	C3
Daletree Court	55	C3
Daletree Cres	55	C2
Daletree Drive	55	C2
Daletree Park	55	C3
Daletree Place	55	C3
Daletree Road	55	C3
Daletree Terrace	55	C3
Daletree View	55	B3
Daleview Road	1	C1
Dalkey	60	F1
Dalkey Ave	60	F2
*Dalkey Court (off Barnhill Road)	60	F2
*Dalkey Grove (off Dalkey Park)	60	F2
Dalkey Park	60	E2
Dalkey Rock	60	F2
Dalriada Avanue	55	C3
Dalriada Close	55	C3
Dalriada Court	55	C3
*Dalriada Square (Dalriada Estate)	55	C3
Dalton Mews	3	B3
Dalymount	70	F1
Damastown Ave	8	F3
Damastown Close	8	F3
Damastown Court	9	A3
Damastown Drive	8	E3
Damastown Green	8	F3
Damastown Road	8	F3
Damastown Walk	8	E3
Damastown Way	9	A3
Dame Court	75	B1
Dame Lane	71	B4
Dame Street	71	B4
Damer Court	71	A2
Damer House	2	E2
Dane Close	11	C4
Dane Road	11	C4
Danes Court (Dollymount)	27	A4
Danesfort	39	B1
Daneswell Road	25	A4
Dangan	41	A2
Dangan Ave	46	D2
Dangan Drive	46	D2
Dangan Park	46	D2
Daniel Street	75	A3
Danieli Drive	26	E2
Danieli Road	26	E2
Dara Court	32	D3
Dara Cres	32	D3
*Dargan Court (between Sidmonton and Albert Ave)	68	D2
*Dargan Street (near Ardee Street)	67	B2
Dargle Bridge	67	A3
*Dargle Court (East of Dargle Heights)	67	B2
*Dargle Cres (East of Hazelwood)	67	B2
Dargle Drive	57	A1
Dargle Heights	67	B2
Dargle Lodge	56	D1
Dargle Road (Drumcondra)	25	A4
Dargle Road (Dean's Grange)	59	A1
*Dargle Terrace (on Lower Dargle Road)	67	B2
Dargle Valley	57	A1
Dargle View	57	A1
Dargle Wood	56	D1
*Darley Cottages (off Vevay Road)	67	C2
Darley Court	70	D3
Darley Street	74	F4
Darley's Terrace	74	E2
Darling Estate	23	C4
Darndale	13	C4
Dartmouth Lane	75	C4
Dartmouth Place	75	C4
Dartmouth Road	75	C4
Dartmouth Square	75	C3
Dartmouth Square East	75	C3
Dartmouth Square North	75	C3
Dartmouth Square South	75	C4
Dartmouth Square West	75	C4
Dartmouth Terrace	75	C4
*Dartmouth Walk (Grand Parade)	75	C3
*Dartry Cottages (off Dartry Road)	47	B3
Dartry Park	47	B2
Dartry Road	47	A2
David Park	25	A4
David Road	25	A4
*Davis Court (Thomas Davis Street West)	36	F3
*Davis Court Apts (off Thomas Davis Street West)	36	F3
Davis Place (off Thomas Davis Street South)	74	F1
Davitt House	73	A3
Davitt Park	60	D4
Davitt Road (Inchicore)	73	B2
Davitt Road (Bray)	67	C2
Davitt Terrace	73	A3
*Dawson Court (off Stephen Street Lower)	75	B1
Dawson Court (Mount Merrion Ave)	48	F3
Dawson Lane	75	C1
Dawson Street	75	C1
*De Bret House (off Stonepark Court)	46	F4
De Burgh Road	70	D4
*De Courcy Square (off Prospect Ave)	25	A4
De Selby	54	D2
De Selby Close	54	D2
De Selby Court	54	D2
De Selby Cres	54	D2
De Selby Downs	54	D2
De Selby Drive	54	D2
De Selby Green	54	D2
De Selby Lane	54	D2
De Selby Lawns	54	D2
De Selby Park	53	C2
De Selby Rise	54	D2
De Selby Road	54	D2
De Velara Place	71	B1
*De Vesci Court (off Sloperton)	49	C4
*De Vesci Court (off Sloperton)	49	C4
*De Vesci House (on Old Dunleary Road)	49	C4
De Vesci Terrace	49	C4
Dean Court	75	A1
*Dean Court (off Back Lane)	75	A1
Dean Street	75	A2
Dean Swift Green	25	A2
Dean Swift Road	25	A2
Dean Swift Square	74	F1
*Deans Court (off Kill Lane)	59	B1
Deans Grange	59	B2
Dean's Grange Road	59	B1
Deansrath Ave	34	F4
Deansrath Cres	43	C1
Deansrath Green	43	C1
Deansrath Grove	34	F4
Deansrath Lawn	34	F4
Deansrath Park	43	C1
Deansrath Road	43	C1
Deanstown Ave	24	D2
Deanstown Drive	24	D2
Deanstown Green	24	D2
Deanstown Park	24	D2
Deanstown Road	24	D2
Decies Road	36	E3
Deepdales	67	B4
Deerhaven	8	F4
Deerhaven Ave	8	F4
Deerhaven Close	8	F4
Deerhaven Cres	8	F4
Deerhaven Green	8	F4
Deerhaven Park	8	F4
Deerhaven View	8	F4
Deerhaven Walk	8	F4
Deerpark	67	B4
*Deerpark Apts (Killarney Street)	72	D2
Deerpark Ave (Castleknock)	23	A4
Deerpark Ave (Kiltipper)	54	F3
Deerpark Close (Castleknock)	23	A3
Deerpark Close (Kiltipper)	54	F3
Deerpark Downs	54	F3
Deerpark Drive (Castleknock)	23	A3
Deerpark Drive (Kiltipper)	54	F3
Deerpark Green	54	F3
*Deerpark House (off Thomas Davis Street West)	36	F3
Deerpark Lawn	23	B3
Deerpark Lodge	54	F3
Deerpark Place	54	F3
Deerpark Rise	54	F3
Deerpark Road (Castleknock Road)	23	A3
Deerpark Road (Mount Merrion)	48	D4
Deerpark Road (Kiltipper)	54	F3
Deerpark Square	54	F3
Deerpark Terrace	54	F3
*Deerpark View (off Deerpark Way)	54	F3
*Deerpark View (Deerpark Way)	54	F3
Deerpark Walk (Kiltipper)	54	F3
Deerpark Way	54	F3
Deey Bridge	19	A4
Del Val Ave	27	C2
Del Val Court	27	C2
Delaford Ave	55	C1
Delaford Drive	55	C1
Delaford Grove	55	C1
Delaford Lawn	55	C1
Delaford Park	55	C1
Delbrook Manor	57	C2
Delbrook Park	57	C2
Delhurst Ave	21	B1
Delhurst Close	21	B1
Delhurst Mews	21	B1

STREET NAME	PAGE / GRID REFERENCE
Delhurst Terrace	21 B1
Delville Road	25 A2
*Delvin Road (off Fassaugh Road)	24 F4
*Delvin Terrace (near Maunsell Place)	71 A2
Delwood Close	22 E3
Delwood Drive	22 E3
Delwood Grove	22 E3
Delwood Lawn	22 E3
Delwood Park	22 E3
Delwood Road	22 E3
Delwood Walk	22 E3
Demesne	26 E3
Denewood Castleknock	23 A3
Denmark Street Great	71 B2
Denville Court	60 D4
Denzille Lane	76 D1
*Derby Square (off Werburgh Street)	75 A1
Dermot O'Hurley Ave	39 A3
Derravaragh Road	46 E2
Derry Drive	46 D1
Derry Park	46 D1
Derry Road	46 D1
Derrynane Court	71 B1
Derrynane Gardens	39 A3
Derrynane Parade	71 B1
Derrynane Square	71 B1
*Desmond Ave (off Cross Ave)	50 D4
*Desmond Cottages (off Ardbrough Road)	60 F2
Desmond Street	75 A3
Devenish Road	46 E1
Deverell Place	71 C3
*Devery's Lane (off Phibsborough Road)	25 A4
*Devitt Villas (off Eden Road Lower)	60 E1
Devlin's Place	76 D1
*Devon Close (off Kill Lane)	59 B1
Devoy Road	73 B2
Dewberry Park	4 D4
Dexter Terrace	75 C4
*Diamond Terrace (north of River Lane)	67 B2
Diamond Valley Apts	67 B2
*Digges Lane (Longford Street Little)	75 B1
Digges Street Upper	75 B2
*Dillon Place South (off John Dillon Street)	75 A1
Dillon's Row	17 C2
Dingle Glen	63 A2
Dingle Road	24 E4
*Dispensary Lane (off Main Street Lucan)	34 D1
Dispensary Lane (Willbrook)	46 F4
*Distillery House Apts (off Martin's Row Chapelizod)	36 E2
Distillery Lane	20 D4
*Distillery Loft Apts (off Richmond Road)	25 B4
Distillery Road	25 B4
Diswellstown Cottages	22 E4
Diswellstown Road	22 D3
*Dixon Villas (off Adelaide Road)	60 E1
Doctor's Lane (Maynooth)	17 C3
Dodder Ave	55 B2
*Dodder Bank (off Dundrum Road)	47 B2
Dodder Court	55 B2
*Dodder Court (on Dundrum Road)	47 C3
Dodder Cres	55 B2
Dodder Dale	46 F4
Dodder Green	55 B2
Dodder Lawn	55 B2
*Dodder Park Drive (off Dodder Road Lower Rathfarnham)	46 F3
Dodder Park Grove	46 F3
Dodder Park Road	46 F3
Dodder Road Lower	47 A3
*Dodder Terrace (off Irishtown Road)	39 A3
*Dodder Vale (off Orwell Gardens)	47 A3
Dodder View Cottages (off Herbert Road)	76 F3
Dodsboro Cottages	33 B2
Dodsboro Road	33 C2
D'Olier Street	71 C4
Dollymount	27 A4
Dollymount Ave	27 A4
Dollymount Grove	26 F4
Dollymount Park	27 A4
Dollymount Rise	27 A4
Dolly's Grove	5 C2
Dolmen Court	12 D4
Dolphin Ave	74 E3
Dolphin Court	73 C3
Dolphin House	74 D3
*Dolphin Market (off Dolphin's Barn Street)	74 D3
Dolphin Park	74 D3
Dolphin Road	73 C3
Dolphin's Barn	74 D3
Dolphins Barn Bridge (Grand Canal)	74 D3
Dolphin's Barn Street	74 D3
*Dominick Court (off Dominick Street Upper)	71 A2
Dominick Lane	71 A3
Dominick Place	71 B3
Dominick Street	50 D4
*Dominick Street Court (Dominick Street Upper)	71 A2
Dominick Street Lower	71 A3
Dominick Street Upper	71 A2
*Domville Court (near Santry Villas)	12 E4
Domville Drive	46 D4
Domville Green	46 D4
*Domville Grove (opposite Cenacle Grove)	64 E1
Domville Road	46 D4
Donaghmede	14 F4
Donaghmede Ave	27 B1
Donaghmede Drive	27 B1
Donaghmede Park	27 B1
Donaghmede Road	27 B1
Donaghmore	18 F3
Donard Road	36 F4
*Donnellan Ave (Saint Johns Terrace)	73 C1
Donnybrook	47 C1
*Donnybrook Castle (off Stillorgan Road)	47 C1
*Donnybrook Close (off Stillorgan Road)	48 D2
Donnybrook Court	47 C2
*Donnybrook Green (off Greenfield Park U.C.D.)	48 D2
Donnybrook Manor	47 C1
Donnybrook Mews	47 C1
Donnybrook Road	47 C1
Donnycarney	26 D3
Donnycarney Road	26 D3
Donomore Ave	54 E2
Donomore Cres	54 E2
Donomore Green	54 E2
Donomore Park	54 E2
Donore Ave	74 E2
Donore Road	74 E2
Donore Terrace	74 E2
Donovan Lane	74 F3
Doon Ave	70 D1
Doon Court	11 C4
Doonamana Road	60 D3
Doonanore Park	60 D3
Doonsalla Drive	60 D3
Doonsalla Park	60 D3
Doreen House Apts (off Nephin Road)	24 D4
Doris Street	76 F1
Dornden Park	48 E2
Dorney Court	64 E3
Dorset Lane	71 B1
Dorset Place	71 B1
Dorset Square	71 B1
Dorset Street Lower	71 B1
Dorset Street Upper	71 A2
Double Lane	17 C3
Dowland Road	46 D1
Dowling's Court	72 D4
Downpatrick Road (Crumlin)	73 C4
Downpatrick Road	46 E1
Dowth Ave	24 F4
Doyles Lane (off Clontarf Road)	27 A4
*Drapier Green (off Drapier Road)	24 F2
Drapier Road	24 F2
*Drayton Close (off Monkstown Road)	49 B4
Drimnagh	73 A3
Drimnagh Road	45 C1
Drinagh Park	58 F4
Drinaghmore	58 F4
Drinaghmore Ave	58 F4
Drinaghmore Close	58 F4
Drinaghmore Court	58 F4
Droim Na Coile Drive	34 F2
Droim na Coille Ave	34 F2
Droim na Coille Court	34 F2
Droim na Coille Place	34 F2
Droim na Coille Place	34 F2
Dromard Road	36 F4
*Dromard Terrace (off Seafort Ave)	39 A4
Dromartin Castle	47 C4
Dromawling Road	25 C2
Drombawn Ave	25 C2
Dromcarra Ave	54 E2
Dromcarra Drive	54 E2
Dromcarra Green	54 D2
Dromcarra Grove	54 E2
Dromeen Ave	25 C2
Dromheath Ave	9 B4
Dromheath Drive	9 B4
Dromheath Gardens	9 B4
Dromheath Grove	9 B4
Dromheath Park	9 B4
Dromlee Cres	25 C2
*Dromnanane Park (off Dromawling Road)	25 C2
*Dromnanane Road (off Dromawling Road)	25 C2
Dromore Road	73 A4
Druid Court	11 C4
Druid Valley	64 D1
Drumahill	58 D1
Drumalee Ave	70 D2
Drumalee Court	70 D2
Drumalee Drive	70 D2
Drumalee Grove	70 D2
Drumalee Park	70 D2
Drumalee Road	70 D2
Drumcairn Ave	54 E1
Drumcairn Drive	54 D1
Drumcairn Gardens	54 D1
Drumcairn Green	54 E1
Drumcairn Parade	54 E1
Drumcairn Park	54 E1
Drumcliffe Drive	24 E4
Drumcliffe Road	24 E4
Drumcondra	25 A4
Drumcondra Park	71 C1
Drumcondra Road Lower	25 B4
Drumcondra Road Upper	25 B3
Drumderg Court	25 C4
Drumfinn Ave	35 C2
Drumfinn Park	36 D3
Drumfinn Road	36 D2
Drumkeen Manor	60 D3
Drummartin Close	48 D4
*Drummartin Cres (off Drummartin Park)	58 D1
Drummartin Link Road	58 D1
Drummartin Park	58 D1
Drummartin Road	48 D4
Drummartin Terrace	48 D4
Drummond Place (off Mount Drummond Ave)	75 A4
Drumnigh	14 E3
Drumnigh Road	14 E3
Drumnigh Wood	14 E2
*Drury Hall Apts (Stephen Street Lower)	75 B1
Drury Street	75 B1
Drynam Ave	2 E3
Drynam Close	2 E3
Drynam Copse	2 E3
Drynam Court	2 D2
Drynam Cres	2 E3
Drynam Drive	2 E3
Drynam Glen	2 E3
Drynam Green	2 E3
Drynam Grove	2 E3
Drynam Hall	2 E3
Drynam Mews	2 E3
Drynam Place	2 E4
Drynam Rise	2 E4
Drynam Road	2 D2
Drynam Square	2 E3
Drynam View	2 E3
Drynam Walk	2 E3
Drynam Way	2 E3
Drysdale Close	55 A2
Dualla Court	48 E4
Dubber Cross	11 B3
Dublin Airport	12 E1
Dublin Road (Swords)	1 C3
Dublin Road (Malahide)	3 A3
Dublin Road (Dunboyne)	7 C3
Dublin Road (Maynooth)	18 D3
Dublin Road (Donaghmore)	18 F3
Dublin Road (Kilbarrack)	27 C2
Dublin Road (Sutton)	29 A1
Dublin Road (Celbridge)	32 D3
Dublin Road (Shankill)	64 E3
Dublin Road (Bray)	67 B1
Dublin Street (Baldoyle)	15 A4
Duck Lane (Smithfield)	70 F3
Dufferin Ave	74 F3
Duke Lane Lower	75 C1
Duke Lane Upper	75 B1
Duke Row	72 D2
Duke Street	75 B1
Dun Aengus	54 F2
Dun an Oir	54 F2
Dun Emer Drive	57 C1
Dun Emer Park	57 C1
Dun Emer Road	57 C1
Dun Gaoithe	58 E3
Dun Laoghaire	50 D4
Dunard Ave	69 B1
Dunard Court	69 C1
Dunard Drive	69 C1
Dunard Park	69 C1
Dunard Road	69 C1
Dunard Walk	69 C1
Dunawley Ave	44 D1
Dunawley Drive	44 D1
Dunawley Grove	44 D1
Dunawley Way	44 D1
Dunbavin Bridge	51 A4
*Dunbo Hill (at Saint Laurence Road, Police Station)	30 D1
*Dunbo Terrace (at Saint Laurence Road, Police Station)	30 D1
Dunboy	59 A4
Dunboyne	7 B2
Dunboyne Bridge	7 C3
Dunboyne Road	18 D2
Dunbro Lane	11 C1
*Dunbur Terrace (near Duncairn Ave)	67 C2
Duncairn Ave	67 C2
Duncairn Terrace	67 C2
Duncarraig	29 B2
Dundaniel Road	26 D1
Dundela Ave	60 E1
Dundela Cres	60 E1
*Dundela Haven (off Dundela Park)	60 E1
Dundela Park	60 E1
Dundrum	57 C1
Dundrum By Pass	57 C1
*Dundrum Gate Apts (off Ballinteer Road)	57 C1
Dundrum Road	47 C3
Dundrum Wood	57 B1
Dunedin Court	59 C1
*Dunedin Drive (off Saint Patrick's Cres)	59 C1
Dunedin Park	59 C1
Dunedin Terrace	59 C1
*Dungar Terrace (off Northumberland Ave Dún Laoghaire)	50 D4
Dungriffan Road	30 D2
*Dungriffan Villas (off Dungriffan Road)	30 D2
Dunleary Hill	49 C4
Dunleary Road	49 C4
Dunluce Road	26 E3
Dunmanus Court	24 E4
Dunmanus Road	24 E4
Dunmore Grove	44 F2
Dunmore Lawn	44 F3
Dunmore Park	44 F2
Dunne Street	72 D2
Dunree Park	26 F1
Dunsandle Court	23 A3
Dunsandle Grove	23 A3
Dunseverick Road	26 E4
Dunsinea Lane	23 B3
Dunsink Ave	24 D2
Dunsink Drive	24 D2
Dunsink Gardens	24 D2

STREET NAME	PAGE / GRID REFERENCE		STREET NAME	PAGE / GRID REFERENCE		STREET NAME	PAGE / GRID REFERENCE		STREET NAME	PAGE / GRID REFERENCE
Dunsink Green	24	D2	Eaton Brae (Shankill)	64	E2	Eklad Close	13	C4	Elmdale Park	35	C3
Dunsink Lane	23	A2	Eaton Close	52	F2	Eklad Park	13	C4	*Elmfield		
Dunsink Park	24	D2	*Eaton Court			*El Greco Apts			(adjacent Kilgobbin Wood)	58	E4
Dunsink Road	24	D2	(off Terenure Road North)	46	F2	(off Serpentine Ave)	39	A4	Elmfield Ave	14	D4
Dunsoghly	23	C1	*Eaton Court (Newcourt Ave)	68	D3	*Elbin House (off Serpentine Ave)	39	A4	Elmfield Close	14	D4
Dunsoghly Ave	23	C1	Eaton Green	52	F2	Elder Park	54	E3	Elmfield Court (Clarehall)	14	D4
Dunsoghly Close	23	C1	*Eaton Hall			Elderberry	34	D3	Elmfield Court (Clondalkin)	44	E1
Dunsoghly Court	23	C1	(off Terenure Road North)	46	F2	Elderwood Road	35	B2	Elmfield Cres	14	E4
Dunsoghly Drive	23	C1	*Eaton House			*Elford Terrace (off Donore Ave)	74	E2	Elmfield Drive	14	D4
Dunsoghly Green	23	C1	(beside Eaton Terrace)	52	F2	Elgin Heights	67	A4	Elmfield Green	14	D4
Dunsoghly Grove	23	C1	Eaton Place	49	B4	Elgin Road	76	E3	Elmfield Grove	14	D4
Dunsoghly Park	23	C1	Eaton Road	46	F2	Elgin Wood	67	B4	Elmfield Lawn	14	E4
*Dunstaffnage Hall Apts			Eaton Square (Terenure)	46	F2	*Elizabeth O'Farrell Park			Elmfield Park	14	E4
(off Church Road)	58	F1	Eaton Square (Monkstown)	49	B4	(Lombard Street East)	72	D4	Elmfield Rise	14	D4
Dunville Ave	47	B1	Eaton Terrace	52	F2	Elizabeth Street	25	B4	Elmfield Vale	14	E4
*Dunville Close			Eaton Way	52	F2	Elkwood	56	E1	Elmfield Walk	14	D4
(off Annesley Park)	47	B1	Eaton Wood Ave	64	E3	*Ellen Hall (off Emmet Road)	73	A2	Elmfield Way	14	D4
*Dunville Court (off Moyne Road)	47	B1	Eaton Wood Court	64	E3	Ellenfield Road	25	C2	Elmgrove	60	D4
*Durham Place (off Corrig Road)	60	D1	Eaton Wood Green	64	E3	Ellensborough	54	F3	*Elmgrove Terrace		
Durham Road	39	B4	Eaton Wood Grove	64	E3	Ellensborough Close	54	F3	(near Duncairn Ave)	67	C2
Durrow Road	46	E1	Eaton Wood Square	64	E2	Ellensborough Copse	54	F3	Elmpark Apts	48	E2
Dursey Row	22	F1	Ebenezer Terrace	74	E2	Ellensborough Court	54	F3	Elmpark Ave	47	B1
Dwyer Park	67	C1	Eblana Ave	50	D4	Ellensborough Cres	54	F3	Elmpark Green	48	E2
			Eblana Villas			Ellensborough Dale	54	F3	Elms	48	F3
			(Lower Grand Canal Street)	76	E1	Ellensborough Downs	54	F3	Elms		
	E		Eblana Villas (off Arbour Hill)	70	E3	Ellensborough Drive	54	F3	(opposite Knockmaroon Gate)	36	D1
			Eccles Court	71	B1	Ellensborough Grange	54	F3	Elmwood Ave Lower	47	B1
*Eagle Hill (off George's Ave)	49	A3	Eccles Place	71	B1	Ellensborough Green	54	F3	Elmwood Ave Upper	47	B1
*Eagle Hill Ave			Eccles Street	71	A1	Ellensborough Grove	54	F3	Elmwood Close	21	B1
(off Terenure Road North)	46	F2	Echlin Street	74	E1	Ellensborough Lane	54	F3	*Elmwood Court		
Eagle Park	26	D1	Eden Ave	57	A1	Ellensborough Lawn	54	F3	(On Elmwood Road)	1	C1
*Eagle Terrace			Eden Court	57	A1	Ellensborough Lodge	54	F3	Elmwood Drive	1	C1
(off Sandyford Road)	57	C1	Eden Cres	57	A1	Ellensborough Meadows	54	F3	Elmwood Park	1	C1
*Eagle Terrace (Dalkey)	60	F2	Eden Grove	57	A1	Ellensborough Park	54	F3	Elmwood Road	1	C1
Eagle Valley	66	E4	Eden Park	60	D1	Ellensborough Rise	54	F3	Elner Court	4	D4
Eagle's Nest	68	D3	Eden Park Ave	58	D1	Ellensborough View	54	F3	*Elton Court (Dunboyne)	7	B3
*Eaglewood Apts			Eden Park Drive	48	D4	Ellensborough Walk	54	F3	*Elton Court (off Philipsburgh Ave)	25	C4
(off Rochestown Ave)	59	C2	Eden Park Road	58	D1	Ellensborough Way	54	F3	*Elton Court (off Clonrosse Drive)	26	F1
*Eaglewood House			Eden Quay	71	C4	Ellerslie	64	D3	Elton Court (Leixlip)	32	F1
(off Rochestown Ave)	59	C2	Eden Road Lower	60	D1	*Ellesmere (off Brewery Road)	58	F2	Elton Court (Dalkey)	60	E1
*Eaglewood Mews			Eden Road Upper	60	D1	Ellesmere Ave	70	D1	Elton Drive (Dunboyne)	7	B2
(off Rochestown Ave)	59	C2	Eden Terrace (Botanic Ave)	25	A4	Ellis Court	70	E4	Elton Drive (Coolock)	27	A1
Earl Place	71	B3	Eden Terrace (Dún Laoghaire)	60	D1	Ellis Quay	70	E4	Elton Grove (Dunboyne)	7	B3
Earl Street North	71	B3	*Eden Villas (off Coldwell Street)	60	D1	Ellis Quay Apts	70	F4	Elton Park (Coolock)	27	A1
Earl Street South	74	F1	*Edenbrook Court			Ellis Street	70	E4	Elton Park (Dalkey)	60	E1
Earls Court (Dolphins Barn)	74	D3	(off Ballyboden Road)	56	F1	Elm Close	34	E3	*Elton Walk (off Clonrosse Drive)	27	A1
Earls Court (Cabra)	69	C1	Edenbrook Drive	46	E4	Elm Court (Lucan)	34	E3	*Elvenden House		
*Earls Court			Edenbrook Park	46	E4	Elm Court (Jobstown)	54	D2	(off Cameron Street)	74	E2
(off Terenure Road East)	46	F2	Edenmore	26	F2	Elm Dene	34	E3	Ely Close	55	B3
Earlscroft	67	C4	Edenmore Ave	26	F1	Elm Drive (Lucan)	34	E3	*Ely Cres (off Allenton Road)	55	B3
*Earlsfield Court			Edenmore Cres	27	A2	Elm Drive (Jobstown)	54	D2	Ely Drive	55	B3
(off Francis Street)	74	F1	Edenmore Drive	26	F2	Elm Green	34	E3	*Ely Green (off Ely Close)	55	B3
Earlsfort	34	F3	Edenmore Gardens	26	F2	Elm Grove (Lucan)	34	E3	Ely Green	55	B3
Earlsfort Ave	34	F3	Edenmore Green	26	F2	Elm Grove	49	A4	Ely Grove	55	B3
Earlsfort Close	34	F3	Edenmore Grove	26	F2	Elm Grove (Jobstown)	54	D2	Ely Place	75	C2
*Earlsfort Court (Earlsfort Terrace)	75	C3	Edenmore Park	26	F2	Elm House	76	D3	Ely Place Upper	75	C2
Earlsfort Court	34	F2	Edenvale	57	A2	*Elm House Apts (off Elm Drive)	54	D2	Ely View	55	B3
Earlsfort Drive	34	F3	Edenvale Road	47	B1	Elm Mount Ave	25	C2	Embassy Lawn	47	C2
Earlsfort Gardens	34	F2	*Edenwood			Elm Mount Close	26	D2	Emerald Cottages	76	F2
Earlsfort Green	34	F3	(off Eden Park Drive Goatstown)	48	D4	Elm Mount Court	26	D3	Emerald Place	72	D3
Earlsfort Grove	34	F3	*Edgewood (off Richmond Road)	25	B4	Elm Mount Cres	26	D2	Emerald Square	74	D2
Earlsfort Lane	34	F3	Edgewood Lawns	22	E1	Elm Mount Drive	26	D2	Emerald Street	72	E3
Earlsfort Lawn	34	F2	Edmondsbury Court			Elm Mount Grove	26	D2	Emerald Terrace	74	E2
Earlsfort Meadows	34	F2	(off Esker Lane)	34	E1	Elm Mount Heights	26	D2	*Emily Lawless Court		
Earlsfort Park	34	F2	Edmondstown	56	E3	Elm Mount Lawn	26	D2	(off Bayside Square South)	27	C1
Earlsfort Rise	34	F3	Edmondstown Green	56	E2	Elm Mount Park	26	D2	Emmet Court	73	A2
Earlsfort Road	34	F2	Edmondstown Road	56	E3	Elm Mount Rise	26	D2	Emmet Cres	73	A2
Earlsfort Terrace	75	C3	Edward Lane	76	D4	Elm Mount Road	26	D2	*Emmet Manor (Emmet Cres)	36	F3
Earlsfort Vale	34	F3	Edward Place	76	D4	Elm Mount View	26	D2	Emmet Place	70	F4
Earlsfort View	34	F3	Edward Road	68	D3	Elm Park (Celbridge)	32	D3	Emmet Road	73	A1
Earlsfort Way	34	F3	Edward Square	76	D4	Elm Park (Nutley Lane)	48	D1	Emmet Square	48	F3
Earman's Wood	14	E2	*Edward Terrace			Elm Park Terrace	46	F2	Emmet Street (Harold's Cross)	74	F4
East Pier (Howth)	30	D1	(off Nerano Road)	60	F2	Elm Road (Donnycarney)	26	D3	*Emmet Street		
East Pier (Dún Laoghaire)	50	E3	Edwards Court	56	E2	Elm Road (Fox and Geese)	45	A1	(North Circular Road)	71	C1
East Road	72	F3	*Edwin Court			Elm Road (Newtown)	11	A2	*Emmet Street		
East Wall	72	F1	(off Albert Road Upper)	60	E2	Elm Vale	34	E3	(off Parnell Street Sallynoggin)	60	D1
East Wall Road (Fairview)	72	F1	Effra Road	47	A1	Elm Way (Lucan)	34	E3	*Emmett Buildings		
East Wall Road (Alexandra Basin)	39	A2	*Eglinton Park			*Elm Way (off Grange Wood)	57	A2	(Watling Street)	70	E4
*Eastmore (Bushy Park Road)	46	F3	(off Tivoli Road Dun Laoghaire)	49	C4	Elm Wood	34	E3	Emor Street	75	A3
Eastmoreland Court	76	E3	*Eglinton Road			Elmbrook	34	E2	Emorville Ave	75	A3
Eastmoreland Lane	76	E3	(off Quinnsborough Road)	67	C2	Elmbrook Cres	34	E2	Empress Place	72	D2
Eastmoreland Place	76	E3	Eglinton Court	47	C1	Elmbrook Lawn	34	E2	Enaville Ave (off Annesley Place)	72	E1
Easton	32	E1	Eglinton Park (Donnybrook)	47	C1	Elmbrook Walk	34	E2	Enaville Road	72	E1
*Easton Drive (Easton)	32	E1	Eglinton Road	47	C1	Elmcastle Close	45	A3	Engine Alley (off Meath Street)	74	F1
*Easton Green (Easton)	32	E1	*Eglinton Square			Elmcastle Court	45	A3	*Engleberg Court		
Easton House	19	B4	(off Eglinton Road)	47	C1	Elmcastle Drive	45	A3	(opposite Glandore Park)	59	C1
*Easton Mews (Easton)	32	E1	*Eglinton Terrace			Elmcastle Green	45	A3	English Row	32	D4
Easton Park	19	C4	(Royal Canal Bank)	71	A2	Elmcastle Park	45	A3	Ennafort Ave	26	F2
Easton Road	19	B4	Eglinton Terrace (Donnybrook)	47	C1	Elmcastle Walk	45	A3	Ennafort Court	26	F3
*Easton Row (Easton)	32	E1	Eglinton Terrace (Dundrum)	47	C4	Elmdale Cres	35	C3	Ennafort Drive	26	F3
Eastwood	23	C2	*Eglinton Wood			Elmdale Drive	35	C3	Ennafort Grove	26	F2
Eaton Brae (Orwell Road)	47	A3	(off Eglinton Road)	47	C1				Ennafort Park	26	F3

STREET NAME	PAGE / GRID REFERENCE
Ennafort Road	26 F3
Ennel Ave	26 F2
*Ennel Court (beside Inagh Court)	64 E1
Ennel Drive	26 F2
Ennel Park	26 F2
*Ennis Grove (off Londonbridge Road)	39 A3
Enniskerry	66 D3
Enniskerry Bridge	66 E3
Enniskerry Demense	66 E4
*Enniskerry Road (off Phibsborough Road)	25 A4
Enniskerry Road (Sandyford)	58 D4
Erne Place (Lansdowne Park)	76 E1
Erne Place Little	76 D1
Erne Place Lower	72 D4
Erne Street Lower	72 D4
Erne Street Upper	76 D1
Erne Terrace Front	76 D1
Erne Terrace Rere	76 D1
Errigal Gardens	73 A4
Errigal Road	36 F4
Erris Road	24 E4
Erris Square	22 F1
Esker Drive	34 D2
Esker Glebe	34 D2
Esker Lane	34 E2
Esker Lawns	34 D1
Esker Lodge	34 E2
Esker Lodge Ave	34 E2
Esker Lodge Close	34 E2
Esker Lodge View	34 E2
Esker Manor	34 E2
Esker Meadow	34 E2
Esker Meadow Close	34 E2
Esker Meadow Court	34 E2
Esker Meadow Green	34 E2
Esker Meadow Grove	34 E2
Esker Meadow Lawn	34 E2
Esker Meadow Rise	34 E2
Esker Meadow View	34 E2
Esker Park	34 E2
Esker Pines	34 E1
Esker Road	34 D2
Esker South	34 D3
*Esker Villas (off Summerville Park)	47 A1
Esker Woods	34 E2
Esker Woods Close	34 E2
Esker Woods Court	34 E2
Esker Woods Drive	34 E2
Esker Woods Grove	34 E2
Esker Woods Rise	34 E2
Esker Woods View	34 E2
Esker Woods Walk	34 E2
Esmond Ave	25 C4
*Esmonde Terrace (Upper Dargle Road)	67 B2
*Esplanade Terrace (Strand Road, Convent Ave)	68 D2
*Esposito Road (off John Mc Cormack Ave)	45 C1
Essex Gate (off Essex Quay)	71 A4
Essex Quay	71 A4
Essex Street East	71 A4
Essex Street West (off Fishamble Street)	71 A4
Estate Ave	48 E1
Estate Cottages (Northumberland Road)	76 E2
Estate Cottages (Ballsbridge)	76 F3
Estuary Court	2 D1
Estuary Road	2 F2
Estuary Roundabout (Swords)	2 D1
Estuary Row	3 B2
Estuary Walk	2 F2
Eugene Street	74 E2
Eustace Bridge (Grand Canal)	75 C3
Eustace Street	71 B4
Everton Apts	56 E1
Everton Ave	70 D2
Evora Cres (end of Grace O' Malley Road)	30 D1
Evora Park	30 D1
Evora Terrace (at Saint Laurence Road, Police Station)	30 D1
Ewington Lane	74 D1
Exchange Court	71 C4
Exchange Street Lower (off Wood Quay)	71 A4

STREET NAME	PAGE / GRID REFERENCE
Exchange Street Upper (off Lord Edward Street)	71 A4
Exchequer Street	75 B1
Excise Walk	72 E3
Eyre Court	2 E2

F

STREET NAME	PAGE / GRID REFERENCE
*Faber Grove (off Rory O'Connor Park)	59 B1
Fade Street	75 B1
*Fagan's Lane (off main street and Pound Lane)	17 C3
*Fair Haven (on Strand Street Malahide)	3 B2
Fairacre	2 F3
Fairbrook Lawn	46 F4
Fairfield Ave	72 E2
*Fairfield Court (off Newbridge Ave)	39 A3
*Fairfield House (off Harrison Row)	46 F2
Fairfield Park	47 A2
Fairfield Road	25 A4
Fairgreen	53 A2
*Fairgreen Court (near Adelaide Villas)	67 C2
*Fairgreen Road (near Maitland Street)	67 B2
*Fairgreen Terrace (near Adelaide Villas)	67 C2
Fairlawn Park	24 E2
Fairlawn Road	24 E2
*Fairlawns (off Saval Park Road)	60 E2
*Fairview Ave (off Irishtown Road)	39 A3
Fairview Ave Lower	25 C4
Fairview Ave Upper	25 C4
Fairview Close	25 C4
*Fairview Court (off Fairview Ave Lower)	25 C4
*Fairview Green (off Fairview Ave Upper)	25 C4
Fairview Lawn	64 D1
*Fairview Passage (off Fairview Strand)	25 C4
Fairview Strand	25 C4
*Fairview Terrace (off Fairview Ave Lower)	25 C4
Fairways	46 E4
Fairway's Ave	24 F2
Fairway's Green	24 F2
*Fairway's Grove	24 E2
Fairway's Park	24 F2
Fairy Castle	61 B2
Fairy Grove	12 E3
Fairyhill (Stillorgan)	59 A1
Fairyhill (Oldcourt)	67 B3
Faith Ave	72 E1
Falcarragh Road	25 B2
*Falcons View Apts (adjacent Blanchardstown Town Centre)	22 E1
Falls Road	64 D2
Farmhill Drive	47 C4
Farmhill Park	47 C4
Farmhill Road	47 C4
Farmleigh	23 A4
Farmleigh Ave (Castleknock)	23 A4
Farmleigh Ave (Stillorgan)	58 F1
Farmleigh Close (Castleknock)	23 A4
Farmleigh Close (Stillorgan)	58 F1
Farmleigh Court	23 A4
Farmleigh Park (Castleknock)	23 A4
Farmleigh Park (Stillorgan)	58 F1
Farmleigh View	23 A4
Farmleigh Woods	23 A4
Farney Park	39 A4
Farnham Cres	24 E2
Farnham Drive	24 E2
Farrenboley Cottages	47 B3
Farrenboley Park	47 B3
Fassaroe	66 F3
Fassaroe	67 A2
Fassaroe Ave	67 A3
Fassaroe Glen	67 A2
Fassaroe Lane	67 A3
*Father Bidone Court (off Saint Mary's Ave West)	36 F3
*Father Colohan Terrace (near Market House)	67 C2

STREET NAME	PAGE / GRID REFERENCE
*Father Didone Court (off Saint Mary's Ave West)	36 F3
*Father Kit Court (off Saint Agnes RoadCrumlin)	46 D1
Father Lemass Court	36 D3
Father Mathew Square	70 F3
Father Matthew Bridge (River Liffey)	70 F4
Father Scully House	71 C2
Fatima Terrace	67 C2
*Faughart Road (off Kells Road)	46 E1
Faulkner's Terrace	73 C1
Faussagh Ave	24 E4
Faussagh Road	24 F4
Fawn Lodge	23 A4
Feltrim	3 A4
Feltrim Hall	2 D3
Feltrim Road	2 F4
Fenian Street	76 D1
Fergus Road	46 F2
Ferguson Road	25 A3
*Fernbrook (north of Connawood)	67 B1
Ferncarrig Ave	58 D3
Ferncarrig Court	58 D3
Ferncarrig Rise	58 D3
Ferncourt Ave	55 B3
Ferncourt Close	55 B3
*Ferncourt Cres (off Ferncourt Ave)	55 B3
*Ferncourt Drive (off Ferncourt Drive)	55 B3
Ferncourt Green	55 B3
Ferncourt Park	55 B3
Ferncourt View	55 B3
Ferndale (Tallaght)	55 A2
Ferndale	8 F4
Ferndale Ave	24 F2
Ferndale Glen	64 D3
Ferndale Hill	64 D4
Ferndale Road (Glasnevin)	24 F2
Ferndale Road (Shankill)	64 D3
Ferndale Road (Bray)	67 A1
Fernhill Ave	45 C3
Fernhill Park	45 C3
Fernhill Road	45 C2
Fernleigh	22 D3
Fernleigh Close	22 D3
Fernleigh Court	22 D3
Fernleigh Cres	22 D3
Fernleigh Dale	22 D3
Fernleigh Dene	22 D4
Fernleigh Drive	22 D3
Fernleigh Grange	22 D4
Fernleigh Green	22 D3
Fernleigh Grove	22 D4
Fernleigh Heath	22 D4
Fernleigh Lawn	22 D3
Fernleigh Park	22 D3
Fernleigh Place	22 D3
Fernleigh Vale	22 D3
Fernleigh View	22 D4
Fernleigh Way	22 D4
Fernley Court	75 A2
Ferns Road	46 E1
Fernvale Drive	46 D1
Fernwood Ave	54 E1
Fernwood Close	54 E1
Fernwood Court	54 E1
Fernwood Lawn	54 E1
Fernwood Park	54 E1
Fernwood Way	54 E1
Ferrard Road	46 F2
Ferrycarrig Ave	13 B4
Ferrycarrig Drive	13 B4
Ferrycarrig Green	13 B4
Ferrycarrig Park	13 B4
Ferrycarrig Road	13 B4
Ferryman's Crossing	72 E3
*Fertullagh Road (off Leix Road)	24 F4
Fettercairn	44 E4
Fettercairn Cres	54 D1
Fettercairn Road	44 E4
*Fey Yerra (off Leopardstown Road)	58 F2
Fforster	34 E2
Fforster Close	34 E2
Fforster Court	34 E2
Fforster Cres	34 E2
Fforster Lawn	34 E2
Fforster Park	34 E2

STREET NAME	PAGE / GRID REFERENCE
Fforster Walk	34 E2
Fforster Way	34 E2
*Field Ave (off Balfe Road)	45 C1
*Field's Terrace (off Charleston Road)	47 B1
*Fieldview Cottages (off Annaville Ave)	49 A4
Fiery Lane	62 D4
*Findlater Building Apts (off Harbour Road, opposite west pier)	30 D1
Findlater Place	71 B3
Findlater Street (North Circular Road)	70 D3
*Findlater Street (off Eden Terrace Dún Laoghaire)	60 E1
Fingal Place	70 E2
Fingal Street	74 E2
Finglas	24 E1
Finglas East	24 E1
Finglas Park	24 E1
Finglas Place	24 E2
Finglas Road	24 E2
Finglas Road Old	24 F3
Finglas South	24 D2
*Finglas Square (off Owenstown Park Fosters Ave)	48 D3
Finglas West	24 D1
Finglaswood Road	24 D1
Finn Street	70 D3
Finneber Fort	24 E2
Finneber Fort Square	24 E2
Finnscourt	34 D3
Finnsgreen	34 D3
Finnsgrove	34 D3
Finnslawn	34 D3
Finnspark	34 D3
Finnstown Cloisters	34 D3
Finnstown Fairways	34 D3
Finnstown Hall	34 D3
Finnsvale	34 D3
Finnsview	34 D3
Finnswalk	34 D3
Finnswood	34 D3
Finsbury Green	47 B4
Finsbury House (off Herbert Road)	76 F3
Finsbury Park	47 B4
*Firgrove (off Military Road Ballybrack)	60 E4
Firhouse	55 C1
Firhouse Road	55 B2
Firhouse Road West	55 A2
First Ave (Seville Place)	72 E3
First Ave (Sarsfield Road)	36 F3
First Ave (Belgard Heights)	44 F4
Fishamble Street	71 A4
*Fisherman's Green (off Gasyard Lane Malahide)	3 B2
*Fishermans Wharf (off York Road)	39 A2
*Fitzgerald Park (off Mounttown Road Lower)	59 C1
Fitzgerald Street	75 A4
Fitzgibbon Lane	71 C1
Fitzgibbon Street	71 C1
Fitzmaurice Road (Glasnevin)	24 F2
Fitzmaurice Road (Rathcoole)	52 F2
*Fitzpatrick's Cottages (off Harold's Cross Road)	46 F1
Fitzroy Ave	25 B4
Fitzwilliam Court (Leeson Park)	76 D4
Fitzwilliam Court (Fitzwilliam Square)	75 C2
Fitzwilliam Court (Stillorgan Road)	48 E3
Fitzwilliam Lane	76 D2
Fitzwilliam Place	75 C3
Fitzwilliam Place North (Grangegorman)	70 F3
*Fitzwilliam Point (off Fitzwilliam Quay)	39 A3
*Fitzwilliam Quay (off Fitzwilliam Quay)	39 A3
Fitzwilliam Square	75 C2
Fitzwilliam Square East	76 D2
Fitzwilliam Square North	76 D2
Fitzwilliam Square South	75 C2
Fitzwilliam Square West	75 C2
*Fitzwilliam Street (off Cambridge Park)	39 A3
Fitzwilliam Street Lower	76 D2

STREET NAME	PAGE	GRID REFERENCE
Fitzwilliam Street Upper	76	D2
*Fitzwilliam Terrace (at Esplanade)	68	D2
Fleet Street	71	B4
Fleming Road	25	A3
Fleming's Hall Apts	76	D3
Fleming's Place	76	D3
Flemingstown Park	47	B4
Flemming House	76	D3
Fleurville	49	A4
Fleurville & Benamore Road	49	A4
Fleurville Road	49	A4
Floraville Ave	44	E1
Floraville Drive	44	E2
Floraville Estate	44	E1
Floraville Lawn	44	E1
Florence Road	67	C2
Florence Street	75	A3
*Florence Terrace (Leeson Park Ave)	76	D4
*Florence Terrace (Florence Road)	67	C2
*Florence Villas (Sandymount)	39	A4
*Florence Villas (Florence Road)	67	C2
Flower Grove	60	D2
Foley Street	71	C3
Fontenoy Street	71	A2
Fontenoy Terrace	68	D3
*Fonthill Abbey (off Fonthill Park)	56	F1
Fonthill Abbey	56	F1
Fonthill Park	56	F1
Fonthill Road (Clondalkin)	35	A2
Fonthill Road (Rathfarnham)	56	F1
Fonthill Road North	35	A3
Fonthill Road South	44	D2
Forbes Lane	74	E2
*Forbes Quay Apts (Forbes Street)	72	E4
Forbes Street	72	E4
Forest Ave (Swords)	1	B3
Forest Ave (Kilnamanagh)	45	A3
Forest Boulevard	1	B3
Forest Close	45	A3
Forest Court	1	B2
Forest Cres	1	B3
Forest Dale	1	B2
Forest Drive (Swords)	1	B3
Forest Drive (Kilnamanagh)	45	A3
Forest Green (Swords)	1	B3
Forest Green (Kilnamanagh)	45	A3
Forest Grove	1	B3
Forest Hills (Swords)	1	C3
Forest Hills (Rathcoole)	52	E2
Forest Lawn	45	A3
Forest Park (Swords)	1	B2
Forest Park (Leixlip)	32	F1
Forest Park (Kilnamanagh)	45	A3
Forest Road	1	B4
Forest View	1	B3
Forest Walk	1	C3
Forest Way	1	C3
Forester Drive	34	F2
Forestfields Road	1	C3
Forestwood Ave	12	D4
Forestwood Close	12	E4
*Forge Court (south of Church on Main Street Howth)	30	D2
Forster Way	2	D2
Fort Ostman	73	C4
*Fort Ostman Wood (off Old County Road)	73	C4
Fortescue Lane	75	B4
Fortfield Ave	46	E3
*Fortfield Court (off Fortfield Road)	46	E3
Fortfield Cres	46	E3
Fortfield Drive	46	E3
Fortfield Gardens	47	A2
Fortfield Grove	46	E3
Fortfield Park	46	E3
Fortfield Road (Kimmage)	46	E2
Fortfield Road (Bushy Park)	46	E3
Fortfield Square	46	E3
Fortfield Terrace	47	A2
Forth Road	72	F2
*Forthill Court (off Fonthill Road)	56	F1
Fortlawn Ave	22	D1
Fortlawn Cres	22	D1
Fortlawn Drive	22	D1
Fortlawn Park	22	D1
Fortlawns	60	E2
Fortrose Park	46	E4
Fortunestown	53	C1
Fortunestown Close	53	C1
Fortunestown Cres	53	C1
Fortunestown Lane	53	B1
Fortunestown Road	54	D2
Fortunestown Way	54	D1
Fortview Ave	39	C1
Fortwilliam	48	E4
Foster Place North	72	D1
Foster Place South (College Green)	71	B4
Foster Terrace	72	D1
Fosterbrook	48	E2
Fosters Ave	48	D3
Fountain Place	70	F3
Fountain Road (Phoenix Park)	69	C3
*Fountain View Apts (James's Street)	74	D1
Fourth Ave (Seville Place)	72	E3
Fourth Ave (Tallaght)	44	F4
Fownes Street Lower (off Temple Bar)	71	B4
Fownes Street Upper	71	B4
Fox and Geese	45	A1
Fox Hill	55	A4
Foxborough Ave	34	E3
Foxborough Close	34	F3
Foxborough Court	34	F3
Foxborough Cres (off Foxborough Road)	34	F3
Foxborough Downes	34	E3
Foxborough Drive	34	E3
Foxborough Gardens	34	F3
Foxborough Glade	34	F3
Foxborough Glen	34	F3
Foxborough Green	34	F3
Foxborough Grove	34	F3
Foxborough Hall (off Newlands Road)	34	F3
Foxborough Heights	34	F3
Foxborough Hill	34	E3
Foxborough Lane	34	F3
Foxborough Lawn	34	F3
Foxborough Manor	34	F3
Foxborough Meadows	34	E3
Foxborough Park	34	E3
Foxborough Place	34	E3
Foxborough Rise	34	E3
Foxborough Road	34	E3
Foxborough Row	34	F3
Foxborough Walk	34	F3
Foxborough Way	34	E3
Foxdene Ave	34	F3
Foxdene Drive	34	F3
Foxdene Gardens	34	F3
Foxdene Green	34	F3
Foxdene Grove	34	F3
Foxdene Park	34	F3
Foxes Grove	64	E3
Foxe's Lane	27	B2
Foxfield	34	D3
Foxfield Ave	27	B2
Foxfield Cres	27	B2
Foxfield Drive	27	B2
Foxfield Green	27	B2
Foxfield Grove	27	B2
Foxfield Heights	27	B2
Foxfield Lawn	27	B2
Foxfield Park	27	B2
Foxfield Road	27	B2
Foxfield Saint John	27	B2
Foxford	34	F2
Foxford Court (off Ballyowen Lane)	34	F2
Foxhill Ave	27	A1
Foxhill Close	27	A1
Foxhill Court	27	A1
Foxhill Cres	27	A1
Foxhill Drive	27	A1
Foxhill Green	14	D4
Foxhill Grove	27	A1
Foxhill Lawn	27	A1
Foxhill Park	27	A1
Foxhill Way	27	A1
Foxpark	34	D3
Foxrock	59	A3
Foxrock Ave	59	A2
Foxrock Close	59	B2
Foxrock Court	59	A2
Foxrock Cres	59	B2
Foxrock Green	59	A2
Foxrock Grove	59	B2
Foxrock Manor	58	F2
*Foxrock Mount (off Foxrock Park)	59	A2
Foxrock Park	59	A2
Foxrock Wood	59	B2
Foxwood (Swords)	2	D2
Foxwood (Lucan)	34	D3
Foyle Road	25	C4
*Frances Ball House (off Stonepark Court)	46	F4
*Francis Court (off Mark's Alley west)	74	F1
Francis Street	74	F1
Frank Sherwin Bridge (River Liffey)	70	D4
*Frankfort (off Dundrum Road)	47	B4
Frankfort Ave	47	A2
Frankfort Cottages	72	D2
*Frankfort Court (off Rathgar Ave)	46	F2
*Frankfort Flats (off Rathgar Ave)	46	F2
Frankfort Mews	47	B4
Frankfort Park	47	B4
*Frascati Court (off George's Ave)	49	A3
*Frascati Hall (off Frascati Road Blackrock)	49	A3
Frascati Park	49	A3
Frascati Road	49	A3
Frederick Court	71	B2
*Frederick House (Fredrick Street South)	75	C1
Frederick Lane North	71	B2
Frederick Street North	71	B2
Frederick Street South	75	C1
*French Mullen Flats (Charlemont Street)	75	B3
French Park	9	B2
Frenchman's Lane	71	C3
*Friar's Walk (off Monastery Park)	44	E1
*Friarsland Ave (off Larchfield Road)	47	C3
Friarsland Cres	47	C3
Friarsland Road	47	C3
Friary Ave	70	F3
*Friary Close (near Cook Street)	71	A4
Friary Court	70	F3
Friary Grove	70	F3
Friel Ave	36	D4
Fumbally Court	75	A2
Fumbally Lane	75	A2
*Fumbally Square (Fumbally Lane)	75	A2
Furry Glen	36	D1
*Furry Hill (off Sandyford Road)	58	D2
Furry Park Court	26	E3
Furry Park Road	26	E3
Furze Road (Phoenix Park)	36	E1
Furze Road (Sandyford)	58	E2

G

STREET NAME	PAGE	GRID REFERENCE
Gables	27	A1
Gaelic Street	72	E2
Gainsborough	2	F3
Gainsborough Ave	2	F3
Gainsborough Close	2	F3
Gainsborough Court	2	F3
Gainsborough Cres	2	F3
Gainsborough Downs	2	F3
Gainsborough Green	2	F3
Gainsborough Lawn	2	F3
Gainsborough Park	2	F3
Gallaun Road	11	C4
Gallery Quay Apts	76	E1
Galloping Green (Stillorgan)	58	F1
*Galloping Green (off Belmont)	59	A1
Gallows Hill	1	C2
Galmoy Road	24	F4
Galtrim Park	67	C2
Galtrim Road	67	C2
Galtymore Close	36	F4
Galtymore Drive	73	B3
Galtymore Park	36	F4
Galtymore Road	73	B3
*Gandon Close (off Harold's Cross Road)	46	F1
*Gandon Court (off Main Street Lucan)	34	D1
Gandon Hall	71	C3
*Gandon Mews (off Main Street Lucan)	34	D1
Garda Terrace (Phoenix Park)	69	C3
Garden Lane	74	F1
Garden Terrace (off Clanbrassil Street Upper)	74	F3
Garden View	75	B4
Garden View Court	74	F1
Gardiner Lane	71	C2
Gardiner Place	71	B2
Gardiner Row	71	B2
Gardiner Street Lower	71	C2
Gardiner Street Middle	71	C2
Gardiner Street Upper	71	B1
Garnett Hall	7	A2
Garnett Vale	7	A2
Garnish Square	22	F1
Garrison Mews	64	D1
Garrynisk Close	44	F3
Garrynisk Road	44	F3
Garrynure	47	B2
Garryowen Road	36	E3
Gartan Ave	25	A4
Gartan Court	2	E1
Gartan Drive	2	E1
Garter Ave	53	C1
Garter Lane	53	B1
Garthy Wood Apts	56	D1
Garville Ave Upper	46	F2
*Garville Court (off Garville Road)	47	A2
*Garville Drive (off Garville Ave)	47	A2
Garville Lane	47	A2
*Garville Place (off Garville Ave)	47	A2
Garville Road	47	A2
Gas Yard Lane	3	B2
*Gascoigne Court (Camben Row)	75	A2
*Gateway Apts (Gateway)	25	A1
Gateway Ave	25	A1
Gateway Court	25	A1
Gateway Cres	25	A1
Gateway Gardens	25	A1
Gateway Mews	25	A1
Gateway Place	25	A1
Gateway View	25	A1
Gaybrook Lawns	3	A3
Gazelle Ave	9	B2
Gazelle Lane	9	B2
Gazelle Mews	9	B2
Gazelle Terrace	9	B2
Gazelle Walk	9	B2
Geoffrey Keating Road	74	F2
*George Reynolds Flats (off Oliver Plunkett Ave)	39	A3
George's Ave (Blackrock)	49	A3
Georges Court	72	D4
George's Dock	72	D3
George's Hill	71	A3
George's Lane	70	F3
George's Place (Temple Street)	71	B1
*George's Place (off George's Ave)	49	A3
George's Place (Dún Laoghaire)	50	D4
George's Quay	71	C4
*Georges Quay House (Georges Quay)	71	C4
Georges Road (off Mckee Ave)	24	E1
George's Street Lower	50	D4
George's Street Upper	50	D4
George's Wharf	71	A1
Georgian Hamlet	15	A4
Georgian Village	23	A4
Gerald Street	76	F1
*Geraldine Court (off Doctors Lane)	17	C3
Geraldine Street	71	A1
Geraldstown Woods	12	D4
*Gertrude Terrace (near Ardee Street)	67	B2
*Gibbon's Cottages (beside De Selby Road)	54	D2
Gilbert Road	74	F3
Gilford Ave	39	B4
*Gilford Court (off Gilford Road)	39	A4
Gilford Drive	39	A4
Gilford Park	39	A4
*Gilford Pines (off Gilford Road)	39	A4
Gilford Place	72	D2
Gilford Road	39	A4
*Gilford Terrace (off Gilford Road)	39	B4
Giltspur Heights	67	B4
Giltspur Lane	67	B4
Giltspur Wood	67	B3
Glandore Park	59	C1
Glandore Road	25	C3
Glasanaon Court	24	E2

STREET NAME	PAGE / GRID REFERENCE
Glasanaon Park	24 E2
Glasanaon Road	24 E2
Glasaree Court	24 E2
Glasaree Road	24 E2
Glasilawn Ave	24 F2
Glasilawn Road	24 F2
Glaslyn	26 D4
Glasmeen Road	24 F2
Glasmore Park	1 C1
*Glasnamana Place (off Glasnamana Road)	24 F2
Glasnamana Road	24 F2
Glasnevin	24 F3
Glasnevin Ave	24 F1
Glasnevin Court	24 E3
Glasnevin Downs	24 F3
Glasnevin Drive	25 A1
Glasnevin Hill	25 A3
Glasnevin North	24 F1
Glasnevin Oaks (off Finglas Road Old)	24 F3
Glasnevin Park	24 F1
Glasnevin Woods	24 E3
Glasson Court	47 B3
*Glasthule Buildings (off Glasthule Road)	60 E1
Glasthule Road	60 E1
*Glaunsharoon (off Eglinton Road)	47 C1
Gleann na Rí	63 C1
Gleann na Smol (Monkstown)	49 B4
Gleann na Smól (Tallaght)	54 F2
Glebe (Airport)	13 B1
Glebe (Newcastle)	41 C3
Glebe (Rathcoole)	52 D3
Glebe Close	41 C3
Glebe Green	41 C3
Glebe Hall	59 C1
Glebe Heights	41 C4
Glebe Square	41 C4
*Glebe View (Church Street Finglas)	24 E2
Glebe Way	41 C4
Gledswood Ave	47 C3
Gledswood Close	47 C3
*Gledswood Drive (off Bird Ave)	47 C3
Gledswood Park	47 C3
Glen Ave	59 B3
Glen Close	59 B3
Glen Dale	59 B3
Glen Drive	59 B3
Glen Druid	64 E1
Glen Ellan Ave	1 C1
Glen Ellan Close	1 C1
Glen Ellan Court	1 C1
Glen Ellan Cres	1 C1
Glen Ellan Drive	1 C1
Glen Ellan Gardens	1 C1
Glen Ellan Green	1 C1
Glen Ellan Grove	1 C1
Glen Ellan Park	1 C1
Glen Ellan Pines	1 C1
Glen Ellan Walk	1 C1
Glen Garth	59 B3
Glen Grove	59 B3
Glen Lawn Drive	59 B3
Glen na Smol	67 C4
*Glen Terrace (off Link Road)	60 E1
Glen Walk	59 B3
Glenaan Road	25 B2
Glenabbey Road	48 E4
Glenacre	62 E4
Glenageary Ave	60 D2
Glenageary Court	60 D2
Glenageary Hall	60 E2
Glenageary Lodge	60 D2
Glenageary Park	60 D2
Glenageary Road Lower (Sallynoggin)	60 D1
Glenageary Road Lower (Dun Laoghaire)	50 D4
Glenageary Road Upper	60 D1
Glenageary Woods	60 D1
Glenalbyn Road	58 F1
Glenalua Heights	60 E3
Glenalua Road	60 E3
Glenalua Terrace	60 E3
Glenamuck Cottages	63 A2
Glenamuck North	62 F1
Glenamuck Road (Golden Ball)	62 F2
Glenamuck Road (Carrickmines)	63 A1

STREET NAME	PAGE / GRID REFERENCE
Glenamuck Road North (Brighton Road)	59 B4
Glenamuck Road South (Carrickmines)	63 A1
Glenamuck Road South (Kilternan)	62 F2
*Glenann (off Willbrook Road)	46 F4
Glenanne	46 E2
Glenard Ave (Cabra)	70 D1
Glenard Ave (Bray)	67 C2
*Glenard Hall (off Roebuck Downs)	47 C3
Glenarm Ave	25 B4
*Glenarm Square Apts (Dargle Road)	25 A4
Glenarriff Road	23 C3
Glenart Ave	48 F4
Glenaulin	36 D2
Glenaulin Drive	36 D2
*Glenaulin Green (off Oakcourt Ave)	35 C2
Glenaulin Park	36 D2
Glenaulin Road	35 C2
*Glenavon Court (off Griffith Ave)	25 A3
Glenavon Park	64 D1
Glenavy Park	46 E2
Glenayle Road	26 F1
Glenayr Road	46 F2
Glenbeigh Park	69 C1
Glenbeigh Road	70 D2
Glenbourne Ave	58 F4
Glenbourne Close	58 F4
Glenbourne Cres	58 F4
Glenbourne Drive	58 F4
Glenbourne Green	58 F4
Glenbourne Grove	58 F4
Glenbourne Park	58 F4
Glenbourne Road	58 F4
Glenbourne View	58 F4
Glenbourne Walk	58 F4
Glenbourne Way	58 F4
*Glenbower Park (off Churchtown Road)	47 B4
Glenbrae	64 E2
*Glenbrian Hall (off Howth Road)	26 D4
Glenbrook (Enniskerry)	66 E3
*Glenbrook (South of Glenlucan)	67 B3
Glenbrook Park	46 F4
Glenbrook Road	23 C3
*Glenburgh Terrace (on River Lane)	67 B2
Glencairn	58 E3
Glencairn Ave	58 E3
Glencairn Chase	58 E3
Glencairn Close	58 E3
Glencairn Copse	58 E4
Glencairn Court	58 E4
Glencairn Cres	58 E4
Glencairn Dale	58 E3
Glencairn Drive	58 E3
*Glencairn Garth (off Glencairn Road)	58 E3
Glencairn Glade	58 E4
Glencairn Glen	58 F4
Glencairn Green	58 E3
Glencairn Grove	58 F4
Glencairn Heath	58 E3
Glencairn Heights	58 E3
Glencairn Lawn	58 E3
Glencairn Oaks	58 E4
Glencairn Park	58 E3
Glencairn Place	58 E4
Glencairn Rise	58 E3
Glencairn Road	58 E3
Glencairn Thicket	58 F3
Glencairn View	58 E3
Glencairn View	58 E3
Glencairn Walk	58 E3
Glencairn Way	58 E3
Glencar Road	69 C2
*Glencarr Court (beside Glencarr Lawn)	64 E1
Glencarr Lawn	64 E1
Glencarraig	29 B1
Glencarrig Court	55 B2
*Glencarrig Court (Near Grace Park Ave)	25 B4
Glencarrig Drive	55 B2
Glencarrig Green	55 B2

STREET NAME	PAGE / GRID REFERENCE
Glencarthy Court Apts	26 D3
Glencloy Road	25 B2
Glencorp Road	25 C2
Glencourt Estate	67 C3
Glencullen	62 E4
Glencullen Bridge	65 B1
Glendale	20 D4
Glendale Drive	67 C3
Glendale Meadows	20 E4
Glendale Park	46 D3
*Glendalough Road (off Hollybank Road)	25 A4
Glendhu Park	23 C3
Glendhu Road	23 C3
Glendinning Lane (off Wicklow Street)	75 B1
Glendoher Ave	56 F1
Glendoher Close	56 E1
Glendoher Drive	56 F1
Glendoher Park	56 E1
Glendoher Road	56 E1
Glendoo Close	45 B3
Glendown Ave	46 D3
Glendown Close	46 D3
Glendown Court	46 D3
Glendown Cres	46 D3
Glendown Drive	46 D3
Glendown Green	46 D3
Glendown Grove	46 D3
Glendown Lawn	46 D3
Glendown Park	46 D3
Glendown Road	46 D3
Glendun Road	25 B2
Glenealy Downs	8 F4
Glenealy Road	74 D4
Gleneaston	19 B4
Gleneaston Ave	19 B4
Gleneaston Close	19 B4
Gleneaston Court	19 B4
Gleneaston Cres	19 B4
Gleneaston Drive	19 B4
Gleneaston Gardens	19 B4
Gleneaston Green	19 B4
Gleneaston Grove	19 B4
Gleneaston Lawns	19 B4
Gleneaston Manor	19 B4
Gleneaston Park	19 B4
Gleneaston Rise	19 B4
Gleneaston Square	19 B4
Gleneaston View	19 B4
Gleneaston Way	19 B4
Gleneaston Woods	19 B4
*Glenesk Court (off Claremont Road)	39 A4
Glenfarne Road	26 F1
Glenfield Ave	35 A2
Glenfield Close	35 A2
Glenfield Drive	35 A2
Glenfield Grove	35 A2
Glenfield Park	35 A2
*Glengara Close (off Glenageary Road Lower)	60 D1
Glengara Park	60 D1
Glengariff Parade	71 A1
Glengarriff Cres	71 B1
Glengarriff Parade	71 B1
Glenhill Ave	24 E2
Glenhill Court	24 E2
Glenhill Drive	24 E2
Glenhill Grove	24 E2
Glenhill Road	24 E2
Glenhill Villas	24 E2
Glenlucan	67 B2
Glenlyon Cres	55 C2
Glenlyon Grove	55 C2
Glenlyon Park	55 C2
*Glenmalure Court (off James's Walk)	73 C2
Glenmalure Park	73 C2
Glenmalure Square	47 B2
*Glenmalure Villas (off Saint Jame's Walk)	74 D2
Glenmaroon Park	35 C2
Glenmaroon Road	35 C2
Glenmore Court	56 F2
Glenmore Green	56 F2
Glenmore Park	56 F2
Glenmore Road	69 C1
Glenmurry Park	45 C3
Glenomena Grove	48 E2
Glenomena Park	48 E2

STREET NAME	PAGE / GRID REFERENCE
Glenpark Close	35 B1
Glenpark Drive	35 B1
Glenpark Road	35 B1
Glenshane Close	54 D1
Glenshane Cres	54 D1
*Glenshane Dale (off Glenshane Lawns)	54 D1
Glenshane Drive	54 D1
Glenshane Gardens	54 D1
Glenshane Green	54 D1
Glenshane Grove	54 D1
Glenshane Lawns	54 D1
Glenshane Park	54 D1
*Glenshane Place (off Glenshane Lawns)	54 D1
Glenshesk Road	25 C2
*Glenside Villas (off Lucan Road Palmerston)	35 C1
Glenthorn	67 B4
Glenties Drive	24 D2
Glenties Park	24 D2
Glentow Road	25 B2
*Glentworth Park (off Slademore Ave)	27 A1
Glenvale	34 E3
Glenvar Park	48 F3
Glenvara Park	55 C2
Glenview (Rochestown Ave)	60 D3
Glenview (Enniskerry)	66 D3
Glenview Drive	55 B1
*Glenview House Apts (opposite Brookmount Ave)	55 C1
Glenview Lawns	55 B1
Glenview Park	55 B1
Glenville Ave	22 E2
Glenville Court	22 E3
Glenville Drive	22 E3
Glenville Garth	22 E3
Glenville Green	22 E2
Glenville Grove	22 E2
Glenville Lawn	22 E2
Glenville Road	22 E3
*Glenville Terrace (off Main Street Dundrum)	47 C4
Glenville Way	22 E2
Glenwood (Bray)	67 B2
Glenwood (Laragcon Lucan)	33 C1
*Glenwood (off Landscape Road)	47 A3
Glenwood Road	26 F1
Glin Ave	13 B4
Glin Close	13 B4
Glin Court	13 B4
Glin Cres	13 B4
Glin Drive	13 B4
Glin Grove	13 B4
Glin Park	13 B4
Glin Road	13 B4
Glitspur Brook	67 C3
Gloucester Diamond	71 C2
Gloucester Lane (off Sean McDermott Street Lower)	71 C2
Gloucester Place	71 C2
Gloucester Place Lower	71 C2
Gloucester Place Upper	71 C2
*Gloucester Square Apts (Gloucester Place Lower)	71 C2
Gloucester Street South	72 D4
Glovers Alley	75 B1
Glovers Court (off York Street)	75 B1
Goatstown	48 D4
Goatstown Ave	47 C4
Goatstown Close	48 D4
Goatstown Road	47 C4
Gobán Saor	58 E4
Godfrey Place (off Oxmanstown Road)	70 D2
Gofton Hall (off Mckee Ave)	24 E1
Golden Ball	62 F2
Golden Lane	75 A1
Goldenbridge Ave	73 B2
Goldenbridge Gardens	73 A2
Goldenbridge Terrace	73 A2
Goldenbridge Walk (Goldenbridge)	73 A2
Goldenbridge Walk (Tyrconnell Road)	36 F4
Goldsmith Hall Apts	72 D4
Goldsmith Street	71 A1
*Goldsmith Terrace (off Quinnsborough Road)	67 C2
Goldstone Court Apts	74 D4

STREET NAME	PAGE / GRID REFERENCE
Golf Links Road (Portmarnock)	15 A2
Gordon Ave	59 A3
Gordon Place	75 B3
Gordon Street	76 F1
*Gorsefield Court (off McAuley Road)	26 F2
Gort na Mona Drive	59 B3
Gortbeg Ave	24 E3
Gortbeg Drive	24 E3
Gortbeg Park	24 E3
Gortbeg Road	24 E3
Gortmore Ave	24 E2
Gortmore Drive	24 E2
Gortmore Park	24 E3
Gortmore Road	24 E3
Gosworth Park	60 E1
*Goulding Mews (Cadogan Road)	25 C4
Gowrie Park	60 D1
Grace O'Malley Drive	30 D2
Grace O'Malley Road	30 D2
Grace Park Ave	25 B4
Grace Park Court	25 C2
Grace Park Gardens	25 B4
Grace Park Heights	25 C3
*Grace Park Lawns (off Grace Park Heights)	25 C2
Grace Park Manor	25 B3
Grace Park Meadows	25 C3
Grace Park Road	25 C3
Grace Park Terrace	25 C3
Gracefield Ave	26 F2
Gracefield Road	26 E2
Grafton Street	75 B1
Graham Court	71 B2
Graham's Row	71 A2
Graigue Court	11 C4
Granby Lane	71 A2
Granby Place	71 B3
Granby Row	71 A2
Grand Canal Bank	74 D2
*Grand Canal Court (off Herberton Road)	73 C3
Grand Canal Docks	76 F1
Grand Canal Place	74 E1
Grand Canal Plaza	76 E1
Grand Canal Quay	76 E1
Grand Canal Square 72 E4	72 E4
Grand Canal Street Lower	76 E1
Grand Canal Street Upper	76 E2
Grand Canal View	73 B2
Grand Central Apts	58 E2
Grand Parade	75 C3
Grange (Meath)	6 E4
Grange (Malahide)	14 E1
Grange	43 A1
Grange Abbey Cres	14 E4
Grange Abbey Drive	14 E4
Grange Abbey Grove	14 E4
Grange Abbey Road	14 E4
Grange Ave	14 F4
Grange Brook	56 F2
Grange Close (Kilbarrack)	27 C1
Grange Close (Pottery Road)	59 C3
*Grange Cottages (off Brewery Road)	58 F1
Grange Court	57 A1
*Grange Court Apts (Stanhope Street)	70 F3
Grange Cres	59 B2
Grange Downs	57 A1
Grange Drive	27 C1
*Grange Grove (off Dean's Grange Road)	59 B1
Grange Hall	57 B3
Grange Hall Apts	27 A2
Grange Lodge Ave	14 E4
Grange Lodge Court	14 E4
Grange Manor	34 D3
Grange Manor Ave	57 A1
Grange Manor Close	57 A1
Grange Manor Drive	57 A1
Grange Manor Grove	57 A1
Grange Manor Road	57 A1
Grange Parade	27 C1
Grange Park (Baldoyle)	14 F4
Grange Park (Willbrook)	56 F1
Grange Park (Cornelscourt)	59 B2
Grange Park Ave	27 A2
Grange Park Close	27 B2
Grange Park Cres	27 B2
Grange Park Drive	27 A2

STREET NAME	PAGE / GRID REFERENCE
Grange Park Green	27 B2
Grange Park Grove	27 A2
Grange Park Rise	27 B1
Grange Park Road	27 A2
Grange Park View	27 B1
Grange Park Walk	27 A2
Grange Rise	14 F4
Grange Road (Baldoyle)	14 F4
Grange Road (Rathfarnham)	46 F4
Grange Road (The Priory)	56 F1
Grange Road (Marley Park)	57 A2
*Grange Terrace (off Dean's Grange Road)	59 B1
Grange View Close	43 B1
Grange View Court	43 B1
Grange View Green	43 B1
Grange View Grove	43 B1
Grange View Lawn	43 B1
Grange View Park	43 B1
Grange View Place	34 E4
Grange View Road	43 B1
Grange View Walk	43 B1
Grange View Way	43 B1
Grange View Wood	43 B1
Grange Way	27 C1
Grange Wood (Ballinteer)	57 A2
Grangebrook Ave	56 F2
Grangebrook Close	56 F2
Grangebrook Park	56 F2
Grangebrook Vale	56 F2
Grangefield	57 B3
Grangegorman Lower	70 F3
Grangegorman Upper	70 F2
Grangegorman Villas	70 F3
Grangemore	14 E4
Grangemore Ave	14 E4
Grangemore Court	14 D4
Grangemore Cres	14 D4
Grangemore Drive	14 E4
Grangemore Grove	14 E4
Grangemore Lawn	14 E4
Grangemore Park	14 E4
Grangemore Rise	14 D4
Grangemore Road	14 D4
Grangewood	59 C1
*Granite Hall (off Rosmeen Gardens)	60 D1
Granite Place (off Gilford Road)	76 F4
*Granite Terrace (off Inchicore Terrace South)	36 F3
Granitefield	59 C3
Granitefield Manor	59 C3
Granitefield Mews	59 C3
Grantham Place	75 B3
Grantham Street	75 A3
Grants Ave (Greenogue Industrial Estate)	42 E4
Grants Court (Greenogue Industrial Estate)	42 E4
Grants Cress (Greenogue Industrial Estate)	42 E4
Grants Drive (Greenogue Industrial Estate)	42 E4
Grants Hill (Greenogue Industrial Estate)	42 E4
Grants Lane (Greenogue Industrial Estate)	42 E4
Grants Park (Greenogue Industrial Estate)	42 E4
Grants Place (Greenogue Industrial Estate)	42 E4
Grants Rise (Greenogue Industrial Estate)	42 E4
Grants Road (Greenogue Industrial Estate)	42 E4
Grants Row (Greenogue Industrial Estate)	42 E4
Grant's Row	76 D1
Grants View (Greenogue Industrial Estate)	42 E4
Grants Way (Greenogue Industrial Estate)	42 E4
Granville Close	60 D3
*Granville Cres (off WoodleyRoad)	60 D3
Granville Park	59 A1
Granville Road (Deans Grange)	59 A2
Granville Road (Cabinteely)	59 C3
Grattan Ave	35 A4
Grattan Bridge (River Liffey)	71 A4
Grattan Court (off Mount Street)	76 E1
Grattan Court (Celbridge)	31 C4

STREET NAME	PAGE / GRID REFERENCE
Grattan Court East	76 E1
Grattan Cres	36 F3
Grattan Hall	14 E4
Grattan Lodge	14 E4
Grattan Parade	25 A4
Grattan Place	76 E1
Grattan Street	76 E1
*Gravel Walk Apts (Hendrick Street)	70 E4
*Gravel Walk Church Apts (Hendrick Street)	70 E4
Gray Square	74 F1
Gray Street (off Meath Street)	74 F1
Great Western Ave	70 F1
Great Western Square	70 F1
Great Western Villas	70 F1
Greeg Court	71 B3
Greek Street	71 A4
Green Acre Court	56 D1
Green Court View Apts	71 A3
*Green Isle Court (off Bushfield Lawns)	44 D2
Green Lane (Leixlip)	19 C4
Green Lane (Rathcoole)	52 E2
Green Park (Rathgar)	47 B3
Green Park Road	67 B2
Green Road (Blackrock)	48 F3
Green Street	71 A3
Green Street East	72 F4
Green Street Little	71 A3
Greencastle Ave	26 E1
Greencastle Cres	26 E1
Greencastle Drive	13 B4
Greencastle Parade	26 F1
Greencastle Park	13 B4
Greencastle Road	13 B4
Greendale Ave	27 C2
*Greendale Court (off Thornville Drive)	27 B2
Greendale Road	27 B2
Greenfield Close	17 C4
Greenfield Cres	48 D2
Greenfield Drive	18 D4
*Greenfield Manor (off Greenfield Park U.C.D.)	48 D2
Greenfield Park (Stillorgan Road)	48 D2
Greenfield Park (Ballycullen Road)	55 C2
Greenfield Place (off Mount Drummond Ave)	75 A4
Greenfield Road (Sutton)	29 B1
Greenfield Road (Mount Merrion)	48 E4
Greenfort Ave	35 A2
Greenfort Close	35 A2
Greenfort Cres	35 A2
Greenfort Drive	35 A2
Greenfort Gardens	35 A2
Greenfort Lawns	35 A2
Greenfort Park	35 A2
Greenfort Walk	35 A2
Greenhills	45 B3
Greenhills Court	55 A1
Greenhills Road	45 A4
Greenisle Road	43 C3
Greenlands	58 D2
*Greenlawns (off Macroom Ave)	13 B4
Greenlea Ave	46 E2
Greenlea Drive	46 E2
Greenlea Grove	46 E2
Greenlea Park	46 E3
*Greenlea Place (off The Laurels)	46 F2
Greenlea Road	46 E3
Greenmount Ave	74 F4
Greenmount Court	74 F4
Greenmount Lane	74 F4
Greenmount Lawns	46 F2
Greenmount Lodge	62 F2
Greenmount Road	46 F2
Greenmount Square	74 F4
Greenoge	42 F4
Greenogue Drive	52 F2
Greenore Court	76 E1
Greenore Terrace	76 E1
Greenpark Road	33 C2
Greenridge Court	22 E1
Greentrees Drive	45 C2
Greentrees Park	45 C2
Greentrees Road	45 C2
Greenview	14 E2
Greenville Ave	74 F3
Greenville Parade (Blackpitts)	74 F3

STREET NAME	PAGE / GRID REFERENCE
Greenville Place	74 F3
Greenville Road	49 B4
Greenville Terrace	74 F3
Greenwood	13 C1
Greenwood Ave	14 D4
Greenwood Close	14 D4
Greenwood Court	14 D4
Greenwood Drive	14 D4
*Greenwood Heights Apts (near The Orchard)	14 D4
*Greenwood Lawn (on Greenwood Drive)	14 D4
Greenwood Lawn	14 D4
Greenwood Park	14 D4
Greenwood Walk	14 D4
Greenwood Way	14 D4
Grenville Lane	71 B2
Grenville Street	71 B2
*Greygates (off Sycamore Cres)	48 E4
Grey's Lane	30 D2
Greythorn Park	60 D1
Griannan Fidh	58 D3
Griffeen	34 E3
Griffeen Ave	34 D3
Griffeen Glen Ave	34 E3
Griffeen Glen Boulevard	34 E3
Griffeen Glen Chase	34 E3
Griffeen Glen Close	34 E3
Griffeen Glen Court	34 E3
Griffeen Glen Court Yard	34 E3
Griffeen Glen Cres	34 E3
Griffeen Glen Dale	34 E3
Griffeen Glen Dene	34 E3
Griffeen Glen Drive	34 E3
Griffeen Glen Green	34 E3
Griffeen Glen Grove	34 E3
Griffeen Glen Lawn	34 E3
Griffeen Glen Park	34 E3
Griffeen Glen Road	34 E3
Griffeen Glen Vale	34 E3
Griffeen Glen View	34 E3
Griffeen Glen Way	34 E3
Griffeen Glen Wood	34 D3
Griffeen Road	34 E3
Griffeen Way	34 E2
Griffin Rath Hall	18 D4
Griffin Rath Manor	18 D4
Griffin Rath Road	18 D4
Griffith Ave	25 B3
Griffith Bridge (Grand Canal)	73 B2
Griffith Close	24 F2
Griffith Court	25 C4
Griffith Cres	24 F2
Griffith Downs	25 B3
Griffith Drive	24 F2
Griffith Hall	25 C3
Griffith Heights	24 F2
Griffith Lawns	25 A3
Griffith Parade	24 F2
Griffith Road	24 F2
Griffith Square	74 F3
Griffith Terrace	74 F1
*Grosvenor Ave (on Newcourt Road)	68 D3
Grosvenor Court (Clontarf)	26 E4
*Grosvenor Court (Templeville Road)	46 D3
*Grosvenor House Apts (off Pakenham Road)	49 C4
Grosvenor Lane	47 A1
Grosvenor Lodge	47 A1
*Grosvenor Park (off Leinster Road)	47 A1
Grosvenor Place	47 A1
Grosvenor Road	47 A1
Grosvenor Square	47 A1
*Grosvenor Terrace (off The Hill Dún Laoghaire)	49 C4
*Grosvenor Terrace (off Sorrento Road)	60 F2
Grosvenor Villas (Rathmines)	47 A1
*Grosvenor Villas (off Sorrento Road)	60 F2
Grotto Ave	48 F2
Grotto Place	48 F2
Grove Ave (Harold's Cross)	75 A4
Grove Ave (Malahide)	3 C3
Grove Ave (Finglas)	24 E1
Grove Ave (Mount Merrion)	48 F4
Grove Court (Blanchardstown)	22 D1
*Grove Court (off Naas Road Bluebell)	36 F4

STREET NAME	PAGE / GRID REFERENCE
*Grove Hall (Linden Court)	48 F4
*Grove House (Grove Ave)	75 A4
*Grove House Apts (off Grove Wood)	59 A3
*Grove House Gardens (off Stillorgan Grove)	48 F4
Grove Lane	13 C4
Grove Lawn (Malahide)	3 C3
Grove Lawn (Stillorgan)	48 F4
Grove Mews	70 F1
Grove Paddock	48 F4
Grove Park (Rathmines)	75 B4
Grove Park (Coolock)	13 C4
Grove Park Ave	24 F1
Grove Park Cres	24 F1
Grove Park Drive	24 F1
Grove Park Road	24 F1
Grove Road (Rathmines)	75 A4
Grove Road (Malahide)	3 C3
Grove Road (Blanchardstown)	22 D2
Grove Road (Finglas)	24 E1
Grove Wood (Finglas)	24 E1
Grove Wood (Foxrock)	59 A3
Grovedale	63 B2
Guild Street	72 E3
*Guilford Terrace (off Lower Road)	64 E3
Gulistan Cottages	47 A1
Gulistan Place	47 A1
Gulistan Terrace	47 A1
Gunny Hill	55 C3
Gurteen Ave	36 D3
Gurteen Park	36 D3
Gurteen Road	36 D2

H

STREET NAME	PAGE / GRID REFERENCE
Hacketsland	64 E1
Haddington Lawns	60 E2
Haddington Park	60 E2
Haddington Place	76 E2
Haddington Road	76 E2
Haddington Square	76 F2
*Haddington Terrace (off Adelaide Street)	50 D4
*Haddington Way East (Canon Mews East)	76 F2
*Haddington Way West (Canon Mews West)	76 F2
*Haddon Court (off Haddon Road)	39 B1
*Haddon Park (Seaview Ave North)	26 D4
Haddon Road	26 E4
Hadleigh Court	23 A3
*Hadleigh Green (near The Pines)	23 A3
*Hadleigh Park	23 A3
Hagan's Court	76 D2
Haigh Terrace	50 D4
Hainault Drive	59 B3
Hainault Grove	59 B3
Hainault Lawn	59 B3
Hainault Park	59 A3
Hainault Road	59 A3
Halliday Road	70 E3
Halliday Square	70 D3
Hallscourt	67 C2
Halston Street	71 A3
Hamilton Court (off Strand Street Little)	71 A4
*Hamilton Court (at Hamilton Hall Dunboyne)	7 B3
*Hamilton Court (Seaview Terrace)	48 D1
Hamilton Hall	7 B3
*Hamilton House (Wellington Lane)	76 E4
Hamilton Street	74 E3
Hammond Lane	70 F4
Hammond Street	74 F2
Hampstead Ave	25 A2
Hampstead Court	25 A2
Hampstead Park	25 A3
Hampton Court	76 E4
Hampton Court (Clontarf)	26 F4
*Hampton Court (off Tyrconnell Road)	36 F3
Hampton Cres	48 E3
Hampton Green (Cabra)	69 B1
*Hampton Lodge Apts (off Grace Park Road)	25 B3
Hampton Park	48 E3
Hampton Square	69 C1
Hampton Wood	11 C4
Hampton Wood Ave	11 B4

STREET NAME	PAGE / GRID REFERENCE
*Hampton Wood Court	11 C4
Hampton Wood Cres	11 B4
Hampton Wood Drive	11 C4
Hampton Wood Green	11 B4
Hampton Wood Lawn	11 C4
Hampton Wood Park	11 B4
Hampton Wood Road	11 B4
*Hampton Wood Square	11 C4
Hampton Wood Way	11 C4
Hamwood	6 F3
Hanbury Court	74 F1
*Hanbury Hall (off Hanbury Lane)	74 F1
Hanbury Lane (The Coombe)	74 F1
*Hanbury Lane (off Main Street Lucan)	34 D1
*Hanbury Mews (Hanbury Lane)	74 F1
Hanlon's Lane	61 B1
Hanna Square	35 A1
Hannaville Park	46 F2
*Hanover Dock Apts (Forbes Street)	72 E4
Hanover Lane	75 A1
Hanover Quay	72 F4
*Hanover Reach Apts (Forbes Street)	72 E4
Hanover Square	75 A1
Hanover Street East	72 D4
Hanover Street West	74 F1
*Hanover Waterfront Apts (Hanover Quay)	72 F4
*Hanover Wharf Apts (Asgard Road)	72 E4
Hansfield	8 E4
Hansted Close	34 D4
Hansted Cres	34 D4
Hansted Dale	34 D4
Hansted Drive	34 D4
Hansted Park	34 D4
Hansted Place	34 D4
Hansted Road	34 D4
Hansted Way	34 D4
Ha'penny or Liffey Bridge (River Liffey)	71 B4
Harbour Court	71 C4
Harbour Cres	60 F1
*Harbour House Apts (off Bond Street)	74 E1
Harbour Master Place	72 D3
Harbour Road (Howth)	30 D1
Harbour Road (Dún Laoghaire)	50 D4
Harbour Road (Dalkey)	60 F1
Harbour Square	50 D4
*Harbour Terrace (off Harbour Road)	49 C4
Harbour View	30 D1
Harbour View (Dún Laoghaire)	50 D4
Harcourt Green	75 B3
Harcourt Hall	75 B3
Harcourt Lane	75 B3
Harcourt Lodge	73 B2
Harcourt Place	75 B3
Harcourt Road	75 B3
Harcourt Street	75 B2
Harcourt Terrace	75 C3
Harcourt Terrace Lane (Charlemont Place)	75 C3
*Harcourt Villas (off Dundrum Rosd/Mulvey Park)	47 C3
*Harcourt Villas (on Dundrum Road)	47 C3
Hardebeck Ave	45 C1
Hardiman Road	25 A3
Hardwicke Arch (off Hardwicke Street)	71 B2
Hardwicke Lane	71 B2
Hardwicke Place	71 B2
Hardwicke Street	71 B2
*Hardwicke Street Flats (Hardwicke Street)	71 B2
Harelawn Ave	35 A3
Harelawn Cres	35 A3
Harelawn Drive	35 A2
Harelawn Green	35 A3
Harelawn Grove	35 A2
Harelawn Park	35 A2
Harlech Cres	48 D3
Harlech Downs	47 C3
Harlech Grove	48 D3
*Harlech Villas (off Harlech Downs)	47 C3
Harmac Court	46 F2
Harman Street	74 E2

STREET NAME	PAGE / GRID REFERENCE
Harmoney Court	76 E1
Harmonstown Road	26 F2
*Harmony Ave (off Eglinton Road)	47 C1
*Harmony Court (off Eglinton Road)	47 C1
Harmony Row	76 D1
Harold Bridge Court	74 F4
*Harold Cres (off Eden Road Lower)	60 E1
Harold Road	70 E3
Harold's Cross	74 F4
Harold's Cross Cottages	74 F4
Harold's Cross Road	74 F4
Harold's Grange Road	57 B3
Haroldville Ave	74 D2
Harrington Court	75 B3
Harrington Street	75 A3
Harrison Row	46 F2
Harristown	5 A2
Harry Street	75 B1
Hartstown Road	21 C1
Harty Ave	45 C1
Harty Court (off Daniel Street)	75 A2
*Harty Court (off Harty Ave)	45 C1
Harty Place	75 A2
Harvard	48 D3
Hastings Street	76 F1
*Hastings Terrace (off Glasthule Road)	60 E1
Hatch Lane	75 C3
Hatch Place	75 C3
Hatch Street Lower	75 C3
Hatch Street Upper	75 B3
Hatter's Lane	74 F4
Havelock Place	76 F2
Havelock Square	76 F2
*Havelock Terrace (off O'Connell Gardens)	39 A3
*Haven View (adjacent The Haven Malahide)	3 B2
Haverty Road	25 C4
Hawkins Street	71 C4
Hawkridge	33 B2
Hawthorn Ave	72 E2
*Hawthorn Drive (off Acorn Road)	57 B1
Hawthorn Lawn	22 F3
Hawthorn Lodge (Castleknock Road)	22 F3
Hawthorn Lodge (Farmleigh)	23 A4
*Hawthorn Manor (off Newtown Park)	59 A1
Hawthorn Park	1 C2
Hawthorn Road (Clondalkin)	44 F1
Hawthorn Road (Bray)	67 B1
Hawthorn Terrace	72 E2
Hawthorn View	32 D2
Hawthorns Road	58 D2
*Hayden Square (off Owenstown Park Fosters Ave)	48 D3
Haydens Lane	34 D4
Hayden's Lane	34 D3
Haydens Lane Place	34 D4
Haydens Park	34 D3
Haydens Park Ave	34 D3
Haydens Park Close	34 D3
Haydens Park Dale	34 D3
Haydens Park Drive	34 D3
Haydens Park Glade	34 D3
Haydens Park Green	34 D3
Haydens Park Grove	34 D3
Haydens Park Lawn	34 D3
Haydens Park View	34 D3
Haydens Park Walk	34 D3
Haydens Park Way	34 D3
Haymarket	70 F4
Haymarket House	70 F4
*Hayworth Close (off Hayworth Drive)	21 B1
Hayworth Court	21 B1
Hayworth Drive	21 B1
Hayworth Mews	21 A1
Hayworth Place	21 A1
Hayworth Rise	21 A1
Hayworth Terrace	21 A1
Hazel Ave	58 D1
Hazel Court	14 F2
Hazel Grove	14 F2
Hazel Lane	26 F4
Hazel Lawn (Blanchardstown)	22 E2
*Hazel Lawn (off Carriglea Ave Kill O'The Grange)	59 C2

STREET NAME	PAGE / GRID REFERENCE
*Hazel Park (off Kimmage Road Lower)	46 E2
Hazel Road	26 D3
Hazel Villas	58 D1
Hazelbrook (Malahide)	14 E1
Hazelbrook (Tymon North)	45 B4
Hazelbrook (Kilmacud)	58 D1
*Hazelbrook Apts (off Hazelbrook Court)	46 E2
Hazelbrook Court	46 E2
Hazelbrook Drive	46 E2
Hazelbrook Road	46 E2
Hazelbrook Square	47 A4
Hazelbury Green	8 E4
Hazelbury Park	8 E4
Hazelcroft Gardens	24 E2
Hazelcroft Green	24 E2
Hazelcroft Park	24 E2
Hazelcroft Road	24 E2
Hazeldene	47 C1
Hazeldine Apts	67 C4
Hazelgrove	54 D2
Hazelgrove Court	54 E2
Hazelhatch	41 B1
Hazelhatch Park	32 D4
Hazelhatch Road	41 C3
Hazelwood (Santry Ave)	12 D4
Hazelwood (Shankill)	64 E2
Hazelwood (Bray)	67 B2
Hazelwood Ave	21 C1
Hazelwood Bank	44 D2
Hazelwood Close	44 D2
Hazelwood Court (Hartstown)	21 C1
Hazelwood Court (Beaumont)	26 D1
Hazelwood Cres (Hartstown)	21 C1
Hazelwood Cres (Clondalkin)	44 D2
Hazelwood Cres (Bray)	67 B2
Hazelwood Drive	26 D2
Hazelwood Green	21 C1
Hazelwood Grove	26 E1
Hazelwood House	75 B4
Hazelwood Lane	44 D2
Hazelwood Park	26 D1
Hazelwood View	44 D2
Hazlebury Park	8 E4
Headford Grove	47 B4
Headfort Court (Hill Street)	71 B2
Healthfield Road	46 F2
Healy Street (off Rutland Place North)	71 C2
Heaney Ave	35 C4
*Heany Ave (off Coliemore Road)	60 F2
Heath Square (off Mckee Ave)	24 E1
Heather Close	57 A2
Heather Court	58 E2
Heather Drive	57 A2
Heather Gardens	4 D4
Heather Grove (Palmerston)	35 B2
Heather Grove (Ballinteer)	57 B2
Heather Lawn	57 A2
Heather Park	57 B2
Heather Road (Ballinteer)	57 A2
Heather Road (Burton Hall)	58 E2
Heather View Ave	54 F2
Heather View Close	54 F2
Heather View Drive	54 F2
Heather View Lawn	54 F2
Heather View Park	54 F2
Heather View Road	54 F2
Heather Walk	4 D4
Heatherwood	67 B4
*Heathfield (off Monkstown Road)	49 B4
Heathfield	23 C1
Heathfield Ave	23 C1
Heathfield Cres	23 C1
Heathfield Green	23 C1
Heathfield Park	23 C1
Heathfield Terrace	23 C1
Heathfield View	23 C1
Heathfield Way	23 C1
*Heatley Villas (on Pearse Road)	59 C2
Heidelberg	48 D3
*Hempenstal Terrace (off Durham Road)	39 B4
Hendrick Lane	70 E4
Hendrick Place	70 E4
Hendrick Street	70 F4
*Henley Court (off Henley Villas)	47 B4
Henley Park	47 B4
Henley Villas	47 B4
Henrietta Lane	71 A2

STREET NAME	PAGE / GRID REFERENCE		STREET NAME	PAGE / GRID REFERENCE		STREET NAME	PAGE / GRID REFERENCE		STREET NAME	PAGE / GRID REFERENCE
Henrietta Place	71 A3		Highland View	59 B3		Holly Tree Square	11 C4		*Honey Park	
Henrietta Street	71 A3		Highridge Green	58 E1		Holly Tree Terrace	11 C4		(off Sallynoggin Road)	60 D2
Henry Place	71 B3		Highthorn Park	59 C1		Hollybank Ave Lower	47 B1		Hope Ave	72 E1
Henry Road	36 D4		*Highthorn Woods			Hollybank Ave Upper	47 B1		Hope Street (off Gordon Street)	76 F1
Henry Street	71 B3		(off Highthorn Park)	59 C1		Hollybank Road	25 A4		*Hopkins Square	
Herbert Ave	48 E1		*Hill Cottages			Hollybrook	59 A3		(off Owenstown Park Fosters Ave)	48 D3
Herbert Cottages			(off Killiney Hill Road)	60 E3		*Hollybrook Court			*Horan Hall	
(off Merrion Road)	76 F3		Hill Court	14 F1		(off Hollybrook Road)	26 D4		(off Belgard Square West)	54 F1
*Herbert Court			Hill Crest	3 C4		*Hollybrook Court Drive			Horan's Lane	54 E3
(off Hollyrood Park)	39 A4		Hill Drive	3 B3		(off Hollybrook Road)	26 D4		Horse Fair	72 E4
Herbert Cres	22 F2		Hill Street	71 B2		Hollybrook Grove	26 D4		Horton Court	46 F2
Herbert House	76 E1		Hillbrook Woods	22 D1		Hollybrook Manor	26 D4		Hotel Yard	71 B3
Herbert Lane	76 D2		Hillcourt	47 A2		*Hollybrook Mews			Houghton Terrace	70 E3
Herbert Park (Ballsbridge)	76 F4		Hillcourt Park	60 D2		(off Hollybrook Park)	26 D4		Howard Street (off Gordon Street)	76 F1
Herbert Park (Oldcourt)	67 B3		Hillcourt Road	60 D2		*Hollybrook Mews			Howth	30 D2
Herbert Park Lane	76 F4		Hillcrest (Malahide)	3 A2		(Copeland Grove)	26 D4		Howth Harbour	30 D1
Herbert Park Mews	47 C1		Hillcrest (Lucan)	34 D2		Hollybrook Park (Clontarf)	26 D4		*Howth House Apts	
Herbert Place			*Hillcrest (off Templeogue Road)	46 D4		Hollybrook Park (Irishtown)	67 C4		(off Harbour Road,	
(Baggot Street Lower)	76 D2		Hillcrest (Rathgar)	47 A2		Hollybrook Road			close to Post Office)	30 D1
*Herbert Place (off Bath Street)	39 A3		Hillcrest Ave	33 C2		(off Hollybrook Park)	26 D4		Howth Junction Cottages	
Herbert Road (Blanchardstown)	22 F2		Hillcrest Close	33 C2		*Hollybrook Wood			(off Kilbarrack Road)	27 B1
Herbert Road (Sandymount)	39 A4		*Hillcrest Court (off Griffith Ave)	25 A3		(off Hollybrook Park)	26 D4		Howth Lodge Apts	29 C1
Herbert Road (Oldcourt)	67 B3		Hillcrest Court	34 D2		*Hollybrook Wood			*Howth Peninsula Apts	
Herbert Street	76 D2		Hillcrest Downs	58 D3		(Hollybrook Grove)	26 D4		(off Harbour Road,	
*Herbert View			Hillcrest Drive	33 C2		*Hollybrooke (off Bluebell Ave)	36 E4		opposite west pier)	30 D1
(Pearse Square, Bray)	67 B2		Hillcrest Green	33 C2		*Hollyrood Apts			Howth Road (Marino)	26 D4
Herberton Apts	74 D2		Hillcrest Grove	34 D2		(off Hollyrood Park)	39 A4		Howth Road (Killester)	26 E3
Herberton Bridge (Grand Canal)	73 C3		Hillcrest Heights	33 C2		Hollystown	9 B1		Howth Road (Saint Anns Park)	26 F3
Herberton Drive	74 D3		Hillcrest Lawns	33 C2		Hollystown Demesne	9 B1		Howth Road (Raheny)	27 B2
Herberton Park	73 C2		*Hillcrest Manor			Hollystown Park	9 B1		Howth Road (Sutton)	29 B1
Herberton Road	73 C2		(off Templeogue Road)	46 D4		Hollyville Lawn	35 C1		Howth Road (Howth)	29 C1
Herberton Street	74 D2		Hillcrest Park (Glasnevin)	24 F2		Hollywell	11 C4		Howth Road Apts	26 E3
Herberton Walk	74 D2		Hillcrest Park (Lucan)	33 C2		Hollywood Drive	48 D4		*Howth Terrace	
Hermitage Ave	56 F1		Hillcrest Road (Lucan)	34 D2		Hollywood Park	48 D4		(at Saint Laurence Road,	
Hermitage Close	56 F1		Hillcrest Road (Sandyford)	58 D3		*Holme's Cottages			Police Station)	30 D1
Hermitage Court	57 A1		Hillcrest View	33 C2		(on Church Ave Rathmines)	47 A1		Howth View Park	27 B1
Hermitage Cres	34 F1		Hillcrest Walk	33 C2		Holmston Ave	60 D1		Huband Bridge (Grand Canal)	76 E2
Hermitage Downs	57 A1		Hillcrest Way	33 C2		Holmwood	59 B4		Huband Road	36 F4
Hermitage Drive	56 F1		Hillsbrook Ave	46 D2		*Holycross Ave			Hudson Road	60 E1
Hermitage Garden	34 F1		Hillsbrook Cres	46 D2		(off Clonliffe Road)	25 B4		Hughes Road East	45 C1
Hermitage Green	34 F1		Hillsbrook Drive	46 D2		*Holycross Cottages			Hughes Road North	45 C1
Hermitage Grove	56 F1		Hillsbrook Grove	46 D2		(off Holycross Ave)	25 B4		Hughes Road South	45 C1
Hermitage Lawn	56 F1		Hillside	60 E2		Holyrood Park	39 A4		Hume Ave	35 C4
Hermitage Manor	34 F1		Hillside Drive	47 A3		Holywell	58 D1		Hume Ave	36 D4
Hermitage Park (Lucan)	34 F1		Hillside Park	56 E1		Holywell Ave (in Holywell Estate)	2 E3		Hume Street	75 C2
Hermitage Park (Grange Road)	56 F1		*Hillside Terrace			Holywell Ave (Kilbarrack)	27 B1		Hunters Ave	55 C3
Hermitage Place	34 F1		(south of Church on			Holywell Close	2 E3		Hunters Court	55 C3
Hermitage Road	34 F1		Main Street Howth)	30 D2		Holywell Court	2 D3		Hunters Cres	55 C3
Hermitage Road	34 F1		Hilltop Lawn	64 D3		Holywell Cres (Kilbarrack)	27 B1		Hunters Green	55 C3
Hermitage Valley	34 F1		Hilltown	1 B3		Holywell Cres North	2 D3		Hunters Grove	55 C3
Hermitage View	56 F1		Hilltown Close	1 C2		Holywell Cres South	2 D3		*Hunters Hall (off Hunters Place)	55 C3
Hermitage Way	34 F1		Hilltown Court	1 C2		Holywell Dale	2 D3		Hunters Hill	55 C3
Heronford Lane	63 C2		Hilltown Cres	1 A2		Holywell Dene	2 D3		Hunters Lane	55 C3
Heskin Court	48 E2		Hilltown Green	1 C2		Holywell Drive	2 D3		Hunters Meadow	55 C3
Heuston Square	73 A1		Hilltown Grove	1 C2		Holywell Gardens	2 D3		Hunters Parade	55 C3
*Heuston Square South			Hilltown Lawn	1 C2		Holywell Green	2 E3		Hunters Place	55 C3
(Military Road)	69 C4		Hilltown Park	1 C2		Holywell Grove	2 E3		Hunters Road	55 C3
Hewardine Terrace			Hilltown Road	1 C2		Holywell Heath	2 D3		*Hunter's Row (off Seapark Road)	26 F4
(off Killarney Street)	72 D2		Hilltown Way	1 C2		Holywell Heights	2 D3		Hunters Run	8 E4
Heytesbury Court			Hillview	52 E2		Holywell Lawn	2 E4		Hunters Run The Close	8 E4
(off Merrion Road)	76 E3		*Hillview Cottages			Holywell Manor	2 D3		Hunters Run The Drive	8 E4
Heytesbury Lane	76 E4		(off Hillview Drive)	59 C2		Holywell Meadows	2 E4		Hunters Run The Glade	8 E4
Heytesbury Street	75 A3		*Hillview Court			*Holywell Mews			Hunters Run The Grove	8 E4
Hibernian Ave	72 E2		(off Beech Lawn Ave)	57 B1		(in Holywell Estate)	2 D3		Hunters Run The Park	8 E4
Hibernian Road	72 E4		Hillview Drive	59 C2		Holywell Park	2 D3		Hunters Run The Rise	8 E4
*Hibernian Terrace			Hillview Estate	57 B1		Holywell Place	2 D3		Hunters Run The View	8 E4
(off Chapelizod Road)	36 E2		*Hillview Glade			Holywell Rise	2 D3		Hunters Run The Way	8 E4
High Park	25 C2		(off Beech Lawn Ave)	57 B1		Holywell Road			Hunters Walk	55 C3
High Street			Hillview Grove	57 B1		(in Holywell Estate)	2 D3		Hunters Way	55 C3
(Christ Church)	75 A1		Hillview Lawns	59 C2		Holywell Road (Kilbarrack)	27 B1		Huntstown Ave	21 C1
*High Street			Hilton Gardens	57 C2		*Holywell Row			Huntstown Close	8 F4
(off Old Blessington Road)	55 A1		Hilton Mews (Harcourt Terrace)	75 C3		(in Holywell Estate)	2 D3		Huntstown Court	8 F4
Highdownhill	51 C1		Hoey Close	14 E4		Holywell Square	2 E3		Huntstown Drive	8 F4
Highfield Ave (Dundrum)	57 A2		Hoey Court	14 E4		Holywell View	2 E3		Huntstown Glen	8 F4
Highfield Close	1 C2		Hoey Place	14 E4		Holywell Villas	2 D3		Huntstown Green	8 F4
*Highfield Court			*Hoeys Court			Holywell Walk	2 D3		Huntstown Grove	8 F4
(off Highfield Road)	47 A2		(off Werburgh Street)	75 A1		Holywell Way	2 E3		Huntstown Lawn	22 D1
Highfield Cres	1 C2		Hogan Ave	76 E1		Holywell Wood	2 D3		Huntstown Park	8 F4
Highfield Downs	1 C2		*Hogan House			Home Farm Park	25 B3		Huntstown Rise	9 A4
Highfield Drive	57 A2		(off Stonepark Court)	46 F4		Home Farm Road	25 A3		Huntstown Road	21 C1
Highfield Green	1 C2		Hogan Place	76 D1		Home Villas	47 C1		Huntstown Way	9 A4
Highfield Grove	47 A2		Hogan Square	76 E1		Homelawn Ave	55 B1		Huntstown Wood	8 F4
Highfield Lawn	1 C2		*Hogan View Apts (Convent Ave)	25 B4		Homelawn Drive	55 B1		Hutchinson's Strand	2 E1
Highfield Manor	47 A2		Holles Place	76 D1		Homelawn Gardens	55 B1		Huttonread	51 C4
*Highfield Mews			Holles Row	76 D1		Homelawn Road	55 A1		Huxley Court	74 E2
(off Rathmines Road Upper)	47 A2		Holles Street	76 D1		Homelawn Villas	55 A1		Huxley Cres	74 E2
Highfield Park (Celbridge Road)	33 A1		Holly Ave	58 D1		*Homelee (off Serpentine Park)	39 A4		Hyacinth Street	72 E2
Highfield Park (Churchtown)	47 B3		Holly Court	64 D1		Homeleigh	22 D4		Hybla Court	23 C4
Highfield Road	47 A2		Holly Park	64 E2		Homestead Court	24 E4		Hybreasal	73 B2
Highland Ave	59 B3		Holly Park Ave	59 A1		*Homeville (off Ballycullen Road)	55 C1		Hybreasal Apts	73 B2
Highland Grove	59 B3		Holly Road (Donnycarney)	26 D3		*Homeville Court			Hyde Park (Templeogue)	46 E3
Highland Lawn	59 B3		Holly Road (Fox and Geese)	44 F1		(off Ballycullen Road)	55 C1		Hyde Park (Dalkey)	60 E1

STREET NAME	PAGE / GRID REFERENCE	
Hyde Park Ave	48	F3
Hyde Park Gardens	48	F3
Hyde Road	60	F1
*Hyde Square (Kilmainham)	73	B2
*Hyde Square (off Owenstown Park Fosters Ave)	48	D3
*Hyde Square Apts (off South Circular Road)	73	B2
Hynestown	42	D2

I

STREET NAME	PAGE	GRID
Idrone Ave	56	D1
Idrone Close	56	D1
Idrone Drive	56	D1
*Idrone Mews (off Idrone Terrace)	49	A3
Idrone Park	56	D1
Idrone Terrace	49	A3
Imaal Road	70	E1
Inagh Court	64	E1
Inagh Road	36	D3
Inbhir Ide	3	A2
Inbhir Ide Close	3	A2
Inbhir Ide Drive	3	A2
Inchicore	73	A1
Inchicore Road	73	A1
*Inchicore Square (off Inchicore Terrace South)	36	F3
*Inchicore Terrace North (off Inchicore Terrace South)	36	F3
Inchicore Terrace South	36	F3
Infirmary Road	69	C3
Inglewood Close	21	C2
Inglewood Cres	21	C2
Inglewood Drive	21	C2
Inglewood Road	21	C2
Ingram Road	74	F3
Inis Fáil	54	F2
Inis Thiar	54	F2
Inishowen	12	F3
*Inkerman Cottages (off Amiens Street)	72	D2
Innisfallen Parade	71	B1
Innishmaan Road	25	B2
Innishmore Terrace (Saint Mary's Road)	46	D1
Innismore	46	D1
*Inns Court (on Winetavern Street)	75	A1
Inns Quay	70	F4
Inver Road	24	E4
*Invermore Grove (off Carraroe Ave)	27	A1
Inverness Road	25	C4
Iona Ave	25	A4
Iona Cres	25	A4
Iona Drive	25	A4
Iona Park	25	A4
Iona Road	25	A4
Iona Villas	25	A4
Iris Grove	48	E3
Irishtown (Ringsend)	39	A3
Irishtown (Bray)	67	C4
Irishtown Road	39	A3
Irvine Cottages	72	F3
Irvine Terrace	72	F3
Irwin Court	73	C1
Irwin Street	73	C1
Island Key	72	F2
Island Street	70	E4
Island View (Malahide)	3	C3
Island View (Kilbarrack)	27	C2
*Island View Apts (off Harbour Road, close to Post Office)	30	D1
Island View Court Apts	27	C2
Island Villa	76	E1
Islandbridge	69	B4
Islandbridge Court	69	B4
Islandbridge Gate (Phoenix Park)	69	A4
Islington Ave	50	E4
Isolda Road	39	A3
*Isolde Gardens (off Martin's Row Chapelizod)	36	E2
*Isolde House Apts (off Martin's Row Chapelizod)	36	E2
Ivar Street	70	E3
Iveagh Buildings	75	A2
Iveagh Court	75	B3
*Iveagh Exchange Apts (Granby Place)	71	B3
Iveagh Gardens	73	B4
*Iveagh Trust (Bride Road)	75	A1
Iveleary Road	25	B2
Iveragh Court (off Seafort Ave)	76	F3
Iveragh Road	25	B2
Ivy Cottages	75	C4
*Ivy Court (off Ballyshannon Road)	25	C1
Ivy Terrace	74	E2

J

STREET NAME	PAGE	GRID
Jackson's Bridge	17	A3
James Connolly Park	35	A4
*James Connolly Square (Saint Kevin's Square)	67	C2
James Everett Park	67	B2
James Joyce Bridge (River Liffey)	70	E4
*James Joyce Court (off Ferguson Road)	25	A3
James Joyce Court (off Sutton Downs)	27	C1
James Joyce Street	71	C3
James Larkin Road	27	B2
*James McCormack Gardens (off Burrowfield Road)	29	A1
James Plunkett House	36	F3
James's Place East	76	D2
James's Street	74	D1
James's Street East	76	D2
James's Street North	72	E1
James's Terrace	3	B2
*James's Terrace Upper (off James Terrace)	3	B2
Jamestown	62	F1
Jamestown Ave	36	F4
Jamestown Cottages	62	E1
Jamestown Court	36	F4
Jamestown Road (Poppintree)	11	B4
Jamestown Road (Finglas)	24	E1
Jamestown Road (Inchicore)	36	F4
Jamestown Road (Grand Canal)	36	E4
*Jamestown Square (Jamestown Road)	36	F4
*Jane-Ville (off Tivoli Road)	50	D4
Jerome Connor Place	69	C3
Jervis Lane Lower	71	A4
Jervis Lane Upper	71	A3
Jervis Street	71	A3
Jobstown	54	D2
Jobstown Road	54	D2
*Jobstown Village Square (off Jobstown Road)	54	D1
*Joe Sartini Court (near Temple Buildings)	71	A2
John Dillon Street	75	A1
John F Kennedy Ave	45	A1
John F Kennedy Drive	45	A1
John F Kennedy Park	36	D4
John F Kennedy Road	36	D4
John Field Road	75	A1
John MacCormack Ave	45	C1
John McCormack Bridge (Tolka River)	72	F1
John Street North (off Ellis Quay)	70	E4
John Street South	74	F2
John Street West	74	F1
Johns Court (Christchurch)	74	F1
*John's Court (Dolphins Barn Street)	74	E2
John's Lane East	75	A1
John's Lane West	74	F1
Johnsbridge	34	D3
Johnsbridge Ave	34	D3
Johnsbridge Close	34	D3
Johnsbridge Green	34	D3
Johnsbridge Grove	34	D3
Johnsbridge Meadows	34	D3
Johnsbridge Park	34	D3
Johnsbridge Walk	34	D3
Johnson Place	75	B1
Johnson's Court	75	B1
Johnstown	51	C4
Johnstown Ave	59	C3
Johnstown Court	59	C2
Johnstown Gardens	24	E2
Johnstown Grove	59	C3
*Johnstown House (off Johnstown Park)	24	F2
Johnstown Lane	59	C3
Johnstown Park (Glasnevin)	24	F2
Johnstown Park (Cornelscourt)	59	C3
Johnstown Road (Rathcoole)	52	E2
Johnstown Road (Cornelscourt)	59	C3
*Jones Terrace (Sidmonton Ave)	68	D2
Jones's Road	71	C1
Jordanstown	42	F4
Jordanstown Ave (Greenogue Industrial Estate)	42	F4
Jordanstown Drive (Greenogue Industrial Estate)	42	F4
Jordanstown Road (Greenogue Industrial Estate)	42	F4
Josephine Ave	71	B1
Joy Street (off Gordon Street)	76	F1
Joyce Ave	59	A3
Joyce Hall	59	B4
Joyce Road (Drumcondra)	25	A3
Joyce Way	35	C4
Jugback Close	1	C1
Jugback Court	1	C1
Jugback Cres	1	C1
Jugback Green	1	Inset
Jugback Lane	1	C1
Juliet Square	35	B1

K

STREET NAME	PAGE	GRID
Kavanagh Ave	36	D4
Keadeen Ave	45	B2
Kearneystown Lower	41	A3
Kearn's Place	73	B1
Keatingspark	52	D2
*Keegan's Cottages (off Merrion Road)	48	E1
Keeloges	42	D3
Keeper Road	73	C3
Kells Road	46	E1
Kelly's Ave	50	D4
Kelly's Lane (Phibsborough)	71	A1
*Kelly's Lane (off main street and Pound Lane)	17	C3
Kelly's Row	71	B1
Kelly's Square	71	B1
Kellystown Lane	19	A3
Kellystown Road	57	B4
Kelston Ave	59	A2
Kelston Drive	59	A2
*Kelston Hall (off Kelston Drive)	59	A2
Kelston Park	59	A2
Kelston View	59	A2
Kelvin Close	4	D4
Kempton	23	C3
Kempton Ave	23	C3
Kempton Court	23	C3
Kempton Green	23	C3
Kempton Grove	23	C3
Kempton Heath	23	C3
Kempton Lawn	23	C3
Kempton Park	23	C3
Kempton Rise	23	C3
Kempton View	23	C3
Kempton Way	23	C3
Kenah Court	60	E3
*Kengar Mews (off Rathgar Ave)	46	F1
Kenilworth Lane	46	F1
*Kenilworth Manor (off Harold's Cross Road)	46	F1
Kenilworth Park	46	F1
Kenilworth Road	47	A1
Kenilworth Square	46	F1
Kenilworth Square East	47	A1
Kenilworth Square North	46	F1
Kenilworth Square South	46	F1
Kenilworth Square West	46	F1
Kenmare Parade	71	B1
*Kennedy Court (off Pembroke Street)	39	A3
*Kennedy Park (off Boghall Road)	67	C3
Kennelsfort Green	35	B2
Kennelsfort Road Lower	35	C1
Kennelsfort Road Upper	35	C2
*Kennilworth Lodge (off Harold's Cross Road)	46	F1
Kennington Close	45	C4
Kennington Cres	45	C4
Kennington Lawn	45	C4
Kennington Road	45	C3
*Kensington Lodge (off Rochestown Ave)	59	C2
*Kent Terrace (on Barnhill Road)	60	F2
Kentfield	64	E2
Kerlogue Road	39	A3
*Kerrygold House (off Harold's Cross Road)	46	F1
Kerrymount Ave	59	A4
*Kerrymount Close (off Kerrymount Rise)	59	B3
Kerrymount Green	59	B3
Kerrymount Mall	59	B3
Kerrymount Rise	59	B3
Kettles Drive	2	E4
Kettles Lane	2	E4
Kettles Place	2	E4
Kevin Barry Flats (off Church Street Upper)	70	F3
*Kevin Street Cross (on New Bride Street)	75	A2
Kevin Street Lower	75	A2
Kevin Street Upper	75	A2
Kew Park	33	C1
Kew Park Ave	33	B2
Kew Park Cres	33	B1
Kickham Road	73	B2
Kilakee Close	45	B3
Kilakee Drive	45	B3
Kilbarrack	27	C1
Kilbarrack Ave	27	C2
Kilbarrack Gardens	27	C2
Kilbarrack Grove	27	C2
Kilbarrack Parade	27	B1
Kilbarrack Road	27	B1
Kilbarrack Way	27	B1
Kilbarron Ave	26	D1
*Kilbarron Court (off Kilbarron Park)	26	D1
Kilbarron Drive	26	D1
Kilbarron Park	26	D1
Kilbarron Road	26	D1
*Kilbegnet Close (off Castle Street Dalkey)	60	F2
Kilbogget Grove	59	C4
*Kilbogget Villas (off Bray Road)	59	C4
Kilbride	43	A3
Kilbride Grove	67	B3
Kilbride Lane	67	B3
Kilbride Road (Killester)	26	E3
Kilbrina	7	B2
Kilcarberry Ave	43	C2
Kilcarberry Close	43	C2
Kilcarberry Court	43	C2
Kilcarberry Lawn	43	C2
Kilcarbery	43	B2
Kilcarrig Ave	44	E4
Kilcarrig Close	54	E1
Kilcarrig Cres	44	E4
Kilcarrig Green	44	E4
Kilclare Ave	54	E2
Kilclare Cres	54	E2
Kilclare Drive	54	E2
Kilclare Gardens	54	E2
Kilcloon	5	A2
Kilcloon Lawns	5	A2
Kilcock Maynooth Leixlip ByPass	32	E1
Kilcock Road	17	C3
Kilcock-Maynooth-Leixlip Bypass	33	A1
*Kilcolman Court (off Glenageary Road Upper)	60	E2
Kilcronan Ave	34	E4
Kilcronan Close	34	E4
Kilcronan Court	34	E4
Kilcronan Cres	34	E4
Kilcronan Grove	34	E4
Kilcronan Lawns	34	E4
Kilcronan View	34	E4
Kilcroney Lane	67	A4
Kilcross Ave	58	D3
Kilcross Close	58	D3
Kilcross Court	57	C3
Kilcross Cres	57	C3
Kilcross Drive	57	C3
Kilcross Grove	57	C3
Kilcross Lawn	58	D3
Kilcross Park	57	C3
Kilcross Road	58	D3
Kilcross Square	57	C3
Kilcross Way	57	C3
Kildare Bridge	18	D2
Kildare Park	46	D1
Kildare Place	75	C1
Kildare Road	46	D1
Kildare Street	75	C1
Kildonan Ave	24	D1
Kildonan Court	24	D1

STREET NAME	PAGE / GRID REFERENCE
Kildonan Drive	24 D1
Kildonan Road	24 D1
Kildress House	76 D2
Kilfenora Drive	27 A1
Kilfenora Road	46 E1
Kilgarran	66 D3
Kilgarron Park	66 D3
Kilgobbin Grove	58 E4
*Kilgobbin Heights	58 E4
Kilgobbin Lane	58 D4
*Kilgobbin Lawn (off Kilgobbin Grove)	58 E4
Kilgobbin Road	58 E3
Kilgobbin Wood	58 E4
Kilgraigue	5 B3
*Kilgrastor Court (Oldcourt Park)	67 B3
Kilkieran Court	24 E4
Kilkieran Road	24 E4
Kill Abbey	59 B1
Kill Ave	59 C1
Kill Lane	59 B2
Kill O' the Grange	59 C1
Killadoon Park	31 C4
Killakee Ave	55 B2
Killakee Close	45 B3
Killakee Court	55 B2
Killakee Drive	45 B2
Killakee Gardens	55 B2
Killakee Green	55 B2
Killakee Grove	55 B2
Killakee Lawns	55 B2
Killakee Park	55 B2
Killakee Rise	55 B2
Killakee Road	56 D4
Killakee View	55 B2
Killakee Walk	55 B2
Killakee Way	55 B2
Killala Road	24 E4
Killan Court	72 F3
Killan Road	72 F3
Killarney Ave	72 D2
Killarney Court (on Killarney Ave)	72 D2
*Killarney Court (Oldcourt Park)	67 B3
Killarney Glen	67 B2
Killarney Heights	67 B3
Killarney Lane	67 B3
Killarney Parade	71 B1
Killarney Park	67 B3
Killarney Road	67 B3
Killarney Street	72 D2
*Killarney Villas (near Market House)	67 C2
Killary Grove	27 B1
Killeany	5 A4
Killeck	1 A2
Killeck Lane	1 A3
Killeen	2 F3
Killeen Ave	2 F3
Killeen Court	2 F3
Killeen Cres	2 F3
Killeen Mews	3 B3
Killeen Park	2 F3
Killeen Road (Bluebell)	36 D4
Killeen Road (Fox and Geese)	45 A1
Killeen Road (Rathmines)	47 B1
Killeen Terrace	3 B2
Killegar	65 C1
*Killery Terrace (on Upper Dargle Road)	67 B2
Killester	26 E3
Killester Ave	26 E3
*Killester Court (off Killester Park)	26 E3
*Killester Park (off Killester Park)	26 E3
Killester Park	26 E3
Killinarden	54 E2
Killinarden Estate	54 E2
Killinarden Heights	54 E2
Killinarden Road	54 E3
Killiney	60 E3
Killiney Ave	60 E4
*Killiney Court (Seafield Road near Seafield Court)	64 E1
Killiney Gate	60 E4
Killiney Grove	60 E2
Killiney Heath	60 E4
Killiney Hill Road	60 E3
Killiney Hill Road	64 E1
*Killiney Oaks (Seafield Road near Seafield Court)	64 E1
Killiney Road	60 E2
*Killiney Terrace (off Breffni Road)	60 E1
*Killiney Towers (off Killiney Road)	60 E2
Killiney View	60 E1
Killininy Cottages	55 B2
*Killininny Court Apts (off Kilakee Grove)	55 B2
Killininny Road	55 B2
*Killshannig (on Crinken Lane)	64 D4
Kilmactalway	42 F3
Kilmacud	58 E1
Kilmacud Ave	58 E1
Kilmacud Park	58 E1
Kilmacud Road Upper	58 E1
Kilmahuddrick Ave	43 B1
Kilmahuddrick Close	43 B1
Kilmahuddrick Court	43 B1
Kilmahuddrick Cres	43 B1
Kilmahuddrick Drive	43 B1
Kilmahuddrick Green	43 B1
Kilmahuddrick Grove	43 B1
Kilmahuddrick Lawn	43 B1
Kilmahuddrick Place	43 B1
Kilmahuddrick Road	43 B1
Kilmahuddrick Walk	43 B1
Kilmahuddrick Way	43 B1
Kilmainham	73 B1
Kilmainham Bank	73 A1
Kilmainham Lane	73 C1
Kilmainham Orchard	73 B1
Kilmainham Square (South Circular/Inchicore Road)	73 B1
Kilmalin	65 C3
*Kilmantain Place (near Market House)	67 C2
Kilmartin Ave	54 D1
Kilmartin Cres	44 D4
Kilmartin Drive	54 D1
Kilmartin Gardens	54 D1
Kilmartin Green	54 D1
Kilmartin Park	54 D1
Kilmashogue Bridge	56 F3
Kilmashogue Close	45 B3
Kilmashogue Drive	45 B3
Kilmashogue Grove	45 B3
Kilmashogue Lane	56 F3
Kilmore	26 D1
Kilmore Ave (Coolock)	26 E1
Kilmore Ave (Killiney)	60 E4
Kilmore Close	26 E1
*Kilmore Court (off Kilmore Road)	26 D1
Kilmore Cres	26 E1
Kilmore Drive	26 E1
Kilmore Place Apts	26 D1
Kilmore Road	26 D1
Kilmorony Close	27 A1
Kilnamanagh	45 A3
Kilnamanagh Court	45 C1
Kilnamanagh Estate	45 A3
Kilnamanagh Road	45 C1
Kilrock Road	30 E2
*Kilronan Court (off Howth Road)	26 D4
Kilshane	10 E2
Kilshane Ave	10 D2
*Kilshane Court (Ratoath Ave)	23 C2
Kilshane Cross	10 F2
Kilshane Drive	10 E3
Kilshane Drive	23 C2
Kilshane Park	10 D2
Kilshane Road (North Road)	10 E3
Kilshane Road (Rathoath Road)	23 C2
Kilshane View	10 D2
Kilshane Way	10 D3
Kiltalown	54 D3
Kiltalown Ave	54 D2
Kiltalown Close	54 D2
Kiltalown Cottages	54 D2
Kiltalown Court	54 D2
Kiltalown Cres	54 D2
Kiltalown Drive	54 D2
Kiltalown Green	54 D2
Kiltalown Grove	54 D2
Kiltalown Heights	54 D2
Kiltalown Hill	54 D2
Kiltalown Park	54 D2
Kiltalown Path	54 D2
Kiltalown Road	54 D2
Kiltalown View	54 D2
Kiltalown Walk	54 D2
Kiltalown Way	54 D2
Kilteel Road	52 E2
Kilteragh Drive	59 A3
*Kilteragh Pines (off Westminister Road)	59 A3
Kilteragh Road	59 A3
Kilternan	62 F2
Kiltiernan Bridge	62 F3
Kiltipper	54 F3
Kiltipper Ave	55 A2
Kiltipper Close	55 A2
Kiltipper Drive	55 A2
Kiltipper Gate	54 F3
Kiltipper Rise	54 F3
Kiltipper Road	55 A3
Kiltipper View	54 F3
Kiltipper Way	54 F3
*Kiltuck Park (beside Medical Centre)	64 E4
Kilvere	46 E4
Kilvere Park	46 D4
Kilwogan Manor	31 C2
Kilworth Road	36 F4
Kimmage	46 D2
*Kimmage Court (off Kimmage Road Lower)	46 E2
Kimmage Grove	46 E2
Kimmage Manor Way	46 D2
Kimmage Road Lower	46 F1
Kimmage Road West	46 D2
Kinahan Street	70 D3
Kincora Ave	26 E4
Kincora Court	39 C1
Kincora Drive	26 E4
Kincora Grove	26 E4
Kincora Park	26 E4
Kincora Road	26 E4
*Kincora Walk (on Hazel Lane)	26 F4
*King Edward Court (King Edward Lane)	67 C2
King Edward Lawn	67 C2
King Edward Park	67 B2
King Edward Road	67 B2
King Street North	70 F3
King Street South	75 B1
King William's Rampart	24 D2
Kingram Place	75 C3
King's Ave	72 D1
King's Court	70 E2
*Kings Court Apts (Beside Chapel Lane)	71 B3
*Kings Court Apts (Brunswick Street North)	70 F3
King's Hall	36 E2
*Kings House Apts (off Bow Bridge)	74 D1
Kings Inns	71 A3
King's Inns Court	71 A2
King's Inns Street	71 A3
Kingsbry	17 C4
Kingsland Parade	75 A3
Kingsland Park Ave	75 A3
*Kingsmill Court (near Yarnhall Street)	71 A3
*Kingsmill Court Apts (Yarnhall Street)	71 A3
Kingsmill Road	67 C2
Kingston	57 B3
Kingston Ave	57 B3
Kingston Close	57 B3
Kingston Court	56 F2
Kingston Cres	57 B3
Kingston Drive	57 C3
Kingston Green	57 B3
Kingston Grove	57 B3
Kingston Hall	57 B3
Kingston Heights	57 C3
Kingston Lawn	57 B3
*Kingston Lodge (off Clonliffe Road)	25 B4
Kingston Park	57 B3
Kingston Rise	57 B3
Kingston View	57 B3
Kingston Walk	57 B3
Kingswood	43 C3
Kingswood Ave (Citywest)	43 C4
Kingswood Ave (Kilnamanagh)	44 F3
Kingswood Castle	45 A2
Kingswood Drive (Citywest)	43 C4
Kingswood Drive (Kilnamanagh)	44 F3
Kingswood Heights	44 F3
Kingswood Interchange (Junction 2)	43 C3
Kingswood Manor	44 F3
Kingswood Manor Apts	44 F3
Kingswood Road	43 C4
Kingswood View	44 F3
Kinsaley	14 D1
Kinsaley Bridge	14 D1
Kinsaley Lane	3 A4
Kinsealy Court	2 E3
Kinsealy Downs	2 E3
Kinsealy Lane	14 D1
Kinvara Ave	24 D4
Kinvara Drive	23 C4
Kinvara Grove	23 C4
Kinvara Park	24 D4
Kinvara Road	23 C4
Kippure Ave	45 B3
Kippure Park	24 D3
Kirbrensis Manor	21 A1
Kirkfield	22 D2
Kirkpatrick Ave	22 D3
Kirkpatrick Drive	22 D3
Kirkwood	39 A4
Kirwan Street	70 E3
Kirwan Street Cottages	70 E2
Kitestown Road	30 E3
*Knapton Court (off York Road Dún Laoghaire)	49 C4
*Knapton Lawn (off Knapton Road)	49 C4
Knapton Road	49 C4
*Knapton Terrace (off Knapton Road)	49 C4
*Knapton Villas (on Knapton Road)	49 C4
*Knights Bridge (off Castle Ave Clontarf)	26 E4
Knights Wood	12 E4
Knock Riada	36 D2
Knockaire	56 D1
Knockandinny	52 E4
Knockaulin	20 D4
Knockcullen	56 D1
Knockcullen Drive	56 D1
Knockcullen Lawn	56 D1
Knockcullen Park	56 D1
Knockcullen Rise	56 D1
Knockdara	3 C3
Knockfield Manor	55 C1
Knocklyon	56 D1
Knocklyon Ave	55 C1
Knocklyon Close	56 D1
Knocklyon Court	56 D1
Knocklyon Drive	56 D1
*Knocklyon Gate Apts (off Knocklyon Hill)	55 C2
Knocklyon Green	56 D1
Knocklyon Grove	56 D1
Knocklyon Heights	55 C1
*Knocklyon Mews (off Knocklyon Ave)	55 C1
Knocklyon Park	55 C1
Knocklyon Road	55 C1
Knockmaree Apts	36 E2
Knockmaroon Gate (Phoenix Park)	36 D1
Knockmaroon Hill	36 D1
Knockmaroon Road (Phoenix Park)	36 D1
Knockmeenagh Lane	44 E2
Knockmeenagh Road	44 E2
*Knockmitten Close (off Knockmitten Lane)	44 F1
Knockmitten Lane	45 A1
*Knockmitten Lane North (off Knockmitten Lane)	44 F1
Knockmore Ave	54 E2
Knockmore Cres	54 E2
Knockmore Drive	54 E2
Knockmore Gardens	54 E2
Knockmore Green	54 E2
Knockmore Grove	54 E2
Knockmore Park	54 E2
Knock-na-Cree Grove	60 F2
Knock-na-Cree Park	60 F2
Knock-na-Cree Road	60 F2
*Knocknagow (off Stradbrook Road)	49 B4
Knocknarea Ave	73 B4
Knocknarea Road	73 A4

STREET NAME	PAGE / GRID REFERENCE
*Knocknarrow Terrace (Kilmainham Lane)	73 C1
Knocknashee	48 D4
Knocksedan Bridge	1 A2
Knocksedan Drive	1 A2
Knocksedan Wood	1 A2
Knocksink Bridge	66 E3
Knocksinna	59 A2
*Knocksinna Court (off Granville Road)	59 A2
Knocksinna Cres	59 A2
*Knocksinna Grove (off Knocksinna Park)	59 A2
Knocksinna Park	59 A2
Knowth Court	11 C4
Kyber Road (Phoenix Park)	36 F2
*Kyle-Clare Road (off Pine Road)	39 A3
Kylemore Ave	36 D3
Kylemore Drive	36 D3
Kylemore Park North	36 D4
Kylemore Park South	36 D4
Kylemore Park West	36 D4
Kylemore Road (Ballyfermot)	36 D2
Kylemore Road (Grand Canal)	36 E4
Kylemore Way	36 E4

L

STREET NAME	PAGE / GRID REFERENCE
La Rochelle Apts	74 F1
*La Touche Court (off Bluebell Ave)	36 F4
La Touche Court (Ballinteer)	57 A2
La Touche Drive	36 E4
La Touche Road	36 F4
La Vallee	67 A3
La Vista Ave	29 B2
Labre Park	36 E4
Laburnum Road	47 C2
Laburnum Walk	35 B2
Lad Lane	76 D2
Lad Lane Apts	76 D3
Lad Lane Upper	76 D3
Lady's Lane	73 B1
Lady's Well Road	9 A4
Lagan Road	24 E3
Lake Drive	53 C1
Lakelands Ave	58 D1
Lakelands Close	58 D1
Lakelands Cres	58 E1
Lakelands Drive	58 E1
Lakelands Grove	58 D1
Lakelands Lawn	58 D1
Lakelands Park	46 E3
*Lakelands Place	58 D1
Lakelands Road	58 E1
Lakeshore Drive	2 D3
Lakeview Drive	2 D3
Lally Road	36 E3
Lamb Alley	74 F1
Lambay Close	64 E1
Lambay Court	3 C3
Lambay Drive	64 E1
Lambay Road	25 A3
*Lambda Apts (on Monkstown Farm)	59 C1
Lambourne Park (Clonsilla)	21 C2
Lambourne Ave	21 C2
Lambourne Court	21 C2
Lambourne Drive	21 C2
Lambourne Road	21 C2
*Lambourne Village (off Kincora Grove)	26 E4
Lambourne Wood	59 C4
Lamb's Brook	58 D3
Lamb's Court (off James Street)	74 D1
Landen Road	36 E3
*Landore (off Orwell Road Rathgar)	47 A3
Landscape Ave	47 A3
*Landscape Court (off Landscape Road)	47 A3
Landscape Cres	47 A4
Landscape Gardens	47 B4
Landscape Park	47 A4
Landscape Road	47 A3
Landsdown Valley Place	45 C1
*Landsdowne Gate (Blank Tony)	45 C1
*Landsdowne Valley (off Slieve Bloom Park)	45 C1
*Landsdowne Valley Apts (Landsdowne Valley)	45 C1

STREET NAME	PAGE / GRID REFERENCE
*Landsdowne Valley Cres (off Kilworth Road)	36 F4
*Landsdowne Valley Park (off Davitt Road)	36 F4
Lanesborough Ave	11 B4
Lanesborough Castle	11 B4
Lanesborough Court	11 B4
Lanesborough Drive	11 B4
Lanesborough Gardens	11 B4
Lanesborough Grove	11 B4
Lanesborough Mews	11 B4
Lanesborough Park	11 B4
Lanesborough Road	11 B4
Lanesborough Square	11 B4
Lanesborough Terrace	11 B4
Lanesborough View	11 B4
Lanesville	59 B1
*Lanesville Mews (off Lanesville)	59 C1
Lanesville Terrace	59 B1
Lanewood Mews (off Wellington Road)	76 E3
Langrishe Place	71 C2
Lanndale Lawns	54 E1
*Lansdowne Court (Lansdowne Park)	76 F3
Lansdowne Cres	76 F2
Lansdowne Gardens (off Sandymount Ave)	76 F3
*Lansdowne Hall (off Sandymount Road)	39 A3
Lansdowne Lane	76 F2
Lansdowne Park (Ballsbridge)	76 F2
Lansdowne Park (Templeogue)	56 D1
Lansdowne Road	76 F3
*Lansdowne Square (off Herbert Road)	39 A4
Lansdowne Terrace	76 F2
Lansdowne Village	39 A3
Lansdowne Villas	76 F2
Lansdowne Woods (off Merrion Road)	76 F3
Lapwing Apts	48 E3
*Laracor Gardens (off Ardara Ave adjacent Kilmorony Close)	27 A1
Laragh	60 E4
Laragh Close	27 A1
*Laragh Flats (off Grace Park Court)	25 C2
Laragh Grove	27 A1
Laraghbryan East	17 B2
Laraghbryan West	17 A2
Laraghcon	34 D1
*Larch Drive (off Brookwood)	56 E2
Larch Grove	21 C2
Larch Grove	47 B1
Larch Hill	12 F4
Larch House (Swords)	1 Inset
Larchfield	7 C3
Larchfield	47 C4
Larchfield Park	47 C4
Larchfield Road	47 C4
Larchford Place	21 B1
Larkfield	34 F2
Larkfield Ave (Liffey Valley)	34 F2
Larkfield Ave (Harold's Cross)	46 F1
Larkfield Close	34 F2
Larkfield Court	34 F2
Larkfield Gardens	46 F1
Larkfield Green	34 F2
Larkfield Grove (Liffey Valley)	34 F2
Larkfield Grove (Harold's Cross)	46 F1
Larkfield Mews	32 D3
Larkfield Park	46 F1
Larkfield Place	34 F2
Larkfield Rise	34 F2
Larkfield Square	34 F2
Larkfield View	34 F2
Larkfield Way	34 F2
Larkhill Road	25 B2
*Larkspur Hall (at Levmoss Estate)	58 F3
*Larrisa Court (off Kimmage Road Lower)	46 E1
Latchford	21 B1
Latchford Close	21 B1
Latchford Court	21 B1
Latchford Green	21 B1
Latchford Park	21 B1
Latchford Row	21 B1
Latchford Square	21 B1
Latchford Terrace	21 B1

STREET NAME	PAGE / GRID REFERENCE
Latouche Bridge (Grand Canal)	75 B4
Latouka Apts (off Ballyowen Lane)	34 F1
Lauderdale Estate	67 C3
Lauderdale Terrace (New Row South)	75 A2
*Lauderdale Terrace (Lauderdale Estate)	67 C3
Lauder's Lane	29 A1
Laundry Lane	46 F1
Laurel Ave (Dundrum)	57 B1
Laurel Ave (Ballybrack)	64 E1
Laurel Bank	59 C1
Laurel Court	22 E3
Laurel Drive	57 B1
*Laurel Hill (off Glenageary Road Upper)	60 D1
Laurel Lodge Road	22 F3
Laurel Park	44 E1
Laurel Place	46 F2
Laurel Road	57 B1
Laurelton (Rathbeale Road)	1 C1
Laurelton (Terenure)	46 F3
Laurence Brook	36 E2
Laurence Court	46 F1
Laurleen	58 F1
Lavarna Grove	46 E2
Lavarna Road	46 E2
Laverna Ave	22 E3
Laverna Dale	22 E3
Laverna Grove	22 E3
Laverna Way	22 E3
Laverty Court	75 C2
Lavery Ave	35 C4
Lavista Ave	26 E3
Lawnswood Park	58 F1
Lawrence Grove	26 D4
*Lawrence Walk (Saint James)	26 D4
Lawrence's Ave	18 D4
Lawson Spinney	3 A3
*Lawson Terrace (off Sandycove Road)	60 E1
Lazer Lane	72 E4
*Le Bas Terrace (off Leinster Road West)	46 F1
*Le Brett Terrace (off Main Street Rathfarnham)	46 F3
Le Brocquy Ave	36 D4
*Le Fanu Drive (off Clover Hill Road)	36 D3
Le Fanu Road	36 D3
Le Vere Terrace	74 F4
Lea Cres	39 B4
Lea Road	39 B4
Leahy's Terrace	39 A3
Lealand Ave	43 C1
Lealand Close	43 C1
Lealand Cres	43 C1
Lealand Drive	43 C1
Lealand Gardens	43 C1
Lealand Grove	43 C1
Lealand Road	43 C1
Lealand Walk	43 C1
Leda Mews (off Waterloo Road)	76 E3
Ledwidge Cres	67 B1
Lee Road	24 E3
Leeson Close	75 C3
Leeson Court	76 D4
Leeson Lane	75 C2
Leeson Mews	75 C4
Leeson Park	75 C4
Leeson Park Ave	76 D4
Leeson Place	75 C3
Leeson Street Lower	75 C2
Leeson Street Upper	76 D4
Leeson Village	76 D4
Leeson Walk	75 C4
Lehaunstown Road	63 C1
Leicester Ave	47 A1
*Leicester Court (off Leicester Ave)	47 A1
Leighlin Road	46 E1
Lein Gardens	26 F2
Lein Park	26 F2
Lein Road	26 F2
Leinster Ave	72 E1
*Leinster Cottages (on Convent Lane)	17 C3
*Leinster Court (adjacent O'Neill's Park)	18 D3
Leinster Lane	75 C1
Leinster Lawn	47 C3

STREET NAME	PAGE / GRID REFERENCE
*Leinster Lodge Apts (adjacent O'Neill's Park)	18 D3
Leinster Market	71 C4
Leinster Park (Maynooth)	18 D3
Leinster Park (Harold's Cross)	46 F1
Leinster Place	46 F1
Leinster Road	47 A1
Leinster Road West	46 F1
*Leinster Square (Leinster Road)	47 A1
Leinster Street	17 C3
Leinster Street East	72 E1
Leinster Street North	24 F4
Leinster Street South	75 C1
*Leinster Terrace (off Nangor Road)	44 D1
Leinster Wood (in Carton Demesne)	18 F1
Leitrim Place	76 E2
Leix Road	70 D1
Leixlip	33 B1
Leixlip Bridge	33 A1
Leixlip Gate	32 E1
Leixlip Park	32 F1
Leixlip Road	33 B1
Lemon Street	75 B1
Lennox Place	75 A3
Lennox Street	75 B3
Lennox Terrace	75 B3
Lentisk Lawn	27 A1
Leo Ave	71 B1
Leo Street	71 B1
Leonard's Court	74 F3
Leopardstown	58 F3
Leopardstown Abbey	58 F4
Leopardstown Ave	58 F2
*Leopardstown Court (off Brewery Road)	58 F2
Leopardstown Drive	58 F2
Leopardstown Gardens	58 F2
Leopardstown Grove	58 F2
Leopardstown Heights	58 E3
*Leopardstown Lawn (off Leopardstown Drive)	58 F2
Leopardstown Oaks	58 F2
Leopardstown Park	58 F2
Leopardstown Rise	58 E3
Leopardstown Road (Leopardstown)	58 D3
Leopardstown Road (Stillorgan Road)	58 F2
Leopardstown Valley	58 F4
*Les Buissonets Apts (off Sweetman's Ave)	49 A3
Leslie Ave	60 F1
Leslie's Buildings	70 F1
*Leukos Road (off Pine Road)	39 A3
Levmoss Estate	58 F3
*Levmoss Hall (at Levmoss Estate)	58 F3
*Liberty Court (Clanbrassil Terrace)	74 F2
*Liberty Court (Corporation Street)	71 C3
*Liberty Court Apts (Clanbrassil Terrace)	75 A2
*Liberty Court Apts (on Clanbrassil Street Lower)	74 F2
Liberty House	71 C2
Liberty Lane	75 B2
Liberty Lane	74 F1
Liberty Square	74 F1
Library Road (Dún Laoghaire)	50 D4
Library Road (Shankill)	64 E2
Library Square	52 F2
Library View Villas	71 A1
Liffey Ave	34 F2
Liffey Close	34 F2
Liffey Court	34 F2
Liffey Cres	34 F2
Liffey Dale	34 F2
Liffey Downs	34 F2
Liffey Drive	34 F2
Liffey Gardens	34 F2
Liffey Glen	34 F2
Liffey Green	34 F2
Liffey Grove	34 F2
Liffey Hall (off Liffey Cres)	34 F2
Liffey Junction	24 E4
Liffey Lawn	34 F2
Liffey Park	34 F2
Liffey Place	34 F2
Liffey Rise	34 F2
Liffey Road	34 F2
Liffey Row	34 F2
Liffey Street Lower	71 B4

STREET NAME	PAGE / GRID REFERENCE
Liffey Street South	36 F3
Liffey Street Upper	71 B3
Liffey Street West	70 E4
*Liffey Terrace (off Saint Laurence Road)	36 E2
Liffey Terrace	34 F2
Liffey Vale	34 F2
Liffey Valley Park	34 F2
Liffey View	34 F2
*Liffey View Apts (off Main Street Leixlip)	33 A1
Liffey Villas	34 F2
Liffey Walk	34 F2
Liffey Way	34 F2
Liffey Wood	34 F2
Lighthouse Apts	72 F1
Lilys Way	21 A1
Lime Street	72 E4
Limekilin Court	45 B3
Limekilin Ave	45 B3
Limekiln Close	45 C3
Limekiln Drive	45 C3
Limekiln Green	45 B3
Limekiln Grove	45 C2
Limekiln Lane (Harold's Cross)	74 F4
Limekiln Lane (Kimmage)	45 C2
Limekiln Park	45 C3
Limekiln Road	45 C3
Limelawn Court	22 D2
Limelawn Glade	22 D2
Limelawn Green	22 D2
Limelawn Hill	22 D2
Limelawn Park	22 D2
Limelawn Rise	22 D2
Limelawn Wood	22 D2
Limes Road	58 D2
Limetree Ave	4 D4
Limewood Ave	26 F1
Limewood Park	26 F1
Limewood Road	27 A1
Lincoln Hall (Swords)	1 Inset
Lincoln House	70 F4
Lincoln Lane	70 F4
Lincoln Place	76 D1
Linden Court	48 F4
Linden Grove	48 F4
Linden Lea Park	58 F1
Linden Square	48 F4
*Lindenvale (off Proby Square)	49 A4
Lindisfarne Ave	43 C1
Lindisfarne Drive	43 C1
Lindisfarne Green	43 C1
Lindisfarne Grove	43 C1
Lindisfarne Lawns	43 C1
Lindisfarne Park	34 F4
Lindisfarne Vale	43 C1
Lindisfarne Walk	43 C1
*Lindsay Grove (off Prospect Road)	25 A4
Lindsay Road	25 A4
Linenhall Parade	71 A3
Linenhall Street (off King Street North)	71 A3
Linenhall Terrace	71 A3
Link Road (off Monkstown Cres)	49 C4
Link Road (Glasthule)	60 E1
*Linnbhlá (adjacent Santry Cross Junction)	12 D4
Linnetfields	21 A1
Linnetfields Ave	8 E4
Linnetfields Close	8 E4
Linnetfields Court	21 A1
Linnetfields Drive	8 E4
Linnetfields Park	21 A1
Linnetfields Rise	8 E4
Linnetfields Square	8 E4
Linnetfields View	8 D4
Linnetfields Walk	21 A1
Lios na Sídhe	54 F2
Lioscian	1 B1
*Lisalea (off Frascati Park Blackrock)	49 A3
*Lisburn Court (King Street North)	71 A3
Lisburn Street	71 A3
Liscannor Road	24 E4
*Liscanor (off Harbour Road)	60 F1
Liscarne Court	35 A3
*Liscarne Dale (off Collinstown Road)	35 A3
Liscarne Dale	35 A3

STREET NAME	PAGE / GRID REFERENCE
Liscarne Gardens	35 A3
Lisin Glen Apts	24 F3
Lisle Road	46 D1
*Lismeen Grove (off Beechpark Ave)	26 E1
Lismore	18 E4
Lismore Road	46 E1
Lissadel Ave	73 B4
Lissadel Court	73 A4
Lissadel Cres	2 F2
Lissadel Drive	73 A4
Lissadel Grove	73 A3
Lissadel Grove	2 F2
Lissadel Park	2 F2
Lissadel Road	73 A4
Lissadel Wood	2 F2
Lissane Apts	22 E1
Lissen Hall	2 E1
Lissen Hall Drive	2 E1
Lissenfield	75 B4
Lissenhall Ave	2 D1
Lissenhall Bridge	2 E1
Lissenhall Court	2 D1
Lissenhall Drive	2 D1
Lissenhall Park	2 D1
Little Britain Street	71 A3
Little Fitzwilliam Place	76 D2
*Little Meadow (off Pottery Road)	59 C3
*Little Orchard (off Pottery Road)	59 C3
Littlepace	8 E4
Littlepace Close	8 E4
Littlepace Court	8 E4
Littlepace Cres	8 E4
Littlepace Drive	8 E4
Littlepace Gallops	8 E4
Littlepace Meadow	8 E4
Littlepace Park	8 E4
Littlepace Road	8 E4
Littlepace View	8 E4
Littlepace Walk	8 E4
Littlepace Way	8 E4
Littlepace Woods	8 E4
Littlewood	58 D4
Litton Lane	71 B4
Llewellyn Close	57 A1
Llewellyn Court	57 A1
Llewellyn Grove	57 A1
Llewellyn Lawn	57 A1
Llewellyn Park	57 A1
Llewellyn Way	57 A1
Llex House	76 D3
Lock Road	34 D3
Lockkeeper's Walk	24 D3
*Loftus Hall (off Belgard Square West)	54 F1
Loftus Lane	71 A3
*Loftus Square (off Main Street Rathfarnham)	46 F4
Lohunda Close	22 D2
Lohunda Court	22 D2
Lohunda Cres	21 C2
Lohunda Dale	22 D2
Lohunda Downs	22 D2
Lohunda Drive	22 D2
Lohunda Green	22 D2
Lohunda Grove	22 D2
Lohunda Park	21 C2
Lohunda Park View	22 D2
Lohunda Road	22 D2
Lombard Court (Clanbrassil Street)	74 F3
Lombard Court (Lombard Street East)	72 D4
Lombard Street East	72 D4
Lombard Street West	75 A3
Lomond Ave	25 C4
*Londonbridge Drive (off Londonbridge Road)	39 A3
Londonbridge Road	39 A3
Long Lane (New Bride Street)	75 A2
*Long Lane (off Mountjoy Street)	71 A2
Long Lane Close (off Long Lane)	75 A2
Long Meadow Apts	69 C4
Long Mile Road	45 B1
*Longbost Quay North Apts (Asgard Road)	72 E4
*Longbost Quay South Apts (Asgard Road)	72 E4
Longdale Terrace	25 A1
Longdale Way	25 A1
Longford Lane	75 B1

STREET NAME	PAGE / GRID REFERENCE
Longford Place	49 C4
Longford Street Great	75 A1
Longford Street Little	75 B1
Longford Terrace	49 C4
Longlands	2 D2
Longmeadow	59 C3
Longmeadow Grove	59 C3
Long's Place	74 E1
Longwood Ave	75 A3
Longwood Park	46 F4
*Looceville Court (off Saint Agnes RoadCrumlin)	46 D1
Lorcan Ave	25 C1
Lorcan Cres	25 C1
Lorcan Drive	25 B1
Lorcan Green	25 C1
Lorcan Grove	25 C1
*Lorcan O'Toole Court (off Lorcan O'Toole Park)	46 D2
Lorcan O'Toole Park	46 D2
Lorcan Park	25 C1
Lorcan Road	25 B1
Lorcan Villas	25 C1
Lord Edward Street	75 A1
Lordello	64 D3
Lordello Road	64 D3
Lords Walk (Phoenix Park)	69 B2
Loreto Abbey	47 A4
Loreto Ave (Nutgrove Ave)	47 A4
Loreto Ave (Dalkey)	60 F1
Loreto Court	47 A4
Loreto Cres	47 A4
Loreto Grange	67 C3
Loreto Park	47 A4
Loreto Road	74 E2
Loreto Row	47 A4
Loreto Terrace	46 F4
*Loretto Ave (Sidmonton Road)	67 C2
*Loretto Terrace (Sidmonton Road)	67 C2
*Loretto Villas (Sidmonton Road)	67 C2
Lorne Terrace (off Almeida Ave)	73 C2
*Losset Hall (off Belgard Square West)	54 F1
Lough Conn Ave	36 D2
Lough Conn Drive	36 D2
Lough Conn Road	36 D2
Lough Conn Terrace	36 D2
Lough Derg Road	27 A2
Lough na Mona	19 C4
Loughlinstown	64 D1
Loughlinstown Drive	64 D1
Loughlinstown Park	64 D1
Loughlinstown Wood	64 D1
*Loughmorne House (off Terenure Road West)	46 F2
Loughoreen Hills	30 D3
Loughsallagh Bridge	7 C3
Loughtown Lower	41 C1
Loughtown Upper	42 D1
*Louis Lane (off Leinster Road)	47 A1
Louisa Bridge	19 C4
Louisa Manor	19 C4
Louisa Vally	19 C4
Lourdes House	71 C2
Lourdes Road	74 D2
Louvain	48 D3
Louvain Glade	48 D3
Love Lane	76 E2
Love Lane East	76 E2
Lower Dargle Road	67 B2
Lower Glen Road (Phoenix Park)	36 D1
Lower Kilmacud Road (Goatstown)	48 D4
Lower Kilmacud Road (Stillorgan)	58 D1
Lower Lucan Road (Strawberry Beds)	21 C4
Lower Lucan Road (Lucan)	34 D1
Lower Road (Strawberry Beds)	35 B1
Lower Road (Shankill)	64 E3
Loyola	67 A3
Luby Road	73 A2
Lucan	34 D2
Lucan Bridge	34 D1
Lucan Bypass	34 D2
Lucan Heights	34 E1
Lucan Newlands Road (Esker)	34 D2
Lucan Newlands Road (Ronanstown)	35 A4
Lucan Road (Palmerstown)	35 C1
Lucan Road (Lucan)	34 D1

STREET NAME	PAGE / GRID REFERENCE
Lucan Road (near Qaurryvale)	35 A1
Lucan Road (Chapelizod)	36 D2
Lucan-Newlands Road	34 F3
Lucky Lane	70 D2
Ludford Drive	57 B1
Ludford Park	57 B1
Ludford Road	57 B2
Lugg	52 F4
Lugmore	54 D3
Lugmore Lane	53 C3
Lugnaquilla Ave	45 B3
Luke Street	71 C4
Lullymore Terrace	74 E3
Lurgan Street	71 A3
Luttrell Park	22 D3
Luttrell Park Close	22 D3
Luttrell Park Court	22 D3
Luttrell Park Cres	22 E3
Luttrell Park Drive	22 E3
Luttrell Park Green	22 E3
Luttrell Park Grove	22 D3
*Luttrell Park Heath (adjacent Oldfarm off Carpenterstown Road)	22 E3
Luttrell Park Lawn	22 D3
Luttrell Park View	22 D3
Luttrellstown Ave	22 E4
Luttrellstown Chase	22 D4
Luttrellstown Close	22 E4
Luttrellstown Court	22 D4
Luttrellstown Dale	22 D4
Luttrellstown Drive	22 D4
Luttrellstown Glade	22 D4
Luttrellstown Green	22 D4
Luttrellstown Grove	22 D4
Luttrellstown Heath	22 D4
Luttrellstown Heights	22 D4
Luttrellstown Lawn	22 D4
Luttrellstown Oaks	22 D4
Luttrellstown Park	22 D4
Luttrellstown Place	22 D4
Luttrellstown Rise	22 D3
Luttrellstown Road (Castleknock)	22 D4
Luttrellstown Road (Clonsilla)	21 C3
Luttrellstown Thicket	22 D4
Luttrellstown View	22 E4
Luttrellstown Walk	22 D4
Luttrellstown Way	22 D4
Luttrellstown Wood	22 E4
Lymewood Mews	12 E4
Lynches Lane	34 E4
*Lynch's Lane (off Ballyfermot Road)	36 E3
Lynch's Place	71 A1
Lyndon Gate (off Blackhorse Ave)	24 D4
*Lynton Court (off Sandymount Ave)	39 A4
Lynwood	57 C1
Lyons	41 A4
Lyons Ave	42 D4
*Lyons Ave North (off Newcastle Boulevard)	42 D4
*Lyons Ave South (off Newcastle Boulevard)	42 D4
Lyons Lane	42 D4
Lyons Road	41 B4
Lyons Street (off Newcastle Boulevard)	42 D4
*Lyre House (off Thomas Davis Street West)	36 F3
Lyreen Court	17 C3
Lyreen Park	18 D2

M

STREET NAME	PAGE / GRID REFERENCE
M1 Junction 1 (M50/M1)	13 A3
M1 Junction 2 (Dublin Airport)	13 A1
M1 Junction 3 (Swords)	2 B1
M4 Junction 4 (Leixlip)	33 B1
M4 Junction 6 (Celbridge)	32 D1
M4 Junction 7 (Maynooth)	17 C4
M50 Junction 1 (Dublin Port)	39 A1
M50 Junction 10 (Ballymount)	45 A3
M50 Junction 11 (N81 Tallagh)	45 C4
M50 Junction 12 (Firhouse)	55 C2
M50 Junction 13 (Dundrum)	57 C3
M50 Junction 14 (N31 Dun Laoghaire)	58 E3
M50 Junction 15 (Carrickmines)	59 A4
M50 Junction 16 (Cherrywood)	63 C2

STREET NAME	PAGE / GRID REFERENCE	STREET NAME	PAGE / GRID REFERENCE	STREET NAME	PAGE / GRID REFERENCE	STREET NAME	PAGE / GRID REFERENCE
M50 Junction 17 (M50/M11)	64 D3	Malahide Road (Balgriffin)	14 D3	Marian Cres	46 E4	Marlfield Close	54 F3
M50 Junction 2 (Santry)	13 A1	Malahide Road (Marino)	26 D4	Marian Drive	46 E4	Marlfield Court	54 F3
M50 Junction 3 (M1/M50)	12 F3	Malahide Road (Artane)	26 E2	Marian Grove	46 E4	Marlfield Cres	54 F3
M50 Junction 4 (Ballymun)	12 D3	Malahide Road (Coolock)	26 F1	Marian Park (Baldoyle)	27 C1	Marlfield Green	54 F3
M50 Junction 5 (N2/M50 Finglas)	11 A4	Malahide Roundabout (Swords)	2 D2	Marian Park (Templeogue)	46 E4	Marlfield Grove	54 F3
M50 Junction 6 (N3/M50 Blanchardstown)	22 F2	Malin House	22 F1	Marian Park (Blackrock)	59 A1	Marlfield Lawn	54 F3
M50 Junction 7 (N4/M50)	35 B1	Mallin Ave	74 D2	Marian Road	46 E4	Marlfield Mall	54 F3
M50 Junction 9 (N7/M50 Red Cow)	44 F1	Malone Gardens	76 F2	Marianella	47 A2	Marlfield Place	54 F3
Ma Tuire Apts	48 D4	Malpas Court	75 A2	Mariavilla	17 C2	Marlfield Row	54 F3
Mabbot House	71 C3	Malpas Place (off Malpas Street)	75 A2	*Marie Villas (Sidmonton Road)	67 C2	*Marlfield Terrace (Marlfield Place)	54 F3
Mabbot Lane	71 C3	Malpas Street (off New Street)	75 A2	Marigold Ave	13 C4	Marmion Court Flats	70 F3
Mabel Street	25 B4	Malpas Terrace	75 A2	Marigold Court	13 C4	Marne Villas	70 F2
Mac Mahon Bridge (Grand Canal)	76 E1	Mandalay	20 D4	Marigold Cres	13 C4	Marrowbone Lane	74 E2
Mac Ullaim	53 C1	Mander's Terrace	75 C4	Marigold Grove	13 C4	Marrowbone Lane Close (off Marrowbone Lane)	74 E1
*Mac Ulliam Ave (Mac Ulliam)	53 C1	Mangerton Road	36 F4	Marigold Park	13 C4	Marrowbone Lane Flats	74 E1
*Mac Ulliam Close (Mac Ulliam)	53 C1	Mannix Road	25 A4	Marigold Road	13 C4	Marrsfield Ave	14 E3
*Mac Ulliam Court (Mac Ulliam)	53 C1	Manor Ave	46 E3	*Marina House Apts (off Clarence Street Dún Laoghaire)	49 C4	Marshal Court Apts	74 E1
*Mac Ulliam Cres (Mac Ulliam)	53 C1	Manor Close	57 A2	Marina Village	3 B2	Marshalsea Court (Merchants Quay)	70 F4
*Mac Ulliam Dale (Mac Ulliam)	53 C1	Manor Court	17 C3	Marine Ave	60 E1	*Marshalsea Lane (off Bridgefoot Street)	70 E4
*Mac Ulliam Drive (Mac Ulliam)	53 C1	Manor Cres	21 B1	*Marine Court (off Crofton Road)	50 D4	Marsham Court	58 E1
*Mac Ulliam Gardens (Mac Ulliam)	53 C1	Manor Drive	14 D4	Marine Court (Dalkey)	60 E1	Mart Lane	59 B3
*Mac Ulliam Green (Mac Ulliam)	53 C1	Manor Green	57 A2	Marine Cove (off Baldoyle Road)	28 D1	*Martello Ave (off Summerhill Road)	50 D4
*Mac Ulliam Lane (Mac Ulliam)	53 C1	Manor Grove	46 D2	Marine Drive	39 A4	Martello Court	4 D4
*Mac Ulliam Lawns (Mac Ulliam)	53 C1	*Manor Hall (Adjacent Cromwells Quarter)	73 C1	Marine Parade	60 E1	Martello Mews	48 E1
*Mac Ulliam Mews (Mac Ulliam)	53 C1	*Manor Hall Apts (Mount Brown)	74 D1	Marine Road	50 D4	Martello Terrace	29 B3
*Mac Ulliam Parade (Mac Ulliam)	53 C1	Manor Heath	57 A1	*Marine Terrace (off Park Road Dún Laoghaire)	50 D4	*Martello Terrace (off Seafort Parade Booterstown)	48 F3
*Mac Ulliam Road (Mac Ulliam)	53 C1	Manor House View	27 A3	*Marine Terrace (at Esplanade)	68 D2	*Martello Terrace (off Windsor Terrace Dún Laoghaire)	50 E4
*Mac Ulliam Walk (Mac Ulliam)	53 C1	Manor Mews (off Norseman Place)	70 E3	Marine View	48 F3	*Martello Terrace (Strand Road Bray)	67 C1
*Mac Ulliam Way (Mac Ulliam)	53 C1	Manor Park (Palmerston)	35 C2	*Marine Villas (off Harbour Road, opposite Howth Station)	30 D1	*Martello View (off Strand Road)	39 B4
*Macken House (near The Point)	72 F3	Manor Park (Ballinteer)	57 A2	Mariners Court (off Kilbarrack Road)	27 C2	*Martello Wood (off Strand Road)	39 B4
Macken Street	76 E1	Manor Place (Stoneybatter)	70 E3	Mariners Cove	30 E2	Martin Grove	24 D4
Macken Villa	76 E1	Manor Place (Clonsilla)	21 A1	Mariner's Port	72 E3	Martin Savage Park	23 C3
Mackies Place	75 C2	Manor Rise	57 A2	Marino	25 C4	Martin Street	75 A3
Mackintosh Park	59 C2	Manor Road	35 C2	Marino Ave	26 D4	*Martin White Chalets (off Herbert Road)	39 A4
Macroom Ave	13 B4	Manor Square	21 A1	Marino Ave East	60 E4	Martin's Row	36 E2
Macroom Road	13 B4	Manor Street	70 E3	Marino Ave West	60 E4	*Martin's Terrace (off Hanover Street East)	72 D4
Madden Road	74 F2	*Manor Villas (off Mount Argus Grove)	46 F1	*Marino Court (off Fairview Ave Lower)	25 C4	*Mary Aikenhead Flats (off Basin Street Lower)	74 D1
*Madden's Court (off Thomas Street)	74 E2	Manorfields	21 B1	Marino Cres	25 C4	Mary Street	71 A3
Madden's Lane	60 E4	Mantua Park	2 D1	Marino Green	25 C4	Mary Street Little	71 A4
*Madison Court Apts	76 E1	Maolbuille Road	25 A2	*Marino Mart (off Haverty Road)	25 C4	*Maryfield Ave (off Ardlea Road)	26 E2
Madison Road	73 C2	Mapas Ave	60 E2	Marino Park	25 C4	Maryfield Cres	26 E2
*Magdalen Terrace (off Oliver Plunkett Ave)	39 A3	Mapas Road	60 E2	Marino Park Ave	25 C4	Maryfield Drive	26 D2
Magennis Place	72 D4	Mapel House	1 Inset	*Marino Villa (off Casino Park)	26 D3	*Maryland (Shanganagh Road near School)	64 E2
Magennis Square	72 D4	Maple Ave (Carpenterstown)	22 E3	Marion Villas	74 E2	Marymount	12 F2
Magenta Cres	25 B1	Maple Ave (off Blackthorn Drive)	58 D2	Mark Street	72 D4	Mary's Abbey	71 A4
Magenta Hall	25 B1	Maple Close	22 E3	Market House	67 C2	Mary's Lane	71 A4
*Magenta Place (off Eden Road Upper)	60 D1	Maple Drive (Dunboyne)	7 B2	Market Square (Smithfield)	70 F3	Maryville Road	26 F3
Magna Ave	53 C2	Maple Drive (Carpenterstown)	22 E3	*Market Square (near Market House)	67 C2	Mask Ave	26 E2
Magna Drive	53 C2	*Maple Drive (off The Cloisters)	46 F2	Market Square Apts	71 A3	Mask Cres	26 E2
*Maher's Terrace (on Main Street Dundrum)	47 C4	Maple Glen	22 E3	Market Street South	74 E1	Mask Drive	26 E2
*Maidens Row (off Martin's Row Chapelizod)	36 E2	Maple Green	22 E3	Mark's Alley West	74 F1	Mask Green	26 E2
Main Road (Tallaght)	55 A1	Maple Grove (Carpenterstown)	22 E3	Mark's Lane	72 D4	Mask Road	26 E2
Main Street (Clongriffin)	14 E4	Maple Grove (Rathcoole)	52 F2	Marlay View	57 B2	Mather Road North	48 E3
Main Street (Swords)	2 D2	Maple Grove (Bray)	67 B2	Marlborough Court (Marlborough Street)	71 C3	Mather Road South	48 D3
Main Street (Malahide)	3 B2	Maple House	76 D3	Marlborough Court (Blackhorse Ave)	70 D2	Matt Talbot Court	71 C2
Main Street (Dunboyne)	7 B2	Maple Lawn	22 E3	*Marlborough Court (off Sharavogue)	60 E2	Maunsell Place	71 A2
Main Street (Ballymun)	12 D4	Maple Lodge	23 A4	*Marlborough Lane (off Marlborough Road)	47 B1	*Maxwell Court (off Maxwell Road)	47 A1
Main Street (Baldoyle)	15 A4	Maple Manor	59 C3	Marlborough Mews	70 D2	Maxwell Lane	47 A2
Main Street (Maynooth)	17 C3	Maple Road	47 C2	*Marlborough Park (off Adelaide Road)	60 D1	Maxwell Road	47 A1
Main Street (Blanchardstown)	22 E2	Maples (opposite Knockmaroon Gate)	36 D1	Marlborough Place	71 C3	Maxwell Street	74 E2
Main Street (Finglas)	24 E2	Maples House	58 D2	Marlborough Road (North Circular Road)	70 D2	May Cottages	71 A1
Main Street (Raheny)	27 A2	Maplewood Ave	54 E1	Marlborough Road (Donnybrook)	47 B1	May Lane	70 F4
Main Street (Howth)	30 D2	Maplewood Close	54 E1	Marlborough Road (Glenageary)	60 E1	May Park	26 D3
Main Street (Celbridge)	32 D3	Maplewood Court	54 E1	Marlborough Street	71 C3	*May Street (off Fitzroy Ave)	71 C1
Main Street (Leixlip)	33 A1	Maplewood Drive	54 E1	*Marlborough Terrace (at Esplanade)	68 D2	Mayberry Park	45 A4
Main Street (Lucan)	34 D1	Maplewood Green	54 E1	Marley	3 C3	Mayberry Road	44 F4
Main Street (Newcastle)	42 D4	Maplewood Lawn	54 E1	Marley Ave	57 A1	Mayeston	11 B3
Main Street (Clondalkin)	44 E1	Maplewood Park	54 E1	Marley Close	57 A1	Mayeston Boulevard (Mayeston)	11 C4
Main Street (Rathfarnham)	46 F4	Maplewood Road	54 E1	Marley Court North	57 A1	Mayeston Close (Mayeston)	11 B3
Main Street (Dundrum)	47 C4	Maplewood Way	54 E1	Marley Court South	57 A1	Mayeston Court (Mayeston)	11 B4
Main Street (Blackrock)	49 A3	Maquay Bridge (Grand Canal)	76 E2	Marley Drive	57 A1	Mayeston Cres (Mayeston)	11 C4
Main Street (Rathcoole)	52 F2	Maretimo Gardens East	49 A3	Marley Grove	57 A1	Mayeston Downs (Mayeston)	11 C4
Main Street (Tallaght)	55 A1	*Maretimo Gardens West (off Newtown Ave Blackrock)	49 A3	Marley Lawn	57 A1	Mayeston Drive (Mayeston)	11 B4
Main Street (Bray)	67 C2	*Maretimo Place (off Newtown Ave Blackrock)	49 A3	Marley Rise	57 A1	Mayeston Green (Mayeston)	11 C3
Main Street (Saggart)	53 A2	*Maretimo Road (off Newtown Ave Blackrock)	49 A3	*Marley Villas (off Marley Walk)	57 A1	Mayeston Lawn (Mayeston)	11 B3
Main Street (Ongar)	21 A1	*Maretimo Terrace (off Newtown Ave Blackrock)	49 A3	Marley Walk	57 A1	Mayeston Rise (Mayeston)	11 C4
Main Street (Chapelizod)	36 E2	*Maretimo Villas (off Temple Road)	49 A3	Marlfield	59 C3	Mayeston Square (Mayeston)	11 B4
Maitland Street	67 B2	Marewood Cres	24 F1			Mayeston Walk (Mayeston)	11 C4
Malachi Place	72 E2	Marewood Drive	11 C4			Mayfair	3 C2
Malachi Road	70 E3	Marewood Grove	24 F1				
Malahide	3 B2	Margaret Place	76 F2				
Malahide Demesne	3 A3	Marguerite Road	25 A4				
Malahide Road (Darndale)	13 C4	Marian Court	14 F4				
Malahide Road (Swords)	2 E2						

STREET NAME	PAGE / GRID REFERENCE
Mayfield	47 A2
*Mayfield Court (Mayfield Park)	35 B4
Mayfield Park	35 B4
Mayfield Road (Kilmainham)	73 C2
Mayfield Road (Terenure)	46 F2
Mayfield Terrace (Ballinteer)	57 C2
*Mayfield Terrace (Vevay Road, Putland Road)	67 C3
Mayne Bridge	14 F3
Maynetown	14 F3
Maynooth	18 D2
Maynooth Park	18 D4
Maynooth Road (Dunboyne)	7 A3
Maynooth Road (Celbridge)	31 C1
Mayola Court	47 B4
Mayor Square	72 E3
Mayor Street Lower	72 D3
Mayor Street Upper	72 F3
*Mayville Terrace (off Leslie Ave)	60 F1
Maywood Ave	27 B2
Maywood Close	27 B2
Maywood Cres	27 B3
Maywood Drive	27 B2
Maywood Grove	27 B2
Maywood Lawn	27 B3
Maywood Park	27 B2
Maywood Road	27 B2
Mc Cartney Bridge (Grand Canal)	76 D3
*Mc Donagh House (Whitefriar Street)	75 A1
Mc Kee Court (Blackhorse Ave)	69 C2
Mc Kenny Bridge (Grand Canal)	76 E2
McAuley Ave	26 F2
McAuley Drive	26 F2
McAuley Park	26 F2
McAuley Road	26 F2
McCabe Villas	48 E3
McCarthy Terrace	74 D2
McCreadies Lane	3 A3
McDowell Ave	74 D1
*McGovern Corner Apts (off Cork Street)	74 E2
*McGrane Court (off Sandyford Road)	57 C1
McKee Ave	24 E1
McKee Park	69 C1
McKee Road	24 E1
McKelvey Ave	11 A4
McKelvey Road	11 A4
McMahon Street	75 A3
*McMorrough Road (off Terenure Road North)	46 F2
Meade's Terrace	76 D1
*Meadow Ave (off Meadow Grove)	57 B1
Meadow Close (Dundrum)	57 A1
Meadow Close (Newtown Park Ave)	59 A1
Meadow Copse	21 C1
*Meadow Court (off Wyattville Road)	60 D4
*Meadow Dale (off Meadow Green)	21 C1
Meadow Downs	21 C1
Meadow Drive	21 C1
Meadow Green	21 C1
Meadow Grove	57 B1
Meadow Mount	57 A1
Meadow Park	57 A1
Meadow Park Ave	47 A4
Meadow Vale	59 B2
Meadow View (Dunboyne)	7 B2
Meadow View (Nutgrove Ave)	57 A1
*Meadow Villas (off Meadow Grove)	57 A1
Meadow Way	21 C1
Meadowbank	46 F3
Meadowbrook	17 C4
Meadowbrook Ave (Maynooth)	17 C4
Meadowbrook Ave (Sutton)	28 D1
Meadowbrook Close	17 C4
Meadowbrook Court	17 C4
Meadowbrook Cres	17 C4
Meadowbrook Drive	17 C4
Meadowbrook Lawn	28 D1
Meadowbrook Lawns	17 C4
Meadowbrook Park	28 D1
Meadowbrook Road	17 C4
Meadowfield	58 E4
Meadowlands	59 C1
Meadowlands Ave	59 C1

STREET NAME	PAGE / GRID REFERENCE
*Meadowlands Court (off Meadowlands Ave)	59 C1
*Meadowlands Mews (off Meadowlands Ave)	59 C1
Meadowview Grove	33 C2
Meagans Lane	53 B4
Meakstown Cottages	11 B3
Meath Place (Meath Street)	74 F1
Meath Place (Bray)	67 C2
Meath Road	68 D2
Meath Square	74 F1
Meath Street	74 F1
*Meath Terrace (on Meath Place)	74 F1
*Meathville Terrace (on Long Lane)	75 A2
*Meenan Square (off Owenstown Park Fosters Ave)	48 D3
*Meeting House Square (on Sycamore Street)	71 B4
Meetinghouse Lane	71 A4
Méile an Rí Cres	34 F3
Méile an Rí Drive	34 F3
Méile an Rí Green	34 F3
Méile an Rí Park	34 F3
Méile an Rí Road	34 F3
Méile an Rí View	34 F3
Mellennium Walkway 71 B3	71 B2
Mellifont Ave	50 D4
Mellowes Ave	24 D1
Mellowes Court	24 D2
*Mellowes Cres (off Mellowes Court)	24 D2
Mellowes Park	24 D1
Mellowes Road	24 D1
Mellows Bridge (River Liffey)	70 F4
*Mellows Quay Apts (adjacent Emmet Place)	70 F4
Melrose Ave (Fairview)	25 C4
Melrose Ave (Clondalkin)	43 C1
*Melrose Court (off Philipsburgh Ave)	25 C4
Melrose Cres	43 C1
Melrose Green	43 C1
Melrose Grove	43 C1
Melrose Lawn	34 F4
Melrose Park (Swords)	2 E3
Melrose Park (Clondalkin)	43 C1
Melrose Park The Ave	2 E3
Melrose Park The Close	2 E3
Melrose Park The Cres	2 E3
Melrose Park The Drive	2 E3
Melrose Park The Green	2 E3
Melrose Park The Grove	2 E3
Melrose Park The Heights	2 E3
Melrose Park The Lawn	2 E3
Melrose Park The Park	2 E3
Melrose Park The Rise	2 E3
Melrose Park The Villa	2 E3
Melrose Park The Walk	2 E3
Melrose Road	34 F4
Melville Close	11 B4
Melville Court	11 B4
Melville Cove	11 B4
Melville Cres	11 B4
Melville Drive	11 B4
Melville Green	11 B4
Melville Grove	11 B4
Melville Lawn	11 B4
Melville Park	11 B4
Melville Rise	11 B4
Melville Square	11 B4
Melville Terrace	11 B4
Melville View	11 B4
Melville Way	11 B4
Melvin Road	46 F2
Memorial Court	69 B4
Memorial Road (Inchicore Road)	73 A1
Memorial Road (Custom House Quay)	71 C3
Mercer House	75 B2
Mercer Street Lower	75 B1
Mercer Street Upper	75 B2
Merchamp	26 F4
Merchants Arch (off Temple Bar)	71 B4
*Merchant's Court	70 F4
*Merchant's Hall (Merchants Quay)	70 F4
Merchant's House	70 F4
Merchant's Quay	70 F4
Merchant's Road	39 A1
Merchant's Square	72 F3

STREET NAME	PAGE / GRID REFERENCE
*Meretimo Villas (on Edward Road)	68 D3
Merlyn Drive	48 D1
Merlyn Park	48 D1
Merlyn Road	48 D1
Merrion	48 E1
Merrion Close	76 D1
*Merrion Court (Ailesbury Road)	48 E1
*Merrion Cres (off Trimleston Road)	48 E2
*Merrion Gates (off Strand Road)	48 E1
Merrion Grove	48 E3
Merrion Hall	48 E4
Merrion Park	48 E3
Merrion Place	75 C2
Merrion Road	39 A4
Merrion Row	75 C2
Merrion Square East	76 D2
Merrion Square North	76 D1
Merrion Square South	76 D2
Merrion Square West	76 D1
Merrion Strand	48 E1
Merrion Street Lower	76 D1
Merrion Street Upper	75 C2
*Merrion View Ave (off Ailesbury Road)	48 D1
Merrion Village	48 E1
*Merrion Woods (Rear of Belfield Park Apts)	48 E3
*Merry Bush (off Tritonville Ave)	39 A4
Merrycourt	8 E2
Merton Ave	74 F3
*Merton Cres (off Milltown Ave)	47 B2
Merton Drive	47 B1
Merton Park	74 F3
Merton Road	47 B2
Merton Walk	47 B2
Merville Ave (Fairview)	25 C4
Merville Ave (Stillorgan)	58 F1
Merville Court	24 E2
Merville Road	58 F1
Mespil Estate	76 D3
Mespil Lodge	76 D3
Mespil Road	76 D3
Metropolitan Apts	73 A1
Michael Collins Park	35 A4
*Michell House	76 D4
Middle Third	26 E3
Middle Third Terrace	26 E3
Milesian Ave	2 E2
Milesian Court	2 E2
Milesian Grove	2 E2
Milesian Lawn	2 E2
Milestown	19 C1
Milford	3 A2
Military Road (Rathmines)	75 B4
Military Road (Kilmainham)	73 C1
Military Road (Phoenix Park)	36 F2
Military Road (Killiney)	60 E4
*Mill Bank (near Hills Industrial Estate)	34 D1
Mill Bridge (Swords)	2 D2
Mill Brook Apts	35 C1
Mill Court Ave	43 C1
Mill Court Drive	43 C1
Mill Field (Enniskerry)	66 E3
Mill House	62 F3
Mill Lane (Newmarket)	74 F2
Mill Lane	23 B3
Mill Lane (Palmerstown)	35 C1
Mill Lane (Leixlip)	33 A1
Mill Lane (Loughlinstown)	64 E2
Mill Park	44 D1
*Mill Race Apts (Martins Row)	36 E2
Mill Road (Blanchardstown)	22 F2
Mill Road (Saggart)	53 A2
Mill Street (The Coombe)	74 F2
*Mill Street (off Cross Ave Dún Laoghaire)	50 D4
Millar's Hall (Bridgefoot Street)	74 F1
Millar's Hall (Cork Street)	74 E2
Millbank	14 F2
Millbourne Ave	25 A4
Millbrook Ave	27 A1
Millbrook Court	73 C1
Millbrook Drive	27 A1
Millbrook Grove	27 A1
Millbrook Lawns	55 A1
Millbrook Road	27 A1
Millbrook Terrace	73 B1

STREET NAME	PAGE / GRID REFERENCE
*Millbrook Village (off Milltown Road)	47 C1
Millennium Bridge (River Liffey)	71 B4
Millers Wood	67 B3
Millfarm	7 C2
Millfield (Portmarnock)	14 F2
Millgate Drive	45 C3
Millmount Ave	25 A4
Millmount Grove	47 B3
Millmount Place	25 B4
*Millmount Terrace (Drumcondra)	25 B4
*Millmount Villas (off Millmount Ave)	25 A4
Millrace Ave	53 A2
Millrace Court	53 A2
*Millrace Court (Millrace Road)	23 B3
Millrace Cres	53 A2
Millrace Drive	53 A2
Millrace Garden	53 A2
Millrace Green	53 A2
Millrace Park	53 A2
Millrace Road	23 B3
Millrace View	53 A2
Millrace Walk	53 A2
*Millrose Estate (off Canal Terrace)	36 E4
Millstead	22 F2
Millstream	14 F2
Millstream Road	33 C2
Milltown (Peamount)	42 F2
Milltown (Clonskeagh)	47 C2
Milltown Ave	47 B2
Milltown Bridge Road	47 C2
*Milltown Collonade (on Milltown Road)	47 B2
Milltown Drive	47 A3
Milltown Grove (Churchtown)	47 A3
*Milltown Grove (off Dundrum Road)	47 B2
*Milltown Hill (off Milltown Road)	47 B2
Milltown Park	47 B1
Milltown Path	47 B2
Milltown Road	47 B2
*Milltown Terrace (off Dundrum Road)	47 B3
*Millview (off Ninth Lock Road)	44 E1
Millview Close	3 A3
Millview Cottages	73 A2
Millview Court	3 A2
Millview Lawns	3 A3
Millview Road	3 A3
Millwood Court	27 A1
Millwood Park	27 A1
Millwood Villas	27 A1
Milner's Square	25 B2
Milton Hall	1 C2
Milton Terrace (Swords)	2 D2
*Milton Terrace (north of Galtrim Park)	67 C2
*Milward Terrace (Meath Road, Victoria Ave)	68 D2
Mimosa Hall	58 F3
Mine Hill Lane	63 B3
Minnow Brook	46 F2
*Minnow Brook (opposite Terenure Park)	46 F2
*Minstrel Court (Charles Sheil's Houses)	58 F2
Misery Hill	72 E4
Mitchelstown	10 D2
Moat Lane	1 A2
Moatfield Ave	26 F1
Moatfield Park	26 F1
Moatfield Road	26 F1
Moatview Ave	13 B4
Moatview Court	13 B4
Moatview Drive	13 B4
Moatview Gardens	13 B4
Moatview Terrace	13 B4
*Mobhi Court (off Saint Mobhi Boithirin)	25 A3
Moeran Road	45 C1
Moira Road (off Oxmanstown Road)	70 D3
Moira Villas	74 F1
Moland House	71 C3
Moland Place	71 C3
Molesworth Close	1 A2
Molesworth Place	75 C1
Molesworth Street	75 C1
Mollison Ave	14 D4
Molyneux Yard	74 F1

STREET NAME	PAGE / GRID REFERENCE		STREET NAME	PAGE / GRID REFERENCE		STREET NAME	PAGE / GRID REFERENCE		STREET NAME	PAGE / GRID REFERENCE	
Monalea Grove	55	C1	Montrose Grove	26	D2	Mount Bellew Way	34	E2	*Mountain View Cottages		
Monalea Park	55	C1	Montrose Park	26	D2	Mount Brown	73	C1	(off Mountain View Road)	47	B1
Monalea Wood	55	C1	Moore Lane	71	B3	Mount Carmel	71	A3	Mountain View Court	71	C2
Monaloe Ave	59	C3	Moore Street	71	B3	Mount Carmel Ave	47	C4	*Mountain View Court		
*Monaloe Court			Moorefield	60	E4	Mount Carmel Park	55	C1	(off Shamrock Villas)	46	F1
(off Clonkeen Road)	59	B3	*Moore's Cottages			Mount Carmel Road	47	C4	Mountain View Drive	57	A1
*Monaloe Cres			(off Annaville Ave)	59	A1	Mount Dillon Court	26	E2	Mountain View Park		
(off Clonkeen Road)	59	B3	Mooretown	1	B1	Mount Drinan Ave	2	E3	(Churchtown)	47	A4
Monaloe Drive	59	C3	Mooretown Ave	1	C1	Mount Drinan Cres	2	E3	Mountain View Road (Ranelagh)	47	B1
Monaloe Park	59	C3	Mooretown Grove	1	C1	Mount Drinan Grove	2	E3	*Mountain View Road		
Monaloe Park Road	59	C3	Mooretown Park	1	C1	Mount Drinan Lawn	2	E3	(off Church Road Ballybrack)	60	E4
Monaloe Way	59	C3	Moorfield	35	A4	Mount Drinan Park	2	E3	*Mountain Villa (off Dale View)	60	E4
Monasterboice Road	46	D1	Moorfield Ave	35	A4	Mount Drinan Walk	2	E3	Mountainview Drive	67	C4
Monastery	66	E3	*Moorfield Close			Mount Drummond Ave	74	F4	*Mountbrook (off Seamount)	48	E3
Monastery Cres	44	E1	(off Moorefield Drive)	35	A4	Mount Drummond Court	74	F4	Mountdown Ave	45	C3
Monastery Drive	44	E1	Moorfield Drive	35	A4	Mount Drummond Square	75	A4	Mountdown Drive	45	C3
Monastery Gate	44	F1	Moorfield Green	35	A4	Mount Eagle Court	58	E3	Mountdown Park	45	C3
Monastery Gate Ave	44	F1	Moorfield Grove	35	A4	Mount Eagle Drive	58	E3	Mountdown Road	45	C3
Monastery Gate Close	44	F1	Moorfield Lawns	35	A4	Mount Eagle Green	58	E3	Mountfield	3	B3
Monastery Gate Copse	44	F1	Moorfield Parade	35	A4	Mount Eagle Grove	58	E3	Mountfield Lawn	3	C3
Monastery Gate Green	44	F1	Moorfield Walk	35	A4	Mount Eagle Lawn	58	E3	Mountfield Lodge	3	C3
Monastery Gate Lawn	44	F1	Moracrete Cottages	73	C4	Mount Eagle Park	58	E3	Mountfield Park	3	C4
Monastery Gate Villas	44	F1	*Moran's Cottages			Mount Eagle Rise	58	D3	Mountgorry Lodge	2	E2
Monastery Grove	66	E2	(off Charleston Road)	47	B1	Mount Eagle View	58	E3	Mountgorry Wood Apts	2	E2
Monastery Heath	44	E1	Moreen Ave	58	D2	Mount Eagle Way	58	E3	Mountjoy Parade	71	C1
Monastery Heath Ave	44	E1	Moreen Close	58	D2	Mount Eden Road	47	C1	Mountjoy Place	71	C2
Monastery Heath Court	44	E1	*Moreen Lawn (off Moreen Ave)	58	D2	Mount Eustace	9	B2	Mountjoy Square	71	C2
Monastery Heath Green	44	E1	Moreen Park	58	D2	Mount Eustace Ave	9	B2	Mountjoy Square Apts		
Monastery Heath Square	44	E1	Moreen Road	58	D2	Mount Eustace Close	9	A2	(Mountjoy Square West)	71	B2
*Monastery Heights			Moreen Walk	58	D2	Mount Eustace Drive	9	B2	Mountjoy Square Apts		
(off Monastery Road)	44	E1	*Morehampton Hall			Mount Eustace Green	9	B2	(Mountjoy Square South)	71	C2
Monastery Park	44	E1	(off Morehampton Terrace)	47	C1	Mount Eustace Grove	9	A2	Mountjoy Square East	71	C2
Monastery Rise	44	E1	*Morehampton Hall			Mount Eustace Park	9	B2	Mountjoy Square North	71	C2
Monastery Road	44	E1	(off Morehampton Terrace)	47	C1	Mount Eustace Rise	9	B2	Mountjoy Square South	71	C2
Monastery Walk	44	E1	Morehampton Lane	76	E4	Mount Eustace Walk	9	B2	Mountjoy Square West	71	B2
Monck Place	70	F1	Morehampton Mews			Mount Gandon (off Lucan Road)	34	D1	Mountjoy Street	71	A2
Monks Hill	66	E2	(off Sandymount Ave)	76	E4	Mount Garrett	9	A2	Mountjoy Street Middle	71	A2
Monks Meadow	4	D4	Morehampton Road	76	E4	Mount Garrett Ave	9	A2	Mountpleasant Ave Lower	75	B4
Monksfield	44	F1	Morehampton Square			Mount Garrett Close	9	A2	Mountpleasant Ave Upper	75	B4
Monksfield Ave	44	F1	(off Serpentine Park)	76	E4	Mount Garrett Drive	9	A2	Mountpleasant Parade	75	B4
Monksfield Court	44	F1	Morehampton Terrace	47	C1	Mount Garrett Rise	9	A2	Mountpleasant Place	75	C4
Monksfield Downs	44	F1	Morgan Place	70	F4	Mount Garrett Walk	9	A2	Mountpleasant Square	75	B4
Monksfield Grove	44	F1	Morgans Place	23	A3	*Mount Harold Terrace			Mountpleasant Terrace	75	B4
Monksfield Heights	44	F1	Moritz House	55	B2	(off Leinster Road)	46	F1	*Mountpleasant Terrace Upper		
Monksfield Lawn	44	F1	Morning Star Ave	70	F3	Mount Hybla Court	23	A4	(Mountpleasant Villas)	75	C4
Monksfield Meadows	44	F1	Morning Star Road	74	D2	Mount Hybla House	23	A4	Mountpleasant Villas	75	C4
Monksfield Walk	44	F1	*Mornington Ave			Mount Merrion	48	E4	*Mountpleasant Villas		
Monkstown	49	B4	(off Sandycove Point)	50	E4	Mount Merrion Ave	48	F3	(East of Dargle Heights)	67	B2
Monkstown Ave	59	B1	Mornington Grove	26	E2	*Mount Norris Villas			Mountsandel	59	B4
Monkstown Cres	49	C4	Mornington Park	26	E2	(South of Hall)	68	D2	Mountseskin Road	53	C4
Monkstown Farm	59	C1	Mornington Road	47	B1	Mount Olive Grove	27	B1	Mountshannon Road	73	C2
*Monkstown Gate			*Morrogh Terrace			Mount Olive Park	27	B1	*Mounttown Cottages		
(off The Hill Dún Laoghaire)	49	C4	(off Philipsburgh Ave)	25	C3	Mount Olive Road	27	B1	(off Mounttown Road)	49	C4
Monkstown Grove	59	C1	Morrow House	14	F4	Mount Prospect Ave	26	F4	*Mounttown Park		
*Monkstown Manor			Moss Street	71	C4	Mount Prospect Drive	26	F4	(off Mounttown Lower)	59	C1
(off Monkstown Farm)	59	B1	Mount Albany	59	A1	Mount Prospect Grove	26	F4	Mounttown Road Lower	59	C1
Monkstown Road	49	B4	Mount Albion Road (Dundrum)	57	B1	Mount Prospect House			Mounttown Road Upper	49	C4
*Monkstown Square			Mount Alton	55	C1	(off Clontarf Road)	27	A4	Mountview Road	22	D2
(off Monkstown Ave)	59	B1	Mount Alton Court	56	D1	Mount Prospect Lawn	26	F4	Mourne Road (Brickfields Park)	73	A3
Monkstown Valley	49	B4	Mount Andrew	34	F2	Mount Prospect Park	26	F4	Mourne Road (Drimnagh)	36	F4
Montague Court	75	B2	Mount Andrew Ave	34	F2	Mount Saint Annes	47	B2	Moy Elta Road	72	E2
Montague Lane	75	B2	Mount Andrew Close	34	F1	Mount Salus Road	60	F2	Moy Glas Ave	34	E3
Montague Place	75	B2	Mount Andrew Court	34	F1	*Mount Sandford			Moy Glas Chase	34	E3
Montague Street	75	B2	Mount Andrew Cres	34	F1	(off Milltown Road)	47	C1	Moy Glas Close	34	E3
*Monte Vella (off Barnhill Road)	60	F2	Mount Andrew Dale	34	F2	Mount Street Cres	76	E2	Moy Glas Court	34	E3
*Montebello Terrace			Mount Andrew Grove	34	F1	Mount Street Lower	76	D1	Moy Glas Dale	34	E3
(at South Esplanade)	68	D2	Mount Andrew Place	34	F1	Mount Street Upper	76	D2	Moy Glas Dene	34	E3
*Montgomery Court			Mount Andrew Rise	34	F1	Mount Symon Ave	21	C2	Moy Glas Drive	34	E3
(West of Connolly Station)	72	D3	*Mount Anthony Estate			Mount Symon Close	21	C2	Moy Glas Glen	34	E3
Montini Road	27	C1	(off Ardee Road)	47	A1	Mount Symon Cres	21	B2	Moy Glas Green	34	E3
Montpelier Court	70	D3	Mount Anville Lawn	48	D4	Mount Symon Dale	21	B2	Moy Glas Grove	34	E3
Montpelier Drive	70	D3	Mount Anville Park	48	D4	Mount Symon Drive	21	C2	Moy Glas Lawn	34	E3
Montpelier Gardens	70	D3	Mount Anville Road	48	D4	Mount Symon Estate	21	B2	Moy Glas Park	34	E3
Montpelier Hill	70	D3	Mount Anville Wood	48	D4	Mount Symon Green	21	B2	Moy Glas Road	34	E3
*Montpelier Manor			Mount Argus Ave	46	F1	Mount Symon Lawn	21	C2	Moy Glas Vale	34	E3
(off Monkstown Road)	49	B4	Mount Argus Close	46	F1	Mount Symon Park	21	C2	Moy Glas View	34	E3
*Montpellier Mews			Mount Argus Court	46	F1	Mount Symon Rise	21	B2	Moy Glas Way	34	E3
(Montpellier Hill)	70	D3	Mount Argus Cres	46	F1	Mount Talbot	44	F1	Moy Glas Wood	34	E3
Montpelier Parade	49	B4	Mount Argus Green	46	F1	Mount Tallant Ave	46	F2	Moyclare Ave	28	D1
Montpelier Park	70	D3	Mount Argus Grove	46	F1	Mount Temple Road	70	E3	Moyclare Close	28	D1
*Montpelier Place			Mount Argus Park	46	F1	Mount Venus Road	56	D4	Moyclare Drive	28	D1
(off Monkstown Road)	49	B4	Mount Argus Road	46	F1	Mount Wood	59	C1	Moyclare Gardens		
Montpelier Square	70	D3	*Mount Argus Square			Mountain Park	55	A1	(off Moyclare Road)	28	D1
Montpelier View	54	D2	(Mount Argus Ave)	46	F1	Mountain View (Jobstown)	54	D2	Moyclare Park	28	D1
*Montpelier Walk			Mount Argus Terrace	46	F1	Mountain View (Shankill)	64	E3	Moyclare Road	28	D1
(off Kiltalown Road)	54	D2	Mount Argus View	46	F1	*Mountain View Apts			Moycullen Road	35	C3
Montpellier Mews	70	D4	Mount Argus Way	46	F1	(Vevay Road, Wolfe Tone Square)	67	C3	Moygaddy	18	D1
Montrose Ave	26	D2	*Mount Auburn			*Mountain View Ave			Moyglare	17	A1
Montrose Close	26	D2	(off Killiney Hill Road)	60	E3	(off Shamrock Villas)	46	F1	Moyglare Abbey	17	B2
Montrose Court	26	D2	Mount Bellew Cres	34	F2	Mountain View Cottages			Moyglare Hall	17	C2
Montrose Cres	26	D1	Mount Bellew Green	34	F2	(Castleknock)	22	D4	Moyglare Meadows	17	C2
Montrose Drive	26	D1	Mount Bellew Rise	34	E2				Moyglare Road	17	C2

STREET NAME	PAGE / GRID REFERENCE
Moyglare Village	17 C2
Moyle Cres	44 E1
Moyle Road	24 E3
*Moyne Court (off Moyne Road)	47 B1
Moyne Lodge	14 F3
Moyne Park	14 F3
Moyne Road (Balgriffin)	14 E3
Moyne Road (Ranelagh)	47 B1
*Moynihan Court	
(off Avonmore Road)	55 B1
Moyville	56 E2
Moyville Lawns	56 E1
Muckross Ave	46 D2
Muckross Cres	46 D2
*Muckross Drive	
(off Muckross Ave)	46 D2
Muckross Green	46 D2
Muckross Grove	46 D2
Muckross Parade	71 B1
Muckross Park	46 D2
*Muirfield Drive	
(off Naas Road Bluebell)	36 F4
Mulally's Lane	52 F2
Mulberry Cres	22 F4
Mulberry Drive	22 E4
Mulberry Park	22 E4
Muldowney Court	3 C3
Mulgrave Street	50 D4
Mulgrave Terrace	50 D4
Mulhuddart	9 A4
Mulhuddart Bridge	9 A4
Mulhuddart Wood	9 A4
Mullauns	42 D1
Mullen Bridge	18 D3
*Mullinahack (Oliver Bond Street)	70 F4
Mullinastill Road	64 D2
*Mullingar Terrace	
(off Martin's Row Chapelizod)	36 E2
Mulroy Road	24 E4
Mulvey Park	47 C3
Munster Street	24 F4
*Munster Terrace	
(off Breffni Road)	60 E1
Murphy's Lane	63 B4
Murphystown Road	58 E3
Murphystown Way	58 E3
Murragh	14 F2
*Murray's Cottages	
(off Sarsfield Road)	36 F3
Murrough Road	1 B1
Murtagh Road	70 E3
Muskerry Road	36 E3
Mutton Lane	56 E4
Myra Close	73 A1
Myra Manor	3 A4
*Myrtle Ave	
(off Royal Terrace East)	60 D1
Myrtle Grove (Stillorgan)	58 F1
*Myrtle Grove (off Beech Road)	67 B1
Myrtle Park	60 D1
Myrtle Square	14 F4
Myrtle Street	71 A2

N

N2 Junction 1 (M50/N2 Finglas)	11 A4
N2/M2 Junction 2	
(Saint Margaret's)	10 D1
N4 Junction 1 (N4/M50)	35 B1
N4 Junction 2 (Liffey Valley)	35 A1
N4 Junction 3 (Lucan)	34 E1
N4 Junction 4 (Newcastle)	34 D2
N4 Junction 4a (Dodsboro)	33 C2
N7 Junction 1 (M50/N7 Red Cow)	44 F2
N7 Junction 1A (Newlands Cross)	44 E2
N7 Junction 2 (Kingswood)	43 C3
N7 Junction 3 (Citywest)	43 B4
N7 Junction 4 (Rathcoole)	52 F1
N7 Junction 5 (Athgoe)	51 B3
Naas Road (Walkinstown)	45 A1
Naas Road (Rathcoole)	52 F1
Naas Road (Saggart)	53 B1
Naas Road (Kingswood)	43 C4
Nagle Court	18 D2
*Nangor Cres	
(off Cherrywood Villas)	44 D1
Nangor Place	
(off Cherrywood Villas)	43 C1
Nangor Road (Grange Castle)	43 A2
Nangor Road (Clondalkin)	44 D1
Nangor Road (Fox and Geese)	44 F1

Nanikin Ave	27 A3
Nash Street	36 F3
Nashville Park	30 E2
Nashville Road	30 D2
Nassau Street	75 C1
Naul Road (Brackenstown Road)	1 A3
Naul Road (Cloghran)	1 C4
Navan Road (Cabra)	69 C1
Navan Road (Dunboyne)	7 B2
Navan Road (Clonee)	8 E3
Navan Road (Mulhuddart)	8 F4
Navan Road (Blanchardstown)	22 E1
Navan Road (Castleknock)	23 A3
Neagh Road	46 E2
Neilstown Ave	35 A3
*Neilstown Cottages	
(off Newlands Road)	35 A4
Neilstown Cres	35 A3
Neilstown Drive	35 A3
Neilstown Gardens	35 A3
Neilstown Park	35 A3
Neilstown Road	35 A3
*Neilstown Village Court	
(off Neilstown Road)	35 A3
Nelson Street	71 A1
Nephin Road	24 D4
*Neptune Terrace	
(off Breffni Road)	60 E1
Nerano Road	60 G2
Nerney's Court	71 B2
Nethercross Court	2 D1
Neville Road	47 A2
Nevinstown Lane	1 C3
*New Bancroft Hall	
(off Main Street Tallaght)	55 A1
*New Bancroft Place	
(off Main Street Tallaght)	55 A1
*New Bancroft Square	
(off Main Street Tallaght)	55 A1
New Bawn Drive	55 A2
New Bawn Park	55 A2
New Bride Street	75 A2
New Bridge	32 F2
*New Brighton Terrace	
(Parnell Road)	67 C2
*New Cornelscourt	
(off Bray Road)	59 B3
*New Court (New Street South)	75 A2
New Grange Road	59 A1
New Grove Estate	14 E4
New Ireland Court	73 C2
New Ireland Road	73 C2
New Lucan Road	35 B1
New Nangor Road	43 C1
*New Park Lodge	
(off Knocksinna Park)	59 A2
New Park Road	59 A1
*New Rathmore Terrace	
(Upper Dargle Road)	67 B2
*New Ravenswell Row	
(near Ardee Street)	67 B2
New River Road	23 A2
New Road (Howth)	30 E3
New Road (Inchicore)	36 F3
New Road (Clondalkin)	44 E2
*New Row	
(off Martin's Row Chapelizod)	36 E2
New Row Place	75 A2
New Row South	74 F2
New Row Square	74 F2
New Street	3 B2
New Street Gardens	
(off New Street)	75 A2
New Street North	
(off Church Street)	70 F3
New Street South	75 A2
New Vale	64 E3
New Vale Cottages	64 D3
New Vale Cres	64 E3
New Wapping Street	72 F3
Newbridge Ave (Irishtown)	39 A3
Newbridge Drive	39 A3
Newbrook Ave	27 B1
Newbrook Road	27 B1
Newbury Ave	13 A4
Newbury Drive	13 A4
Newbury Grove	13 A4
*Newbury Heights	
(on Clonshaugh Road)	13 A4
Newbury Lawns	13 B4
Newbury Park	13 A4

*Newbury Terrace	
(on Clonshaugh Road)	13 A4
Newbury Wood	13 A4
Newcastle	41 C4
Newcastle Apts	20 D4
Newcastle Boulevard	42 D4
Newcastle Demesne	41 B4
Newcastle Farm	41 B4
Newcastle Lyons	42 D4
Newcastle Manor	42 D4
Newcastle Manor (The Square)	42 D4
Newcastle Manor Green	42 D4
Newcastle Manor Heights	42 D4
Newcastle Manor Park	42 D4
*Newcastle Manor Place	
(Newcastle Manor)	42 D4
Newcastle Manor Square	42 D4
Newcastle Manor: The Close	42 D4
Newcastle Manor: The Court	42 D4
Newcastle Manor: The Cres	42 D4
Newcastle Manor: The Green	42 D4
Newcastle Manor: The Heights	42 D4
Newcastle Manor: The Park	42 D4
*Newcastle Manor: The Place	
(Newcastle Manor)	42 D4
Newcastle Manor: The Rise	42 D4
Newcastle Road (Lucan)	34 D2
Newcastle Road (Rathcoole)	52 E1
Newcomen Ave	72 D1
Newcomen Bridge (Royal Canal)	72 D2
Newcomen Court	72 D1
Newcourt (Bray)	68 D4
Newcourt Ave	68 D3
Newcourt Mews	2 D1
Newcourt Road	68 D3
*Newcourt Villas	
(start of Putland Road)	67 C3
Newgrange Road	24 F4
Newgrove Ave	39 B4
Newhall Court	54 D2
*Newington Terrace	
(off Castlewood Ave)	47 A1
Newlands Ave	44 E2
Newlands Court	26 D2
Newlands Drive	44 E2
Newlands Manor	44 D3
Newlands Manor Court	44 D3
Newlands Manor Drive	44 D3
Newlands Manor Fairway	44 D3
Newlands Manor Green	44 D3
Newlands Manor Park	44 D3
Newlands Park	44 E2
Newlands Road (Ronanstown)	34 F3
Newlands Road (Clondalkin)	44 E2
Newman Place	18 D3
Newmarket	74 F2
*Newmarket Hall (off Newmarket)	74 F2
*Newmarket Square	
(off Ward's Hill)	74 F2
*Newmarket Street	74 F2
Newpark	59 A2
Newport Street	74 E1
Newtown (Dunboyne)	7 A3
Newtown (Rathfarnham)	56 E3
Newtown (Glencullen)	62 D3
Newtown (Tinnehinch)	66 E4
Newtown Ave (Coolock)	26 F1
Newtown Ave (Blackrock)	49 A3
Newtown Bridge	7 A2
Newtown Close	13 C4
Newtown Cottages	
(Saint Margaret's)	11 A1
Newtown Cottages (Coolock)	26 F1
Newtown Court (Coolock)	13 C4
Newtown Court (Maynooth)	17 B4
*Newtown Court	
(off Eaton Brae Rathgar)	47 A3
Newtown Drive	26 F1
Newtown Glendale	20 D4
Newtown Grove	17 C3
Newtown Hall	17 B3
*Newtown House	
(off Eaton Brae Rathgar)	47 A3
Newtown Lower	51 C4
Newtown Park (Leixlip)	20 D4
Newtown Park (Coolock)	26 F1
Newtown Park (Tallaght)	55 B1
Newtown Park (Blackrock)	59 A1
*Newtown Park Court	
(off Mount Albany)	59 A1
Newtown Road (Coolock)	13 C4
Newtown Road (Maynooth)	17 B4

Newtown Road (Celbridge)	32 D4
Newtown Upper	52 D4
*Newtown Villas	
(off Braemor Road)	47 A3
*Newtown Villas	
(off Newtown Ave Blackrock)	49 A3
Newtown Way	13 C4
Newtownpark Ave	49 A4
*Newtownpark House	
(off Mount Albany)	59 A1
Newtownsmith	50 E4
Niall Street	70 D2
Nicholas Ave	70 F3
Nicholas Street	75 A1
Ninth Lock Road	44 D1
No2 Nth. Road Extension	39 B1
Noel Purcell Park	75 B1
Nore Road	24 E3
Norfolk Road	24 F4
Norseman Court	
(off Norseman Place)	70 E3
Norseman Place	70 E3
North Ave	48 E3
North Bull Island	27 B4
North Circular Road	
(Phibsborough)	71 C1
North Circular Road	
(Phoenix Park)	70 D2
North Circular Road Gate	
(Phoenix Park)	69 C3
North Clarence Street Flats	72 D2
North Great George's Street	71 B2
North Lotts	71 B4
North Quay Extension	39 A2
North Road	
(Phoenix Park North Circular)	69 B1
North Road (Finglas)	24 D1
North Road	
(Phoenix Park Ashtown)	23 B4
North Road (Kilshane)	10 F2
North Strand Road	72 E1
North Street	2 D1
North Street	21 A1
North Wall	72 E3
North Wall Quay	72 E4
*Northbank Apts	
(Alexander Terrace)	72 F3
Northbrook Ave (Ranelagh)	75 C4
Northbrook Ave Lower	72 E1
Northbrook Ave Upper	72 E1
Northbrook Lane	75 C4
Northbrook Road	75 C4
Northbrook Terrace	72 E1
Northbrook Villas	75 C4
Northbrook Walk	75 C4
Northcote Ave	49 C4
*Northcote Place	
(off North Cote Ave)	49 C4
*Northcote Terrace	
(off North Cote Ave)	49 C4
Northern Close	13 B3
Northern Cross Route (Poppintree)	11 B3
Northern Cross Route	
(Abbotstown)	23 A2
Northland Drive (off Tolka Estate)	24 F3
Northland Grove (off Tolka Estate)	24 F3
Northumberland Ave	50 D4
Northumberland Court	76 E2
*Northumberland Park	
(off Northumberland Ave	
Dún Laoghaire)	50 D4
Northumberland Place	
(Grand Canal Street Upper.)	76 E2
*Northumberland Place	
(off Northumberland Ave	
Dún Laoghaire)	50 D4
Northumberland Road	76 E2
Northumberland Square	71 C3
Northway Estate	11 A4
Northwood	12 E4
Northwood Ave	12 E4
Northwood Road	12 D4
Norton's Ave	70 F1
Norwood	64 E1
*Norwood Park	
(off Sandford Road)	47 C1
Nottingham Street	72 E1
Novara Ave	67 C2
*Novara Mews (Novara Ave)	67 C2
*Novara Park (Novara Ave)	67 C2
*Novara Terrace (Novara Ave)	67 C2
Nugent Road	47 A4

STREET NAME	PAGE / GRID REFERENCE
Nunciature Road (Phoenix Park)	23 C4
Nun's Lane	26 E3
Nuns Walk	26 E3
Nurney Lawn	14 D4
Nutgrove Ave	47 A4
*Nutgrove Ave (off Nutgrove Ave)	47 B4
*Nutgrove Court (off Nutgrove Ave)	47 A4
Nutgrove Cres	57 A1
Nutgrove Park (Clonskeagh)	47 C2
Nutgrove Way	57 A1
Nutley Ave	48 D1
Nutley Lane	48 D2
Nutley Park	48 D2
Nutley Road	48 D1
*Nutley Square (off Greenfield Park U.C.D.)	48 D2

O

O Neill's Park	18 D3
Oak Apple Green	47 A2
Oak Ave	12 F4
Oak Close	44 F1
Oak Court	12 F4
Oak Cres	12 F4
Oak Dene	60 E3
Oak Downs	44 D2
Oak Drive (Santry)	12 F4
Oak Drive (Fox and Geese)	44 F1
Oak Glen Park	67 C4
Oak Glen View	67 C4
Oak Green	12 F4
Oak Grove	12 F4
Oak Hall	3 B3
Oak House (Sussex Road)	76 D3
Oak House (Swords)	1 Inset
Oak Lawn (Santry)	12 F4
Oak Lawn (Castleknock)	22 F3
Oak Lodge	23 A4
Oak Rise (Santry)	12 F4
Oak Rise (Clondalkin)	44 D2
Oak Road (Donnycarney)	26 D3
Oak Road (Fox and Geese)	44 F1
Oak View	12 E4
Oak Way	44 D2
*Oakbury Court (off Serpentine Ave)	39 A4
Oakcourt Ave	35 C2
Oakcourt Close	35 C2
Oakcourt Drive	35 C2
Oakcourt Grove	35 C2
Oakcourt Lawn	35 C2
Oakcourt Park	35 C2
Oakdale Close	55 B3
Oakdale Cres	55 B3
Oakdale Drive (Firhouse)	55 B3
Oakdale Drive (Sallynoggin)	59 C2
Oakdale Grove	55 B3
Oakdale Park	55 B3
Oakdale Road	55 B3
Oakdown Road	47 A4
Oakfield Place	75 A3
Oaklands Ave	2 D2
*Oaklands Court (off Claremont Road)	39 A4
Oaklands Cres	47 A2
Oaklands Drive (Sandymount)	39 A4
Oaklands Drive (Rathgar)	47 A2
Oaklands Park (Swords)	2 D2
Oaklands Park (Sandymount)	39 A4
Oaklands Terrace	46 F2
Oaklawn	19 C4
Oaklawn Close	19 C4
Oaklawn West	19 C4
Oakleigh	31 C4
Oakleigh Court	3 A3
*Oakley Court (off Oakley Road)	47 B1
Oakley Grove	49 A4
Oakley Park (Clontarf)	26 F4
*Oakley Park (off Oakley Road)	47 B1
Oakley Park (Blackrock)	49 A4
Oakley Road	47 B1
*Oakley Square (off Oakley Road)	47 B1
Oakpark Ave	25 C1
Oakpark Close	25 C1
Oakpark Drive	25 C1
Oakpark Grove	25 C1
Oaks (opposite Knockmaroon Gate)	36 D1

*Oakton Court (off Oakton Park)	60 E4
Oakton Drive	60 D4
*Oakton Green (off Oakton Park)	60 D4
Oakton Park	60 D1
Oaktree Ave	22 E3
Oaktree Drive	22 E3
Oaktree Green	22 E3
Oaktree Grove	22 E3
Oaktree Lawn	22 E3
Oaktree Road	58 F1
Oakview	66 D3
Oakview Ave	21 C1
Oakview Close	21 C1
Oakview Court	21 C1
Oakview Drive	21 C1
*Oakview Grove (off Oakview Ave)	21 C1
Oakview Lawn	21 C1
Oakview Park	21 C1
Oakview Rise	21 C1
Oakview Walk	21 C1
Oakview Way	21 C1
*Oakwood (off Tivoli Road)	49 C4
*Oakwood Apts (off The Glen Raheny)	27 B3
Oakwood Ave (Swords)	1 C2
Oakwood Ave (Glasnevin)	24 E1
Oakwood Close	24 E1
Oakwood Grove Estate	35 A4
Oakwood Park	24 E1
Oakwood Road	24 E1
Oatfield Ave	35 B3
Oatfield Close	35 B3
*Oatfield Cres (off Oatfield Drive)	35 B2
Oatfield Drive	35 B3
Oatfield Grove	35 B3
Oatfield Lawn	35 B3
Oatfield Park	35 B3
*Obelisk Ave (off Obelisk Grove)	59 A1
Obelisk Court	3 C2
Obelisk Court (Stillorgan)	59 A1
Obelisk Grove	59 A1
Obelisk Lane	18 E4
Obelisk Rise	59 A1
Obelisk Walk	59 A1
*Oblate Drive (off Nash Street)	36 F3
*Oblate View Apts (Tyrconnell Road opposite Church)	36 F3
O'Brien Road	45 C1
*O'Brien's Place North (off Joyce Road)	25 A3
Observatory Court	75 B4
*Observatory Lane (off Rathmines Road Lower)	47 A1
O'Byrne Road	67 C3
O'Byrne Villas (O'Byrne Road)	67 C3
*O'Callaghan Court	76 D1
O'Carolan Road	74 F2
O'Casey Ave	35 C4
O'Connell Ave	71 A1
O'Connell Bridge (River Liffey)	71 B4
O'Connell Gardens	39 A3
O'Connell Street	71 B3
O'Curry Ave (off O'Curry Road)	74 F2
O'Curry Road	74 F2
O'Daly Road	25 A3
Odd Lamp Road (Phoenix Park)	36 F1
O'Devaney Gardens	70 D3
*O'Donnell Gardens (off Eden Road Lower)	60 D1
O'Donoghue Street	36 F3
O'Donovan Road	74 F3
O'Donovan Rossa Bridge (River Liffey)	71 A4
*O'Dwyer Road (off O'Brien Road)	45 C1
Offaly Bridge	18 E1
Offaly Road	24 F4
Offington Ave	29 B2
Offington Court	29 B2
Offington Drive	29 B2
Offington Lawn	29 B2
Offington Manor Apts	29 B1
Offington Park	29 B1
Ogham	60 D3
O'Hanlon's Lane	3 B2
O'Hara Ave	75 A4
*O'Hogan Road (off O'Hogan Road)	36 E3
O'Hogan Road	36 E3
*Oisin Court (off Claremont Road)	39 A4

*Olaf Hall (off Balally Hill)	58 D2
*Olaf House Apts (Ushers Quay)	70 F4
Olaf Road	70 E3
Olcovar	64 E3
Old Bawn Ave	55 A2
Old Bawn Bridge	55 A2
Old Bawn Close	55 A2
*Old Bawn Court (off Old Bawn Road)	55 A1
Old Bawn Drive	55 A2
Old Bawn Park	55 A2
Old Bawn Road	55 A1
Old Bawn Terrace	55 A2
Old Bawn Way	55 A2
Old Belgard Road	44 F4
Old Blessington Road	55 A1
Old Brazil Way	1 A2
Old Bridge Road	46 D4
*Old Brighton Terrace (Parnell Road)	67 C2
Old Cabra Road	70 D1
Old Camac Bridge (Camac River)	73 B1
Old Carrickbrack Road	30 D4
Old Connaught	67 A1
Old Connaught Ave	67 B1
Old Connaught Grove	67 B2
Old Connaught View	67 B2
Old Corduff Road	22 E1
Old Cornmill Road	33 C2
Old County Glen	73 C4
Old County Road	73 B4
Old Dublin Road (Stillorgan)	48 E4
Old Dunleary	49 C4
Old Estuary Mill	2 F2
Old Fairgreen	7 B2
Old Fort Road	1 A2
Old Greenfield	17 C4
Old Hill	20 D4
Old Kilmainham	73 C1
Old Kilmainham Village	74 D1
Old Mill Court	74 F2
Old Mountpleasant	75 C4
Old Naas Road (Bluebell)	36 E4
Old Naas Road (Brownsbarn)	43 C4
*Old Naas Road Cottages (off Old Naas Road)	36 E4
Old Navan Road	22 F2
Old Orchard	46 E4
*Old Orchard Terrace (near Owendore Ave)	46 F4
Old Quarry (Kilshane)	10 D2
Old Quarry (Dalkey)	60 F2
Old Quay	29 B2
Old Quay Mews	29 B2
Old Quay Terrace	29 B2
Old Rathmichael	64 D3
*Old Rathmore Terrace (Upper Dargle Road)	67 B2
*Old Ravenswell Row (Upper Dargle Road)	67 B2
*Old Rectory (off Chapel Hill)	34 D1
Old Rectory Park	47 C4
Old Road	14 E2
Old Street	3 B2
Old Yellow Walls Road	3 A2
Oldbawn	55 A2
Oldbridge	34 E3
Oldbridge Close	34 E3
Oldbridge Court	34 E3
Oldbridge Glen	34 E3
Oldbridge Green	34 E3
Oldbridge Grove	34 E3
Oldbridge Park	34 E3
Oldbridge View	34 E3
Oldbridge Walk	34 E3
Oldbridge Way	34 E3
Oldcarton	18 F1
Oldcastle Ave	29 B2
Oldcastle Drive	43 B1
Oldcastlepark	43 B1
Oldcastlepark Close	43 B1
Oldcastlepark Green	43 B1
Oldcastlepark Grove	43 B1
Oldcastlepark Lawn	43 B1
Oldcastlepark View	43 B1
Oldchurch Ave	43 C1
Oldchurch Close	43 C1
Oldchurch Court	43 C1
Oldchurch Cres	43 C1
Oldchurch Drive	43 C1
Oldchurch Grove	43 C1

Oldchurch Lawn	43 C1
Oldchurch Park	43 C1
Oldchurch Way	43 C1
Oldcourt	67 B3
Oldcourt Ave (Bohernabreena)	55 B2
Oldcourt Ave (Boghall Road)	67 B3
Oldcourt Close	55 B2
Oldcourt Cottages	55 B3
Oldcourt Drive	67 B3
Oldcourt Farm	55 B2
Oldcourt Grove	67 B4
*Oldcourt Lawn (off Oldcourt Ave)	55 B2
Oldcourt Lodge	55 B2
Oldcourt Manor	55 B3
*Oldcourt Mill (off Oldcourt Road)	55 B3
Oldcourt Park	67 B3
Oldcourt Road	55 B3
*Oldcourt Terrace (Vevay Road, Lauderdale Estate)	67 C3
Oldcourt View	55 B2
Oldfarm	22 E3
Oldfield Hall	57 C3
Oldtower Cres	35 A2
Oldtown Ave	25 A1
Oldtown Cottages	31 C3
Oldtown Mill	31 C3
Oldtown Mill Road	31 C3
*Oldtown Park (off Shanliss Road)	25 A1
Oldtown Road	25 A1
Oldtown Road	31 B3
O'Leary Road	73 B2
*Olivemount Grove (off Olivemount Road)	47 C3
Olivemount Road	47 C3
*Olivemount Terrace (off Olivemount Road)	47 C3
Oliver Bond House Flats	70 F4
Oliver Bond Street	70 F4
Oliver Plunkett Ave (Ringsend)	39 A3
Oliver Plunkett Ave (Dún Laoghaire)	59 C1
Oliver Plunkett Road	59 C1
*Oliver Plunkett Square (off Oliver Plunkett Road)	59 C1
*Oliver Plunkett Terrace (off Oliver Plunkett Road)	59 C1
*Oliver Plunkett Villas (off Oliver Plunkett Ave)	59 B1
*Oliver's Alley (off Wood Street)	75 A1
Olney Cres	46 F2
*Olney Grove (off Olney Cres)	46 F2
*Olympic Apts (Pleasants Street)	75 A2
Omni Park	25 B1
O'Moore Road	36 E3
*O'Neachtain Road (off Ferguson Road)	25 A3
O'Neill's Buildings	75 A2
Ongar Chase Estate	21 A1
Ongar Green	21 A1
Ongar Green Ave	21 A1
Ongar Green Cres	21 A1
Ongar Green Drive	21 A1
Ongar Green Green	21 A1
Ongar Green Place	21 A1
Ongar Park Estate	21 B1
Ongar Road	21 B2
Ongar Square	21 A1
Ongar Village	21 A1
Ongar-Hartstown Relief Road	21 C2
Ontario Terrace	75 B4
Onward Close	3 C4
Onward Walk	3 C4
Ophaly Court	47 C4
*O'Rahilly House Flats (off Thorncastle Street)	39 A3
O'Rahilly Parade	71 B3
Oranmore Road	35 C3
*Oratory Mews Court (off Library Road)	50 D4
Orby Ave	58 E3
Orby Close	58 F3
Orby Court	58 F3
Orby Lawn	58 E3
Orby Park	58 F3
Orby View	58 E3
Orby Village	58 E3
Orby Way	58 E3
Orchard Ave (Clonsilla)	21 C2
Orchard Ave (Citywest)	53 B1
Orchard Close	22 D2
*Orchard Cottages (off Newtown Park)	59 A1

STREET NAME	PAGE / GRID REFERENCE
Orchard Court	22 E2
Orchard Green	22 D2
Orchard Grove (Blanchardstown)	22 E2
Orchard Grove (Newcastle)	42 D4
Orchard Lane (Ranelagh)	75 C4
Orchard Lane (Clondalkin)	44 E1
Orchard Lane (Blackrock)	59 A1
Orchard Lawns	35 C3
Orchard Lodge	44 E1
Orchard Road (Ballybough)	25 B4
Orchard Road (Raheny)	27 B2
Orchard Road South	47 B2
Orchard Square	47 C3
Orchard Terrace (Grangegorman Upper)	70 F1
*Orchard Terrace (Vevay Road, Putland Road)	67 C3
*Orchard View (Near Marne Villas)	70 F2
Orchardstown Ave	46 E4
Orchardstown Drive	46 E4
Orchardstown Park	46 E4
Orchardstown Villas	56 E1
*Orchardton (off Willow Bank Drive)	56 E1
Ordnance Survey Road (Phoenix Park)	36 E1
O'Reilly Ave	73 C1
O'Reilly's Cottages	74 F4
Oriel Hall	72 D3
Oriel Street Lower	72 E2
Oriel Street Upper	72 D3
Orlagh Ave	56 D2
Orlagh Close	56 D2
Orlagh Court	56 D2
Orlagh Cres	56 D2
Orlagh Downs	56 D2
Orlagh Grange	56 D2
Orlagh Green	56 D2
Orlagh Grove	56 D2
Orlagh Lawn	56 D2
Orlagh Lodge	56 D2
Orlagh Meadows	56 D2
Orlagh Park	56 D2
Orlagh Pines	56 D2
Orlagh Rise	56 D2
Orlagh View	56 D2
Orlagh Way	56 D2
Orlagh Wood	56 D2
*Ormeau Drive (off Carysfort Road)	60 F1
Ormeau Street	76 F1
Ormond Ave	1 B1
Ormond Close	1 B1
Ormond Cres	1 B1
Ormond Drive	1 B1
Ormond Grove	1 B1
Ormond Lawn	1 B1
Ormond Market (off Ormond Quay Upper)	71 A4
Ormond Place	71 A4
Ormond Quay Lower	71 B4
Ormond Quay Upper	71 A4
Ormond Road	25 B4
Ormond Road South	47 B1
Ormond Square	71 A4
Ormond Street	74 F2
*Ormond Terrace (off Sorrento Road)	60 F2
Ormond View	1 B1
Ormond Way	1 B1
O'Rourke Park	59 C2
Orpen	58 F1
Orpen Close	48 F4
*Orpen Dale (off Stillorgan Grove)	48 F4
Orpen Green	58 F1
Orpen Hill	58 F1
Orpen Rise	58 F1
Orr's Terrace	74 F4
*Orwell Bank (off Orwell Park)	47 A3
*Orwell Court (off Braemor Road)	47 A3
Orwell Gardens	47 A3
*Orwell Mews (off Orwell Road Rathgar)	47 A2
Orwell Park (Templeogue)	45 C4
Orwell Park (Rathgar)	47 A3
Orwell Park Ave	46 D3
Orwell Park Close	46 D3
Orwell Park Cres	46 D3
Orwell Park Dale	45 C4
Orwell Park Drive	46 D3
Orwell Park Glade	45 C3
Orwell Park Glen	46 D3
Orwell Park Green	46 D3
Orwell Park Grove	45 C3
Orwell Park Heights	45 C4
Orwell Park Lawns	45 C3
Orwell Park Rise	45 C4
Orwell Park View	45 C4
Orwell Park Way	46 D3
Orwell Road	47 A2
Orwell Walk	47 A3
*Osborne Court (off Seapoint Ave)	49 B3
*Osborne Terrace (Northbrook Road)	75 C4
Oscar Square	74 F2
Oscar Traynor Road (Kilmore)	13 A4
Oscar Traynor Road (Coolock)	26 E1
*O'Shea's Cottages (off Bray Road Cabinteely)	59 C3
Osprey Ave	45 C3
*Osprey Court (beside Telephone Exchange)	64 E3
Osprey Drive	45 C3
Osprey Lawn	45 C3
Osprey Park	45 C3
Osprey Road	45 C3
Ossory Road	72 E2
*Ossory Road Apts (near Ossory Industrial Estate)	72 E2
Ostman Place	70 E3
O'Sullivan Ave	72 D1
Oswald Road	39 A3
Otranto Place	60 E1
*Otterbrook (off Willbrook Road)	46 F4
Oulart	1 C3
Oulton Road	26 E4
Ounavarra	33 C1
Our Lady's Close (off Our Lady's Road)	74 E2
Our Lady's Road	74 E2
Outer Ring Road	43 B2
Outfarm Lane	22 E3
Outlands	1 B1
*Ovenden House (off Dean Street)	75 A2
Overend Way	57 C1
Ovoca Road	75 A3
Owendoher Haven	56 E1
Owendoher Lodge	56 E1
Owendore Ave	46 F4
Owendore Cres	46 F4
Owen's Ave	73 C1
Owensilla	24 F1
Owenstown Park	48 D3
*Oxford Grove (off Oxford Road)	47 B1
Oxford Lane	75 C4
Oxford Road	47 B1
Oxford Terrace (on Hawthorn Terrace)	72 E2
Oxmantown Lane	70 F4
Oxmantown Road	70 D2

P

STREET NAME	PAGE / GRID REFERENCE
Pace Ave	8 E4
Pace Cres	8 E4
Pace Road	8 E4
Pace View	8 E4
Pacelli Ave	27 C1
Pairc Gleann Trasna	55 A3
Páirc Mhuire	53 A2
Páirc View	53 A2
*Pakenham (off Sloperton)	49 C4
Pakenham Bridge	21 A2
Pakenham Road	49 C4
*Palace Garden Apts (Palace Street)	71 B4
Palace Street (off Dame Street)	71 B4
Palmer Park	56 F2
Palmers Ave	35 B2
Palmers Close	35 B2
Palmers Copse	35 B2
Palmers Court	35 B2
Palmers Cres	35 B2
Palmers Drive	35 B2
Palmers Glade	35 B2
Palmers Grove	35 B2
Palmers Lawn	35 B2
Palmers Park	35 B2
Palmers Road	35 B2
Palmers Walk	35 B2
Palmerston	35 C1
*Palmerston Close (off Windsor Road)	47 B1
Palmerston Court	47 A1
Palmerston Gardens	47 B2
*Palmerston Grove (off Milltown Road)	47 C2
*Palmerston Hall Apts (Palmerston Place)	71 A2
Palmerston Lane	47 B2
Palmerston Park (Rathgar)	47 B2
Palmerston Place	71 A2
Palmerston Road	47 B1
Palmerston Villas	47 A2
Palmerstown Ave	35 C2
Palmerstown Close	35 B2
Palmerstown Court	35 C2
Palmerstown Drive	35 C2
Palmerstown Green	35 B2
Palmerstown Heights	35 B2
Palmerstown Lawn	35 B2
Palmerstown Manor	35 B2
Palmerstown Park (Kennelsfort Road)	35 B2
Palmerstown Woods	35 B4
Paradise Place	71 A2
*Paramount Court Apts (off Corrig Road)	58 E2
Park Ave (Brackenstown Road)	1 B2
Park Ave (Castleknock)	22 F3
Park Ave (Sandymount)	39 B4
Park Ave (Willbrook)	56 F1
Park Ave (Deans Grange)	59 A1
Park Ave West	70 D3
Park Boulevard	9 B2
Park Close (Sallynoggin)	60 D2
*Park Court (off Park Lane Sandymount)	39 A4
Park Court Apts	23 A3
Park Cres (Blackhorse Ave)	69 A1
Park Cres (Kimmage)	46 D2
*Park Cres House (adjacent Lydon Gate)	24 D4
Park Drive (Ranelagh)	47 B1
Park Drive (Cabinteely)	59 B3
Park Drive Ave	22 F3
Park Drive Close	22 F3
Park Drive Court	22 F3
Park Drive Cres	22 F3
Park Drive Green	22 F3
Park Drive Grove	22 F3
Park Drive Lawn	22 F3
*Park Hall (off Merton Walk)	47 B2
*Park Lane (off Martin's Row Chapelizod)	36 E2
Park Lane (Sandymount)	39 A4
*Park Lane (off Park Road Dún Laoghaire)	50 D4
Park Lane 72 E4	72 E4
Park Lawn	27 A4
Park Lodge	69 C3
Park Lodge	22 F3
Park Manor	22 E3
Park Place	69 B4
Park Road (off Navan Road)	23 C3
Park Road (Dún Laoghaire)	50 D4
Park Road (Sallynoggin)	60 D2
*Park Spring's (off Nephin Road)	24 D4
*Park Street (off Hanover Street West)	74 F1
*Park Street (off First Ave)	36 F3
Park Terrace (Coombe)	74 F1
Park View	75 C4
Park View (Cabra)	69 C1
Park View (Portmarnock)	15 A1
Park View (Castleknock)	23 B4
*Park View (Mount Prospect Lawns off Kincora Court)	26 F4
*Park View (off Orwell Road Rathgar)	47 A3
Park View (Enniskerry Road)	58 D4
*Park View Apts (off Old Bawn Road)	55 A1
Park View House	9 B2
Park View Lawns	44 D2
Park View Manor	9 B2
Park Villas (Castleknock)	23 A3
*Park Villas (off Stillorgan Grove)	48 F4
Park West Ave	35 C4
Park West Pointe	35 C4
Park West Road	36 D4
*Parker Hill (off Rathmines Road Lower)	47 A1
Parker House	14 F4
Parkgate Place (off Parkgate Street)	70 D4
Parkgate Street	70 D4
Parkgate Street Gate 70 D4	70 D4
Parkhill Ave	44 F3
Parkhill Close	45 A3
Parkhill Court	44 F3
Parkhill Drive	44 F3
Parkhill Green	44 F3
*Parkhill Heights (off Greenhills Road Kilnamanagh)	45 A3
Parkhill Lawn	44 F3
Parkhill Rise	44 F3
Parkhill Road	44 F3
Parkhill Way	45 A3
Parkhill West	44 F4
*Parkhouse Apts (Benson Street)	72 F4
Parklands (Santry)	12 E4
Parklands (Maynooth)	18 D3
Parklands (Castleknock)	22 F3
Parklands Ave	55 B2
Parklands Close	18 D3
Parklands Court (Maynooth)	18 D3
Parklands Court (Scholarstown Link Road)	55 B2
Parklands Cres	18 D3
Parklands Drive	55 B2
Parklands Grove	18 D3
Parklands Lawns	18 D3
Parklands Lodge	18 D3
Parklands Rise	18 D3
Parklands Road	55 B2
Parklands Square	18 D3
Parklands View	55 B2
Parklands Way	18 D3
Parkmore	23 A3
Parkmore Drive	46 E2
Parknasilla Ave	64 D2
Parknasilla Close	64 D2
Parknasilla Lane	64 D2
Parknasilla Rise	64 D2
Parknasillog	65 C2
*Parkside View (off Nephin Road)	24 D4
Parkvale (Sutton)	28 D1
Parkvale (Dundrum)	57 C1
Parkview (Swords)	1 B2
Parkview (Ashtown)	23 C3
*Parkview (off Greenhills Road Kilnamanagh)	45 A3
*Parkview (Robswall)	3 C3
Parkview Ave (Harold's Cross)	46 F1
Parkview Court (Blackhorse Ave)	69 B1
*Parkview Court (off Harold's Cross Road)	46 F1
*Parkview Place (off Bridge Street)	39 A3
*Parkview Road	24 E1
*Parkview Terrace (north of River Lane)	67 B2
Parkwood Ave	55 A2
Parkwood Grove	55 A2
Parkwood Lawn	55 A2
Parkwood Road	55 A2
Parliament Street	71 A4
Parnell Ave	74 F4
Parnell Bridge (Grand Canal)	74 E4
Parnell Cottages	3 B3
Parnell Court	74 F4
Parnell Drive	9 A4
Parnell Green	9 A4
*Parnell Hall	74 E4
Parnell Lane	9 A4
Parnell Place	71 B2
Parnell Road (Harold's Cross)	74 E3
Parnell Road (Bray)	67 C2
Parnell Square East	71 B2
Parnell Square North	71 B2
Parnell Square West	71 B2
Parnell Street (O'Connell Street)	71 B3
Parnell Street (Sallynoggin)	60 D1
*Parochial Ave (Between College Street and Main Street Baldoyle)	15 A4
Parslickstown Ave	9 A4
Parslickstown Close	9 A4
Parslickstown Court	9 A4
Parslickstown Drive	9 A4

STREET NAME	PAGE / GRID REFERENCE	STREET NAME	PAGE / GRID REFERENCE	STREET NAME	PAGE / GRID REFERENCE	STREET NAME	PAGE / GRID REFERENCE
Parslickstown Gardens	9 A3	Peter Row	75 A2	Pines (opposite Knockmaroon Gate)	36 D1	Portmarnock Grove	4 D4
Parslickstown Green	9 A4	Peter Street	75 A2	*Pinetree Cres (off Parkhill Road)	44 F4	Portmarnock Park	4 D4
Parson Court	17 C3	Peterson's Court	72 D4	*Pinetree Grove (off Parkhill Road)	44 F3	Portmarnock Rise	15 A1
Parson Lodge	17 C3	Petrie Road	74 F3	Pineview Ave	55 A2	Portmarnock Walk	4 D4
Parson Street	17 C3	Peyton	52 F4	Pineview Drive	55 A2	*Portobello Dock (Lennox Street)	75 B3
Parsons Court	42 D4	Peyton Ave	52 F2	Pineview Grove	55 A2	Portobello Harbour	75 B3
*Parson's Court (opposite Newcastle Manor)	42 D4	Peyton Court	52 F2	Pineview Lawn	55 A2	Portobello Harbour Apts	75 B4
Parsons Hall	17 B3	Peyton Drive	52 F2	Pineview Park	55 A2	Portobello Place	75 B3
*Partridge Terrace (off Nash Street)	36 F3	Pheasant Run	8 F4	Pineview Rise	55 A2	Portobello Road	75 A4
Pass If You Can	11 A1	Pheasant Run The Drive	8 F4	Pineview Road	55 A2	*Portobello Wharf Apts (off Windsor Terrace)	74 F4
*Patrician Park (off Kill Ave)	59 C1	Pheasant Run The Green	8 F4	Pinewood	60 D4	Portside Court	72 E1
Patrician Villas	48 F4	Pheasant Run The Grove	8 F4	Pinewood Ave	24 F1	Pottery Road	59 C2
Patrick Doyle Road	47 B2	Pheasant Run The Park	8 F4	Pinewood Close	67 C4	Pound Hill	17 C1
*Patrick Heeney House (Summerhill)	71 C2	Phelan Ave	24 D3	Pinewood Court	8 F4	Pound Lane	17 C3
Patrick Street (Kevin Street Upper.)	75 A1	Phibblestown Ave	21 A1	Pinewood Cres	24 F1	Pound Park	17 C3
Patrick Street (Dún Laoghaire)	50 D4	Phibblestown House Apts	21 B1	Pinewood Drive	24 F1	Pound Street	33 A1
*Patrick's Row (off George's Ave)	49 A3	Phibblestown Wood	21 A1	Pinewood Green	24 F1	Power's Court	76 E2
*Patricks Terrace	71 A2	Phibsborough	71 A1	*Pinewood Grove (off Pinewood Drive)	25 A1	Power's Square (off John Dillon Street)	75 A1
*Patrickswell Court (off Patrickswell Place)	24 D2	Phibsborough Ave	70 F1	Pinewood Park	56 E1	Powerstown Ave	9 A3
Patrickswell Place	24 D2	Phibsborough Place	71 A2	Pinewood Villas	24 F1	Prebend Street	70 F3
Paul Street	70 F3	Phibsborough Road	71 A1	Pinewoods	44 D2	Premier Business Park	23 B1
Pavillion Gate	59 A4	Philipsburgh Ave	25 C4	Pinnockhill Roundabout	1 C3	Premier Square	24 E2
*Pavillion View Apts. (off Rathmines Road Lower)	47 A1	Philipsburgh Terrace	25 C4	Pipe Hill	1 C2	Preston Street	72 D2
Pea Field	48 F3	*Philomena Terrace (off Oliver Plunkett Ave)	39 A3	Plaza Apts.	25 A1	*Price's Lane (Aston Quay)	71 B4
Peamount	42 D2	Phoenix Ave	23 A3	Pleasants Lane	75 B2	Price's Place (Ranelagh)	75 B4
Peamount Road (Newcastle)	42 D3	Phoenix Court (North Circular Road)	70 D2	Pleasants Place	75 B2	Priestfield Cottages	74 E3
Peamount Road (Peamount)	42 E2	Phoenix Court (Arbour Hill)	70 D3	Pleasants Street	75 A2	Priestfield Drive	74 E3
*Pear Tree Field (off Carysfort Downs)	58 F1	Phoenix Court (Castleknock)	23 A3	Pluckstown	51 A2	Primeside Park	10 D3
Pearse Ave	60 D2	Phoenix Court Apts	69 C3	Plums Road	58 D1	Primrose Ave	71 A2
Pearse Brothers Park	56 F2	Phoenix Drive	23 A3	Plunket Hall	2 E2	Primrose Forge	32 D4
*Pearse Close (off Pearse Street Sallynoggin)	60 D2	Phoenix Gardens	23 A3	Plunkett Ave (Finglas)	24 D1	Primrose Gate	32 E4
Pearse Drive	60 D2	*Phoenix House (Leinster Street South)	75 C1	Plunkett Ave (Foxrock)	59 A3	Primrose Grove	13 C4
Pearse Gardens	59 C2	Phoenix Manor	70 D2	Plunkett Cres	11 A4	Primrose Hill (Celbridge)	32 D4
Pearse Green	60 D2	Phoenix Park	69 A2	Plunkett Drive	24 D1	*Primrose Hill (off Tivoli Road)	49 C4
Pearse Grove	76 E1	Phoenix Park Way	23 B3	Plunkett Green	24 D1	Primrose Lane	34 D1
Pearse House	72 D4	Phoenix Place	23 A3	Plunkett Grove	24 D1	Primrose Street (off Wellington Street Upper)	71 A2
Pearse Park	60 D2	*Phoenix Street (off First Ave)	36 F3	Plunkett Hall	7 A2	*Prince Arthur Terrace (Leinster Road)	47 A1
Pearse Road (Sallynoggin)	60 D2	Phoenix Street North	70 F4	Plunkett Road	24 D1	*Prince Edward Terrace Lower (off Carysfort Ave Blackrock)	49 A4
*Pearse Road (near Ardee Street)	67 B2	*Phoenix Street West (off Phoenix Street North)	70 F4	Poddle Close	46 E1	*Prince Edward Terrace Upper (off Carysfort Ave Blackrock)	49 A4
Pearse Square (Pearse Street)	76 E1	Phoenix Terrace	48 F3	*Poddle Green (off Poddle Park)	46 E1	*Prince of Wales Terrace (off Sandymount Ave)	39 A4
Pearse Square (Bray)	67 B2	Phoenix View	74 D1	Poddle Park	46 E2	*Prince of Wales Terrace (off Quinnsborough Road)	67 C2
Pearse Street (Westland Row)	71 C4	Phrompstown	66 F1	Polo Road (Phoenix Park)	69 B2	Prince's Street North	71 B3
Pearse Street (Sallynoggin)	60 D2	Pickford's Terrace	72 F3	Poolbeg Quay	39 A3	Prince's Street South	72 D4
Pearse Villas	60 D2	*Pier 19 Apts (Bridgefoot Street)	70 F4	Poolbeg Street	71 C4	Princeton	48 D3
Pebble Hill	18 D2	Pig Lane	71 C2	Poole Street	74 F2	Prior Hall	74 D1
Pebble Hill Lodge	18 D2	Pigeon House Road (Ringsend)	39 B3	Poplar Row	72 E1	*Prior's Gate (off Main Road Tallaght)	55 A1
Peck's Lane	23 A3	Pike Bridge	18 F3	Poplar Row Flats	72 E1	Priorswood Road	13 C4
Pelletstown Ave	23 C3	*Pile's Terrace (Sandwith Street Upper)	76 D1	Poppintree	11 C4	Priory Ave	48 F4
Pemberton	67 A3	*Pilot View (off Harbour Road)	60 F1	Poppintree Lane	11 C4	Priory Chase	31 C4
Pembroke Cottages (Ringsend)	39 A2	Pim Street	74 E1	Poppintree Parade	11 C4	Priory Close	31 C4
*Pembroke Cottages (off Donnybrook Mews)	47 C1	Pimlico	74 F1	Poppintree Park Lane West	11 C4	Priory Court (Celbridge)	31 C4
*Pembroke Cottages (off Main Street Dundrum)	47 C4	Pimlico Cottages	74 E1	Poppintree Terrace	11 C4	*Priory Court (off Grange Road)	57 A2
*Pembroke Cottages (off Rosemount Terrace Booterstown)	48 F3	Pimlico Terrace	74 F1	Port Tunnel (East Wall Entrance)	72 F1	Priory Cres	31 C4
Pembroke Court (off Pembroke Road)	76 F3	Pine Ave	59 A2	Port Tunnel (Santry Entrance)	25 C1	Priory Drive (Celbridge)	31 C4
Pembroke Gardens	76 E3	Pine Copse Road	57 B1	Port View House	39 A2	Priory Drive (Stillorgan)	48 F4
Pembroke Lane (Lower Baggot Street)	76 D2	Pine Court (Portmarnock)	15 A1	Porters Ave	22 D2	Priory East	24 D4
Pembroke Lane (Pembroke Road)	76 E3	Pine Court (Deans Grange)	59 A1	Porters Gate	21 B2	Priory Green	31 C4
Pembroke Park	76 E4	*Pine Grove (off Firhouse Road)	56 D1	Porters Gate Ave	21 C2	Priory Grove (Celbridge)	31 C4
Pembroke Place (off Sandymount Ave)	76 F4	Pine Grove Park	1 C1	Porters Gate Close	21 B2	Priory Grove (Stillorgan)	48 F4
Pembroke Place (Pembroke Street Upper)	75 C3	Pine Grove Road	1 C1	Porters Gate Court	21 B2	Priory Hall (Donaghmede)	14 E4
Pembroke Road	76 E3	Pine Haven	48 F3	Porters Gate Drive	21 B2	Priory Hall (Kimmage)	46 D2
Pembroke Row	76 D2	Pine Hurst	24 E4	Porters Gate Green	21 B2	Priory Hall (Stillorgan)	48 F4
Pembroke Square	76 E2	Pine Lawn (Tallaght)	55 A2	Porters Gate Grove	21 B2	Priory Lodge	31 C4
Pembroke Street	39 A3	Pine Lawn (Deans Grange)	59 A1	Porters Gate Heights	21 C2	Priory North	24 D3
Pembroke Street Lower	75 C2	Pine Road	39 A3	Porters Gate Lawn	21 B2	Priory Road	46 F1
Pembroke Street Upper	75 C2	Pine Valley Ave	57 B2	Porters Gate Rise	21 C2	Priory Square	31 C4
*Pembroke Terrace (off Main Street Dundrum)	47 C4	Pine Valley Drive	57 B3	Porters Gate View	21 B2	Priory View	31 C3
Penrose Street	76 F1	Pine Valley Grove	57 B3	Porters Gate Way	21 B2	Priory Walk (Celbridge)	31 C4
*Percy Close (off Haddington Road)	76 E2	Pine Valley Park	57 B3	Porters Road	22 D2	Priory Walk (Kimmage)	46 D2
*Percy French Road (off Balfe Ave)	45 C1	Pine Valley Way	57 B3	Portersfield Apts	22 D2	Priory Way (Celbridge)	31 C3
Percy Lane	76 E2	Pinebrook Ave	26 D2	Porterstown	5 A3	Priory Way (Kimmage)	46 D2
Percy Place	76 E2	Pinebrook Close	21 C1	Porterstown Link Road	22 D3	Priory West	24 D4
Peter Place	75 B3	Pinebrook Cres	26 D2	Porterstown Road	22 D2	Proby Garden	49 A4
		Pinebrook Downs	21 C1	Portland Close	72 D2	Proby Hall	60 E2
		Pinebrook Drive	26 D2	Portland Court (off Portland Place)	71 C1	Proby Park	60 E2
		Pinebrook Glen	21 C1	*Portland Lock (off Portland Place)	71 C1	Proby Square	49 A4
		Pinebrook Grove	26 E2	Portland Lock Apts	71 C1	Proby's Lane	71 B3
		Pinebrook Heights	21 C1	Portland Place	71 B1	Promenade Road	39 A1
		Pinebrook Lawn	21 C1	Portland Row	72 D2	Prospect Ave (Finglas Road)	25 A4
		Pinebrook Rise	26 D2	Portland Square	71 C1	Prospect Ave (Stocking Lane)	56 E2
		Pinebrook Road	26 D2	Portland Street North	71 C1	*Prospect Court (off Prospect Ave)	25 A4
		Pinebrook Vale	21 C1	Portland Street West	74 E1	Prospect Court (Edmondstown)	56 E2
		Pinebrook View	21 C1	Portmahon Drive	73 C2	Prospect Drive	56 E2
		Pinebrook Way	21 C1	Portmarnock	15 A1		
		Pinecroft	62 F1	Portmarnock Ave	4 D4		
				Portmarnock Cres	4 D4		
				Portmarnock Drive	4 D4		

STREET NAME	PAGE / GRID REFERENCE
Prospect Glen	56 E2
Prospect Grove	56 E2
Prospect Heath	56 E2
Prospect Heights	56 E2
Prospect Hill	24 E2
*Prospect Lane (off Milltown Road)	47 C2
Prospect Lawn	59 B3
*Prospect Lodge (off Knocklyon Road)	55 C1
Prospect Meadows	56 E2
Prospect Road	25 A4
*Prospect Square (off Prospect Ave)	25 A4
*Prospect Square (beside Premier Square)	24 E2
Prospect Terrace (Kilmainham)	73 B1
*Prospect Terrace (off Marine Drive Sandymount)	39 B3
Prospect View	56 E2
Prospect Way	25 A4
Protestant Row	75 B2
Proud's Lane	75 B2
Provost Row	70 E3
Prussia Street	70 E2
Pucks Castle Lane	63 C3
*Purcell Lane (Saint Kevin's Square)	67 C2
Purley Park	3 C4
*Purser Gardens (off Summerville Park)	47 A1
Putland Road	67 C3
*Putland Villas (Vevay Road, Wolfe Tone Square)	67 C3
Pyro Villas	74 E2

Q

STREET NAME	PAGE / GRID REFERENCE
*Quarry Cottages (off Killester Ave Middle)	26 E3
Quarry Drive	45 C2
Quarry Road (Cabra)	24 E4
Quarry Road (Ferndale Road)	64 D4
Quarryfield Court	44 E2
Quarryvale	35 A1
Quarryvale Park	35 A2
Quartiere Bloom	71 B4
Queen's Park	49 B4
Queen's Road	50 D4
Queen's Street	70 F4
Quinn Ave	74 D1
Quinn's Lane	75 C2
Quinn's Road	64 E3
Quinsborough	51 A4
Quinsborough Road	67 C2

R

STREET NAME	PAGE / GRID REFERENCE
*Radcliff Hall (off Saint John's Road East)	39 B4
*Radcliffe (adjacent Binn Eadair View)	29 A1
Radharc na hAbhann	55 A2
Radlett Grove	4 D4
Rafter's Ave	73 A4
Rafter's Lane	73 A4
Rafter's Road	73 A4
Raglan Hall Apts (off Seafort Ave)	76 E4
*Raglan House (off Serpentine Ave)	39 A4
Raglan Lane	76 E4
Raglan Road	76 E4
Raheen Ave	54 E1
Raheen Close	54 E1
Raheen Court	54 E1
Raheen Cres	54 E1
Raheen Drive (Ballyfermot)	36 D3
Raheen Drive (Tallaght)	54 E1
Raheen Green	54 E1
Raheen Park (Ballyfermot)	36 D3
Raheen Park (Tallaght)	54 E1
Raheen Park (Bray)	68 D3
Raheen Park Ave	68 D3
Raheen Road	54 E1
Raheny	27 A2
Raheny Park	27 A3
Raheny Road	27 A1
Rail Park	18 D4
Railway Ave (Malahide)	3 B2
Railway Ave (Baldoyle)	28 D1
Railway Ave (Inchicore)	36 F3
Railway Close	14 F4
*Railway Cottages (off Serpentine Park)	39 A4
*Railway Court (off Railway Ave Malahide)	3 B2
Railway Mews	14 F4
Railway Road	14 F4
*Railway Road (off Castle Street Dalkey)	60 F2
Railway Street	71 C2
Railway Terrace (off Macken Street)	76 E1
Rainsford Ave	74 E1
*Rainsford Lane (off Military Road Ballybrack)	60 E4
Rainsford Street	74 E1
Ralahine	60 D4
Raleigh Square	73 B4
*Ralph Mews (off Newtownpark Ave)	59 A1
*Ralph Square (off Main Street Leixlip)	33 A1
Ramillies Road	36 E3
Ramleh Close	47 C2
Ramleh Park	47 C2
Ramor Park	22 E2
Ranelagh	75 C4
Ranelagh Ave	75 C4
*Ranelagh Close (opposite Manders Terrace)	75 C4
*Ranelagh Mews (near Mountpleasant Parade)	75 B4
Ranelagh Road	75 C4
Raphoe Road	46 D1
Rath Geal	43 C1
Rathbeale Court	1 C1
Rathbeale Cres	1 C1
Rathbeale Rise	1 C2
Rathbeale Road	1 C1
Rathborne (opposite Knockmaroon Gate)	36 D1
Rathborne Ave	23 C3
Rathborne Close	23 C3
Rathborne Drive	23 C3
Rathborne Place	23 C3
Rathborne Way	23 C3
*Rathbourne Court (adjacent Courtview Apts)	23 C3
*Rathclaren (near Glenlucan)	67 B3
Rathcoole Interchange (N7)	52 F1
Rathcoole Park	52 F2
Rathcreedan	52 D1
Rathdown Ave	46 F3
*Rathdown Court (off Corrib Road)	46 F2
Rathdown Cres	46 F3
Rathdown Drive	46 E3
*Rathdown Grove (off Sandyford Road)	58 D2
Rathdown Park	46 F3
Rathdown Road	70 F1
Rathdown Square	70 E2
*Rathdown Terrace (off Sandyford Road)	58 D2
Rathdown Villas	46 F3
Rathdrum Road	74 D4
Rathelawns	52 E2
Rathfarnham	46 F3
*Rathfarnham Mill (off Main Street Rathfarnham)	46 F4
Rathfarnham Park	46 F3
Rathfarnham Road	46 F3
Rathfarnham Wood	46 F4
Rathgar	47 A2
Rathgar Ave	46 F2
*Rathgar Court (off Rathgar Road)	47 A1
*Rathgar Park (off Terenure Road East)	46 F2
*Rathgar Park (off Orwell Road Rathgar)	47 A2
Rathgar Place	47 A1
Rathgar Road	47 A1
*Rathgar Villas (off Rathgar Ave)	46 F2
Rathingle Road	1 B3
*Rathland Drive (off Ravensdale Drive)	46 E2
Rathland Road	46 E2
Rathlin House	22 F1
Rathlin Road	25 A3
Rathlyon Grove	55 C2
Rathlyon Park	55 C2
Rathmichael	63 C3
Rathmichael Dales	64 D3
Rathmichael Haven	64 D3
Rathmichael Hill	63 C2
Rathmichael Lane	63 C2
Rathmichael Manor	64 D2
Rathmichael Park	64 E2
Rathmichael Road	63 C2
Rathmichael Woods	64 E2
Rathmines	75 A4
Rathmines Ave	47 A1
*Rathmines Ave Court (off Rathmines Road Upper)	47 A1
Rathmines Close	47 A1
*Rathmines Park (off Rathmines Road Upper)	47 A1
Rathmines Road Lower	75 B4
Rathmines Road Upper	47 A1
*Rathmines Square Apts (off William's Park)	47 A1
*Rathmines Wood (off William's Park)	47 A1
Rathmintan Close	54 D2
Rathmintan Court	54 D2
Rathmintan Cres	54 D2
Rathmintan Drive	54 D2
Rathmore	14 F2
Rathmore Ave	9 B2
Rathmore Ave	58 D1
Rathmore Cres	9 B2
Rathmore Drive	9 B2
Rathmore Grove	9 B2
Rathmore Park	27 A2
Rathmore Villas	46 F2
Rathsallagh Ave	64 E2
Rathsallagh Bridge	64 E2
Rathsallagh Drive	64 E2
Rathsallagh Grove	64 E2
Rathsallagh Park	64 E2
Rathvale Ave	26 F1
Rathvale Drive	26 F1
Rathvale Grove	26 F1
Rathvale Park	26 F1
Rathvilly Drive	24 D2
Rathvilly Park	24 D2
Ratoath Ave	24 D2
Ratoath Drive	23 C1
Ratoath Estate	24 D3
Ratoath Road (Hollystown)	9 B1
Ratoath Road (Cabra)	24 E4
Ratoath Road (Finglas)	23 C2
Ratra Park	23 C4
Ratra Road	23 C4
*Ravens Court (off Cardiff Castle Road)	24 D2
Ravens Rock Road	58 E2
*Ravensdale Drive (off Ravensdale Park)	46 E2
Ravensdale Park	46 E2
Ravensdale Road	72 F2
Ravenswell Road	67 C2
*Ravenswood (adjacent to Lawson Spinney)	3 A3
Ravenwood Ave	21 B1
Ravenwood Cres	21 B1
Ravenwood Drive	21 B1
Ravenwood Estate	21 B1
Ravenwood Green	21 B1
Ravenwood Lawn	21 B1
Ravenwood Rise	21 B1
Ravenwood Road	21 B1
Ravenwood View	21 B1
*Raverty Villas (off Beech Road)	67 B1
Rawson Court	76 E2
Raymond Street	74 F3
Rectory Slopes	67 B3
Rectory Way	67 A3
*Red Arches Ave (Red Arches Estate)	14 F4
*Red Arches Close (Red Arches Estate)	14 F4
*Red Arches Drive (Red Arches Estate)	14 F4
*Red Arches Park (Red Arches Estate)	14 F4
Red Arches Road	14 F4
*Red Brick Terrace (off Annaville Ave)	59 A1
*Red Cow Cottages (off Lucan Road Palmerston)	35 C1
Red Cow Interchange	44 F1
Red Cow Lane	70 F3
Redberry	34 D3
Redesdale Cres	48 D4
Redesdale Road	48 D4
Redfern Ave	3 C4
Redgap	52 E3
*Redmond's Court (off Kilbarrack Road)	27 B1
Redmond's Hill	75 B2
Redwood	9 B1
Redwood Ave	45 A4
Redwood Close	45 A4
Redwood Court (Tallaght)	44 F4
Redwood Court (Churchtown)	47 A3
Redwood Drive	44 F4
Redwood Grove	48 F3
Redwood Heights	45 A4
Redwood Lawn	44 F4
Redwood Park	45 A4
Redwood Rise	45 A4
Redwood View	45 A4
Redwood Walk	44 F4
Regal Park	69 B1
Reginald Square	74 F1
Reginald Street	74 F1
Rehoboth Ave	74 E3
Rehoboth Place	74 D3
Reilly's Ave	74 D3
*Renoir Apts (off Serpentine Ave)	39 A4
Reuben Ave	74 D2
Reuben Square Apts (Reuben Street)	74 D3
Reuben Street	74 D2
Reuben Walk	74 D2
*Rexton Court (Merrion Road, Sandymount Ave)	39 A4
*Rhodaville (off Mountpleasant Ave)	75 B4
*Riachville (off Collinswood)	25 C2
Rialto Bridge	73 C2
Rialto Buildings	74 D2
Rialto Cottages	73 C2
*Rialto Court (off Rialto Buildings)	74 D2
Rialto Drive	73 C3
Rialto Park	73 C2
Rialto Street	74 D2
Ribh Ave	26 F2
Ribh Road	26 F2
Richelieu Park	48 E1
Richmond	59 A1
*Richmond Apts	70 F3
Richmond Ave (Fairview)	25 B4
Richmond Ave (Monkstown)	49 C4
Richmond Ave South	47 B2
Richmond Cottages (Summerhill)	72 D1
Richmond Cottages North	72 D1
Richmond Court (Marino)	25 C4
Richmond Court (Milltown)	47 B2
Richmond Cres	72 D1
Richmond Estate	25 C4
*Richmond Gardens (Richmond Ave)	25 C4
*Richmond Green (off Carrickbrennan Road)	49 C4
Richmond Grove	49 C4
*Richmond Hall (off Richmond Road)	25 B4
Richmond Hill (Rathmines)	75 B4
Richmond Hill (Monkstown)	49 C4
*Richmond House (off Richmond Road)	25 B4
Richmond Lane	71 C1
Richmond Lodge	25 B4
*Richmond Manor (Richmond Hill)	75 B4
*Richmond Manor (Richmond Hill)	75 B4
Richmond Mews	75 B4
Richmond Parade	72 D1
Richmond Park (Monkstown)	49 B4
Richmond Park (Herbert Road)	67 A4
Richmond Place (Rathmines)	75 B4
Richmond Place South (South Richmond Street)	75 B3
Richmond Road	25 B4
Richmond Row	75 B3
Richmond Street North	72 D1
Richmond Street South	75 B3
*Richmond Terrace (west side of text Meath)	68 D2
Richmond Villas	75 B3
Richview	47 C2
Richview Park	47 B2

STREET NAME	PAGE	GRID
*Richview Villas (off Whitethorn Road)	47	C2
Riddlesford	67	C4
Ridge Hall	64	E1
Ridge Hill	64	E1
Ridgeford Apts	57	C1
*Ridgeway Villas (on Rowserstown Lane)	73	B1
Ridgewood Ave	1	B3
Ridgewood Close	1	B3
Ridgewood Court	1	B3
Ridgewood Green	1	B3
Ridgewood Grove	1	B3
Ridgewood Park	1	B3
Ridgewood Place	1	B3
Ridgewood Square	1	B3
Rinawade Ave	32	E1
Rinawade Close	32	E1
Rinawade Cres	32	E1
Rinawade Downs	32	E1
Rinawade Glade	32	E1
Rinawade Green	32	E1
Rinawade Grove	32	E1
Rinawade Lawns	32	E1
Rinawade Park	32	F1
Rinawade Rise	32	E1
Rinawade Vale	32	E1
Rinawade View	32	E1
*Ring Street (off Ring Terrace)	36	F3
Ring Terrace	36	F3
Ringsend	39	A3
Ringsend Park	39	A2
Ringsend Road	76	F1
*Rinn na Mara (off Doyles Lane)	27	A4
Ripley Court	67	B3
Ripley Hills	67	B3
*River Close (near Brookdene)	64	E1
River Court	7	B3
*River Court Apts (off Camac Close)	73	A1
River Drive	24	D3
River Forest	20	D4
River Forest View (Leixlip)	19	C3
*River Gardens (off Glasnevin Hill)	25	A3
*River Lane (at Clifton Park)	64	E2
River Lane (Bray)	67	B2
*River Lane Grove (at Clifton Park)	64	E2
River Lawns	31	C4
River Mall	2	D2
River Road (Blanchardstown)	22	F2
River Road (Ashtown)	23	C3
River Road Cottages	23	A2
River Valley Ave	1	C2
River Valley Close	1	B2
River Valley Court	1	B2
River Valley Drive	1	C2
River Valley Grove	1	C3
River Valley Heights	1	C2
River Valley Lawn	1	C2
River Valley Park	1	C2
River Valley Rise	1	C3
River Valley Road	1	C2
River Valley View	1	B2
River Valley Way	1	B2
River View	31	C4
Riverbank (Braemor Road)	47	A3
*Riverbank (off Overend Way Dundrum)	57	C1
Riverbank Hall	24	F3
*Riverbank House	69	B4
Riverdale	20	D4
Riverpark Apts	69	C4
Riverpark View	9	A4
Riverrun Apts	74	D1
Riversdale (Palmerston)	35	C1
*Riversdale (off Overend Way Dundrum)	57	C1
Riversdale Ave (Palmerston)	35	C1
Riversdale Ave (Clondalkin)	44	E1
Riversdale Ave (Terenure)	46	F3
Riversdale Court	35	C1
Riversdale Cres	44	E1
Riversdale Drive	44	E1
Riversdale Green	35	B4
Riversdale Grove (Palmerston)	35	B1
*Riversdale Grove (off Kimmage Road Lower)	46	E2
Riversdale Park (Palmerston)	35	C1
Riversdale Park (Clondalkin)	44	E1
Riversdale Road	44	E1
*Riversdale View (off Boden Wood)	46	F4
Riverside	9	A4
*Riverside (off Watery Lane)	44	E1
*Riverside (off Poddle Park Kimmage)	46	F2
*Riverside Apts (off Milltown Road)	47	B2
Riverside Ave	13	A4
Riverside Cottages	46	E4
Riverside Cres	13	A4
Riverside Drive (Coolock)	13	B4
Riverside Drive (Palmerston)	35	C1
Riverside Drive (Rathfarnham)	47	A3
Riverside Grove	13	A4
Riverside Park	13	A4
Riverside Road	13	A4
*Riverside Walk (off Clonskeagh Road)	47	C1
Riverston Abbey	24	D4
*Riverstown Gardens (beside Ashington Gardens)	24	D3
Rivervale	23	C3
*Rivervale Apts (off Upper Dargle Road)	67	B2
*Riverview (Grand Canal Docks)	76	E1
Riverview (Palmerstown)	35	C1
Riverview (Oldbawn)	55	A2
Riverview (opposite Knockmaroon Gate)	36	D1
Riverview Apts	32	D4
*Riverview Court (off Lucan Road Chapelizod)	36	E2
Riverwood Chase	22	D3
Riverwood Close	22	D3
Riverwood Copse	22	D3
Riverwood Court	22	D3
Riverwood Cres	22	D3
Riverwood Dale	22	D3
Riverwood Dene	22	D3
Riverwood Drive	22	D3
Riverwood Gardens	22	D3
Riverwood Glebe	22	D3
Riverwood Glen	22	D3
Riverwood Green	22	D3
Riverwood Grove	22	D3
Riverwood Hall	22	D3
Riverwood Heath	22	D3
Riverwood Lawn	22	D3
Riverwood Park	22	D3
Riverwood Place	22	D3
Riverwood Road	22	D3
Riverwood Terrace	22	D3
Riverwood Vale	22	D3
Riverwood View	22	D3
Riverwood Way	22	D3
Robert Emmet Bridge (Grand Canal)	74	F4
Robert Emmet Walk	70	E4
Robert Emmett Close	74	E1
*Robert Place (off Mabel Street)	25	B4
Robert Street	74	E1
*Robert Street (Jones's Road off Mabel Street)	25	B4
*Robin Hill Apts (on Blackthorn Drive)	58	D2
Robin Villas	35	C1
Robinhood Park	45	B1
Robinhood Road	45	A1
Robinsons Court	74	F2
Robswall	3	C3
Robswall Path	4	D3
Robswall Walk	4	D3
Rochestown Ave	59	C2
*Rochestown House (off Rochestown Ave)	59	C2
*Rochestown House Apts (off Rochestown Ave)	59	C2
Rochestown Park	60	D2
Rochfort Ave	34	F2
Rochfort Close	34	F2
Rochfort Cres	34	F3
Rochfort Downs	34	F2
Rochfort Green	34	F2
Rochfort Park	34	F2
Rochfort Way	34	F3
Rock Bridge	32	D4
Rock Hall	49	A3
Rock Hill	49	A3
*Rock Lane (Baggot Street Lower)	76	D2
Rock Lodge	60	E3
Rock Road	49	A3
Rockbrae Hall	57	C3
Rockbrook	56	E4
Rockfield (Maynooth)	18	D4
Rockfield (Lucan)	34	D3
Rockfield (Dundrum)	57	C1
Rockfield Ave (Maynooth)	18	D4
Rockfield Ave (Kimmage)	46	D2
Rockfield Close	22	D3
Rockfield Drive (Coolmine)	22	D3
Rockfield Drive (Clondalkin)	44	D2
Rockfield Drive (Kimmage)	46	D2
Rockfield Gardens	18	D3
Rockfield Green	18	D3
Rockfield Lodge	18	D4
Rockfield Manor	18	D4
Rockfield Park (Maynooth)	18	D4
Rockfield Park (Coolmine)	22	D2
Rockfield Rise	18	D3
Rockfield Square	18	D3
Rockfield Walk	18	D3
Rockford Manor	59	B1
Rockford Park	59	B1
*Rockford Terrace (off Rowan Park)	49	B4
Rockfort Ave	60	F2
Rockingham Ave	19	C4
Rockingham Green	19	C4
Rockingham Grove	19	C4
Rockingham Park	19	C4
Rockingham Terrace	2	D2
*Rocklands (off Harbour Road)	60	F1
*Rockmeade Court (off Windmill Road Crumlin)	46	D1
Rockstown	30	E2
Rockview	57	C3
Rockville	62	F2
Rockville Cres	49	B4
Rockville Drive (Monkstown)	49	B4
Rockville Drive (Carrickmines)	63	A1
*Rockville Estate (off Rockville Road)	49	A4
Rockville Park	49	B4
Rockville Road	49	A4
*Rockwell Cove Apts (off Idrone Terrace)	49	A3
Rockwood	34	D3
Rocwood	58	F2
Roebuck Ave	48	E3
Roebuck Castle	48	D3
*Roebuck Cres (off Roebuck Road)	47	C3
Roebuck Downs	47	C3
Roebuck Drive	46	D2
Roebuck Hill	48	D3
*Roebuck Lawn (off Beechmount Drive)	47	C3
Roebuck Park	47	C4
Roebuck Road	48	D3
Roger Casement Park	67	B2
Roger's Lane	75	C2
*Roland Court (off Rathgar Road)	47	A1
*Rollins Court (off Rollins Villas)	60	D1
Rollins Villas	60	D1
Ronanstown	35	A4
Roncalli Road	27	C1
Rookwood View	56	E2
Roosevelt Cottages	24	D4
Rooske Road	7	B3
*Ropewalk Place (off Cambridge Park)	39	A3
Rory O'Connor Park	59	B1
Rory O'More Bridge (River Liffey)	70	E4
Ros Mór View	56	D2
*Rosary Gardens East (off Library Road)	50	D4
*Rosary Gardens West (off Library Road)	49	C4
Rosary Road	74	D2
Rosary Terrace (Ringsend)	39	A3
*Rosary Terrace (off Library Road)	50	D4
Rosbeg Court	27	C2
Rosberry	34	E3
Rosberry Ave	34	E3
Rosberry Court	34	E3
Rosberry Lane	34	E3
Rosberry Park	34	E3
Rosberry Place	34	E3
Rose Park	59	C1
Rose Vale Court	22	D1
Roseacre	58	E3
Rosebank	55	A2
*Rosebank Court (off Nangor Road)	35	B4
*Rosebank Hall (off Nangor Road)	35	A4
*Rosebank Place (off Nangor Road)	35	A4
*Rosebank View (off Nangor Road)	35	B4
Rosedale (Dunboyne)	7	B2
Rosedale (Clonsilla)	21	B1
*Rosedale Apts (off Tyrconnell Road)	36	F3
*Rosedale Apts (off Tyrconnell Road)	36	F3
Rosedale Close	21	B1
Rosedale Cres	21	B1
Roscdale Terrace (Lower Clanbrassil Street)	74	F3
Roseglen Ave	27	B2
*Roseglen Manor (off Roseglen Ave)	27	B2
Roseglen Road	27	B2
Rosehall	46	E4
Rosehaven	22	E3
*Rosehill (off Carysfort Ave)	59	A1
Roselawn	34	E1
Roselawn Ave	22	E2
Roselawn Close	22	F2
Roselawn Court	22	F2
Roselawn Cres	22	E2
Roselawn Drive (Blanchardstown)	22	E2
Roselawn Drive (Oldcourt)	67	C3
Roselawn Glade	22	E2
Roselawn Grove	22	E2
*Roselawn Park (off Boghall Road)	67	C3
Roselawn Road	22	E2
Roselawn View	22	E2
Roselawn Walk	22	E2
Roselawn Way	22	F2
*Rosemount (off Charlemont)	25	C3
Rosemount (Malahide Road Donnycarney)	26	D3
Rosemount (Churchtown)	47	C4
Rosemount Ave	26	E2
Rosemount Court (Inchicore Road)	73	B1
Rosemount Court (Dundrum)	47	C4
Rosemount Court (Booterstown)	48	F3
Rosemount Cres (Roebuck Road)	47	C3
Rosemount Glade	47	C4
Rosemount Hall	47	C4
Rosemount Park	47	C4
Rosemount Park Drive	10	D4
Rosemount Park Road	10	D4
Rosemount Road	70	F1
Rosemount Terrace (Arbour Hill)	70	E3
*Rosemount Terrace (off Dundrum Road)	47	B4
Rosemount Terrace (Booterstown)	48	E3
Rosevale Court	26	F3
Rosevale Mansions	26	F3
*Roseville Court (near Church)	67	B1
*Roseville Terrace (off Dundrum Road)	47	C4
Rosewood Grove	34	F3
Rosmeen Gardens	50	D4
Rosmeen Park	60	D1
*Ross Cottages (adjacent Townyard Lane)	3	B2
Ross Road	75	A1
Ross Street	70	D2
Ross View	35	C1
*Rossaveal Court (off Drumfinn Road)	36	D2
Rossberry Terrace	34	E4
Rossecourt Ave	34	F3
Rossecourt Green	34	F3
Rossecourt Grove	34	F3
Rossecourt Heights	34	F3
Rossecourt Lane	34	F3
Rossecourt Rise	34	F3
Rossecourt Square	34	F3
Rossecourt Terrace	34	F3
Rossecourt Way	34	F3
Rossfield Ave	54	D1
*Rossfield Close (off Glenshane Cres)	54	D1
*Rossfield Court (off Rossfield Gardens)	54	D1
Rossfield Cres	54	D1

STREET NAME	PAGE / GRID REFERENCE		STREET NAME	PAGE / GRID REFERENCE		STREET NAME	PAGE / GRID REFERENCE		STREET NAME	PAGE / GRID REFERENCE
Rossfield Drive	54	D1	Rusheeney View	21	C1	*St. Aidan's Park			St. Bridget's Drive	45	B2
Rossfield Gardens	54	D1	Rusheeney Way	21	B1	(off St. Aidan's Park Road)	25	C4	*St. Bridget's Flats		
Rossfield Green	54	D1	*Rus-in-Urbe Terrace			St. Aidan's Park Ave	25	C4	(off Embassy Lawn)	47	C2
Rossfield Grove	54	D1	(off Glenageary Road Lower)	60	D1	St. Aidan's Park Road	25	C4	St. Brigid's Close	26	E2
Rossfield Park	54	D1	Russel Street Bridge			*St. Aidan's Terrace			St. Brigid's Green	26	E2
Rossfield Way	54	D1	(Royal Canal)	71	C1	(near Duncairn Ave)	67	C2	St. Brigid's Grove	26	E2
*Rosslyn (Rosslyn Court)	67	C2	Russell Ave (Jones's Road)	71	C1	St. Alban's Park	48	E1	St. Brigid's Ave	14	F2
Rosslyn Court	67	C2	Russell Ave (Fortunestown Way)	54	D1	St. Alban's Road	74	F3	St. Brigid's Church Road	58	F1
*Rosslyn Grove (Rosslyn Court)	67	C2	Russell Ave East	72	E2	*St. Alphonsus Ave			St. Brigid's Cottages		
Rossmeen Park			Russell Close	54	D2	(off St. Joseph's Ave)	25	A4	(North Strand)	72	E1
(off Sumerhill Road)	50	E4	Russell Court	54	D2	St. Alphonsus Road	25	A4	St. Brigid's Cottages		
Rossmore Ave (Ballyfermot)	36	D3	*Russell Court Apts			St. Andrew Street	75	B1	(Blanchardstown)	22	F2
Rossmore Ave (Templeogue)	45	C4	(Little Britain Street)	71	A3	St. Andrews	34	F2	St. Brigid's Cottages (Clondalkin)	44	F2
Rossmore Close	46	D4	Russell Cres	54	D1	*St. Andrews Court			*St. Brigid's Court		
Rossmore Cres	46	D4	Russell Downs	54	D1	(off Main Street Lucan)	34	D1	(off Killester Park)	26	E3
Rossmore Drive (Ballyfermot)	36	D2	Russell Drive	54	D2	St. Andrews Drive	34	F2	St. Brigid's Cres	26	E2
Rossmore Drive (Templeogue)	45	C4	Russell Green	54	D2	St. Andrews Fairway	34	F2	*St. Brigid's Drive		
Rossmore Grove	45	C4	Russell Grove	54	D2	St. Andrews Green	34	F2	(off Killester Park)	26	E3
Rossmore Lawns	46	D4	Russell House	2	E2	St. Andrew's Grove	3	B3	St. Brigid's Drive (Clondalkin)	44	E2
Rossmore Park	46	D4	Russell Lane	54	D1	St. Andrew's Lane			St. Brigid's Lawn	26	E2
Rossmore Road (Ballyfermot)	36	D2	Russell Lawns	54	D2	(off Exchequer Street)	75	B1	St. Brigid's Park (Blanchardstown)	22	F2
Rossmore Road (Templeogue)	46	D4	Russell Meadows	54	D1	St. Andrews Park	1	C1	*St. Brigid's Park		
Rostrevor Court	76	E1	Russell Place	54	D1	St. Andrews Wood	34	F2	(St. Brigid's Road)	44	E2
Rostrevor Road	47	A3	Russell Rise	54	D1	*St. Anne's Court			St. Brigid's Park (Cornelscourt)	59	B3
Rostrevor Terrace			Russell Street	71	C1	(beside All St.'s Close)	27	A3	St. Brigid's Road (Artane)	26	E2
(Lower Grand Canal Street)	76	E1	Russell View	54	D2	St. Anne's (Ranelagh)	75	C4	St. Brigid's Road (Clondalkin)	44	E2
Rostrevor Terrace (Orwell Road)	47	A2	Russell Walk	54	D1	St. Anne's (Kimmage)	46	E2	St. Brigid's Road Lower	25	A4
*Roth Abbey Court			Russell's Mews	2	E3	St. Anne's Ave	27	A3	St. Brigid's Road Upper	25	A4
(off Roth Abbey)	73	B2	Russell's Place	2	E3	St. Anne's Drive	27	A3	*St. Brigid's Terrace		
Rothe Abbey	73	B2	Russell's Terrace	2	E4	St. Anne's Park	64	E3	(near Adelaide Villas)	67	C2
Round Gardens	53	B1	Rutland Ave (Crumlin Road)	74	D4	St. Anne's Road North	25	A4	*St. Broc's Cottages		
Rowan Ave	58	D2	Rutland Ave (Clogher Road)	46	E1	St. Anne's Road South	74	E3	(off Victoria Ave)	47	C1
Rowan Close	32	D3	Rutland Cottages	71	C2	*St. Anne's Square			St. Canice's Court	23	C1
Rowan Grove	67	B2	Rutland Court	71	C2	(off St. Marnock's Ave)	14	F2	St. Canice's Park	24	F2
*Rowan Hall (off Milltown Road)	47	C1	Rutland Grove	46	F1	*St. Anne's Square			St. Canice's Road	25	A2
Rowan Hamilton Court	24	E4	Rutland Place North	71	C2	(off Frascati Road Blackrock)	49	A3	St. Canice's Square	24	E2
Rowan House	76	D3	Rutland Place West	71	B2	St. Anne's Terrace (Ranelagh)	75	C4	St. Catherine's Ave	74	E3
Rowan Park	49	B4	Rutland Street 71 C2	71	C2	St. Anne's Terrace (Raheny)	27	A3	*St. Catherine's Court		
Rowan Park Ave	49	B4	Rutland Street Lower	71	C2	St. Anne's Terrace (Rathcoole)	52	E2	(off Oliver Bond Street)	74	F1
Rowanbyrn	59	B1	Rutledge Terrace	74	E3	*St. Anns Close (off Temple Road)	49	A3	St. Catherines Grove		
Rowans Road	58	D2	*Ryan's Cottages			St. Anns Court	71	B2	(off St. Cutberth's Road)	43	C1
Rowlagh Ave	35	A3	(off Harold's Cross Road)	46	F1	*St. Ann's Square Lower			St. Catherine's Lane West	74	F1
Rowlagh Cres	35	A3	Ryder's Row	71	A3	(off St. Marnock's Ave)	14	F2	St. Catherine's Park	60	E1
Rowlagh Gardens	35	A3	Rye Bridge	33	A1	St. Anthony's Ave	44	E2	St. Catherine's Road	60	E1
Rowlagh Green	35	A3	Rye River Ave	20	D4	St. Anthony's Cres	74	D2	St. Catherine's Terrace	29	A1
Rowlagh Park	35	A3	Rye River Close	20	D4	St. Anthony's Cres	45	C2	St. Catherine's View	20	E4
Rowserstown Lane	73	B1	Rye River Court	20	D4	St. Anthony's Place	71	B2	St. Catherines West	74	E3
Royal Canal Ave	23	C3	Rye River Cres	20	D4	St. Anthony's Road	74	D2	*St. Catheryn's Court		
Royal Canal Bank (Phibsborough)	71	A1	Rye River Gardens	20	D4	St. Aongus Court	45	B4	(off Durham Road)	39	B4
Royal Canal Bank (Phibsborough)	25	A4	Rye River Grove	20	D4	St. Aongus Cres	45	B4	*St. Cathryn's Court		
*Royal Canal Court			Rye River Mall	20	D4	St. Aongus Green	45	B4	(Newgrove Ave)	39	B4
(Saint Peters Close)	71	A1	Rye River Park	20	D4	St. Aongus Grove	45	B4	St. Clair's Lawn	67	B3
Royal Canal Terrace	70	F2	Ryecroft	67	C3	St. Aongus Lawn	45	B4	*St. Clair's Terrace (Oldcourt Park)	67	B3
*Royal Canal View (Weaver Lane)	71	A1	Ryemont Abbey	20	D4	*St. Aongus Mews			*St. Clare's Ave		
Royal Hibernian Way	75	C1	Ryevale Lawns	20	D4	(St. Aongus Road)	45	B4	(off Harold's Cross Road)	74	F4
*Royal Marine Terrace			Rynville Manor	67	B4	St. Aongus Park	45	B4	*St. Clare's Terrace		
(at Strand Road)	67	C2				St. Aongus Road	45	B4	(Greenfield Place)	75	A4
Royal Oak	12	F4				*St. Aongus Yard			*St. Clement's Road		
Royal Terrace East	60	D1	**S**			(St. Aongus Road)	45	B4	(off St. Anne's Road North)	25	A4
*Royal Terrace Lane						St. Assam's Ave	27	A2	St. Colmcille's Way	55	C2
(off Royal Terrace West)	60	D1	Sackville Ave	72	D1	St. Assam's Drive	27	A2	St. Columbanus Ave	47	B3
*Royal Terrace North			Sackville Court Apts	71	B2	St. Assam's Park	27	A2	*St. Columbanus Place		
(off Royal Terrace East)	60	D1	Sackville Gardens	72	D1	St. Assam's Road East	27	B2	(off St. Columbanus Road)	47	B3
Royal Terrace West	60	D1	Sackville Place	71	B3	St. Assam's Road West	27	A2	St. Columbanus Road	47	B3
Royse Road	25	A4	Saddlers Ave	9	A4	St. Attracta Road	24	F4	St. Columbas Heights	1	C2
Royston	46	D2	Saddlers Close	9	A4	*St. Aubyn's Court			St. Columbas Rise	1	C2
Royston Village	46	D2	Saddlers Court	75	B4	(opposite Arran Drive)	64	E1	St. Columba's Road	45	B2
Ruben Square	74	D3	Saddlers Cres	9	A4	St. Audoen's House Flats	70	F4	St. Columba's Road Lower	25	A4
Ruby Hall	59	C2	Saddlers Drive	9	A4	St. Audoen's Terrace			St. Columba's Road Upper	25	A4
Rugby Road	47	B1	Saddlers Glade	9	A4	(off High Street)	75	A1	St. Columcille's Cres		
Rugged Lane	21	C4	Saddlers Grove	9	A4	St. Augustine Street	70	F4	(on Chapel Lane)	2	D2
*Rugby Villas (off Oxford Road)	47	B1	Saddlers Lawn	9	A4	St. Augustine's Park	59	A1	St. Columcille's Drive	2	D2
Rushbrook	22	E2	*Saddlers Place			St. Barnabas Gardens	72	E2	*St. Columcille's Terrace		
Rushbrook Ave	45	C3	(off Military Road)	75	A4	St. Begnet's Villas	60	E1	(at Ashbrook)	67	C2
Rushbrook Court	45	C4	Sadleir Hall	7	A2	St. Benedicts Gardens	71	B1	St. Columcills Park	2	D2
Rushbrook Cres	45	C3	Saggart	53	B2	St. Berach's Place	27	B1	St. Conleth's Road	45	C2
Rushbrook Drive	45	C3	Saggart Abbey	53	C2	*St. Bernadette's Hall			St. Cronan`s Cottages	1	C2
Rushbrook Grove	45	C3	Saggart Lakes	53	B2	(Richmond Hill)	75	B4	St. Cronan's Close	1	B2
Rushbrook Park	45	C3	Saggart Lodge Court	53	B2	St. Brendan's Ave	26	E2	St. Cronan's Court	1	B1
Rushbrook Road	45	C3	Saint Agatha Court			*St. Brendan's Cottages			St. Cronan's Grove	1	C1
Rushbrook View	45	C3	(off William Street North)	72	D2	(off Irishtown Road)	39	A3	St. Cronan's Lawn	1	B1
Rushbrook Way	45	C4	St. Agnes Park	46	D1	St. Brendan's Cres	45	B2	*St. Cronan's Road		
Ru sheeney	21	B1	St. Agnes Road	46	D1	St. Brendan's Drive	26	E2	(at Ashbrook)	67	C2
Rusheeney Ave	21	B1	*St. Agnes Terrace			St. Brendan's Park	26	F2	St. Cronan's View	1	B2
Rusheeney Close	21	B1	(off St. Agnes RoadCrumlin)	46	D1	*St. Brendan's Road			St. Cronan's Way	1	C2
Rusheeney Court	21	C1	*St. Agnes Terrace			(off St. Anne's Road North)	25	A4	St. Cuthberts Court	43	C1
Rusheeney Cres	8	F4	(on St. Agnes Road)	46	D1	St. Brendan's Terrace (Coolock)	26	E1	St. Cuthbert's Road	43	B1
Rusheeney Green	21	C1	*St. Agnes Terrace			*St. Brendan's Terrace			St. David's	26	D2
Rusheeney Grove	21	B1	(off Dodder Road Lower			(off North Cote Ave)	49	C4	*St. David's Court		
Rusheeney Manor	21	B1	Rathfarnham)	46	F3	St. Brendan's Terrace (Rockbrook)	56	E4	(off Castle Ave Clontarf)	26	E4
Rusheeney Park	21	B1	St. Aidan's Drive	48	D4	St. Bricin's Park	70	D3	St. David's Park	26	D2
						St. Bridget's Ave (North Strand)	72	E1	St. David's Terrace		
									(Blackhorse Ave)	70	D2

STREET NAME	PAGE / GRID REFERENCE	
*St. David's Terrace (off Glasnevin Hill)	25	A3
St. Davids Wood	26	D2
St. Declan's Road	25	C4
*St. Declan's Terrace (off St. Declan's Road)	25	C4
St. Domhnach's Well Street (off Baldoyle Road)	28	D1
St. Dominic's Ave	55	A1
*St. Dominic's Court (off St. Dominic's Terrace)	55	A1
St. Dominic's Road	55	A1
St. Dominic's Terrace	55	A1
St. Donagh's Cres	27	B1
St. Donagh's Park	27	B1
St. Donagh's Road	27	B1
St. Edmunds	35	A1
St. Eithne Road	24	F4
St. Elizabeth's Court	70	E1
St. Enda's Drive	56	F1
St. Enda's Park	56	F1
St. Enda's Road	46	F2
*St. Finbarr's Court (on St. Finbarrs Road)	24	E4
St. Finbarr's Close	45	B3
St. Finbarr's Road	24	E4
St. Finian's Green	34	D2
St. Finian's Grove	34	D2
St. Finian's Ave	34	D2
St. Finian's Close	34	D2
St. Finian's Cres	34	D2
St. Fintan Road	24	F4
St. Fintan Terrace	24	F4
St. Fintan's Cres	29	B3
St. Fintan's Grove	29	B3
St. Fintan's Park (Sutton)	29	B2
St. Fintan's Park (Deans Grange)	59	B1
St. Fintan's Road	29	B3
*St. Fintan's Terrace (off Lucan Road Palmerston)	35	C1
St. Fintan's Villas	59	B1
St. Francis Square	75	A1
St. Gabriel's	59	C3
*St. Gabriel's Court (off St. Gabriel's Road)	27	A4
St. Gabriel's Road	26	F4
*St. Gall Gardens North (off St. Columbanus Road)	47	B3
*St. Gall Gardens South (off St. Columbanus Road)	47	B3
*St. Gatien Road (off Whitechurch Road)	56	F1
St. George's Ave (Clonliffe Road)	25	B4
St. George's Ave (Killiney)	60	E3
*St. George's Villas (off Inchicore Terrace South)	36	F3
St. Gerard's Road	45	C2
*St. Helena's Court (off St. Helena's Drive)	24	E2
St. Helena's Drive	24	E2
St. Helena's Road	24	E2
*St. Helen's (off Marine Parade)	60	E1
St. Helen's Road	48	E2
St. Helen's Terrace	73	A2
*St. Helen's Villas (off St. Helen's Road)	48	F2
St. Helen's Wood	48	E3
*St. Helier's Copse (off Coppinger Wood)	48	F4
St. Ignatius Ave	71	B1
St. Ignatius Road	71	B1
*St. Ita's Road (off Botanic Ave)	25	A3
St. Ives	3	B2
St. James Ave (Clonliffe Road)	72	D1
*St. James Court (off Mount Brown)	73	C1
*St. James Court (off Serpentine Ave)	39	A4
*St. James Place (Sandymount Road)	39	A3
*St. James Place (off Sandymount Road)	39	A4
*St. James Terrace (off Sandymount Road)	39	A3
St. Jame's Wood	73	B2
St. James's	26	D4
St. James's Ave (James's Street)	74	D1
St. James's Court Apts	74	E1
*St. James's Place (off Tyrconnell Road)	36	F3
St. James's Road	45	B2
St. James's Terrace (Dolphin's Barn)	74	D3
St. James's Walk	74	D2
St. James's Walk	74	D2
St. Jarlath Road	24	F4
St. John Street	74	F2
*St. John's Close (off Mounttown Road. Lower)	59	C1
St. John's Court (Donnycarney)	26	D3
*St. John's Wood (off Orwell Road)	47	A2
St. John's	48	E1
St. John's Ave (The Coombe)	74	F2
St. John's Ave (Clondalkin)	44	D2
*St. Johns Close (opposite Glandore Park)	59	C1
St. John's Close	44	D2
St. John's Cottages	73	C1
St. John's Court	25	B1
St. John's Court (Beaumont)	26	D1
St. John's Court (Clondalkin)	44	D2
St. John's Cres	44	D2
St. John's Drive	44	D2
St. John's Gate	44	D2
St. John's Green	44	D2
St. John's Grove	44	D2
*St. John's Lane (off Strand Road)	48	E1
St. John's Lawn	44	D2
St. John's Park (Dún Laoghaire)	49	C4
St. John's Park East	44	D2
St. Johns Park West	44	D2
St. John's Road	44	D2
St. John's Road East	48	E1
St. John's Road West (Islandbridge)	69	C4
St. John's Road West (Clondalkin)	44	D2
*St. Johns Terrace (Donnellan Ave)	73	C1
*St. John's Terrace (Mount Brown)	73	C1
St. John's Well Way	73	C1
*St. John's Wood (off Castle Ave Clontarf)	26	E4
St. John's Wood (Clondalkin)	44	D2
St. John's Wood West	44	D2
St. Joseph Street (off Leo Street)	71	B1
St. Joseph's	23	C2
St. Joseph's Ave (Drumcondra)	25	A4
*St. Joseph's Ave (off Clonliffe Road)	25	B4
St. Joseph's Cottages	23	C4
St. Joseph's Court	70	E2
*St. Joseph's Grove (off Rosemount Park)	47	C4
*St. Joseph's Mansions	72	D2
St. Joseph's Parade	71	A1
St. Joseph's Place (Dorset Street Lower)	71	B2
St. Joseph's Place (Prussia Street)	70	E2
St. Joseph's Road (Aughrim Street)	70	E2
St. Joseph's Road (Walkinstown)	45	C2
*St. Joseph's Square (off Vernon Ave)	39	C1
*St. Joseph's Terrace (off Dolphin's Barn)	74	D3
St. Joseph's Terrace (North Circular Road)	71	C1
St. Joseph's Terrace	71	A2
*St. Joseph's Terrace (off Philipsburgh Ave)	25	C4
*St. Joseph's Terrace (off Pembroke Street)	39	A3
*St. Joseph's Terrace (on Tivoli Road)	50	D4
St. Joseph's Villas (Summerhill)	72	D1
*St. Judes Apts (adjacent to The Close)	31	C3
St. Kevin's Ave (off Blackpitts)	74	F2
St. Kevins Church Apts	75	A3
St. Kevin's Cottages	75	A3
St. Kevin's Court	47	A2
St. Kevin's Gardens	47	A2
St. Kevin's Parade	75	A3
St. Kevin's Park (Rathgar)	47	A2
St. Kevin's Park (Stillorgan)	58	D1
St. Kevin's Road	75	A4
St. Kevin's Square	67	C2
*St. Kevin's Terrace (New Bride Street)	75	A2
*St. Kevin's Terrace (St. Kevin's Square)	67	C2
St. Kevin's Villas	60	D1
St. Killian's Ave	45	B2
St. Killians Cres	67	B4
*St. Killian's Park (off Watery Lane)	44	E1
St. Laurence Court	36	E3
*St. Laurence Grove (off St. Laurence Road)	36	E2
*St. Laurence O'Toole Court (off Oriel Street Upper)	72	D3
St. Laurence Park	48	F4
St. Laurence Place (Western Way)	71	A2
St. Laurence Place East (Lower Sheriff Street)	72	E3
St. Laurence Road	36	E2
*St. Laurence Terrace (off Lucan Road Chapelizod)	36	E2
*St. Laurence's Terrace (near Adelaide Villas)	67	C2
*St. Lawrence Building Apts (off Harbour Road, opposite west pier)	30	D1
*St. Lawrence Glen (off St. Lawrence Road)	36	E3
St. Lawrence O'Toole Ave	14	F2
*St. Lawrence Quay (off Harbour Road, close to Post Office)	30	D1
St. Lawrence Road (Clontarf)	26	D4
St. Lawrence Road (Howth)	30	D1
St. Lawrence's Court	26	D4
St. Lawrence's Terrace	30	D2
St. Loman's Road	34	F2
St. Luke's Ave	74	F2
*St. Luke's Court (off Cromcastle Green)	26	D1
*St. Luke's Cres (off Dundrum Road)	47	B2
St. Luke's Gate	74	F2
*St. Maelruans Courtyard (off St. Maelruans Park)	55	A1
St. Maelruans Park	55	A1
St. Maignenn's Terrace	73	C1
St. Malachy's Drive	45	C2
*St. Malachy's Road (off Botanic Ave)	25	A3
*St. Margaret's Close (off Castlepark Road)	60	E1
St. Margaret's (North Road)	11	B1
St. Margaret's (Booterstown)	48	F3
St. Margaret's Ave (off Pimlico)	74	F1
St. Margaret's Ave (Malahide)	3	B3
St. Margaret's Ave (Kilbarrack)	27	C2
*St. Margaret's Ave North (Richmond Lane)	71	C1
St. Margaret's Court	11	A4
St. Margaret's Park	3	B3
St. Margaret's Road (Poppintree)	11	C4
St. Margaret's Road (Malahide)	3	B3
St. Margaret's Road (Finglas)	11	A4
St. Margaret's Road (Ballymun)	12	D4
St. Margaret's Terrace	74	E2
St. Mark's Ave	35	A2
St. Mark's Cres	35	A3
St. Mark's Drive	35	A3
St. Mark's Gardens	35	A3
St. Mark's Green	35	A3
St. Mark's Grove	35	A3
St. Marnock's Ave	14	F2
St. Martin's Drive	46	E2
St. Martin's Park	46	E1
St. Mary's Ave (Rathfarnham)	46	F4
St. Mary's Ave North (Mountjoy Street)	71	A2
St. Mary's Ave West	36	F3
*St. Mary's Court (on Church Road)	72	F2
St. Mary's Cres	45	C1
St. Mary's Drive	45	C1
St. Mary's Lane	76	E2
St. Mary's Mansions	71	C2
St. Mary's Park (Leixlip)	20	D4
St. Mary's Park (Finglas)	23	C2
St. Mary's Park (Crumlin)	45	C1
*St. Mary's Place (south of Church on Main Street Howth)	30	D2
St. Mary's Place North	71	A2
*St. Mary's Road (south of Church on Main Street Howth)	30	D2
St. Mary's Road (Crumlin)	46	D1
St. Mary's Road North (East Wall)	72	E2
St. Mary's Road South (Ballsbridge)	76	E3
*St. Mary's Street (off North Cote Ave)	49	C4
*St. Marys Terrace (South of Hall)	68	D2
St. Mary's Terrace (Mountjoy Street)	71	A2
St. Mary's Terrace (Arbour Hill)	70	E3
St. Mary's Terrace (Dunboyne)	7	B2
*St. Mary's Terrace (off Martin's Row Chapelizod)	36	E2
*St. Mary's Terrace (Bath Street)	39	A3
*St. Mary's Terrace (off Grange Road Rathfarnham)	46	F4
*St. Mary's Terrace (entrance to Bentley Road)	67	C4
St. Mathias Wood	60	D4
St. Mel's Ave	45	B3
*St. Michael's Villas (Sarsfield Road)	36	E3
St. Michael's Close (off High Street)	75	A1
St. Michael's Estate	73	A2
St. Michael's Hill (off High Street)	75	A1
St. Michael's House	47	C4
St. Michael's Place	71	A2
*St. Michael's Road (off Botanic Ave)	25	A3
St. Michael's Terrace (Blackpitts)	74	F2
*St. Michael's Terrace (off York Road Dún Laoghaire)	49	C4
St. Michan's House Flats	71	A4
St. Michan's Park	71	A3
St. Michan's Place (off Chancery Street)	71	A4
St. Michan's Street	71	A4
*St. Mobhi Ave (on St. Mobhi Road)	25	A3
St. Mobhi Boithirin	25	A3
St. Mobhi Drive	25	A3
*St. Mobhi Grove (off Botanic Road)	25	A3
*St. Mobhi Mews (St. Mobhi Boithrin)	25	A3
St. Mobhi Road	25	A3
St. Mochtas Ave	22	D3
St. Mochtas Chase	22	D2
St. Mochtas Close	22	D3
St. Mochtas Drive	22	D3
St. Mochtas Green	22	D3
St. Mochtas Grove	22	D3
St. Mochtas Lawn	22	D2
St. Mochtas Road	22	D3
St. Mochtas Vale	22	D3
St. Mura's Terrace	72	F2
*St. Nathy's House (off Churchtown Road)	47	B4
*St. Nathy's Villas (off Nutgrove Ave)	47	B4
St. Nessan's Apts	30	E2
*St. Nessan's Close (streets between Tuckett's Lane and Main Street)	30	D2
*St. Nessans Court (streets between Tuckett's Lane and Main Street)	30	D2
*St. Nessan's Terrace (streets between Tuckett's Lane and Main Street)	30	D2
St. Nicholas Place	75	A1
St. Oliver's Park	35	B3
St. Pappin's Green	24	F2
St. Pappin's Road	25	A2
*St. Pappin's Street (adjacent Santry Cross Junction)	12	D4
St. Patrick's Ave (Fairview)	72	E1
St. Patrick's Ave (Portmarnock)	14	F2
*St. Patrick's Ave (St. Patrick's Park)	44	D1
*St. Patrick's Ave (off Castle Street Dalkey)	60	F2
St. Patrick's Close (Kevin Street Upper)	75	A2
*St. Patrick's Close (off St. Patrick's Cres)	59	C1
St. Patrick's Cottages	46	F4
St. Patrick's Court	74	F3
St. Patrick's Cres (Rathcoole)	52	E2
St. Patrick's Cres (Kill O'The Grange)	59	C1
St. Patrick's Parade	25	A4
St. Patrick's Park (Dunboyne)	7	B2
St. Patrick's Park (Blanchardstown)	22	E2

STREET NAME	PAGE / GRID REFERENCE	
St. Patrick's Park (Celbridge)	31	C3
St. Patrick's Park (Celbridge)	32	D3
St. Patrick's Park (Clondalkin)	44	D1
St. Patrick's Park (Stepaside)	58	E4
St. Patrick's Place	71	A2
*St. Patrick's Place		
(off Royal Canal Bank)	25	A4
St. Patrick's Road (Drumcondra)	25	A4
St. Patrick's Road (Clondalkin)	35	A4
St. Patrick's Road (Walkinstown)	45	C2
*St. Patrick's Road		
(off Castle Street Dalkey)	60	F2
*St. Patrick's Square		
(off Castle Street Dalkey)	60	F2
*St. Patrick's Square		
(off Castle Street Bray)	67	C1
*St. Patrick's Terrace		
(Russell Street)	71	C1
*St. Patrick's Terrace		
(North Brunswick Street)	70	F3
*St. Patrick's Terrace		
(off Fitzroy Ave)	25	B4
*St. Patrick's Terrace		
(off Inchicore Terrace South)	36	F3
*St. Patrick's Terrace		
(off Oliver Plunkett Road)	59	C1
*St. Patrick's Villas		
(off Thorncastle Street)	39	A3
*St. Paul's Court (Slademore Ave)	26	F1
*St. Pauls Drive (Limekiln Lane)	45	C2
*St. Paul's Terrace		
(off Adelaide Road)	60	E1
St. Peter's Ave	70	F1
St. Peter's Close	71	A1
St. Peter's Court	71	A1
St. Peter's Cres	45	C2
St. Peter's Drive	45	C2
St. Peter's Park	7	B2
St. Peter's Road (Phibsborough)	24	F4
St. Peter's Road (Walkinstown)	45	C2
St. Peter's Road (Bray)	67	B1
St. Peter's Square	71	A1
St. Peter's Terrace (Howth)	30	D2
*St. Peter's Terrace		
(off St. Peter's Drive		
Walkinstown)	45	C2
*St. Peter's Terrace		
(off Adelaide Road)	60	E1
*St. Peter's Terrace		
(St. Peters Road)	67	B1
St. Philomenas	9	C4
St. Philomena's Court	9	C4
St. Philomena's Park	9	C3
*St. Philomena's Road		
(off Dalcassian Downs)	24	F4
St. Raphaels Ave	31	C4
St. Ronan's Ave	35	A3
St. Ronan's Close	35	A3
St. Ronan's Cres	35	A3
St. Ronan's Drive	35	A3
St. Ronan's Gardens	35	A3
St. Ronan's Green	35	A3
St. Ronan's Grove	35	A3
St. Ronan's Park	35	A3
St. Ronan's Way	35	A3
St. Samson Court	14	D3
St. Samson Square	14	D3
St. Stephen's Green East	75	C2
St. Stephen's Green North	75	C2
St. Stephen's Green South	75	B2
St. Stephen's Green West	75	B2
St. Sylvester Villas	3	B3
St. Teresa's Gardens	74	E2
*St. Teresa's Place		
(off Prospect Ave)	25	A4
*St. Teresa's Road		
(off Botanic Road Glasnevin)	25	A4
St. Teresa's Road (Crumlin)	46	D2
St. Thomas Mead	48	E3
St. Thomas Road (Ardee Street)	74	F2
*St. Thomas Wood		
(opposite Belfield Park Apts)	48	E3
St. Thomas's Road		
(Mount Merrion)	48	E3
St. Ultan's Flats	75	B3
St. Vincent Street North	71	A1
St. Vincent Street South	75	A3
St. Vincent Street West	73	A2
St. Vincent's Cottages	23	C4
*St. Vincent's Court		
(off Collins Ave)	25	C3
St. Vincent's Court	26	D3
St. Vincent's Park	49	A4

STREET NAME	PAGE / GRID REFERENCE	
St. Werburghs	2	E2
St. Wolstan's Abbey	32	E3
St. Wolston's Abbey	32	D4
St.doolaghs	14	D3
St.sbury Ave	60	E4
Salamanca	48	D4
*Salem Court		
(off Maxwell Road)	47	A1
Salestown	6	D4
*Salisbury Court Apts		
(off Dufferin Ave)	74	F3
Sallowood View	12	E4
Sally Park	55	C1
Sally Park Close	55	C1
Sallyglen Road	60	D2
Sallymount Ave	47	B1
*Sallymount Gardens		
(off Sallymount Ave)	47	B1
*Sallymount Terrace		
(off Sallymount Ave)	47	B1
Sallynoggin	60	D2
Sallynoggin Park	59	C2
Sallynoggin Road	59	C2
Salmon Pool Apts	69	A4
Salthill	49	C4
*Salthill Place (off Crofton Road)	50	D4
Saltzburg	48	D4
Sampson's Lane	71	B3
Samuel Beckett Bridge	72	E4
Sanderling Apts	48	E3
Sandford Ave (Donore Ave)	74	E3
Sandford Ave (Donnybrook)	47	C1
Sandford Close	47	B1
Sandford Gardens	74	F3
*Sandford Gardens		
(off Sandford Ave)	47	C1
Sandford Lodge	47	B1
Sandford Park (Sandford Gardens)	74	F3
Sandford Road	47	B1
Sandford Row	47	B1
Sandford Square	47	B1
Sandford Terrace	47	B1
Sandford Wood	1	C1
Sandon Cove	26	E4
Sandsfords Bridge	19	A3
Sandwith Street Lower	72	D4
Sandwith Street Upper	76	D1
Sandycove Ave East	60	E1
Sandycove Ave North	50	E4
Sandycove Ave West	60	E1
Sandycove Lane East	60	E1
Sandycove Point	50	E4
Sandycove Road	60	E1
Sandyford	58	D2
Sandyford Downs	58	D3
Sandyford Hall	58	E3
Sandyford Hall Ave	58	E3
Sandyford Hall Close	58	E4
Sandyford Hall Court	58	E3
Sandyford Hall Cres	58	E3
Sandyford Hall Drive	58	E4
Sandyford Hall Green	58	E3
Sandyford Hall Grove	58	E4
Sandyford Hall Lawn	58	E3
Sandyford Hall Park	58	E3
Sandyford Hall Place	58	E3
Sandyford Hall Rise	58	E3
Sandyford Hall View	58	E4
Sandyford Hall Walk	58	E3
Sandyford Park	58	D3
Sandyford Road	57	C1
Sandyford View	57	C3
Sandyford Village	58	D3
Sandyhill Ave	24	F1
Sandyhill Court	11	C4
Sandyhill Gardens	24	F1
Sandyhill Terrace	11	C4
Sandyhill Way	11	C4
Sandymount	39	A4
Sandymount Ave	39	A4
*Sandymount Castle		
(off Gilford Road)	39	A4
*Sandymount Castle Drive		
(off Gilford Road)	39	A4
*Sandymount Castle Park		
(off Gilford Road)	39	B4
*Sandymount Castle Road		
(off Gilford Road)	39	A4
*Sandymount Court		
(off Beach Road)	39	A3
*Sandymount Green		
(off Gilford Road)	39	A4

STREET NAME	PAGE / GRID REFERENCE	
Sandymount Road	39	A3
Sans Souci Park	48	F3
Sans Souci wood	67	C3
Santa Sabina Manor	29	B2
Santry	25	B1
Santry Ave	12	E4
Santry Close	12	E4
Santry Court	12	F4
Santry Cross (Ballymun)	12	D4
Santry Villas	12	E4
Sarah Bridge (River Liffey)	69	B4
Sarah Curran Ave	56	F1
*Sarah Curran Road		
(off Sarah Curran Ave)	56	F1
Sarah Place	69	B4
Saran Wood	67	B4
Sarney	6	E2
*Sarsfield Court		
(off Main Street Lucan)	34	D1
Sarsfield Court (Inchicore)	36	F3
Sarsfield Park	34	D1
Sarsfield Quay	70	E4
Sarsfield Road	36	F3
Sarsfield Street (Phibsborough)	71	A1
Sarsfield Street (Sallynoggin)	60	D1
*Sarsfield Terrace		
(off Main Street Lucan)	34	D1
Sarto Lawn	27	C1
Sarto Park	27	C1
Sarto Rise	27	C1
Sarto Road	27	C2
Saul Road	46	E1
Saval Grove	60	E2
Saval Park Cres	60	E2
Saval Park Gardens	60	E2
Saval Park Road	60	E2
Scariff House	22	F1
Scholarstown Park	56	D2
Scholarstown Road	56	D2
School Ave	26	E2
School Lane	28	D1
School Street	74	E1
*School Street Flats		
(off Marrowbone Lane)	74	E1
School Walk	52	E2
Schoolhouse Court	25	B1
Schoolhouse Lane (Kildare Street)	75	C1
Schoolhouse Lane (Santry)	25	B1
Schoolhouse Lane West		
(off High Street)	75	A1
*Schoolhouse Mews		
(off Schoolhouse Lane)	25	B1
Schools Road	67	B4
Scotchstone Bridge	2	D1
Scott Park	67	C3
Scribblestown	23	C3
Scribblestown Ave	23	C3
Scribblestown Close	23	C3
Scribblestown Grove	23	C3
Scribblestown Park	24	D3
Scribblestown Place	23	C3
Scribblestown Road	23	C3
Sea Road	3	A2
Seabank Court (Malahide)	3	C2
*Seabank Court		
(off Marine Parade)	60	E1
Seabrook Manor	14	E2
Seabury	48	E1
Seabury Ave	2	F2
Seabury Close	2	F2
Seabury Court	2	F2
Seabury Cres	2	F2
Seabury Dale	2	F2
Seabury Downs	2	F2
Seabury Drive	3	A2
Seabury Gardens	2	F2
Seabury Glen	2	F2
Seabury Green	2	F2
Seabury Grove	2	F2
Seabury Heights	2	F2
Seabury Lane	2	F2
Seabury Lawns	2	F2
Seabury Meadows	2	F2
Seabury Orchard	2	F2
Seabury Parade	2	F2
Seabury Park	2	F2
Seabury Place	2	F2
Seabury Road	2	F2
Seabury Vale	2	F2
Seabury View	2	F2
Seabury Walk	2	F2

STREET NAME	PAGE / GRID REFERENCE	
Seabury Wood	2	F2
Seacliff Ave	27	C1
Seacliff Drive	27	C1
Seacliff Road	27	C1
Seacourt	26	F4
Seacrest	67	C3
Seafield (off Baldoyle Road)	28	D1
Seafield (Shankill)	64	F2
Seafield Ave (Clontarf)	26	F4
Seafield Ave (Monkstown)	49	B4
Seafield Close	48	E3
Seafield Close	26	F4
Seafield Court (Malahide)	3	B2
Seafield Court (Loughlinstown)	64	E1
Seafield Cres	48	E3
Seafield Downs		
(off Kincora Road Clontarf)	26	F4
Seafield Drive	48	E2
Seafield Grove		
(off St. Gabriel's Road)	27	A4
*Seafield Park (off Seafield Road)	48	E2
Seafield Road (Booterstown)	48	E2
Seafield Road (Killiney)	60	E4
Seafield Road (Ballybrack)	64	E1
Seafield Road East	26	F4
Seafield Road West	26	E4
*Seafield Terrace		
(off Coliemore Road)	60	F2
Seafort Ave	39	A4
*Seafort Cottages		
(off Seafort Ave)	39	A4
*Seafort Gardens		
(off Sandymount Road)	39	A3
Seafort Parade	48	F3
*Seafort Terrace		
(off Seafort Ave)	39	A4
*Seafort Villas (off Seafort Ave)	39	A4
Seagrange Ave	14	F4
Seagrange Drive	27	C1
Seagrange Road	27	C1
Seagrave	14	F2
Seagrave Close	11	B4
Seagrave Court	11	B4
Seagrave Drive	11	B4
Seagrave Rise	11	B4
Seagrave Terrace	11	B4
Seagrave Way	11	B4
Seamount	3	C3
Seamount	48	E3
Seamount Drive	3	C3
Seamount Grove	3	C3
Seamount Heights	3	C3
Seamount Park	3	C3
Seamount Road	3	C3
Seamount View	2	E2
Seamus Ennis Road	24	E1
Seán Heuston Bridge		
(River Liffey)	70	D4
Sean MacDermott Street Lower	71	C2
Sean MacDermott Street Upper	71	C2
Sean Moore Road	39	A3
Sean O'Casey Ave	71	C2
Seán O'Casey Bridge		
(River Liffey)	72	D4
Sean Tracey House	72	D2
*Seanchlos Apts		
(Johnstown Road Rathcoole)	52	E2
Seapark (Malahide)	3	C3
Seapark (Dollymount)	26	F4
Seapark Drive	26	F4
Seapark Hill	3	C3
Seapark Road	26	F4
*Seapoint Ave		
(Between College Street and		
Main Street Baldoyle)	15	A4
Seapoint Ave (Blackrock)	49	B3
*Seapoint Court		
(Between College Street and		
Main Street Baldoyle)	15	A4
Seapoint Court (Bray)	67	C1
Seapoint Road	67	C2
*Seapoint Terrace		
(off Strand Street Ringsend)	39	A3
*Seapoint Terrace		
(off Belgrave Road)	49	B3
*Seapoint Terrace		
(near Duncairn Ave)	67	C2
*Seapoint Villas		
(near Duncairn Ave)	67	C2
Seascout Den	40	D1
Seatown Park	2	D1
Seatown Park The Ave	2	D1

STREET NAME	PAGE / GRID REFERENCE
Seatown Park The Court	2 D1
Seatown Park The Cres	2 D1
Seatown Park The Drive	2 D1
Seatown Park The Green	2 D1
Seatown Park The Grove	2 D1
Seatown Road	2 D1
Seatown Roundabout (Swords)	2 D1
Seatown Terrace	2 D2
Seatown Villas	2 D1
Seatown Walk	2 D2
Seatown West	2 D1
Seaview Ave East	72 E1
Seaview Ave North	26 D4
Seaview Cottages	63 C4
Seaview Lawn	64 E2
Seaview Park	64 E2
*Seaview Terrace (streets between Tuckett's Lane and Main Street)	30 D2
Seaview Terrace (Donnybrook)	48 D1
*Seaview Terrace (off Clarence Street Dún Laoghaire)	49 C4
Seaview Wood	64 E2
Second Ave (Seville Place)	72 E3
Second Ave (Tallaght)	44 F4
Sefton	59 C2
Sefton Green	59 C2
*Sefton Hall (off Kelston Ave)	59 A2
*Selskar Terrace (Old Mountpleasant)	75 C4
Serpentine Ave	39 A4
Serpentine Park	39 A4
Serpentine Road	39 A4
Serpentine Terrace	39 A4
Seskin View Ave	55 A2
Seskin View Drive	55 A2
Seskin View Park	55 A2
Seskin View Road	55 A2
Setanta Place	75 C1
*Seven Houses (off Glenageary Road Lower)	60 D1
Seven Oaks (Whitehall)	25 B3
Seven Oaks (Inchicore)	36 F3
*Seven Oaks (off Belgrave Road)	47 A1
Seventh Lock Cottages	36 D4
Seventh Lock Place	36 D4
Seville Place	72 D2
Seville Terrace	72 D2
Seymour Road	67 C2
Shackelton	8 F4
Shackelton Road	31 C3
Shaldon Grange	62 F2
*Shalimar Apts (off Monastery Road)	44 F1
Shamrock Cottages	72 D2
*Shamrock Hill Mews (off Stillorgan Road)	47 C1
Shamrock Place	72 D2
Shamrock Street	71 A2
Shamrock Terrace	72 D2
Shamrock Villas	46 F1
*Shanagarry (off Milltown Road)	47 B2
Shanard Ave	25 A1
Shanard Road	25 A1
Shanboley Road	25 C1
Shancastle Ave	35 A2
Shancastle Close	35 A2
Shancastle Cres	35 A2
Shancastle Drive	35 A2
Shancastle Lawns	35 A2
Shancastle Park	35 A2
Shandon Cres	24 F4
Shandon Drive	24 F4
Shandon Gardens	24 F4
*Shandon Green (off Shandon Cres)	24 F4
Shandon Mill (off Shandon Park)	24 F4
Shandon Park (Phibsborough)	24 F4
Shandon Park (Monkstown)	49 B4
Shandon Road	24 F4
Shangan Ave	25 B1
Shangan Court	25 A1
Shangan Cres	25 A1
Shangan Drive	25 B1
Shangan Gardens	25 B1
Shangan Green	25 B1
*Shangan Hall Apts (off Shangan Road)	25 A1
Shangan Park	25 B1
Shangan Road	25 A1
Shanganagh Cliffs	64 E2
Shanganagh Grove	64 E3
Shanganagh Road	64 E1
Shanganagh Terrace	60 F4
Shanganagh Vale	60 D4
*Shanganagh Wood (west off Railway Station)	64 E2
Shanglas Road	25 C1
Shanid Road	46 F2
Shankill	64 E3
*Shankill View (near Bray Bridge)	67 C2
Shanliss Ave	25 B1
Shanliss Drive	25 B1
*Shanliss Gardens (off Shanliss Road)	25 A1
Shanliss Grove	25 B1
Shanliss Park	25 B1
Shanliss Road	25 A1
Shanliss Walk	25 B1
Shanliss Way	25 B1
Shannon Terrace	73 C1
Shanowen Ave	25 A1
Shanowen Cres	25 B1
Shanowen Drive	25 B1
Shanowen Grove	25 A1
Shanowen Hall	25 B2
Shanowen Park	25 A1
Shanowen Road	25 B1
Shanowen Square	25 B2
Shanrath Road	25 B1
Shantalla Ave	25 C1
Shantalla Drive	25 C2
Shantalla Park	25 C2
Shantalla Road	25 C2
Shanvarna Road	25 B1
Sharavogue	60 E2
Shaw Court Apts	75 B3
Shaw Street	71 C4
Shaw's Lane	76 F2
Shea's Court	70 E2
Shea's Lane	70 E2
Sheelin Ave	64 E1
Sheelin Drive	64 E1
*Sheelin Grove (off Sheelin Ave)	64 E1
*Sheelin Hill (off Ridge Hill)	64 E1
*Sheelin Walk (off Sheelin Ave)	64 E1
Sheephill Ave	9 C4
Sheephill Green	9 C4
Sheephill Park	9 C4
Sheepmoor Ave	22 D1
Sheepmoor Close	22 D1
Sheepmoor Cres	22 D1
Sheepmoor Gardens	22 D1
Sheepmoor Green	22 D1
Sheepmoor Grove	22 D1
Sheepmoor Lawn	22 D1
Sheepmoor Way	22 D1
Shelbourne Ave (off Gilford Road)	76 F3
Shelbourne Lane (off Gilford Road)	76 F3
*Shelbourne Park Apts	76 F1
Shelbourne Park Mews	76 F1
Shelbourne Place	76 F2
Shelbourne Road	76 F2
Shelbourne Village	76 F1
Shelerin Road	21 C2
Shellys Banks Road	39 B3
Shelmalier Road	72 F2
Shelmartin Ave	25 C4
*Shelmartin Terrace (off Shelmartin Ave)	25 C4
Shelton Drive	46 D2
Shelton Gardens	46 D2
Shelton Grove	46 D2
Shelton Park	46 D2
Sherborne	47 A2
Sheridan Court	71 B2
Sheridan Place	71 B2
Sheriff Street Lower	72 D3
Sheriff Street Upper	72 E3
Sherkin Court	25 B3
Sherkin Gardens	25 B3
Sherrard Ave	71 B1
*Sherrard Court (off Portland Place)	71 B1
Sherrard Street Lower	71 C1
Sherrard Street Upper	71 B1
Sherrards Court	71 B1
Shieling Square	27 B2
Shielmartin Drive	29 B3
*Shielmartin Park (off Shielmartin Road)	29 B3
Shielmartin Road	29 B3
Shinkeen Bridge	32 E3
Ship Street Great	75 A1
Ship Street Little	75 A1
Shrewsbury	39 A4
Shrewsbury Court	59 C3
Shrewsbury Hall	64 E3
Shrewsbury House	59 C4
Shrewsbury Lawn	59 C4
Shrewsbury Lodge	59 C3
Shrewsbury Park	48 D1
Shrewsbury Road (Ailesbury Road)	48 D1
Shrewsbury Road (Shankill)	64 E3
*Shrewsbury Square (off Sandymount Ave)	39 A4
Shrewsbury Woods	59 C4
Sibthorpe Lane	76 D4
*Sidbury Court (between Sidmonton and Albert Ave)	68 D2
Sidmonton Ave	67 C2
*Sidmonton Court (west side of Meath Road)	68 D3
Sidmonton Gardens	67 C2
Sidmonton Park	68 D2
*Sidmonton Place (Kingsmill Road)	67 C2
Sidmonton Road	67 C2
*Sidmonton Square (Sidmonton Ave)	67 C2
Sigurd Road	70 E3
Silchester Court	60 D1
Silchester Cres	60 D1
Silchester Park	60 D1
Silchester Road	60 D1
*Silchester Wood (off Adelaide Road)	60 D1
Silken Park	43 C4
Silken Park Ave	43 C4
Silken Vale	17 C3
Silleachain Lane	20 D4
Silloge Ave	25 A1
Silloge Cres	25 A1
Silloge Gardens	25 A1
Silloge Road	25 A1
Silver Birches (Dunboyne)	7 B2
Silver Birches (Dundrum)	47 C4
Silver Birches Close	7 B2
Silver Birches Cres	7 B2
*Silver Pines (off Brewery Road)	58 F2
Silverberry	34 D3
Silverdale	34 D3
Silverdale Court	67 B2
Silverpine	67 B3
Silverwood	34 D3
Silverwood Drive	46 E4
Silverwood Road	46 E4
Simmon's Place (off Thompson's Cottages)	71 C2
*Simmonscourt Ave (off Simmonscourt Road)	48 D1
Simmonscourt Castle	48 D1
Simmonscourt Road	39 A4
*Simmonscourt Square (off Simmonscourt Road)	48 D1
*Simmonscourt Terrace (off Beaver Row)	47 C1
*Simmonscourt View (off Simmonscourt Road)	48 D1
Simmonstown	41 A1
Simmonstown Manor	32 D4
Simmonstown Park	32 D4
Simons Ridge	57 C3
*Simpsons Lane (off Bath Street)	39 A3
Sion Hill Ave	46 F1
*Sion Hill Court (off Sion Hill Road)	25 C3
Sion Hill Road	25 C3
*Sion House (off Thomas Davis Street West)	36 F3
Sion Road	60 D2
Sionhill	48 F3
*Sir Ivor Mall (off Leopardstown Road)	58 F2
Sir John Rogerson's Quay	72 E4
Sitric Place (off Sitric Road)	70 E3
Sitric Road	70 E3
Skeagh	41 A3
Skelligs Court	22 F1
Skelly's Lane	26 D2
Skreen Road	69 B1
Slade	53 A3
Slade Castle Ave	53 A2
Slade Castle Close	53 A2
Slade Castle Heights	53 A2
Slade Castle View	53 A2
Slade Road	53 A3
Slade Row	70 D3
Slademore Ave	26 F1
Slademore Close	26 F1
Slademore Court	13 C4
Slademore Drive	26 F1
Slane Road	73 C4
Slaney Close	24 E3
Slaney Road	24 E3
Slate Cabin Lane	57 C3
Slemish Road	69 B1
Slieve Rua Drive	58 D1
Slievebloom Park	45 C1
Slievebloom Road	45 C1
Slievemore Road	73 A4
Slievenamon Road	73 B3
*Sloan Terrace (east side of text Meath)	68 D2
Sloperton	49 C4
Smithfield	70 F4
*Smithfield Apts (Near Ellis Quay Apts)	70 F4
Smithfield Gate Apts	70 F3
*Smithfield Market Square Apts (Smithfield)	70 F4
*Smithfield Terrace (Smithfield)	70 F4
*Smith's Cottages (off Bushfield Terrace)	47 B1
*Smith's Lane (off Harold's Cross Road)	46 F1
*Smith's Villas (off York Road Dún Laoghaire)	49 C4
*Smyth Gardens (off York Road Dún Laoghaire)	49 C4
Snowdrop Walk	13 C4
Snugborough	14 E3
Snugborough Road	22 F1
Snugborough Road Extention	22 D2
Somerset Street	76 F1
Somerton	59 C2
*Somerton Mews	59 C2
Somerton Road	22 E4
Somerville Ave	45 C1
*Somerville Court (off St. Agnes RoadCrumlin)	46 D1
Somerville Drive	46 D1
*Somerville Park (off Somerville Ave)	45 C1
Sommerville	47 C4
Sonesta	3 A2
*Sophie Baret Residence (off Lower Kilmacud Road)	48 D4
Sorbonne	48 D4
Sorrel Dale	22 D2
Sorrel Drive	21 C2
Sorrel Heath	21 C2
Sorrel Park	21 C2
Sorrell Hall	57 C3
*Sorrento Close (off Sorrento Road)	60 F2
*Sorrento Court (off Sorrento Road)	60 F2
*Sorrento Drive (off Sorrento Road)	60 F2
*Sorrento Heights (off Sorrento Road)	60 F2
*Sorrento Lawn (off Sorrento Road)	60 F2
*Sorrento Mews (off Sorrento Road)	60 F2
*Sorrento Park (on Sorrento Road)	60 F2
Sorrento Road	60 F2
Sorrento Terrace	60 G2
South Ave	48 E4
South Bank	2 D1
South Bank (Swords)	1 C1
South Bank Road	39 B3
South Circular Road (Dolphin's Barn)	74 D3
South Circular Road (Portobello)	74 E3
South Circular Road (Kilmainham)	73 C2
South Circular Road (Islandbridge)	69 B4
South City Market (on South Great Georges Street)	75 B1
*South Dock Apts	76 F1

STREET NAME	PAGE / GRID REFERENCE
South Dock Place	76 F1
South Dock Road	76 F1
South Dock Street	76 F1
South Esplanade	68 D2
*South Gate Apts (off Ardee Street)	74 F2
South Great George's Street	75 B1
South Hill (Howth)	29 C3
South Hill (Milltown)	47 B2
South Hill Ave	48 F3
South Hill Park	48 E3
South Lotts Road	76 F1
South Park (Cornelscourt)	59 B3
South Park Drive	59 B2
South Richmond View	75 B3
*South Winds (off Ulverton Road Dalkey)	60 F1
South Wood Park	48 F3
*Southdene (off Monkstown Valley)	49 B4
Southern Cross Ave	73 A2
Southern Cross Route	57 B3
Southfield	74 E3
Southlands	64 E4
Southmede	57 C1
Southview Terrace	74 D1
Spa Road	73 A2
Spa Road (Phoenix Park)	69 B2
Spa Road (Inchicore)	36 F3
*Spafield Terrace (off Sandymount Ave)	39 A4
*Spawell Cottages (off Tallaght Road)	45 C4
Spawell Roundabout	46 D4
Spencer Dock	72 E3
Spencer Place (off Spencer Street North)	72 E1
Spencer Row	71 C3
Spencer Street North	72 E1
Spencer Street South	75 A3
Spencer Villas	60 E1
Spences Terrace	74 E2
Sperrin Road	73 A4
Spiddal Park	35 C3
Spiddal Road	35 C3
Spire View	70 F1
Spire View	24 D4
*Spire View Court (off Spire View Lane)	47 A1
Spire View Lane	47 A1
Spitalfields	74 F1
Spring Garden Lane	71 C4
Spring Garden Street	72 D1
Springbank Cottages	53 A2
Springdale Court Apts	26 F2
Springdale Road	26 F2
Springfield (Cabra)	69 B1
Springfield (Tallaght)	54 F1
Springfield Ave	46 E4
Springfield Close	31 C4
Springfield Cres	46 E4
Springfield Drive	46 E4
Springfield Drive	31 C4
Springfield Lane	63 A1
Springfield Park (Templeogue)	46 E4
Springfield Park (Deans Grange)	59 A2
Springfield Road	46 E3
Springhill Ave	59 A1
*Springhill Cottages (off Brookville Park)	59 B1
Springhill Park (Deans Grange)	59 B1
Springhill Park (Dalkey)	60 E2
Springlawn	22 E2
Springlawn Close	22 E2
Springlawn Court	22 E2
Springlawn Drive	22 E2
Springlawn Heights	22 E2
Springlawn Park	22 E2
Springlawn Road	22 E2
Springmount Apts	24 D2
Springvale	56 E2
Springvale Hall	57 C3
Spruce Ave	58 D2
*St Andrews Court	76 D1
*St Augustine Apts (Oliver Bond Street)	70 F4
St Josephs Terrace	71 A2
Stable Lane (Harcourt Street)	75 B2
Stable Lane (Leeson Street Lower)	75 C2
Stable Lane (Smithfield)	70 F4
Stackstown	61 B1
Stacummy Bridge	32 F4

STREET NAME	PAGE / GRID REFERENCE
Staffordstown	5 C2
Staffordstown Little	5 C1
Stamer Street	75 A3
*Stanford (Harlech Vale)	48 D3
Stanford Green	45 C1
Stanhope Street	70 F3
Stanley Street	70 F3
Stannaway Ave	46 D1
*Stannaway Court (off Stannaway Ave)	46 D2
Stannaway Drive	46 E1
Stannaway Road	46 E1
Stapolin	14 F4
Stapolin Ave	14 F4
Stapolin House	14 F4
Stapolin Lawns	14 F4
Station Close	35 A4
Station Hill	14 F4
Station Road (Dunboyne)	7 B3
Station Road (Portmarnock)	14 E2
Station Road (Leixlip)	19 C4
*Station Road (off Clover Hill Road)	35 A4
Station Road (Raheny)	27 A2
Station Road (Sutton)	29 A1
Station Road (Glenageary)	60 E1
Station Road (Killiney)	60 E4
*Station Road (east of Library Road)	64 E2
*Station View Apts (adjacent Oldfarm off Carpenterstown Road)	22 E3
Station Way	14 E4
Stationcourt	22 D3
Stationcourt Hall	22 D3
Stationcourt Park	22 D3
Stationcourt View	22 D3
Stationcourt Way	22 D3
Steamstown Wood	2 F4
Steelstown	51 C3
Steelstown Interchange (N7)	51 B3
*Steeple Gate (off Sandymount Road)	39 A3
Steeven's Gate Apts	74 D1
Steeven's Lane	70 D4
Stella Ave	25 A3
Stella Gardens	39 A3
Stella Maris Apts	17 C4
Stepaside	58 E4
Stepaside	62 E1
Stepaside Lane	62 E1
Stepaside Park	58 E4
Stepaside Park	62 E1
Stepaside Village	58 E4
Stephen Street Lower	75 B1
Stephen Street Upper	75 B1
Stephen's Lane	76 D2
Stephen's Place	76 D2
Stephen's Road	73 B2
Sterling Square Apts	8 D3
Stewart Hall	71 A3
Stillorgan	58 F1
*Stillorgan Court (off Upper Kilmacud Road Extension)	58 E1
Stillorgan Grove	48 F4
Stillorgan Heath	58 E1
Stillorgan Park	48 F4
Stillorgan Park	49 A4
Stillorgan Park Ave	58 F1
Stillorgan Road (Donnybrook)	48 D1
Stillorgan Road (Mount Merrion)	48 E3
Stillorgan Road (Stillorgan)	58 F1
Stillorgan Road (Foxrock)	59 A2
Stillorgan Wood	58 E1
*Stirling Park (off Orwell Road)	47 A3
Stirrup Lane (off Church Street)	70 F3
Stockhole	13 A2
Stockhole Lane	12 F1
Stocking Ave	56 D2
Stocking Lane	56 D3
Stocking Well	56 D2
Stocking Wood	56 D3
Stocking Wood Copse	56 D3
Stocking Wood Drive	56 D3
Stocking Wood Green	56 D3
Stocking Wood Hall	56 D3
Stocking Wood Heath	56 D3
Stocking Wood Manor	56 D3
Stocking Wood Rise	56 D3
Stocking Wood Walk	56 D3

STREET NAME	PAGE / GRID REFERENCE
Stocking Wood Way	56 D3
Stockton Court	23 A3
Stockton Drive	23 A3
Stockton Green	23 A3
Stockton Grove	23 A3
Stockton Lawn	23 A3
Stockton Park	23 A3
Stokes Place	75 B2
*Stone Mews (off Rathgar Road)	47 A1
Stonebridge	21 B2
Stonebridge Ave	21 B2
*Stonebridge Close (beside Post Office)	64 E3
Stonebridge Court	64 D3
Stonebridge Drive	21 B2
Stonebridge Grove	64 D3
*Stonebridge Lane (off Stonebridge Road)	64 D2
Stonebridge Road (Clonsilla)	21 B2
Stonebridge Road (Shankill)	64 D2
*Stonemasons Green (Broadford Cres)	57 A2
Stonemasons Way	57 A2
Stonepark Abbey	46 F4
Stonepark Court	46 F4
*Stonepark Orchard (off Stonepark Abbey)	46 F4
*Stoneview Place (off George's Street Upper)	50 D4
*Stoney Court (near James Street North)	72 E1
Stoney Park	52 F2
Stoney Road (East Wall)	72 E2
Stoney Road (Dundrum)	47 C4
Stoneybatter	70 E3
*Stoneylea Terrace (Vevay Road, Wolfe Tone Square)	67 C3
Store Street	71 C3
Stormanstown Road	25 A2
Stradbrook Close	59 B1
*Stradbrook Cottages (on Stradbrook Road)	49 B4
*Stradbrook Gardens (off Stradbrook Road)	49 B4
Stradbrook Grove	49 B4
*Stradbrook Hall (off Stradbrook Road)	49 B4
*Stradbrook Hill (off Abbey Road Monkstown)	59 B1
Stradbrook Lawn	49 B4
Stradbrook Park	49 B4
Stradbrook Road	49 B4
Straffan Ave	17 C4
Straffan Close	17 C4
Straffan Court	17 C4
Straffan Cres	17 C4
Straffan Drive	17 C4
Straffan Green	17 C4
Straffan Grove	17 C4
Straffan Lawn	17 C4
Straffan Park	17 C4
Straffan Place	17 C4
Straffan Road	17 C4
Straffan Way	17 C4
Straffan Wood	17 C4
Straleek	41 B1
Stralem Court	21 B1
Stralem Cres	21 B1
Stralem Grove	21 B1
Stralem Mews	21 B1
Stralem Terrace	21 B1
*Strand Court (on Strand Street Malahide)	3 B2
*Strand Lane (off St. John's Road East)	48 E1
*Strand Mews (Strand Road)	39 B4
Strand Road (Portmarnock)	4 D4
Strand Road (Portmarnock)	14 F2
Strand Road (Portmarnock)	15 A1
Strand Road (Baldoyle)	15 A4
Strand Road (Sutton)	29 B2
Strand Road (Sandymount)	39 B4
Strand Road (Merrion)	48 E1
Strand Road (Ballybrack)	64 E4
Strand Road (Bray)	68 D2
Strand Street (Malahide)	3 B2
Strand Street (Ringsend)	39 A3
Strand Street Great	71 A4
Strand Street Little	71 A4
*Strand Terrace (off Milltown Road)	47 B2
Strandmill Ave	14 F2

STREET NAME	PAGE / GRID REFERENCE
Strandmill Park	15 A2
Strandmill Road	15 A2
Strandville Ave (North Strand)	72 E1
Strandville Ave East (Clontarf)	26 D4
*Strandville House (off Strandville Ave East)	26 D4
Strandville Place	72 E1
Strangford Gardens	72 E2
Strangford Road	72 E2
*Strasburg Terrace (off Strand Street Ringsend)	39 A3
*Stratford (off Orwell Road Rathgar)	47 A2
Strathmore Road	60 E4
Stratton Grove	33 C3
Stratton Walk	33 C3
Streamstown Lane	2 F4
Streamstown Wood	2 F4
*Streamville Court (Abberley)	64 E1
Streamville Road	27 A1
Strong's Court	71 B2
Suffolk Street	75 B1
Sugarloaf Cres	67 C3
*Sugarloaf Terrace (Vevay Road, Putland Road)	67 C3
Suir Road	73 B2
Sullivan Street	69 C3
Summer Arch	71 C1
Summer Place	71 C2
*Summer Row (off Summer Street North)	71 C1
Summer Street North	71 C2
Summer Street South	74 E1
Summerfield (Blanchardstown)	22 E2
*Summerfield (off Irishtown Road)	39 A3
*Summerfield (off Watermeadow Park Tallaght)	55 A2
Summerfield Ave	22 E2
Summerfield Close	22 E2
*Summerfield Close (off Dalkey Ave)	60 F2
Summerfield Green	22 E2
Summerfield Lawns	22 E2
Summerfield Meadows	22 E2
Summerfield Rise	22 E2
Summerhill	71 C2
*Summerhill Court (Summerhill)	71 C2
*Summerhill Court (off Islington Ave)	50 E4
Summerhill Parade (Summerhill)	72 D1
*Summerhill Parade (off Summerhill Road)	50 D4
Summerhill Place	71 C2
Summerhill Road (Dunboyne)	7 A2
Summerhill Road (Dún Laoghaire)	50 D4
Summerseat	8 D4
Summerseat Cottage	8 D4
Summerseat Court	8 D4
Summerseat Cres	8 D4
Summerseat Drive	8 D4
Summerseat Estate	8 D4
Summerseat Walk	8 D4
Summerville	39 B1
Summerville Park	47 A1
*Summerville Terrace (on Dalkey Ave)	60 F2
Sunbury Court	47 A2
Sunbury Gardens	47 A2
*Sunbury Park (off Sunbury Gardens)	47 A2
Suncroft Ave	14 F2
Suncroft Drive	54 D2
Suncroft Park	54 D2
Sundale Ave	54 D2
Sundale Close	54 D2
Sundale Cres	54 D1
Sundale Green	54 D1
Sundale Grove	54 D2
Sundale Heights	54 D1
Sundale Lawn	54 D1
Sundale Meadows	54 D1
Sundale Parade	54 D1
Sundale Park	54 D2
Sundale Road	54 D2
Sundale Villas	54 D1
Sundale Walk	54 D1
Sundrive Park	46 E1
Sundrive Road	73 C4
Sunnybank Apts	69 B4

STREET NAME	PAGE / GRID REFERENCE
*Sunnybank Court (off Dundrum Road)	47 C4
*Sunnybank Court (off Upper Dargle Road)	67 B1
Sunnyside	62 F3
*Sunnyside Apts (Malahide Road)	26 E2
*Sunville Green (off Summerville Drive)	46 D1
Susan Terrace	74 F2
Susanville Road	25 B4
Sussex Road	76 D3
*Sussex Street (off Eblana Ave)	50 D4
Sussex Terrace	76 D3
Sutton	29 A1
Sutton Castle Apts	29 B3
Sutton Court (off Sutton Downs)	28 D1
Sutton Downs	28 D1
Sutton Grove	28 D1
Sutton Lane	63 A3
Sutton Lawns	28 D1
Sutton Park	28 D1
*Sutton Road (Pearse Square, Bray)	67 B2
*Sutton Villas (Pearse Square, Bray)	67 B2
Swallowbrook	8 F4
Swallowbrook Cres	8 F4
Swallowbrook Park	8 F4
Swallowbrook View	8 F4
Swan Alley	74 F1
Swan Grove	75 C4
*Swan Hall (off Belgard Square West)	54 F1
Swan Place	76 D4
Swan Yard (off Harry Street)	75 B1
Swanbrook	67 C4
Swan's Nest Ave	27 B1
Swan's Nest Court (Swan's Nest Ave)	27 B1
Swan's Nest Road	27 B1
*Swanville Place (off Rathmines Road Lower)	47 A1
Swanward Court	74 E4
Sweeney's Terrace	74 F2
Sweetbriar Lane	58 D1
Sweetman House	14 F4
*Sweetman's Ave (off Frascati Road Blackrock)	49 A3
Sweetman's Ave	49 A3
Sweetmount Ave	47 B4
Sweetmount Drive	57 B1
*Sweetmount House (off Beaumont Ave)	47 B4
Sweetmount Park	47 B4
Sweetmount Park	57 B1
Swift Hall	59 B4
Swiftbrook (Tallaght)	54 D1
Swiftbrook Ave	54 D1
Swiftbrook Close	54 D1
Swiftbrook Drive	54 D1
Swiftbrook Park	54 D1
Swift's Alley	74 F1
Swift's Grove	13 A3
Swift's Row (off Ormond Quay)	71 B4
Swiftwood	53 B1
Swilly Road	24 E4
Swords	2 E2
Swords Manor Ave	1 B2
Swords Manor Court	1 B1
Swords Manor Cres	1 B1
Swords Manor Drive	1 B1
Swords Manor Grove	1 B2
Swords Manor View	1 B1
Swords Manor Way	1 B1
Swords Road (Santry)	12 F4
Swords Road (Malahide)	3 A3
Swords Road (Collinstown)	12 F2
Swords Road (Santry)	25 B1
Swords Street	70 D3
Sybil Hill Ave	26 F3
Sybil Hill Road	26 F3
Sycamore Ave (Castleknock)	22 E3
Sycamore Ave (Tallaght)	45 A3
Sycamore Ave (Cabinteely)	59 B3
Sycamore Close (Kilnamanagh)	44 F3
Sycamore Close (Cornelscourt)	59 B3
*Sycamore Court (off Carriglea Ave Kill O'The Grange)	59 C2
Sycamore Cres (Mount Merrion)	48 E4
Sycamore Cres (Cabinteely)	59 B3

STREET NAME	PAGE / GRID REFERENCE
Sycamore Drive (Castleknock)	22 E3
Sycamore Drive (Tallaght)	45 A3
*Sycamore Drive (off Sycamore Road Dundrum)	57 B1
Sycamore Drive (Cabinteely)	59 B3
Sycamore Green (Cabinteely)	59 B3
*Sycamore Grove (off Pine Ave Foxrock)	59 A2
Sycamore Grove (Cabinteely)	59 B4
Sycamore House	76 D3
Sycamore House (Swords)	1 Inset
Sycamore House (Sutton)	28 D1
*Sycamore House (at Eaton Wood Square)	64 E2
Sycamore Lawn (Castleknock)	22 E3
Sycamore Lawn (Cabinteely)	59 B3
Sycamore Park (Castleknock)	22 E3
Sycamore Park (Finglas)	24 E1
Sycamore Park (Tallaght)	45 A3
Sycamore Road (Finglas)	24 E1
Sycamore Road (Fox and Geese)	45 A1
Sycamore Road (Mount Merrion)	48 E4
Sycamore Road (Dundrum)	57 B1
Sycamore Street	71 B4
Sycamore View	22 E3
Sycamore Walk	59 B4
*Sydenham (off Corrig Ave)	50 D4
*Sydenham Court (off Sandymount Ave)	39 A4
Sydenham Mews	68 D3
*Sydenham Place (on Kilmacud Rd Upr)	47 C4
*Sydenham Road (off Merrion Road)	39 A4
Sydenham Road (Dundrum)	47 C4
Sydenham Villas (Dundrum)	57 C1
*Sydenham Villas (near Sydenham Mews)	68 D3
Sydney Ave	49 A3
Sydney Parade Ave	48 E1
Sydney Terrace	49 A3
Sylvan Ave	45 A3
Sylvan Close	44 F3
Sylvan Drive	44 F3
Symphony House	75 C3
Synge House	47 A3
Synge Lane	75 A3
Synge Place	75 B3
Synge Street	75 B3
Synge Way	35 C4
Synnott Lane	71 B1
Synnott Place	71 B1
Synnott Row	71 B1
*Synnott Terrace (off Dunleary Road)	49 C4
Synod Hall	75 A1

T

STREET NAME	PAGE / GRID REFERENCE
Taaffe's Place	72 E1
Tailors Court	75 A1
Tailor's Hall	75 A1
Talbot	2 F3
Talbot Ave	2 F3
Talbot Court (Malahide)	3 A2
Talbot Court (Blanchardstown)	22 F2
Talbot Downs	22 F2
Talbot Hall (Swords)	1 Inset
*Talbot House (Granby Lane)	71 A2
Talbot Lane (Talbot Street)	71 C3
*Talbot Lane (off Ballinclea Road)	60 E3
Talbot Lodge	48 F4
Talbot Memorial Bridge (River Liffey)	71 C4
Talbot Park	2 F3
Talbot Place	71 C3
Talbot Road (Swords)	2 F3
*Talbot Road (off Killiney Hill Road)	60 E3
Talbot Street	71 C3
Tallaght	55 A1
Tallaght Bypass	54 F1
Tallaght Bypass	55 A1
Tallaght Road	55 B1
*Tallow Hall (off Belgard Square West)	54 F1
Tamarisk Ave	45 A3
Tamarisk Close	45 A3
Tamarisk Court	45 A3
Tamarisk Dale	45 A3
Tamarisk Drive	45 A3

STREET NAME	PAGE / GRID REFERENCE
Tamarisk Grove	45 A3
Tamarisk Heights	45 A3
Tamarisk Lawn	45 A3
Tamarisk Park	45 A3
Tamarisk View	45 A3
Tamarisk Walk	45 A3
Tamarisk Way	45 A3
*Tandy Court Apts (off Spitalfields)	74 F1
Tandys Lane	33 C3
Tandys Lane	34 D3
Taney Ave	47 C4
Taney Court	47 C4
Taney Cres	47 C4
Taney Drive	47 C4
Taney Grove	47 C4
*Taney Hall (off Eglinton Terrace)	47 C4
Taney Lawn	47 C4
Taney Manor	47 C4
Taney Park	47 C4
Taney Rise	47 C4
Taney Road	47 C4
Tangier Lane (off Grafton Street)	75 B1
*Tara Cres (off Kilakee Green)	55 B2
Tara Hill Cres	46 F4
*Tara Hill Grove (off St. Patrick's Cottages)	46 F4
Tara Hill Road	46 F4
Tara Lawn	27 A1
Tara Street	71 C4
Tassagard Greens	53 B2
Tassagart Drive	53 A2
*Tathony House Apts (off Mount Brown)	74 D1
Tay Lane	52 E2
Taylors Court	56 E1
Taylor's Hill	57 A3
Taylor's Lane (Pimlico)	74 E1
Taylor's Lane (Ballyboden)	56 E1
Teeling Way	72 F2
Temple Bar	71 B4
Temple Buildings	71 A2
Temple Cottages	71 A2
Temple Court (off Hogan Place)	76 E1
Temple Court (Arbour Hill)	70 D3
*Temple Court (off Temple Road)	49 A3
Temple Court Apts	12 E4
Temple Cres	49 B4
Temple Gardens (Santry)	12 E4
Temple Gardens (Milltown)	47 B2
Temple Grove	32 D3
*Temple Hall Apts. (off Milltown Road)	47 B2
*Temple Hill (on Terenure Road West)	46 E2
Temple Hill	49 B4
Temple Lane North	71 B2
Temple Lane South	71 B4
*Temple Lawns (at Temple Gardens Santry)	12 E4
Temple Lawns (Celbridge)	32 D4
Temple Manor (Dunboyne)	7 B2
Temple Manor (Celbridge)	31 C4
Temple Manor (Greenhills)	45 C3
Temple Manor Ave	45 C3
Temple Manor Close	45 C3
Temple Manor Court	45 C3
Temple Manor Drive	45 C3
Temple Manor Grove	45 C3
Temple Manor Way	45 C3
Temple Park	47 B2
*Temple Park Apts	12 E4
Temple Park Ave	49 B4
Temple Place	75 C4
Temple Place	71 B2
Temple Road (Rathgar)	47 B2
Temple Road (Blackrock)	49 A3
*Temple Square (off Orchard Road South)	47 B2
Temple Street North	71 B2
Temple Street West	70 D4
*Temple Terrace (off Coliemore Road)	60 F2
Temple Villas (Arbour Hill)	70 D3
*Temple Villas (on Palmerston Road)	47 B1
*Temple Villas (off Cowper Road)	47 B2
Templemore Ave	47 A2
Templeogue	46 D4
Templeogue Lodge	46 D4

STREET NAME	PAGE / GRID REFERENCE
Templeogue Road	46 E3
Templeogue Wood	46 D4
Templeroan	56 D1
Templeroan Ave	56 D1
Templeroan Close	56 E1
Templeroan Court	56 D1
Templeroan Cres	56 D1
Templeroan Downs	56 E1
Templeroan Drive	56 D1
Templeroan Green	56 D2
Templeroan Grove	56 D1
Templeroan Lodge	56 D2
Templeroan Meadows	56 E1
Templeroan Mews	56 D1
Templeroan Park	56 D1
Templeroan View	56 D1
Templeroan Way	56 D1
Templeview Ave	14 D4
Templeview Close	14 D4
Templeview Copse	14 D4
Templeview Court	14 D4
Templeview Cres	14 D4
Templeview Downs	14 D4
Templeview Drive	14 D4
Templeview Green	14 D4
Templeview Grove	14 D4
Templeview Lawn	14 D4
Templeview Park	14 D4
Templeview Place	14 D4
Templeview Rise	14 D4
Templeview Row	14 D4
Templeview Square	14 D4
Templeview Vale	14 D4
Templeview View	14 D4
Templeview Walk	14 D4
Templeview Way	14 D4
Templeville Ave	46 D3
Templeville Drive	46 D3
*Templeville Park (off Templeville Road)	46 E3
Templeville Road	46 D3
Tenterfields	74 E2
Terenure	46 F2
Terenure Park	46 F2
*Terenure Place (off Hannaville Park)	46 F2
Terenure Road East	46 F2
Terenure Road North	46 F2
Terenure Road West	46 E2
Terminal Road North	39 C2
Terminal Road South	39 C2
Termon	60 F2
Termon Court (off Gallaun Road)	11 C4
Terrace Place (off Bella Street)	71 C2
Tetrarch Grove	7 C1
Texas Lane	3 A2
*The Alders (off Monkstown Valley)	49 B4
*The Alders (off Northwood Ave)	12 E4
*The Alders (Carrington)	12 E4
*The Anchora Apts (adjacent Townyard Lane)	3 B2
*The Anchorage (off Clarence Street Dún Laoghaire)	49 C4
The Anchorage (Robswall)	4 D3
*The Anchorage Apts	76 F1
The Appian Way	76 D4
The Arches	17 C3
*The Atrium Apts (Island Street)	70 E4
The Ave (Plunkett Hall)	7 A2
The Ave (Lutterell Hall)	7 B2
The Ave (Dunboyne Castle)	7 B3
The Ave (Mulhuddart Wood)	9 A4
The Ave (Louisa Valley)	19 C4
The Ave (Manorfields)	21 B1
The Ave (Celbridge)	32 D3
The Ave (St. Wolston's Abbey)	32 D4
The Ave (Grange Manor)	34 D3
The Ave (Tallaght)	44 F3
The Ave (Templeogue)	46 D3
The Ave (Ballyboden)	56 E2
The Ave (Ballinteer)	57 C2
The Ave (Carrickmines)	63 A1
The Ave (Ongar)	21 A1
*The Barley Store Apts (off Portland Street North)	71 C1
The Bawn	3 B3
The Bawn Grove	3 B3
The Bay Apts (Merrion Road)	48 E2

STREET NAME	PAGE	GRID REFERENCE
*The Beaches (off Northwood Ave)	12	E4
*The Beaches (at The Gallops)	58	E4
The Beeches (Donaghmede)	27	A1
*The Beeches (off Monkstown Valley)	49	B4
*The Beeches (off Barton Drive Willbrook)	56	F1
The Beeches (Kilmacud)	58	D1
*The Beeches (Abberley)	64	E1
*The Beeches (Carrington)	12	E4
The Belfry (Inchicore)	73	A1
The Belfry (Kilbarrack)	27	B1
The Belfry (Citywest Road)	53	C2
*The Belfry Apts (off Collins Ave West)	25	C2
*The Birch (off Overend Way Dundrum)	57	C1
The Birches	59	A3
*The Birches Apts (adjacent Courtview Apts)	23	C3
The Black Ave	33	B1
*The Blackthorn (off Overend Way Dundrum)	57	C1
The Boulevard	9	A2
The Bramblings	26	E3
The Briars	35	C1
The Bridge	64	E3
The Brokerage Apts	71	C4
The Burgage	60	F2
*The Castlelands (off The Courtyard)	46	F4
*The Cedars (off Monkstown Valley)	49	B4
*The Cedars (Abberley)	64	E1
*The Cedars (off Northwood Ave)	12	E4
*The Cedars (Carrington)	12	E4
*The Cedars Apts	76	F4
The Chandler Apts	23	B3
*The Charter (adjacent Santry Cross Junction)	12	D4
The Chase	58	F2
*The Cherries (off Grange Wood)	57	A2
*The Claremont (adjacent Santry Cross Junction)	12	D4
*The Cloisters (off Grace Park Road)	25	B3
The Cloisters (Mount Tallant Ave)	46	F2
The Close (Plunkett Hall)	7	A2
The Close (Dunboyne Castle)	7	A3
The Close (Lutterell Hall)	7	B2
The Close (Manorfields)	21	B1
The Close (Beaumont)	25	C1
The Close (Oldtown Mill)	31	C3
The Close (Celbridge)	31	C3
The Close (Temple Manor)	31	C4
The Close (Grange Manor)	34	D3
The Close (Tallaght)	44	F3
The Close (Templeogue)	46	D3
The Close (Mount Merrion)	48	E3
*The Close (off The Wood Tallaght)	55	A2
The Close (Ballyboden)	56	E2
The Close (Ballinteer)	57	C2
*The Close (Robswall)	3	C3
The Close (Moyglare Hall)	17	C1
The Clovers	23	A3
The Coachworks	75	A3
The Coombe	74	F1
The Coppice (Palmerstown)	35	C1
The Coppins (Celbridge)	32	D3
The Coppins (Foxrock)	59	A3
The Copse (Drumcondra)	25	B3
The Copse (Weston)	33	B2
*The Copse (off The Heights Ballinteer)	57	B2
The Court (Lutterell Hall)	7	B2
The Court (Plunkett Hall)	7	A2
The Court (Sadleir Hall)	7	A2
The Court (Dunboyne Castle)	7	B3
The Court (Mulhuddart Wood)	9	A4
The Court (Larch Hill)	12	F4
The Court (Whitehall)	25	C2
The Court (Clontarf)	26	D4
The Court (off The Village Raheny)	27	B3
The Court (Celbridge)	31	C3
The Court (Oldtown Mill)	31	C3
The Court (Temple Manor)	31	C4
The Court (Tallaght)	44	F3
The Court (Tallaght)	44	F4
The Court (Templeogue)	46	D3
The Court (Donnybrook)	47	C2
The Court (Ballinteer)	57	B2
The Court (Carrickmines)	59	B4
The Court (Ballybrack)	60	E4
The Court (Glenamuck Road)	63	A1
The Court (Shankill)	64	E3
*The Court (Glasnevin)	25	A4
*The Court (Robswall)	4	D3
The Court (Moyglare Hall)	17	C2
The Court (Blanchardstown)	22	F2
*The Court Apts (adjacent Emmet Place)	70	F4
The Courthouse	52	F2
The Courtyard (Grants Row)	76	D1
The Courtyard (Hill Street)	71	B2
The Courtyard (in Parkview Estate)	1	A2
The Courtyard (Clonsilla)	22	D3
The Courtyard (Celbridge)	31	C4
The Courtyard (Templelogue)	46	E3
The Courtyard (Rathfarnham)	46	F4
The Courtyard (Leopardstown)	58	E2
The Courtyard (Bray)	67	B2
*The Courtyard (Robswall)	3	C3
*The Courtyard (off Foxrock Park)	59	A2
The Cove	3	A2
*The Covert (off The Coppice)	35	C1
*The Cres (on Foster Way)	2	D2
The Cres (Malahide)	4	D3
The Cres (Plunkett Hall)	7	A2
The Cres (Lutterell Hall)	7	A2
The Cres (Dunboyne Castle)	7	B3
The Cres (Mulhuddart)	9	A4
The Cres (Larch Hill)	12	F4
The Cres (College Grove)	22	F3
The Cres (Whitehall)	25	B3
*The Cres (off Beaumont Road)	25	C2
The Cres (Oldtown Mill)	31	C3
The Cres (Abbeyfarm)	31	C4
The Cres (Temple Manor)	31	C4
The Cres (St. Wolston's Abbey)	32	D4
The Cres (Lucan)	33	C2
The Cres (Grange Manor)	34	D3
The Cres (Tallaght)	44	E4
The Cres (Tallaght)	44	F3
The Cres (Ranelagh)	47	B1
*The Cres (off Donnybrook Road)	47	C1
The Cres (Tallaght)	55	A1
The Cres (Ballyboden)	56	E2
*The Cres (off The Walk Ballinteer)	57	B2
The Cres (Carrickmines)	63	A1
*The Cres (Robswall)	4	D3
The Cres (Moyglare Hall)	17	C1
The Cres (Ongar)	21	A1
The Cres (Park West)	35	C4
The Cres (Kimmage)	46	E3
The Croft	32	D2
The Dale (Dunboyne)	7	B2
The Dale (Manorfields)	21	B1
The Dale (Celbridge)	31	C3
The Dale (Kilnamanagh)	44	F3
The Dale (Belgard)	44	F4
*The Dale (off The Heights Ballinteer)	57	B2
The Dale (Carrickmines)	63	A1
The Dale (Bray)	67	B2
*The Dale (Moyglare Hall)	17	C2
*The Deanery (beside Vanessa Lawns)	31	C3
The Dell	57	A2
The Dingle	35	B2
*The Distillery Apts (Distillery Road)	25	B4
*The Distillery Building Apts (off Distillery Road)	25	B4
The Downs (Dunboyne Castle)	7	A3
The Downs (St. Wolston's Abbey)	32	D4
The Drive (Sadlier Hall)	7	A2
The Drive (Lutterell Hall)	7	B2
The Drive (Dunboyne Castle)	7	B3
The Drive (Mulhuddart Wood)	9	A4
The Drive (Manorfields)	21	B1
The Drive (Oldtown Mill)	31	C3
The Drive (Abbeyfarm)	31	C4
The Drive (Temple Manor)	31	C4
The Drive (Grange Manor)	34	D3
The Drive (Kilnamanagh)	44	F3
The Drive (Tallaght)	55	A1
The Drive (Ballyboden)	56	E1
The Drive (Ballinteer)	57	B2
The Drive (Woodbrook Glen)	67	C1
*The Drive Apts	56	E1
The Dunes	15	A1
The Elm (Rockfield)	57	C1
The Elms (Dunboyne)	7	B2
The Elms (Celbridge)	32	D2
The Elms (Elm Park)	48	E2
*The Elms (opposite Sheelin Drive)	64	E1
The Elms (Crinken Lane)	64	E3
*The Elms (off Northwood Ave)	12	E4
*The Elms (Carrington)	12	E4
*The Elms Apts (adjacent Courtview Apts)	23	C3
The Fairways (Portmarnock)	14	E2
The Fairways (Woodbrook Glen)	67	C1
*The Fairways Apts	8	D3
*The Falls (off Dodder Road Lower Rathfarnham)	46	F3
The Forum	58	E2
The Fosters	48	E3
*The Foundary Apts (Beaver Street)	72	D2
The Gables (Old Cabra Road)	70	D1
The Gables (Grange View Road)	43	B1
The Gables (Rathgar)	47	A2
The Gables (Nutgrove)	57	A1
The Gables (Dundrum)	57	B1
*The Gables (off Torquay Road Foxrock)	59	A3
The Gallan	60	D3
The Gallops	58	E3
The Gardens	63	A1
The Garth (Cookstown)	44	E4
The Garth (Kingswood Heights)	44	F3
The Gasworks	76	F1
The Gate	44	D1
The Gate Lodge	30	E3
The Glade (Palmerstown)	35	B2
The Glade (Oldtown Mill)	31	C3
The Glade (St. Wolston's Abbey)	32	D4
The Glade (Kingswood Heights)	44	F3
The Glade (Ballinteer)	57	B2
The Glebe	34	E2
The Glen (Louisa Valley)	19	C4
The Glen (Raheny)	27	B3
The Glen (Ballyboden)	56	E1
The Glen (Ballinteer)	57	B2
The Glen (Clon Burgh)	58	D3
*The Glen (off Glenageary Road Lower)	60	D1
The Glen (Oldtown Mill)	31	C2
The Glens	63	A1
*The Goulding (adjacent Santry Cross Junction)	12	D4
The Grainhouse	74	E2
*The Granary (Long's Place)	74	E1
The Grange (Malahide)	3	B4
The Grange (Terenure)	46	F2
The Grange (Deans Grange)	59	B1
*The Grange Apts (off Brewery Road)	58	F1
The Green (Malahide)	3	B2
The Green (Lutterell Hall)	7	B2
The Green (Dunboyne Castle)	7	B3
The Green (Mulhuddart Wood)	9	A4
The Green (Larch Hill)	12	F4
The Green (Moyglare Abbey)	17	B2
The Green (Manorfields)	21	B1
The Green (Beaumont)	25	C1
The Green (Celbridge)	31	C3
The Green (Oldtown Mill)	31	C3
The Green (Tallaght)	44	F3
The Green (Templeogue)	46	D3
The Green (Ballyboden)	56	E1
The Green (Ballinteer)	57	B2
The Green (Carrickmines)	63	A1
The Green (Woodbrook Glen)	67	C1
*The Green (Robswall)	3	C3
The Green (Moyglare Hall)	17	C2
The Green Road	60	G2
The Greenlands	46	F4
The Grove (Plunkett Hall)	7	A2
The Grove (Sadleir Hall)	7	A2
The Grove (Dunboyne Castle)	7	A3
The Grove (Lutterell Hall)	7	B2
The Grove (Louisa Valley)	19	C4
The Grove (Whitehall)	25	B3
The Grove (off The Village Raheny)	27	B3
The Grove (Abbeyfarm)	31	C4
The Grove (St. Wolston's Abbey)	32	D4
The Grove (Grange Manor)	34	D3
The Grove (Tallaght)	44	E4
The Grove (Tallaght)	44	F3
The Grove (Tallaght)	55	A1
The Grove (Dundrum)	57	A1
The Grove (Ballinteer)	57	B2
The Grove (Woodbrook Glen)	67	C1
*The Haggard (streets between Tuckett's Lane and Main Street)	30	D2
The Hall	46	F2
*The Hampton (adjacent Santry Cross Junction)	12	D4
*The Hardwick Apts (near Catherine Lane)	70	F3
*The Hardwicke Apts (Church Street Upper)	70	F3
The Haven (Malahide)	3	B2
*The Haven (off St. Mobhi Boithirin)	25	A3
*The Hawthorns (Abberley)	64	E1
*The Hawthorns (off Northwood Ave)	12	E4
*The Hawthorns (Carrington)	12	E4
The Heath (Tallaght)	44	F4
The Heath (Templeogue)	46	D3
The Heath (Ballinteer)	57	B2
The Hedgerows	59	A3
The Heights (Dunboyne Castle)	7	B3
The Heights (Ballinteer)	57	B2
*The Heights (Robswall)	3	C3
*The Hibernian Apts	76	F1
The Hill (Malahide)	3	B3
The Hill (Mulhuddart Wood)	9	A4
The Hill (Monkstown)	49	C4
The Hill (Ballinteer)	57	C2
The Hill (Clon Burgh)	58	D3
The Hill (Stillorgan)	58	F1
The Hole in the Wall Road	14	E4
*The Hollows (adjacent Adamstown Court)	34	D2
The Holly (Rockfield)	57	C1
*The Hops (off Basin Street Lower)	74	D2
*The Innings Apts (off Rathmines Road Lower)	47	A1
The Island	36	E2
*The Ivory Buildings Apts (Hanover Street East)	72	E4
The Killigeen	52	D4
*The Kilmore (adjacent Santry Cross Junction)	12	D4
The Kilns	14	F2
*The Lakelands (off Rathfarnham Wood)	46	F4
*The Landey (adjacent Santry Cross Junction)	12	D4
*The Larches (Abberley)	64	E1
The Laurels (Dollymount)	26	F4
*The Laurels (off Bluebell Ave)	36	E4
The Laurels (Terenure)	46	F2
*The Laurels (off Main Street Rathfarnham)	46	F4
*The Laurels (off Main Street Tallaght)	55	A1
The Laurels (Churchtown)	47	B4
The Laurels (Hazelhatch)	41	B1
The Lawn (Plunkett Hall)	7	A2
The Lawn (Moyglare Abbey)	17	B2
The Lawn (Finglas)	24	E2
The Lawn (Oldtown Mill)	31	C3
The Lawn (Tallaght)	44	E4
The Lawn (Ballyboden)	56	E2
The Lawn (Ballinteer)	57	B2
The Lawn (Woodbrook Glen)	67	C1
The Lawns (Abbeyfarm)	31	C4
The Lawns (Temple Manor)	31	C4
*The Lighthouse (Robswall)	4	D3
The Lime (Rockfield)	57	C1
*The Linden (off Overend Way Dundrum)	57	C1
The Links	14	F2
The Links Apts (Merrion Road)	48	E2
The Little Grove	32	D4
The Lodge (Clontarf)	26	D4
The Lodge (Glenageary)	60	D1
*The Lodge Apts (adjacent Courtview Apts)	23	C3
*The Maieston (adjacent Santry Cross Junction)	12	D4
The Mall (Malahide)	3	B2

STREET NAME	PAGE / GRID REFERENCE
The Mall (Baldoyle)	15 A4
The Mall (Leixlip)	33 A1
The Mall (Lucan)	34 D1
*The Mall (off Main Street Ongar)	21 A1
The Malt House	74 E2
The Maltings	67 C2
The Maltings Apts	70 E4
*The Manor (off Kimmage Road West)	46 D2
The Manor (Templeogue)	46 D4
The Maples (Bird Ave)	47 C3
*The Maples (off Monkstown Valley)	49 B4
The Mayne	8 E2
The Meadow	57 B2
The Meadows (Dunboyne)	7 B2
The Meadows (Killester)	26 F3
The Meadows (Oldtown Mill)	31 C3
The Meadows (Newtownpark Ave)	59 A1
The Meadows East	44 F4
The Meadows West	44 E4
The Mews (Hill Street)	71 B2
The Mews (Killester)	26 E3
The Mews (Clontarf)	26 E4
*The Mews (off Clontarf Road)	27 A4
The Mews (Templeogue)	46 E3
*The Mews (off Castlewood Ave)	47 A1
*The Mews (Robswall)	4 D3
The Mews (Ribh Road)	26 F2
*The Mews Apts (adjacent Courtview Apts)	23 C3
The Mill	74 E2
*The Mill Pond Apts (off Nangor Road)	44 D1
The Mills	22 F2
The Moorings (Portobello Harbour)	75 B4
The Moorings (Malahide)	3 C3
The Moorings (Chapelizod)	36 E2
*The Moorings (off Fitzwilliam Quay)	39 A3
The Moorings (Clontarf)	26 F4
The Moorings Apts (off Merrion Road)	76 E3
The New Road	23 B1
The Northumberlands	76 E2
The Nurseries (Swords)	1 C3
The Nurseries (Mulhuddart)	9 B4
*The Nurseries (off Wyattville Road Ballybrack)	60 E4
The Nurseries (Oldcourt)	67 B3
The Oaks (Swords)	1 B3
The Oaks (Hollystown)	9 C1
The Oaks (Dollymount)	27 A4
The Oaks (Celbridge)	32 D3
The Oaks (Belgard)	44 E4
The Oaks (Churchtown)	47 B4
The Oaks (Ballinteer)	57 B2
*The Oaks (off Loughlinstown Drive)	64 D1
*The Oaks (Abberley)	64 E1
*The Oaks (Rockfield)	57 C1
*The Oaks (off Northwood Ave)	12 E4
*The Oaks (at The Gallops)	58 E4
*The Oaks (Carrington)	12 E4
*The Oaks Apts	76 F4
*The Oar House Apts (off Portland Street North)	71 C1
*The Observatory (Windmill Lane)	72 D4
*The Old Convent Apts (off Basin Street Lower)	74 D1
*The Old Distillery Apts (off Allingham Street)	74 E2
The Old Forge	34 D3
The Old Golf Links	3 C3
*The Old Presbytery (off Cambridge Park)	39 A3
*The Old Schoolhouse (off Milltown Ave)	47 B2
*The OldeDock Apts (Ship Street Little)	75 A1
The Orchard (Clarehall)	14 D4
The Orchard (Carpenterstown)	22 D3
The Orchard (Killester)	26 E3
The Orchard (Palmerston)	35 B1
The Orchard (Oldtown Mill)	31 C3
*The Orchard (near Primrose Lane)	34 D1
The Orchard (Kimmage)	46 E2
*The Orchard (off Seapoint Ave)	49 B3
The Orchard (Deans Grange)	59 A1
The Orchard (Fassaroe)	67 A2
The Orchard (Lucan)	34 D1
*The Orchard (off Hollybank Ave Upper)	47 B1
*The Orchard Apts	35 B3
*The Orchards (Seafield Road)	60 E4
The Oval	35 C2
The Paddock (Moyglare Abbey)	17 B2
The Paddock (Ashtown)	23 C4
The Paddock (Oldtown Mill)	31 C2
The Paddocks (Kilmainham)	73 B2
The Paddocks (Swords)	2 D2
The Paddocks (Dunboyne)	7 B2
*The Paddocks (off Ulverton Road Dalkey)	60 F1
*The Paddocks (Ongar Village)	21 A1
*The Paddock's (off Seaview Ave North Clontarf)	26 E4
The Paddocks Cres	33 C2
The Paddocks Drive	33 C2
The Paddocks Place	33 C2
The Paddocks Rise	33 C2
The Paddocks Road	33 C2
The Paddocks Square	33 C3
The Paddocks View	33 C2
The Paddocks Walk	33 C2
The Paddocks Way	33 C2
The Palms	48 D3
The Park (Plunkett Hall)	7 A2
The Park (Dunboyne Castle)	7 B3
The Park (Larch Hill)	12 F4
The Park (Louisa Valley)	19 C4
The Park (Beaumont)	25 C1
The Park (Celbridge)	31 C3
The Park (Oldtown Mill)	31 C3
The Park (Abbeyfarm)	31 C4
The Park (Grange Manor)	34 D3
The Park (Tallaght)	44 F3
The Park (Templeogue)	46 D3
The Park (Tallaght)	55 A2
The Park (Clon Burgh)	58 D3
The Park (Lutterell Hall)	7 A2
The Park Apts	75 B4
*The Park Lands (off Castleside Drive)	46 F4
*The Pidgeon House Apts	76 F1
The Pines (Castleknock)	23 A3
The Pines (Killester)	26 E3
The Pines (Ballinteer)	57 B2
*The Pines (off Woodley Park Kilmacud)	58 D1
The Pines (Oldcourt)	67 B3
*The Pines Apts	76 F4
The Place (Dunboyne Castle)	7 B3
The Place (Carrickmines)	63 A1
The Place	42 D4
The Plantation	76 D2
*The Plaza (Forster Way Swords)	2 D2
The Plaza Apts	9 B2
*The Poplars (off Monkstown Valley)	49 B4
*The Priory (off St. Margarets Ave Malahide)	3 B2
The Priory (Cabra)	24 D4
The Priory (Grange Road)	56 F1
The Quarry	4 D4
The Ramparts	63 C1
The Rectory (Raheny)	27 A2
The Rectory (Stepaside)	58 D4
*The Red Mill Apts (Brunswick Street North)	70 F3
*The Richmond Apts (Brunswick Street North)	70 F3
The Rise (Malahide)	3 B3
The Rise (Manorfields)	21 B1
The Rise (Glasnevin)	25 A2
The Rise (Newcastle)	42 D4
The Rise (Tallaght)	44 E4
The Rise (Tallaght)	44 F3
The Rise (Mount Merrion)	48 E4
The Rise (Ballyboden)	56 E2
The Rise (Ballinteer)	57 B2
The Rise (Dalkey)	60 E2
The Rise (Carrickmines)	63 A1
The Road (Manorfields)	21 B1
The Rookery	56 D2
The Rose	9 B2
The Rowan (Rockfield)	57 C1
*The Rowans (Abberley)	64 E1
The Sand Holes	22 F4
The Scalp	63 A4
The Slopes	49 C4
The Spinnaker (Robswall)	4 D3
The Spruce	9 B2
The Square (Larch Hill)	12 F4
*The Square (off Main Street Lucan)	34 D1
*The Square (off Irishtown Road)	39 A3
The Square (Greenogue Industrial Estate)	42 E4
The Square (Tallaght)	54 F1
*The Stables (off Hampton Cres)	48 E3
*The Stables Apts (adjacent Courtview Apts)	23 C3
The Steeple (Moyglare Abbey)	17 B2
The Steeples	36 E3
*The Steps Apts (on Kilmainham Lane)	73 B1
The Stiles Road	26 E4
The Summit (Howth)	30 E3
*The Sweepstakes (off Merrion Road)	39 A4
The Sycamore (Rockfield)	57 C1
*The Sycamore (at The Gallops)	58 E4
*The Sycamores (opposite Sheelin Drive)	64 E1
*The Sycamores (off Northwood Ave)	12 E4
The Sycamores (Malahide)	3 C3
*The Sycamores (Carrington)	12 E4
*The Tallow Apts (north of Ashtown Station)	23 C3
*The Tap Apts (King Street North)	70 F3
The Terrace	63 A1
The Thatch Road	25 C2
The Thicket	59 A3
*The Tower (Smithfield)	70 F4
*The Tramyard Apts (off Thomas Davis Street West)	36 F3
*The Turnpike (adjacent Santry Cross Junction)	12 D4
The Vale	35 C1
The View (Dunboyne Castle)	7 A3
The View (Larch Hill)	12 F4
The View (Manorfields)	21 B1
The View (Celbridge)	31 C3
The View (Oldtown Mill)	31 C3
The View (St. Wolston's Abbey)	32 D4
The View (Tallaght)	44 F3
The View (Tallaght)	55 B1
The View (Ballinteer)	57 B2
The View (Carrickmines)	63 A1
*The View (Robswall)	3 C3
*The Village (Clonsilla)	21 C3
*The Village (off Drumcondra Road Upper)	25 B3
The Village (Raheny)	27 B3
*The Village Centre (Lucan Village)	34 D1
*The Village Court (Lucan Village)	34 D1
The Village Gate	60 F2
The Walk (Dunboyne Castle)	7 B3
The Walk (Louisa Valley)	19 C4
The Walk (Manorfields)	21 B1
The Walk (Oldtown Mill)	31 C3
The Walk (Templeogue)	46 D3
The Walk (Tallaght)	55 A1
The Walk (Ballinteer)	57 B2
The Walk (Carrickmines)	63 A1
*The Walk (Robswall)	3 C3
The Walk (Moyglare Hall)	17 C2
The Walled Gardens	32 D2
The Walled Orchard	33 B1
*The Warehouse Apts (Clanbrassil Terrace)	74 F2
The Warren	2 F3
*The Watercourse (off Rossmore Road)	46 D4
*The Waterfront (Cian Park)	25 B4
*The Waxworks Apts (north of Ashtown Station)	23 C3
The Way (Dunboyne Castle)	7 B3
*The Weaver Apts (off Meath Place)	74 F1
The Weir	36 E2
*The Wheat Barn Apts (off Portland Street North)	71 C1
The Wicklow Way	61 C4
The Willow	9 B2
The Willow (Rockfield)	57 C1
The Willows (Glasnevin)	24 F3
The Willows (Celbridge)	32 D3
*The Willows (off Claremont Road)	39 A4
*The Willows (off Orwell Road)	47 A3
*The Willows (off Monkstown Valley)	49 B4
*The Willows (Abberley)	64 E1
*The Willows (off Northwood Ave)	12 E4
*The Willows (Carrington)	12 E4
*The Windmill Apts (near Windmill Lane Apts)	72 D4
The Wood (Tallaght)	55 A2
The Wood (Clon Burgh)	58 D3
The Wood (Carrickmines)	63 A1
The Wood (Crinken Lane)	64 E3
*The Wooden Buildings Apts (Exchange Street Upper)	71 A4
The Woodlands (Celbridge)	32 D3
*The Woodlands (off Rathfarnham Wood)	46 F4
*The Woods (off Charlemont)	25 C3
*The Works (Inchicore terrace South)	36 F3
*Theresa House (off Stonepark Court)	46 F4
Third Ave (Seville Place)	72 E3
Third Ave (Tallaght)	44 F4
Thirlestane Terrace	74 F1
Thomas Court	74 E1
*Thomas Court Barn (off Marrowbone Lane)	74 E1
*Thomas Court Bawn (at School Street)	74 E1
*Thomas Davis Court (on Sutton Downs near Bayside Square South)	27 C1
Thomas Davis Street (West)	36 F3
Thomas Davis Street South	74 F1
Thomas Lane	71 B3
*Thomas Moore Court (off Bayside Square South)	27 C1
Thomas Moore Road	45 C1
Thomas Street	74 F1
Thomas Street West	74 E1
*Thomastown Cres (off Sallynoggin Road)	60 D2
Thomastown Road	60 D3
*Thomond (at Eaton Wood Square)	64 E2
Thomond Road	36 E3
Thompson's Cottages	71 C2
Thor Place	70 D3
*Thormanby Grove (south of Church on Main Street Howth)	30 D2
Thormanby Lawns	30 D2
Thormanby Lodge	30 E2
Thormanby Road	30 E2
Thormanby Woods	30 E2
Thorn Wood	48 E3
Thornberry Apts	8 F4
*Thorncastle Court Apts (off Thorncastle Street)	39 A2
Thorncastle Street	39 A2
*Thorncliff (off Dundrum Road)	47 B2
Thorncliffe Park	47 B3
Thorndale Ave	26 D2
*Thorndale Court (off Collinswood)	25 C2
Thorndale Cres	26 D2
Thorndale Drive	26 D3
Thorndale Grove	26 D3
Thorndale Lawns	26 D2
Thorndale Park	26 D2
Thornfield Square	44 E1
Thornhill Court	31 C2
Thornhill Gardens	31 C2
Thornhill Heights	31 C2
Thornhill Lane	27 A4
Thornhill Meadows	31 C2
Thornhill Road (Kilmacud)	48 E4
Thornhill Road (Bray)	67 A2
*Thornhill View (north of Old Connaught Grove)	67 B1
Thornleigh Ave	1 Inset
Thornleigh Close	1 Inset
Thornleigh Court	1 Inset
Thornleigh Green	1 Inset
Thornleigh Grove	1 Inset
Thornleigh Lane	1 Inset
Thornleigh Park	1 Inset
Thornleigh Place	1 Inset
Thornleigh Road	1 Inset
Thornleigh Row	1 Inset
Thornville Ave	27 B1

STREET NAME	PAGE / GRID REFERENCE
Thornville Drive	27 B2
Thornville Park	27 C1
Thornville Road	27 B1
*Thornville Terrace	
(on Thornville Road)	27 B2
*Three Rock Close	
(off Kipure Ave)	45 B3
Three Rock Grove	57 B3
Three Rock Road	58 E2
Thundercut Alley	70 F3
*Tibradden Close	
(off Tibradden Drive)	45 B2
Tibradden Drive	45 B2
Tibradden Grove	45 B3
Tibradden Lane	56 F4
Tibradden Road	56 F3
Ticknick	63 B2
Ticknock Ave	57 C3
Ticknock Dale	57 C3
Ticknock Drive	57 C3
Ticknock Grove	57 C3
Ticknock Hill	57 C3
Ticknock Park	57 C3
Ticknock Road	57 B4
Ticknock Way	57 C3
Tiknock	61 B1
Tiknock Bridge	61 B1
Timard	17 A1
Timber Mills Apts	26 E2
*Timberyard	
(off Brabazon Street)	74 F2
*Time Place Apts	
(off Corrig Road)	58 E2
Tinkers Hill	21 A4
Tinkler's Path	36 E1
Tinnehinch	66 E4
Tinnehinch Bridge	66 E4
Tivoli Ave	46 F1
Tivoli Close	59 C1
Tivoli Road	49 C4
Tivoli Terrace East	50 D4
Tivoli Terrace North	49 C4
Tivoli Terrace South	49 C4
*Tobernea Terrace	
(off Seapoint Ave)	49 B3
Tolka Cottages	24 F3
Tolka Estate	24 F2
Tolka Estate Road	24 F3
Tolka Quay	39 A2
Tolka Quay Road	39 A2
Tolka Road	25 B4
Tolka Vale	24 E3
Tolka Valley Road	24 D3
Tolka Valley View	24 D2
Tolka View	22 E2
*Tom Clarke House	
(off Ballybough Road)	25 B4
Tom Kelly Road	75 B3
Tomar Court 70 D3	70 D3
Tonduff Close	45 B3
*Tonguefield Road	
(off Blarney Park)	46 E1
Tonlegee Ave	26 F1
Tonlegee Drive	26 F1
Tonlegee Road	27 A1
Tootenhill	52 D2
Tootenhill (Rathcoole)	52 E2
Tor an Rí Close	34 F3
Tor an Rí Court	34 F3
Tor an Rí Lane	34 F3
Tor an Rí Parade	34 F3
Tor an Rí Terrace	34 F3
Tor an Rí Walk	34 F3
Torca Road	60 F2
*Torca View (off Sorrento Road)	60 F2
Torcaill	3 C4
*Torlogh Gardens	
(off Philipsburgh Ave)	25 C4
*Torlogh Parade (off Griffith Ave)	25 C3
Torquay Road	58 F2
Torquay Wood	58 F2
Tory Square	22 F1
*Tourmakeady Road	
(off Innishmaan Road)	25 B2
*Tourville Lodge	
(off Church Lane)	46 F3
Tower Ave	46 F2
Tower Road (Castleknock)	22 F4
Tower Road (Clondalkin)	44 D1
Tower Road	36 D1
Tower Terrace	
(off Kilmainham Lane)	73 B1

STREET NAME	PAGE / GRID REFERENCE
Tower View Cottages	24 F4
*Tower Villas (on Tower Ave)	46 F2
Townsend Street	71 C4
*Townyard House Apts	
(adjacent Townyard Lane)	3 B2
Townyard Lane	3 B2
Tracy Bonham Lane	70 E4
Traders Wharf	49 C3
*Traders Wharf Apts	
(Ushers Quay)	70 F4
Trafalgar Lane	49 B4
Trafalgar Terrace (Blackrock)	49 B3
*Trafalgar Terrace	
(near Meath Place)	67 C2
Tramway Court (Sutton)	29 A1
*Tramway Court	
(off Old Blessington Road)	55 A1
Tranquility Grove	26 D1
Traverslea Close	60 D1
Traverslea Woods	60 D1
*Traynor Place (O'Reilly Ave)	73 C1
Treepark Ave	45 A3
Treepark Close	45 A3
Treepark Drive	45 A3
Treepark Road	45 A3
Trees Ave	48 E4
Trees Road Lower	48 E4
Trees Road Upper	48 E4
Treesdale	48 F4
Tresilian	59 A3
*Trideat Apts (off Claremont Road)	39 A4
Trim Road	26 D1
Trimbleston Apts	47 C3
Trimleston Ave	48 E2
Trimleston Drive	48 E2
Trimleston Gardens	48 E2
Trimleston Park	48 E2
Trimleston Road	48 E2
Trinity Hall (Rathgar)	47 A2
Trinity Square	72 D4
Trinity Street	71 B4
Trinity Terrace	72 D1
*Tristan House Apts	
(off Martin's Row Chapelizod)	36 E2
*Tritonville Ave	
(off Cranfield Place)	39 A3
*Tritonville Close	
(off Sandymount Road)	39 A3
Tritonville Court	39 A4
*Tritonville Cres	
(off Tritonville Road)	39 A3
*Tritonville Mews	
(off Sandymount Road)	39 A3
Tritonville Road	39 A3
*Trosyrafon Terrace	
(at South Esplanade)	68 D2
*Tuansgate Apts	
(off Belgard Square East)	54 F1
Tubber Lane Road	33 B2
Tubbermore Ave	60 F2
Tubbermore Road	60 F2
Tuckett's Lane	30 D2
Tudor Court	2 F2
Tudor Lawns	58 F2
Tudor Road	47 B1
Tulip Court	13 C4
Tullyhall	34 D4
Tullyhall Ave	34 D4
Tullyhall Close	34 D4
Tullyhall Court	34 D4
Tullyhall Cres	34 E4
Tullyhall Drive	34 E4
Tullyhall Green	34 D4
Tullyhall Park	34 D4
Tullyhall Rise	34 E4
Tullyhall Way	34 D4
Tullyvale	63 C1
Turnapin Cottages	12 F3
Turnapin Green	12 F3
Turnapin Grove	12 F3
Turnapin Lane	12 F3
Turnberry	28 D1
Turnberry Square	28 D1
Turnpike Lane	44 F2
Turnpike Road	45 A2
Turnstone Apts	48 E3
Turret Road	35 C2
*Turrets Flats	
(off Summerville Park)	47 A1
Turvey Road	73 B1
Tuscany Downs	27 A2
Tuscany Park	28 D1

STREET NAME	PAGE / GRID REFERENCE
*Twin Cottages	
(off Yankee Terrace)	49 A4
Tymon Close	55 A2
Tymon Cres	54 F2
Tymon Farm Apts	45 C4
Tymon Grove	55 A2
*Tymon Heights	55 B2
Tymon Lane	45 B4
Tymon Lane	45 C4
Tymon Lawn	55 A2
Tymon Lodge Apts	45 B3
Tymon North	45 B4
Tymon North Ave	45 B4
*Tymon North Court	
(off Tymon North Road)	45 B4
Tymon North Gardens	45 B4
Tymon North Green	45 B4
Tymon North Grove	45 B4
Tymon North Lawn	45 B4
Tymon North Park	45 B4
*Tymon North Place	
(off Tymon North Ave)	45 B4
Tymon North Road	45 B4
Tymonville Ave	45 B4
Tymonville Court	45 A4
Tymonville Cres	45 A4
Tymonville Drive	45 A3
Tymonville Grove	45 B3
Tymonville Lawn	45 B4
Tymonville Park	45 B4
Tymonville Road	45 A4
Tynan Hall	44 F3
Tynan Hall Ave	44 F3
Tynan Hall Grove	44 F3
Tynan Hall Park	44 F3
Tyrconnell Park	36 F3
Tyrconnell Road	36 F3
*Tyrconnell Street	
(off Tyrconnell Road)	36 F3
*Tyrconnell Villas	
(off Gratten Cres)	36 F3
Tyrellstown Boulevard	9 B2
Tyrellstown Way	9 B2
Tyrone House	71 C3
Tyrone Place	73 A2
Tyrrell Place	71 C1
*Tyrrel's Lane	
(off Fitzwilliam Street Ringsend)	39 A3
Tyrrelstown Ave	9 B2

U

UCD Village Belgrove	48 D3
*Ullardmor (off Ardeevin Road)	60 F2
Ulster Street	24 F4
Ulster Terrace (North Strand)	72 D1
*Ulster Terrace	
(off Stillorgan Grove)	58 F1
*Ulverton Close	
(off Ulverton Road Dalkey)	60 F1
*Ulverton Court	
(off Ulverton Road Dalkey)	60 F1
Ulverton Road	60 F1
*Ulysses House Apts	
(Little Britain Street)	71 A3
University Village Apts	17 C2
Upper Cliff Road	30 E2
Upper Dargle Road	67 A2
Upper Garville Ave	47 A2
Upper Glen Road (Phoenix Park)	36 E1
Upper Kilmacud Road Extension	58 E1
Uppercross	34 F1
*Uppercross Court	
(off Old Blessington Road)	55 A1
Uppercross Road	73 C2
*Urney Grove (off Killiney Road)	60 E2
Usher Lane	1 A2
Usher Street	70 F4
Ushers Court Apts	70 F4
Usher's Island	70 E4
Usher's Quay	70 F4

V

*Vale Terrace	
(on lower Dargle Road)	67 B2
*Vale View (Upper Dargle Road)	67 B2
Vale View Ave	59 B3
Vale View Close	59 B3
Vale View Grove	59 B3

STREET NAME	PAGE / GRID REFERENCE
*Vale View Lawn	59 B3
Valentia House	71 B1
Valentia Parade	71 B1
Valentia Road	25 B3
Valeview Cres	24 D2
Valeview Drive	24 D2
Valeview Gardens	
(off St. Helena's Road)	24 D2
Valley Ave	64 D1
Valley Close	64 D1
Valley Drive	63 C1
*Valley Park Ave	
(off Valley Park Road)	23 C2
Valley Park Drive	23 C2
Valley Park Road	23 C2
Valley View	1 B1
Valley View	64 D1
Valley Walk	64 D1
Vallombrosa	67 A2
Vanessa Close	31 C3
Vanessa Lawns	31 C3
Vauxhall Ave	74 D2
Vavasour Square	76 F2
Venetian Hall	26 E3
Ventry Drive	24 D4
Ventry Park	24 E4
Ventry Road	24 E4
Verbena Ave (Kilbarrack)	27 C1
Verbena Ave (Foxrock)	59 A3
Verbena Grove	27 C1
Verbena Lawn	27 C1
Verbena Park	27 C1
Verdemont	22 D2
*Vergemount	
(off Clonskeagh Road)	47 C1
*Vergemount Hall	
(off Clonskeagh Road)	47 C1
*Vergemount Park	
(off Clonskeagh Road)	47 C1
Verney House	62 F3
Vernon Ave	26 F4
Vernon Court (Vernon Ave)	26 F4
*Vernon Court (off Clontarf Road)	39 C1
Vernon Drive	26 F3
Vernon Gardens	26 F4
Vernon Grove (Clontarf)	26 F4
Vernon Grove (Rathgar)	47 A2
Vernon Heath	26 F4
Vernon Park	26 F4
Vernon Rise	26 F3
Vernon Street	75 A2
*Vernon Wood (off Vernon Ave)	39 C1
*Veronica Terrace	
(off Oliver Plunkett Ave)	39 A3
Verschoyle Ave	53 C2
Verschoyle Close	53 C2
Verschoyle Court	76 D2
Verschoyle Cres	53 C2
Verschoyle Drive	53 C2
Verschoyle Glen	53 C2
Verschoyle Green	53 C2
Verschoyle Heights	53 C2
Verschoyle Mews	76 D2
Verschoyle Park	53 C2
Verschoyle Place	
(off Lower Mount Street)	76 E2
Verschoyle Rise	53 C2
Verschoyle Vale	53 C2
Verville Court	26 E4
Vesey Mews	49 C4
Vesey Park	34 D2
Vesey Place	49 C4
*Vesey Terrace	
(off Main Street Lucan)	34 D1
*Vevay Arcade (on Vevay Road)	67 C3
*Vevay Cres (Vevay Road)	67 C2
Vevay Road	67 C3
*Vevay Villas	
(Vevay Road, Putland Road)	67 C3
Vicar Street	74 F1
Vicars Court	8 F4
Vico Road	60 F3
*Vico Terrace (off Vico Road)	60 F3
Victoria Ave (Donnybrook)	47 C1
Victoria Ave (Bray)	68 D2
*Victoria Cottages (off Bath Street)	39 A3
*Victoria Lane (off Botanic Ave)	25 B4
*Victoria Lane	
(off South Zion Road)	47 A2
Victoria Quay	70 E4
Victoria Road (Clontarf)	26 E4
Victoria Road (Killiney)	60 E3

STREET NAME	PAGE / GRID REFERENCE
Victoria Road (Dalkey)	60 F2
Victoria Road	46 F2
Victoria Street	75 A3
Victoria Terrace (Clontarf)	39 B1
Victoria Terrace (Dundrum)	47 C4
*Victoria Terrace (off Mellifont Ave)	50 D4
*Victoria Terrace (off Dalkey Ave)	60 F2
*Victoria Village (off Rathgar Ave)	46 F2
Victoria Village (Rathgar)	47 A2
Victoria Villas (Clontarf)	26 D4
*Victoria Villas (off Rathgar Ave)	46 F2
Viking Harbour (Ushers Island)	70 E4
Viking Place	70 E3
Viking Road	70 E3
*Villa Bank (Royal Canal Bank)	71 A1
Villa Blanchard	22 F2
*Villa Building Apts (off Harbour Road, opposite west pier)	30 D1
Villa Nova	48 F4
Villa Park Ave	24 D4
Villa Park Drive	24 D4
Villa Park Gardens	24 D4
Villa Park Road	24 D4
*Village Court Apts (off Butterfield Ave)	46 F4
Village Gate Arcade	67 C2
*Village Green (off Main Street Rathfarnham)	46 F3
Village Green (Tallaght)	55 A1
Village Heights	9 A4
*Village House (Reilly's Ave)	74 D3
Village Road (Beside Aiken's Village)	58 D4
Village Square (Tallaght)	55 A1
*Village Weir (off Main Street Lucan)	34 D1
Villarea Park	60 E1
Villiers Road	47 A2
Vintage Court	74 E2
Violet Hill	60 D3
Violet Hill Drive	24 F3
Violet Hill Park	24 F3
Violet Hill Road	24 F3
Virginia Drive	24 D2
*Virginia Hall (off Belgard Square West)	54 F1
Virginia Heights	54 F1
Virginia Park	24 D2
Viscount Ave	12 F4

W

Wadelai Green	25 A2
Wadelai Road	25 A2
Wade's Ave	27 A3
Wainsfort Ave	46 D3
Wainsfort Cres	46 D3
Wainsfort Drive	46 D2
Wainsfort Gardens	46 D3
Wainsfort Grove	46 E3
Wainsfort Manor	46 D3
Wainsfort Manor Cres	46 D3
Wainsfort Manor Drive	46 D3
Wainsfort Manor Green	46 D3
Wainsfort Manor Grove	46 D3
Wainsfort Park	46 E3
Wainsfort Road	46 D3
*Waldemar Terrace (off Dundrum Road)	47 B4
Walker's Cottages	75 B4
Walker's Court	75 B4
Walkinstown	45 B1
Walkinstown Ave	45 B1
Walkinstown Close	45 B1
Walkinstown Cres	45 B1
Walkinstown Cross	45 C2
Walkinstown Drive	45 B1
Walkinstown Green	45 B1
Walkinstown Parade	45 B1
Walkinstown Park	45 B1
Walkinstown Road	45 C1
*Wallace Road (off Bunting Road)	45 C1
Walnut Ave (Whitehall)	25 B3
Walnut Ave (Clondalkin)	44 F3
Walnut Close	44 F3
Walnut Court	25 B2
Walnut Drive	44 F3
Walnut Lawn	25 B3

STREET NAME	PAGE / GRID REFERENCE
Walnut Park	25 B3
Walnut Rise	25 B3
*Walnut View (off Brookwood)	56 E2
Walsh Road	25 A3
Waltersland Road	58 F1
Waltham Terrace	48 F4
Walton Hall (Swords)	1 Inset
Waltrim Grove	67 B4
Walworth Road	75 A3
Walworth Terrace (Walworth Road)	75 A4
*Warburton Terrace (west side of text Meath)	68 D2
Ward's Hill	74 F2
Warner's Lane	75 C3
Warren Ave	22 E3
Warren Close	22 E3
Warren Court (off Warrenhouse Road)	28 D1
Warren Cres	22 E4
Warren Green (Carpenterstown)	22 E3
Warren Green (Sutton)	28 D1
Warren Manor	2 F3
Warren Park	22 E3
Warren Street	75 A3
Warrenhouse Road	28 D1
Warrenmount	74 F2
Warrenmount Place	74 F2
*Warrenpoint (off Clontarf Road)	26 E4
Warrenstown	9 B4
Warrenstown Close	9 B4
Warrenstown Court	9 B4
Warrenstown Drive	9 B4
Warrenstown Garth	9 B4
Warrenstown Green	9 B4
Warrenstown Grove	9 B4
Warrenstown Lawn	9 B4
Warrenstown Park	9 B4
Warrenstown Place	9 B4
Warrenstown Rise	9 B4
Warrenstown Row	9 B4
Warrenstown Vale	9 B4
Warrenstown View	9 B4
Warrenstown Walk	9 B4
Warrenstown Way	9 B4
Warrington Lane	76 E2
Warrington Place	76 E2
Warwick Terrace	76 D4
Wasdale Grove	46 F2
*Wasdale House (off Wasdale Park)	46 F3
Wasdale Park	46 F3
*Washerwoman Lane (off Orwell Road)	47 A2
*Washington Grove (off Washington Lane)	46 E4
Washington Grove	46 E4
Washington Lane	46 E4
Washington Park	46 E4
Washington Street	74 F3
Waterfall Ave	25 B4
Waterfall Road	26 F3
Watergate Estate	55 A1
Waterloo Ave	72 E1
Waterloo Lane	76 D4
Waterloo Mews (off Shelbourne Road)	76 E3
Waterloo Road	76 D4
Watermeadow Drive	54 F2
Watermeadow Park	55 A2
Watermill	27 B3
Watermill Ave	27 A3
Watermill Close	55 A2
Watermill Drive	27 A3
Watermill Grove	55 A2
Watermill Lawn	27 A3
Watermill Lawn (Tallaght)	55 A2
Watermill Park	27 A3
Watermill Road	27 A3
*Watermint Court (at Lockkeeper's Walk)	24 D3
Waterside Apts	76 F1
Waterside Ave	2 E2
Waterside Close	2 E2
Waterside Court	2 E2
Waterside Cres (Swords)	2 E2
Waterside Cres (Portmarnock)	3 C4
Waterside Drive	2 E2
Waterside Green	2 E3
Waterside Grove	2 E2
Waterside King`s Hall	2 E2

STREET NAME	PAGE / GRID REFERENCE
Waterside Lawn	2 E2
Waterside Park	2 E2
Waterside Place	2 E3
Waterside Rise	2 E2
Waterside Road	2 E2
Waterside Walk	2 E2
Waterside Way	2 E2
Waterstown	35 C1
Waterstown Ave	35 C1
Waterville Road	22 F1
Waterville Row	22 F1
Waterville Terrace	22 F1
Watery Lane	2 D1
Watery Lane (Swords)	1 C1
Watery Lane (Clondalkin)	44 E1
Watkins Buildings	74 F2
Watling Street	70 E4
Watson Ave	60 D4
Watson Drive	60 D4
Watson Park	60 D4
Watson Road	60 D3
Watson's Estate	60 D3
Waverley Ave	25 C4
*Waverley Terrace (off Harold's Cross Road)	46 F1
*Waverley Terrace (Adelaide Road)	67 C2
Waynestown	5 C1
Wayside Cottages	62 F2
Weaver Court	35 A2
Weaver Lane	71 A1
Weaver's Close	74 F2
*Weavers Hall (at Levmoss Estate)	58 F3
Weavers Row (The Coombe)	74 E2
Weaver's Row (Clonsilla)	21 C2
Weaver's Square	74 F2
Weaver's Street	74 F2
Weaver's Walk	21 C2
*Webster's Cottages (off Annaville Ave)	49 A4
Wedgewood Estate	58 D2
*Weir House (opposite Convent Ave)	25 B4
Weirview	34 D1
Weirview Drive	58 F1
Weldon's Lane	15 A4
Well Road	2 D2
Wellesley Place	71 C1
*Wellington Cottages (off Willington Green)	45 C3
*Wellington Court (off Whitehall Road West)	46 D2
*Wellington Court (Novara Ave)	67 C2
*Wellington Gardens (off Oakley Road)	47 B1
Wellington House (off Seafort Ave)	76 E4
Wellington Lane (Wellington Road)	76 E4
Wellington Lane (Tallaght Road)	45 C3
*Wellington Lodge (off Serpentine Ave)	39 A4
*Wellington Mews (Wellington Lane)	76 E4
Wellington Park	46 D3
Wellington Place (Leeson Street)	76 E4
Wellington Place North	71 A2
Wellington Quay	71 B4
Wellington Road (Ballsbridge)	76 E4
Wellington Road (Phoenix Park)	69 B4
*Wellington Road (off Whitehall Road Templeogue)	46 D3
*Wellington Street (off George's Place Dún Laoghaire)	50 D4
Wellington Street Lower	71 A2
Wellington Street Upper	71 A2
Wellmount Ave	24 D2
Wellmount Court	24 D2
Wellmount Cres	24 D2
Wellmount Drive	24 D2
Wellmount Green	24 D2
Wellmount Parade	24 D2
Wellmount Park	24 D2
Wellmount Road	24 D2
Wellpark Ave	25 B3
Wellview Ave	9 A3
Wellview Cres	9 A3
Wellview Green	9 A3
Wellview Grove	9 A3
Wellview Park	9 A3
Wendell Ave	4 D4
Wentworth Apts	76 E1

STREET NAME	PAGE / GRID REFERENCE
Werburgh Street	75 A1
Wesbury	58 E1
Wesley Heights	57 C2
Wesley House	76 D4
Wesley Lawns	57 C2
Wesley Place	74 F3
Wesley Road	47 A2
West Park Drive	24 F2
West Pier (Howth)	30 D1
West Pier (Dún Laoghaire)	49 C3
West Road	72 E2
West Terrace	36 F3
Westbourne Ave	43 C1
Westbourne Close	43 C1
Westbourne Court	46 F3
Westbourne Drive	43 C1
Westbourne Green	43 C1
Westbourne Grove	43 C1
Westbourne Lawn	43 C1
Westbourne Lodge	56 D1
Westbourne Park	43 C1
Westbourne Rise	43 C1
Westbourne Road	46 F3
*Westbourne Terrace (near Bray Bridge)	67 C2
Westbourne View	43 C1
Westbrook	46 D2
Westbrook Lawns	53 C2
Westbrook Park	33 C2
Westbrook Road	47 B3
Westbury	34 D3
Westbury Ave	34 D3
Westbury Close	34 D3
Westbury Drive	34 D2
Westbury Grove	33 C3
Westbury Park	34 D3
Westcourt	74 D1
*Westend Gate (Castleknock)	22 F3
Westend Gate (Tallagh)	54 F1
Westend Village	22 E2
Western Parkway	35 B2
Western Parkway Motorway	22 E4
Western Road	74 E3
Western Way	71 A2
*Westerton Rise (off Ballinteer Road)	57 C1
Westfield Park	68 D3
Westfield Road	46 F1
*Westfield Terrace (off Rock Road)	49 A3
*Westgate Apts (off St. Augustine Street)	74 F1
*Westhampton Place (off Terenure Road North)	46 F2
Westhaven	8 F4
Westland Row	76 D1
*Westland Square Apts (Westland Square Business Park)	72 D4
Westmanstown	42 D3
*Westminster Court (off Brighton Road Foxrock)	59 A3
Westminster Lawns	58 F2
Westminster Park	59 A2
Westminster Road	59 A3
*Westmoreland Park (off Sandford Road)	47 B1
Westmoreland Street	71 B4
Weston Ave (Leixlip)	33 B1
Weston Ave	47 B4
Weston Close (Leixlip)	33 B1
Weston Close (Churchtown)	47 B4
Weston Court	33 B2
Weston Cres	33 B1
Weston Drive	33 B1
Weston Green	33 B1
Weston Grove	47 B4
Weston Heights	33 B2
Weston Lane (Leixlip)	33 B1
Weston Lawn	33 B1
Weston Meadow	33 B2
Weston Park (Churchtown)	47 B4
Weston Road	47 B4
*Weston Terrace (off Weston Park)	47 B4
Weston Way	33 B2
Westpark (Coolock)	26 F2
Westpark (Rathcoole)	52 F2
Westpark (Tallaght)	55 A1
Westpark Apts	53 B1
*Westview Terrace (Adelaide Road)	67 C2
Westway Close	9 C4
Westway Grove	9 C4

STREET NAME	PAGE / GRID REFERENCE
Westway Lawns	22 F1
Westway Park	9 C4
Westway Rise	9 C4
Westway View	9 C4
Westwood Ave	23 C2
Westwood Road	23 C2
Wexford Street	75 B2
Wharton Terrace	74 F4
Whately Hall	8 F4
*Whately Road (off Upper Kilmacud Road)	58 E1
Wheatfield	67 C3
Wheatfield Grove	4 D4
Wheatfield Road (Portmarnock)	4 D4
Wheatfield Road (Palmerstown)	35 C2
Wheatfields Ave	35 B3
Wheatfields Close	35 B3
Wheatfields Court	35 B3
Wheatfields Cres	35 B3
Wheatfields Drive	35 B3
Wheatfields Grove	35 B3
Wheatfields Park	35 B3
*Wheaton Court (off Inchicore Terrace South)	36 F3
*Whelan House Flats (off Thorncastle Street)	39 A3
*Whelan's Terrace (off Temple Road)	49 A3
Whitaker Hall	71 A2
White Gables	64 D2
White Hall (Ballymount Road)	44 F3
White Oak	47 C3
White Oaks	67 B4
Whiteacre Close	25 B1
Whiteacre Court	25 B1
Whiteacre Cres	25 B1
Whitebank Road	39 B3
Whitebarn Road	47 A4
Whitebeam Ave	47 C2
Whitebeam Road	47 C2
Whitebeams Road	58 D2
Whitebrook Park	54 E1
Whitechapel Ave	22 D2
Whitechapel Court	22 D2
Whitechapel Cres	22 D2
Whitechapel Green	22 D2
Whitechapel Grove	22 D2
Whitechapel Lawn	22 D2
Whitechapel Park	22 D2
Whitechapel Road	22 D2
*Whitechurch Abbey (off Grange Park)	56 F1
Whitechurch Ave	56 F2
Whitechurch Close	56 F2
Whitechurch Court	56 F2
Whitechurch Cres	56 F2
Whitechurch Drive	56 F2
Whitechurch Green	56 F2
Whitechurch Grove	56 F2
Whitechurch Heights	56 F2
Whitechurch Hill	56 F2
Whitechurch Lawn	56 F2
Whitechurch Park	56 F2
Whitechurch Pines	56 F1
Whitechurch Place	56 F2
Whitechurch Road	56 F2
Whitechurch Stream	56 F1
Whitechurch View	56 F2
Whitechurch Walk	56 F2
Whitechurch Way	56 F2
Whitecliff	56 F1
Whitefriar Garden Flats (off Whitefriar Street)	75 A1
Whitefriar Place	75 B1
Whitefriar Street	75 A1
Whitehall	25 B2
Whitehall Close	46 D3
Whitehall Gardens	46 D2
Whitehall Mews	59 A2
Whitehall Park	46 D3
Whitehall Road (Kimmage)	46 D2
Whitehall Road (Churchtown)	47 A4
Whitehall Road West	46 D2
Whitehall Square	45 C2
Whites Gate (Phoenix Park)	23 A4
White's Lane North	71 A2
White's Road	23 A4
*White's Villas (off Carysfort Road)	60 F1
Whitestown	22 D1
Whitestown Ave	22 D1
Whitestown Cres	22 D1
Whitestown Drive (Blanchardstown)	22 D1
Whitestown Drive (Tallaght)	54 E2
Whitestown Gardens	22 D1
Whitestown Green	22 D1
Whitestown Grove	22 D1
Whitestown Park	22 D1
Whitestown Road	54 F2
Whitestown Walk	22 D1
Whitestown Way	54 F2
Whitethorn	35 B3
Whitethorn Ave	26 D2
Whitethorn Close	26 D2
Whitethorn Cres (Artane)	26 D2
Whitethorn Cres (Coldcut Road)	35 B3
Whitethorn Drive	35 B3
Whitethorn Gardens	35 B3
Whitethorn Grove (Artane)	26 D2
Whitethorn Grove (Celbridge)	32 D3
Whitethorn Park (Artane)	26 D2
Whitethorn Park (Coldcut Road)	35 B3
Whitethorn Rise	26 D2
Whitethorn Road (Artane)	26 D2
Whitethorn Road (Milltown)	47 C2
*Whitethorn Walk (off Pine Ave Foxrock)	59 A2
*Whitethorn Walk (off Carriglea Ave Kill O'The Grange)	59 C2
Whitethorn Way	35 B3
Whitton Road	46 F2
Whitworth Ave	71 C1
*Whitworth Hall Apts (Behind District Court)	70 F3
*Whitworth Parade (off St. Patrick's Road)	25 A4
Whitworth Place (off Binns Bridge)	71 B1
Whitworth Road	25 A4
Whitworth Terrace (off Russell Ave)	71 C1
Wicklow Lane (off Wicklow Street)	75 B1
Wicklow Street	75 B1
Wicklow Way	65 A4
Wigan Road	25 A4
Wikeford Hall (Swords)	1 Inset
Wilderwood Grove	45 C4
*Wilfield (off Sandymount Ave)	39 A4
Wilfield Park	39 A4
Wilfield Road	39 A4
Wilford Court	67 B1
Wilfrid Road	46 F1
*Wilfrid Terrace (off Tivoli Ave)	46 F1
Willans Ave	21 A1
*Willan's Court (Willan's Ave)	21 A1
Willans Drive	21 A1
Willans Green	21 A1
*Willan's Grove (Willan's Ave)	21 A1
*Willan's Lane (Willan's Ave)	21 A1
*Willan's Place (Willan's Ave)	21 A1
Willans Rise	21 A1
Willans Row	21 A1
Willans Way	21 A1
Willbrook	46 F4
Willbrook Downs	56 F1
Willbrook Estate	56 F1
*Willbrook Grove (off Willbrook Street)	46 F4
Willbrook House	75 C4
Willbrook Lawn	46 F4
Willbrook Park	46 F4
Willbrook Road	46 F4
Willbrook Street	46 F4
*Willbrook Villas (Willbrook Street)	46 F4
William Beckett House	76 D3
William Dargan Bridge	47 B4
*William Pallister House (off Stonepark Court)	46 F4
William Street North	72 D1
William Street South	75 B1
William's Lane	71 B3
William's Park	47 A1
Williams Place Lower (Buckingham Street Upper)	71 C1
William's Place South	75 A2
William's Place Upper (off Portland Place)	71 B1
Willie Bermingham Place	73 C1
Willie Nolan Road	15 A4
Willington Ave	45 C3
Willington Court	45 C3
Willington Cres	45 C3
Willington Drive	45 C3
Willington Green	45 C3
Willington Grove	45 C3
*Willington Lawn (off Willington Grove)	45 C3
Willington Park	45 C3
Willow Ave	32 E4
Willow Ave (Clondalkin)	44 D2
Willow Ave (Loughlinstown)	64 D1
Willow Bank	49 C4
Willow Bank Drive	56 E1
Willow Bank Park	56 E1
Willow Brook	32 E4
Willow Court (Clondalkin)	44 D2
Willow Court (Loughlinstown)	64 D1
Willow Cove	32 E4
Willow Cres	32 E4
Willow Cres	64 D1
Willow Drive	32 E4
Willow Drive	44 D2
Willow Gate	57 B1
Willow Green	32 E4
Willow Grove (Clondalkin)	44 D2
Willow Grove (Cornelscourt)	59 B3
*Willow Grove (off Carriglea Ave)	59 C1
Willow House	76 D3
Willow Lawn	32 E4
Willow Lodge	23 A4
Willow Mews	48 E1
Willow Park (Dunboyne)	7 B2
*Willow Park (off Pine Ave Foxrock)	59 A2
Willow Park (Loughlinstown)	64 D1
Willow Park Ave	24 F1
Willow Park Close	24 F1
Willow Park Cres	24 F1
Willow Park Drive	25 A1
Willow Park Grove	24 F1
Willow Park Lawn	24 F1
Willow Park Road	24 F1
Willow Place (Booterstown)	48 F3
Willow Place (Loughlinstown)	64 D1
Willow Rise	32 E4
Willow Road (Fox and Geese)	45 A1
Willow Road (Dundrum)	57 B1
Willow Terrace	48 F2
Willow Vale	60 D4
Willow View	32 E4
Willow Wood Close	21 C2
Willow Wood Downs (off Willow Wood Grove)	21 C2
Willow Wood Green	21 C2
Willow Wood Grove	21 C2
Willow Wood Lawn	21 C2
Willow Wood Park	21 C1
Willow Wood Rise	21 C1
Willow Wood View	21 C2
Willow Wood Walk	21 C1
Willowbank	57 C1
Willowbrook Grove	31 C3
Willowbrook Lawns	31 C3
Willowbrook Lodge	31 C3
Willowbrook Park	31 C3
Willowfield	39 B4
Willowfield Ave	47 C4
Willowfield Park	47 C4
*Willowmount (off Willow Place)	48 F3
Willows (opposite Knockmaroon Gate)	36 D1
Willows Court	21 C2
Willows Drive	21 C2
Willows Green	21 C2
Willows Road	21 C2
*Willsbrook Apts (on Clonshaugh Road)	13 A4
Willsbrook Ave	34 E2
Willsbrook Cres	34 F1
Willsbrook Drive	34 E2
Willsbrook Gardens	34 E1
Willsbrook Green	34 E2
Willsbrook Grove	34 E1
Willsbrook Park	34 E1
Willsbrook Place	34 E1
Willsbrook Road	34 E2
Willsbrook View	34 E2
Willsbrook Way	34 E1
*Wilmont Ave (off Glasthule Road)	60 E1
Wilson Cres	48 D4
Wilson Road	48 E4
Wilson's Place	76 D1
Wilson's Terrace	74 F1
Wilton Court	76 D3
Wilton Place	76 D3
Wilton Terrace	76 D3
*Windele Road (off Joyce Road)	25 A3
Windermere	21 B2
*Windermere (off Gilford Road)	39 B4
Windgate Rise	30 D3
Windgate Road	30 D3
Windmill Ave (Swords)	1 C2
Windmill Ave (Crumlin)	46 D1
Windmill Cres (Swords)	1 A2
*Windmill Cres (off Windmill Road Crumlin)	46 D1
Windmill Lands	1 C2
Windmill Lane	72 D4
Windmill Lane Apts	72 D4
*Windmill Lodge (Windmill Road)	46 D1
Windmill Park	22 D3
Windmill Park	46 D1
Windmill Rise	1 C2
Windmill Road	73 B4
Windmill Square	22 D3
Windmill Terrace	22 D3
Windmillhill	51 C3
*Windrush (north of Church)	64 D2
Windsor Ave	25 C4
*Windsor Court (off Stradbrook Road)	59 B1
Windsor Drive	59 B1
*Windsor Mews (off St. Margarets Ave Malahide)	3 B2
Windsor Park	59 B1
Windsor Place	75 C2
*Windsor Place (off Lanesville)	59 B1
Windsor Road	47 B1
Windsor Terrace (Ranelagh)	75 A4
Windsor Terrace (Malahide)	3 B3
Windsor Terrace (Dún Laoghaire)	50 D4
*Windsor Villas (off Philipsburgh Ave)	25 C4
Windy Arbour	47 C3
Windy Ridge	64 D4
Winetavern Street	71 A4
Wingfield	62 E1
*Winston Ville (off Charlemont Road Clontarf)	26 D4
Winter Garden Apts	72 E4
Winton Ave	47 A2
*Winton Grove (off Terenure Road North)	46 F2
Winton Road	76 D4
Wogansfield	33 A1
*Wolfe Tone Ave (off Cross Ave)	50 D4
Wolfe Tone Close	71 A3
Wolfe Tone Quay	70 D4
Wolfe Tone Square East	67 C3
Wolfe Tone Square Middle	67 C3
Wolfe Tone Square North	67 C3
Wolfe Tone Square South	67 C3
Wolfe Tone Square West	67 C3
Wolfe Tone Street	71 A3
Wolseley Street	74 F3
Wolstan Haven Ave	31 C3
Wolverton Glen	60 E2
Wood Avens	35 A3
Wood Dale Close	55 B2
Wood Dale Cres	55 B2
Wood Dale Drive	55 B2
Wood Dale Green	55 B2
Wood Dale Green	55 C2
Wood Dale Grove	55 C2
*Wood Dale Oak (Wood Dale Green)	55 C2
Wood Dale View	55 C2
Wood Lane	70 E4
Wood Quay	71 A4
Wood Street	75 A1
Woodbank Ave	23 C2
Woodbank Drive	23 C2
Woodberry (Carpenterstown)	22 E3
Woodberry (Lucan)	34 D3
Woodbine Ave	48 E2
Woodbine Close	27 A1
Woodbine Drive	27 A1
*Woodbine House (off Woodbine Road)	48 E2
Woodbine Park (Raheny)	27 A1
Woodbine Park (Booterstown)	48 E2

STREET NAME	PAGE / GRID REFERENCE
Woodbine Road (Raheny)	27 A1
Woodbine Road (Booterstown)	48 E2
*Woodbine Terrace	
(off Dundrum Road)	47 C4
Woodbrook Court	22 D3
Woodbrook Cres	22 D3
Woodbrook Downs	64 E4
Woodbrook Glen	67 C1
Woodbrook Hall	22 D3
Woodbrook Lawn	67 C3
Woodbrook Park (Carpenterstown)	22 D3
Woodbrook Park (Templelogue)	46 D4
Woodbrook Square	22 D3
*Woodchester House	
(Golden Lane)	75 A1
Woodcliff Heights	30 E2
Woodfarm Ave	35 C2
*Woodfarm Cottages	
(off Lucan Road Palmerston)	35 C1
Woodfarm Drive	35 C2
Woodfield	56 D2
*Woodfield Cottages	
(off Sarsfield Road)	36 F3
*Woodfield Place	
(off Sarsfield Road)	36 F3
*Woodfield Terrace (Blank Tony)	36 F3
Woodford	58 E2
Woodford Ave	44 F1
Woodford Close	44 F1
Woodford Court (Monksfield)	44 F1
*Woodford Court	
(off Leinster Road West)	46 F1
Woodford Cres	44 E1
Woodford Downs	44 F1
Woodford Drive	44 E1
Woodford Garth	44 E1
Woodford Green	44 F1
Woodford Grove	44 F1
Woodford Heights	44 F1
Woodford Hill	44 F1
Woodford Lawn	44 F1
Woodford Meadows	44 E1
Woodford Parade	44 E1
Woodford Park	44 F1
Woodford Park Road	44 E1
Woodford Rise	44 F1
Woodford Road	44 E1
Woodford Terrace	44 F1
Woodford View	44 F1
Woodford Villas	44 E1
Woodford Walk	44 F1
Woodford Way	44 F1
*Woodhaven	
(off Milltown Bridge Road)	47 C2
Woodhazel Close	25 A1
Woodhazel Terrace	25 A1
Woodlands (Malahide)	14 F1
Woodlands (Maynooth)	17 B3
Woodlands	22 D1
*Woodlands	
(off Orwell Road Rathgar)	47 A2
Woodlands Ave (Stillorgan)	48 E4
Woodlands Ave (Cornelscourt)	59 C3
Woodlands Court	15 A1
Woodlands Drive (Stillorgan)	48 E4

STREET NAME	PAGE / GRID REFERENCE
Woodlands Drive	
(Johnstown Road)	59 C3
Woodlands Park (Mount Merrion)	48 F4
Woodlands Park	
(Johnstown Road)	59 C3
Woodlands Road	59 C3
Woodlawn	12 F4
Woodlawn Ave	12 F4
Woodlawn Close	12 F4
Woodlawn Court	12 F4
Woodlawn Cres (Coolock Lane)	12 F4
Woodlawn Cres (Churchtown)	47 B4
Woodlawn Drive	12 F4
Woodlawn Green	12 F4
Woodlawn Grove (Coolock Lane)	12 F4
*Woodlawn Grove	
(off Churchtown Road Lower)	47 B4
Woodlawn Park (Coolock Lane)	12 F4
Woodlawn Park (Churchtown)	47 B4
Woodlawn Park (Tallaght)	55 C2
*Woodlawn Park	
(off Mounttown Lower)	59 C1
Woodlawn Park Ave	55 B1
Woodlawn Park Drive (Firhouse)	55 B1
Woodlawn Park Grove	55 C2
Woodlawn Rise	12 F4
*Woodlawn Terrace	
(off Churchtown Road)	47 B4
Woodlawn View	12 F4
*Woodlawn Villas	
(off Mounttown Road Lower)	59 C1
Woodlawn Walk	12 F4
Woodlawn Way	12 F4
*Woodleigh	
(off Rathmines Road Upper)	47 A2
*Woodley Court	
(off Woodley Park Kilmacud)	58 D1
Woodley Park	58 D1
Woodley Road	60 D3
Woodpark (Blanchardstown)	22 F2
*Woodpark (off The Rise)	25 A3
Woodpark (Ballinteer)	57 B2
Woods End	22 F2
Woodscape	34 D3
Woodside (Leixlip)	19 C4
Woodside (Clontarf)	26 F4
Woodside (Howth)	30 D2
Woodside (Rathfarnham)	47 A3
Woodside Drive	47 A3
Woodside Grove	47 A3
Woodside Hall	57 C3
Woodside Road	57 C3
*Woodstock Court	
(off Sandford Road)	47 B1
*Woodstock Gardens	
(off Sandford Road)	47 B1
*Woodstock Hill	55 C2
Woodstock Park	56 D1
Woodstown	55 C2
Woodstown Abbey	56 D2
Woodstown Abbey	55 C2
Woodstown Ave	55 C2
Woodstown Close	55 C2
*Woodstown Court	
(Woodstown Ave)	55 C2
Woodstown Cres	55 C2
Woodstown Dale	55 C2

STREET NAME	PAGE / GRID REFERENCE
Woodstown Drive	55 C2
Woodstown Gardens	55 C2
Woodstown Green	55 C2
Woodstown Heath	55 C2
Woodstown Height	55 C2
Woodstown Hill	55 C2
*Woodstown House	
(off Stonepark Court)	46 F4
Woodstown Lane	56 D2
Woodstown Lawn	55 C2
Woodstown Meadow	55 C2
Woodstown Parade	55 C2
Woodstown Park	55 C2
Woodstown Place	55 C2
Woodstown Rise	55 C2
Woodstown Vale	55 C2
Woodstown Walk	55 C2
Woodstown Way	55 C3
*Woodthorpe	
(off Coolnevaun Kilmacud)	58 E1
Woodtown Way	56 D3
Woodvale Ave	21 C1
Woodvale Cres	21 C1
Woodvale Drive	21 C1
Woodvale Garth	21 C1
Woodvale Green	21 C1
Woodvale Grove	21 C1
Woodvale Park	21 C1
Woodvale Way	21 C1
Woodview (Celbridge)	32 D2
Woodview (Lucan)	33 C2
*Woodview (on Commons Road)	64 E2
Woodview (Mount Merrion Ave)	48 F3
Woodview Close	27 A1
*Woodview Cottages	
(off Church Lane)	46 F3
Woodview Court (Dunboyne)	7 B3
*Woodview Court	
(off Ard Lorcain Stillorgan)	58 F1
Woodview Court Apts	33 C2
*Woodview Drive	
(on Boghall Road)	67 C3
Woodview Grove	22 E2
Woodview Heights (Dunboyne)	7 B3
Woodview Heights (Lucan)	33 C2
Woodview House	48 F3
Woodview Park (Castleknock)	23 A3
Woodview Park (Ardara Ave)	27 A1
Woodville Ave	34 E1
Woodville Close	34 E1
Woodville Court	26 E1
Woodville Green	34 E1
Woodville Grove	34 E1
*Woodville House	
(off Kilmore Road)	26 D1
Woodville Lawn	34 E1
*Woodville Road	
(off Botanic Ave)	25 A4
Woodville Walk	34 E1
Wormwood Gate	
(off Bridge Street Lower)	70 F4
Wyattville	64 D1
Wyattville Close	64 D1
Wyattville Hill	64 D1
Wyattville Link Road	63 C2

STREET NAME	PAGE / GRID REFERENCE
Wyattville Park	64 D1
Wyattville Road	64 D1
*Wyckham Ave	
(off Wyckham Place)	57 C1
Wyckham Grove	57 C1
Wyckham Park Road	57 B1
Wyckham Place	57 C1
*Wyckham Point Apts.	
(Gort Muire)	57 C1
Wyckham Way	57 C1
Wynberg Park	49 B4
*Wyndham Court (Chancery Lane)	75 A1
Wyndham Park	67 C2
*Wynnefield Park	
(off Charleville Road)	47 A1
Wynnefield Road	47 A1
Wynnsward Drive	47 C2
Wynnsward Park	47 C2
Wytclcaf Grove	14 D4
Wyvern Estate	60 E3

X

Xavier Ave	72 E1
*Xavier Court	
(Sherrard Street Upper)	71 B1

Y

Yale	48 D3
Yankee Terrace	49 A4
Yarnhall Street	71 A3
Yeates Hall	59 B4
Yeates Way	35 C4
*Yeats Court	
(off Sandymount Ave)	39 A4
Yellow Meadows Ave	44 F1
Yellow Meadows Drive	44 E1
Yellow Meadows Estate	44 F1
Yellow Meadows Grove	44 E1
Yellow Meadows Lawn	44 E1
Yellow Meadows Park	44 E1
Yellow Meadows Vale	44 E1
Yellow Road	25 C2
Yellow Walls	3 A2
Yellow Walls Road	3 A2
Yellownook Ave	59 C3
Yewlands Terrace	46 F2
York Ave	47 A1
York Road (Ringsend)	39 A2
York Road (Rathmines)	47 A1
York Road (Dún Laoghaire)	49 C4
York Street	75 B2
*York Terrace	
(off York Road Dún Laoghaire)	49 C4

Z

Zardoz Court	
(off Claremont Road)	76 F4
Zion Road	47 A2
Zoo Road (Phoenix Park)	69 B3
Zuma Terrace	
(on Mount Drummond Ave)	74 F4